Architecture in America
A Battle of Styles

The H. C. Price Tower, 1953-1955, Bartlesville, Oklahoma; a detailed view of the tower showing the abstract design in the concrete paneling.

Architecture in America:
A Battle of Styles

Edited by

William A. Coles
University of North Carolina

and

Henry Hope Reed, Jr.

New York

APPLETON-CENTURY-CROFTS, INC.

PRINTED IN THE UNITED STATES OF AMERICA

E 20272

Preface

ARCHITECTURE is the most available and public of the arts. It surrounds us in our daily lives, houses the complex and varied functions of our civilization, and provides a setting for the other arts. It at once demonstrates and symbolizes the extent to which man can come to terms with and arrange his natural environment. We all respond to it at least on the simplest level, if not necessarily with conscious awareness. We all have on occasion found ourselves awed and exalted by its monumental forms and arrangements, reverent before its sacred or venerable works, delighted by its moments of festive gaiety, arrested by its novelty, or soothed by its comfort and restful charm. Conversely, we have all felt oppressed by the absence of its rule in a crowded, dingy slum or in the endless monotony of a jerry-built suburb.

The intention of this book is to bring these reactions more fully to the level of conscious and useful understanding by providing materials for thought about architecture, in order that we may make critically informed judgments about its aims and achievements. This task is particularly necessary today, not only because ours is a century that has witnessed deep conflicts about architecture—many inherited from the previous century—but also because our age has produced a varied literature of architectural theory and criticism. Because that literature gives frequent evidence of intellectual confusion, the way to sound understanding is especially perilous. But our dangers only serve to underscore more emphatically our urgent needs.

The subtitle of this anthology reads "A Battle of Styles." At this point, we might well ask ourselves what is meant by the word "style" if we are to understand the nature of the battle. The term means a definite type or manner of architecture, characterized by distinctive patterns of structure or ornamentation, a special form of skilled construction and execution. Different historical epochs have had different styles, and the historian, in order to help us identify them, has given them names such as the

Romanesque Style, the Gothic Style, the Renaissance Style, and so forth. In America the predominant current in our architectural heritage has been the classical way of building; in order to see its different phases the historian has given them special names such as the Colonial Style of the Eighteenth Century, the Greek Revival Style of the 1830's and 1840's or the American Renaissance Style for the period from 1880 to 1930. Today we have predominantly what we call, for want of a better phrase, the Modern Style.[1] Although the classical manner of building continues, and there are Romanesque and Gothic churches still being built, what is termed Modern dominates the contemporary scene.

The central fact in the history of contemporary architecture is the rise to dominance of a new style which represents a startling break with past traditions and values. This style has overthrown classical architecture's emphasis upon formal values, ornament, and symmetry, together with its refined and idealized stylistic vocabulary, sometimes denying the validity of traditional aims themselves and sometimes substituting for these older concepts new and different visual interpretations. It has itself emphasized the claims of function as dominant, has eagerly sought innovation in constructive technique, and has encouraged originality in design and in the use of materials. This phenomenon, from the time when its guiding theoretical precepts were first advocated, has been attended by a violent controversy which focuses on such fundamental problems as the relative merits of permanence or change and the nature and role of beauty in architecture. At the present moment the restlessness and soul-searching of architectural thought are, if anything, more acute than ever. Is not this situation in itself a further indication that our generation must have the intellectual initiative, the critical freedom, and the adequate information that alone will enable it to rethink the terms of the architectural controversy in as dispassionate a frame of mind as possible?

This book presupposes no prior knowledge of architectural

---

[1] The word "Modern" has been capitalized in the editorial apparatus of this volume wherever it refers to a specific style of architecture. This has been done to avoid confusion since the word is applied by some writers to the architecture of the last hundred years, irrespective of style.

history or criticism on the part of the student. It is a self-contained introduction to architectural thought. For this reason it opens with an extensive anthology of major statements, ranging from antiquity to the present, on the nature of architecture, its aims, and the problems of architectural theory and practice as they shed light on modern controversies. Thus introduced to the terms of the conflict and armed with a critical apparatus and terminology, the student can proceed to a concrete examination of the values, aims, and achievements of five specific examples of American architecture of the last seventy years, two classical and three Modern. The examples have been singled out for very definite reasons. They are all examples of public buildings and several of them, notably the National Capitol and the United Nations, are familiar to all. Also, all five have excited an unusual amount of commentary both for and against their aims and achievements.

To judge the buildings for himself the student is supplied with photographs of the buildings, descriptions and analyses of each building, and an array of varied and controversial critical commentary. As further aids to comprehension, an illustrated glossary of technical terms is provided along with questions and theme topics intended to focus the student's attention on some of the crucial issues involved. There is also a brief annotated bibliography of works suggested for further reading in courses where students may be asked to pursue independent research beyond the limits of this text.

We have taken pains wherever possible to extend the range of architectural thought by including relevant material from men of letters and others not specifically architects or critics of architecture. We have done so in the hope that teachers will take advantage of the profound general import of the subject matter to relate problems involved here with similar problems found in the history of ideas, literature, and the other arts.

While the design of the book provides ample opportunity for many different kinds of writing assignments—for descriptive, narrative, digestive, or summary papers—it is also our express intention as editors to give students the opportunity to evaluate complex ideas and materials and to form enlightened, independent judgments, not only on the contents of the book, but on architecture in their own communities and on their own campuses.

The editors have tried to provide as wide and controversial a selection of material as possible within the necessary limits of the book. Coverage in the several case studies does, nevertheless, vary. To some extent the differences are due to the nature of the buildings themselves. Major public buildings ought to, and do, evoke more commentary, since they affect larger numbers of people. But the differences also reflect the lamentable and increasing poverty of recent architectural criticism. No one who is familiar with architectural periodicals of the last seventy years can fail to note this. Too often the magazines of today are little more than glossy picture books. Attempts at close analysis by contemporary writers such as Lewis Mumford are all too rare and deserve to be valued whether or not one fully endorses their judgments.

While this book is primarily designed for college writing courses employing controlled research methods, it is also intended for use as a primer in courses in architecture, art history, and American studies. Readers will find here a collection of writings, past and contemporary, which in range, variety, and freshness is virtually unrivaled in the present literature of architecture.

The authors wish to thank Messrs. Henry Large, Donald Welles, James Welles, O. B. Hardison, Jr., Lawrence Costello, James Ferguson, Myron Simmons, and Mr. and Mrs. Robert Kaske for their assistance, as well as George Pettengill, librarian of the American Institute of Architects, Miss Ruth E. Schoneman and Miss Nancy W. Boone of the Burnham Library of the Art Institute of Chicago, Mrs. Marian Vanderbilt of Skidmore, Owings & Merrill, the public relations staff of the National Gallery of Art, and particularly Mr. Adolph Placzek, Librarian of Avery Library, Columbia University, whose magnificent collection made this book possible.

To Klara Majthenyi the editors are most grateful, not only for the book's format and careful copyediting through all phases, but more especially for her fine drawings in the glossary.

W. A. C.

H. H. R., Jr.

Contents

Contents

part II

Five Controversies
of Modern American Architecture

1

The World's Columbian Exposition, Chicago, 1893

3

The United Nations Building, New York City, 1947-1952

4

Lever House, New York City, 1952

5

The Price Tower, Bartlesville, Oklahoma, 1953-1955

Aims of Architecture

The Pantheon, 120-124 A.D., Rome, the most perfectly preserved of all ancient buildings in Rome. Andrea Palladio, who measured it in the course of his career, wrote that thanks to stately edifices such as the Pantheon "we come to a certain knowledge of the *Roman* virtue and greatness, which otherwise perhaps had not been believed."

VITRUVIUS

The Fundamental Principles of Architecture

Vitruvius, *The Ten Books on Architecture,* trans. by Morris Hicky Morgan (Cambridge, Harvard University Press, 1914. Book I, Chapter ii.*

1. Architecture depends on Order . . . , Arrangement . . . , Eurythmy, Symmetry, Propriety, and Economy. . . .

2. Order gives due measure to the members of a work considered separately, and symmetrical agreement to the proportions of the whole. . . . Arrangement includes the putting of things in their proper places and the elegance of effect which is due to adjustments appropriate to the character of the work. . . .[13]

3. Eurythmy is beauty and fitness in the adjustments of the members. This is found when the members of a work are of a height suited to their breadth, of a breadth suited to their length, and, in a word, when they all correspond symmetrically.

4. Symmetry is a proper agreement between the members of the work itself, and relation between the different parts and the whole general scheme, in accordance with a certain part selected as a standard. . . .

5. Propriety is that perfection of style which comes when a work is authoritatively constructed on approved principles.[14]

* Reprinted by permission of Harvard University Press, copyright, 1914, by the President and Fellows of Harvard College.

JOHN RUSKIN

The Seven Lamps of Architecture

John Ruskin, *The Seven Lamps of Architecture* (London, Smith, Elder, and Co., 1849).

Architecture is the art which so disposes and adorns the edifices raised by man for whatsoever uses, that the sight of them may contribute to his mental health, power, and pleasure.

It is very necessary, in the outset of all inquiry, to distinguish between Architecture and Building.

To build, literally, to confirm, is by common understanding to put together and adjust the several pieces of any edifice or receptacle of a considerable size. . . . But building does not become architecture merely by the stability of what it erects. . . .

Let us, therefore, at once confine the name to that art which,[7] taking up and admitting, as conditions of its working, the necessities and common uses of the building, impresses on its form certain characters venerable or beautiful, but otherwise unnecessary. . . . It may not be always easy to draw the line so sharply and simply; because there are few buildings which have not some pretence or colour of being architectural; neither can there be any architecture which is not based on building; but it is perfectly easy, and very necessary, to keep the ideas distinct, and to understand fully that Architecture concerns itself only with those characters of an edifice which are above and beyond its common use.[8]

JOHN RUSKIN

The Stones of Venice

John Ruskin, *The Stones of Venice* (London, Smith, Elder, and Co., 1851), I.

The two virtues of architecture which we can justly weigh, are, we said, its strength or good construction, and its beauty or good decoration. Consider first, therefore, what you mean when you say a building is well constructed or well built; you do not merely mean that it answers its purpose,—this is much, and many modern buildings fail of this much; but if it be verily well built, it must answer this purpose in the simplest way, and with no over-expenditure of means. We require of a light-house, for instance, that it shall stand firm and carry a light; if it do not this, assuredly it has been ill built; but it may do it till the end of time, and yet not be well built. It may have hundreds of tons of stone in it more than were needed, and have cost thousands of pounds more than it ought. To pronounce it well or ill built, we must know the utmost forces it can have to resist, and the best arrangements of stone for encountering them, and the [38] quickest ways of effecting such arrangements: then only, so far as such arrangements have been chosen, and such methods used, is it well built. . . .[39]

Then as regards decoration . . .[43] do not try to . . . connect the delight which you take in ornament with that which you take in construction and usefulness. They have no connexion; and every effort that you make to reason from one to the other will blunt your sense of beauty, or confuse it with sensations altogether inferior to it. You were made for enjoyment, and the world was filled with things which you will enjoy, unless you are too proud to be pleased by them, or too grasping to care for what you cannot turn to other account than mere delight. Remember that the most beautiful things in the world are the most useless. . . .[44]

SIR GILBERT SCOTT

Lectures on the Rise and Development
of Mediaeval Architecture

Sir Gilbert Scott, *Lectures on the Rise and Development of Mediaeval Architecture;*
delivered at the Royal Academy (London, John Murray, 1879). Vol. II.

Our art, as has so often been remarked, differs from the sister
arts of painting and sculpture in this, that whereas they arise
directly from the artistic[291] aspirations of our nature, apart
from practical necessities and utility, ours arises first from these
necessities, and then from the desire to clothe the results with
beauty. It may be said that the yearning after abstract beauty
unlinked with utility is the higher and more spiritual sentiment;
but on the other hand, if we look around us throughout the
creations of nature, we are prompted to reply that, in linking
beauty with utility, we are more directly imitating Him Who
made man in His own image, and in Whose works this union of
the useful and the beautiful is one of the most universal characteristics.

Architecture, then, as distinguished from mere building, is
the *decoration of construction.* If I were lecturing on architecture, in the broadest form of the expression, I must treat throughout of construction, and of its decoration, *pari passu,* as the latter
has but little meaning if severed from the former, which is its
groundwork. . . .[292]

Make yourselves, then, artists, not alone in respect of mere
architecture itself, but in respect also of its allied arts;
in respect of architectural sculpture, in respect of painted decoration, in respect of figure-sculpture and of figure-painting in
forms suited to architecture; of painted glass, mosaic work, metal
work, and all the subordinate arts. I do not say that you should

really practise these arts yourselves, but by training yourselves
in them you will become fitted to direct, guide, and check those
whom you employ, or who are made your art colleagues.[325]

ABBOT SUGER

On the Abbey Church of St. Denis

Abbot Suger, On the Abbey Church of St.-Denis and Its Art Treasures. Edited,
translated, and annotated by Erwin Panofsky (Princeton, Princeton University Press,
1946).*

OF THE CAST AND GILDED DOORS

The verses on the door, further, are these:
"Whoever thou art, if thou seekest to extol the glory of these
    doors,
Marvel not at the gold and the expense but at the craftsmanship
    of the work.
Bright is the noble work; but, being nobly bright, the work
Should brighten the minds, so that they may travel, through
    the true lights,[47]
To the True Light where Christ is the true door.
In what manner it be inherent in this world the golden door
    defines:
The dull mind rises to truth through that which is material
And, in seeing this light, is resurrected from its
    former submersion." [49]

* Reprinted by permission of Princeton University Press, Princeton,
New Jersey, 1946.

LEON BATTISTA ALBERTI

The Architecture of Leon Battista Alberti in Ten Books

Leon Battista Alberti, *The Architecture of Leon Battista Alberti in Ten Books*, trans. by James Leoni (London, printed by Thomas Edlin, 1726), II.*

Book VI, Chapter II

Of Beauty and Ornament, their effects and difference, that they are owing to art and exactness of proportion; as also of the birth and progress of Arts.

It is generally allowed that the pleasure and delight which we feel on the view of any Building, arise from nothing else but Beauty and Ornament, since there is hardly any man so melancholy or stupid, so rough or unpolished, but what is very much pleased with what is beautiful, and pursues those things which are most adorned, and rejects the unadorned and neglected; and if in any thing that he views he perceives any Ornament is wanting, he declares that there is something difficient which wou'd make the work more delightful and noble. We shou'd therefore consult Beauty as one of the main and principle requisites in any thing which we have a mind shou'd please others. How necessary our Forefathers, men remarkable for their wisdom, look'd upon this to be, appears, as indeed from almost every thing they did, so particularly from their Laws, their Militia, their sacred and all other publick Ceremonies; which it is almost incredible what pains they took to adorn; insomuch that one wou'd almost imagine they had a mind to have it thought, that

* U.S. edition: Joseph Rykwert, ed. (Hollywood-by-the-Sea, Florida, Transatlantic Arts, 1955).

all these Things (so absolutely necessary to the life of mankind) if stript of their pomp and ornament, wou'd be somewhat stupid and insipid. When we lift up our Eyes to Heaven, and view the wonderful Works of God, we admire him more for the beauties which we see, than for the conveniences which we feel and derive from them. But what occasion is there to insist upon this? when we see that Nature consults beauty in a manner to excess, in every thing she does, even in painting the flowers of the field. If Beauty therefore is necessary in any thing, it is so particularly in Building, which can never be without it, without giving offence both to the skilful and the ignorant. How are we moved by a huge shapeless ill-contrived pile of Stones? the greater it is, the more we blame the folly of the expence, and condemn the builder's inconsiderate lust of heaping up stone upon stone without contrivance. The having satisfied necessity is a very small matter, and the having provided for conveniency affords no manner of pleasure, where you are shocked by the deformity of the work. . . . Your whole care, diligence, and expence, therefore shou'd all tend to this, that whatever you build may be not only useful and convenient, but also handsomely adorned, and by that means delightful to the sight, that whoever views it may own the [2] expence cou'd never have been better bestowed. But what Beauty and Ornament are in themselves, and what difference there is between them, may perhaps be easier for the Reader to conceive in his mind, than for me to explain in words. In order therefore to be as brief as possible, I shall define Beauty to be a harmony of all the parts, in whatsoever subject it appears, fitted together with such proportion and connection, that nothing cou'd be added, diminished, or altered, but for the worse. A quality so noble and divine, that the whole force of wit and art has been spent to procure it; and it is but very rarely granted to any one, or even to Nature herself, to produce any thing every way perfect and compleat. . . . If this be granted we may define Ornament to be a kind of an auxiliary brightness and improvement to Beauty. So that then Beauty is somewhat lovely which is proper and innate, and diffused over the whole body, and ornament somewhat added or fastened on, rather than proper and innate. To return therefore where we left off. Whoever wou'd build so as to have their Building commended, which every reasonable Man wou'd desire, must build according to a justness of proportion, and this justness of proportion must be owing to Art. Who therefore will affirm, that a handsome and just Structure can be raised any otherwise than by the means of Art? and consequently this part of building, which relates to beauty and ornament, being the chief of all the rest, must without doubt be directed by some sure rules of art and proportion, which whoever neglects will make himself ridiculous. But there are some who will by no means allow of this, and say that men are guided by a variety of opinions in their judgment of beauty and of buildings; and that the forms of structures must vary according to every man's particular taste and fancy, and not be tied down to any rules of Art. A common thing with the ignorant, to despise what they do not understand! It may not therefore be amiss to confute this error; not that I think it necessary to enter into a long discussion about the origin of Arts, from what principles they were deduced, and by what methods improved. I shall only take notice that all Arts were begot by Chance and Observation, and nursed by Use and Experience, and improved and perfected by Reason and Study. . . .[3]

ANDREA PALLADIO

The Architecture of A. Palladio;
In Four Books

[Andrea Palladio] *The Architecture of A. Palladio; In Four Books, Revis'd, Design'd,* and Publish'd by Giacomo Leoni, a Venetian . . . Translated from the Italian Original (London: Printed by John Watts, for the Author, MDCCXV).

The First Book, Chap. 1

OF THINGS TO BE CONSIDERED AND PROVIDED, BEFORE ONE BEGINS TO BUILD

The first thing that requires our consideration, when we are about Building, is the Plan and the Upright of the Edifice we propose to erect. Three things, according to *Vitruvius*, are chiefly to be consider'd, without which a Building cannot be of any value. These are *Conveniency, Solidity,* and *Beauty.* For no Edifice can be allow'd to be perfect, if it be commodious and not durable; or, if being durable, it be subject to many inconveniences; or, if having both solidity and conveniency, it has no beauty nor conformity.

An Edifice may be reckon'd Commodious, when every part of it has its proper place and situation, in respect to its dignity and uses; having neither more nor less than these require: as when the Halls, Rooms, Closets, Galleries, Cellars, Garrets, &c. are fitly dispos'd, and in their proper places. The Solidity of an Edifice depends upon the care of erecting the Walls very *plum,* and thicker below than above, with good and stout Foundations: taking care that the *pillars* above be exactly perpendicular over the *pillars* below, and that all the openings, as Doors and Windows, be one above the other, so that the solid be upon the solid, and the void upon the void. As for the beauty of an Edifice, it

The Colosseum, 70-82 A.D., Rome, the center for gladiatorial combats and other public spectacles. The Colosseum illustrates well the fundamental principles of architecture enunciated by Vitruvius: "eurythmy, symmetry, propriety and economy."

consists in an exact Proportion of the parts within themselves, and of each part with the whole; for a fine Building ought to appear as an entire and perfect body, wherein every member agrees with its fellow, and each so well with the whole, that it may seem absolutely necessary to the being of the same.[1]

Book the Third
THE PREFACE TO THE READER

. . . 'Tis highly convenient, that turning my Discourse to more excellent and magnificent fabricks, I shou'd now proceed to treat of publick Edifices: wherein (because they consist of larger dimensions, and that they are beautify'd with more curious ornaments than private ones, as serving for the use and conveniency of every body) Princes have a most ample field to show the world the greatness of their Souls, and Architects are furnish'd with the fairest opportunity, to demonstrate their own abilities in excellent and surprizing inventions. Wherefore, as well in this book, in my *Antiquities*, as in those others, which (God willing) are to follow, it is my desire, that by so much the greater application may be us'd in considering the little I shall say, and the designs I shall give: by how much greater fatigue and longer watchings I have been reducing those fragments that remain of ancient buildings into such a form, that I hope the lovers of Antiquity may reap pleasure from the same, and the studious of Architecture receive much benefit: especially seeing that much more is learnt [1] in a little time from good examples, or originals by measuring them, and by seeing entire edifices with all their parts describ'd on a little piece of paper; than can in a long time be learnt from words, by which the Reader becomes able only in Idea, and not without some difficulty, to attain to a firm and certain knowledge of what he reads, and to bring it afterwards into practice with great fatigue. Every person who is not altogether depriv'd of Judgment, may very manifestly perceive, how excellent the manner was, which the Ancients us'd in their buildings: seeing that after so long a space of time, after so many destructions and mutations of empires, there still remain in *Italy*, and out of it, the vestigies or ruins of so great a number of their stately Edifices, by the means whereof we come to a certain knowledge of the *Roman* virtue and greatness, which otherwise perhaps had not been believ'd.[2]

CHRISTOPHER WREN

Of Architecture; and Observations on Antique Temples, &c

Parentalia: or Memoirs of the Family of the Wrens; Viz. of Mathew Bishop of Ely, Christopher Dean of Windsor, &c. But Chiefly of Sir Christopher Wren, Late Surveyor-General of the Royal Buildings, President of the Royal Society, Compiled by his Son Christopher, Now published by his Grandson, Stephen Wren . . . with the Care of Joseph Ames (London, 1750).

[From some rough Draughts, imperfect]

Architecture has its political Use; publick Buildings being the Ornament of a Country; it establishes a Nation, draws People and Commerce; makes the People love their native Country, which Passion is the Original of all great Actions in a Commonwealth. . . .

Architecture aims at Eternity; and therefore the only Thing uncapable of Modes and Fashions in its Principals, the *Orders*.

The *Orders* are not only *Roman* and *Greek*, but *Phoenician*, *Hebrew*, and *Assyrian*; therefore being founded upon the Experience of all Ages, promoted by the vast Treasures of all the great Monarchs, and Skill of the greatest Artists and Geometricians, every one emulating each other; and Experiments in this kind being greatly expenceful, and Errors incorrigible, is the Reason that the Principles of Architecture are now rather the Study of Antiquity than Fancy. . . .

There are natural Causes of Beauty. Beauty is a Harmony of Objects, begetting Pleasure by the Eye. There are two Causes of Beauty, natural and customary. Natural is from *Geometry*, consisting in Uniformity (that is Equality) and Proportion. Customary Beauty is begotten by the Use of our Senses to those Objects which are usually pleasing to us for other Causes, as Familiarity or particular Inclination breeds a Love to Things not in themselves lovely. Here lies the great Occasion of Errors; here is tried the Architect's Judgment: but always the, true Test is natural or geometrical Beauty. . . .[351]

Views contrary to Beauty are Deformity, or a Defect of Uniformity, and Plainness, which is the Excess of Uniformity; Variety makes the Mean.

Variety of Uniformities makes compleat Beauty: Uniformities are best tempered, as Rhimes in Poetry, alternately, or sometimes with more Variety, as in Stanza's.

In Things to be seen at once, much Variety makes Confusion, another Vice of Beauty. In Things that are not seen at once, and have no Respect one to another, great Variety is commendable, provided this Variety transgress not the Rules of *Opticks* and *Geometry*.

An Architect ought to be jealous of Novelties, in which Fancy blinds the Judgment; and to think his Judges, as well as those that are to live five Centuries after him, as those of his own Time. That which is commendable now for Novelty, will not be a new Invention to Posterity, when his Works are often imitated, and when it is unknown which was the Original; but the Glory of that which is good of itself is eternal.[352]

JAMES BOSWELL

The Life of Samuel Johnson, LL. D.

James Boswell, *The Life of Samuel Johnson, LL.D.* . . . (Printed by Henry Baldwin, for Charles Dilly, in the Poultry, London, 1791), I.

We then fell into a disquisition whether there is any beauty independent of utility. The General maintained there was not. Dr. Johnson maintained that there was; and he instanced a coffee-cup which he held in his hand, the painting of which was of no real use, as the cup would hold the coffee equally well if plain; yet the painting was beautiful.[364]

EDMUND BURKE

A Philosophical Inquiry into the Origin of Our Idea of the Sublime and Beautiful

Edmund Burke, "A Philosophical Inquiry into the Origin of Our Ideas of the Sublime and Beautiful," from The Works of the Right Honorable Edmund Burke, Revised Edition (Boston, Little, Brown and Company, 1865), I.

If, where parts were well adapted to their purposes, they were constantly beautiful, and when no use appeared, there was no beauty, which is contrary to all experience; we might conclude that beauty consisted in proportion or utility. But since, in all respects, the case is quite otherwise, we may be satisfied that beauty does not depend on these, let it owe its origin to what else it will.[187]

JOHN RUSKIN

Influence of Imagination in Architecture

John Ruskin, The Two Paths (New York, John Wiley, 1859); an Address Delivered to the Members of the Architectural Association in Lyon's Inn Hall, 1857.

If we were to be asked abruptly, and required to answer briefly, what qualities chiefly distinguish great artists from feeble artists, we should answer, I suppose, first, their sensibility and tenderness; secondly, their imagination; and thirdly, their industry. Some of us might, perhaps, doubt the justice of attaching so much importance to this last character, because we have all known clever men who were indolent, and dull men who were industrious. But though you may have known clever men who were indolent, you never knew a *great* man who was so; and, during such investigation as I have been able to give to the lives of the artists whose works are in all points noblest, no fact ever looms so large upon me—no law remains so steadfast in the universality of its application, as the fact and law that they are all great workers: nothing concerning them is matter of more astonishment than the quantity they have accomplished in the given length of their life; and when I hear a young man spoken of, as [113] giving promise of high genius, the first question I ask about him is always—

Does he work?

But though this quality of industry is essential to an artist, it does not in anywise make an artist; many people are busy, whose doings are little worth. Neither does sensibility make an artist; since, as I hope, many can feel both strongly and nobly, who yet care nothing about art. But the gifts which distinctively mark the artist—*without* which he must be feeble in life, forgotten in death—*with* which he may become one of the shakers of the earth, and one of the signal lights in heaven—are those of sympathy and imagination. I will not occupy your time, nor incur the risk of your dissent, by endeavouring to give any close definition of this last word. We all have a general and sufficient idea of imagination, and of its work with our hands and in our hearts: we understand it, I suppose, as the imaging or picturing of new things in our thoughts; and we always show an involuntary respect for this power, wherever we can recognise it, acknowledging it to be a greater power than manipulation, or calculation, or observation, or any other human faculty. If we see an old woman spinning at the fireside, and distributing her thread dexterously from the distaff, we respect her for her manipulation —if we ask her how much she expects to make in a year, and she answers quickly, we respect her for her calculation —if she is watching at the same time that none of [114] her grandchildren fall into the fire, we respect her for her observation— yet for all this she may still be a commonplace old woman enough. But if she is all the time telling her grandchildren a fairy tale out of her head, we praise her for her imagination, and say, she must be a rather remarkable old woman.

Precisely in like manner, if an architect does his working-drawing well, we praise him for his manipulation—if he keeps closely within his contract, we praise him for his honest arith-metic—if he looks well to the laying of his beams, so that nobody shall drop through the floor, we praise him for his observation. But he must, somehow, tell us a fairy tale out of his head beside all this, else we cannot praise him for his imagination, nor speak of him as we did of the old woman, as being in any wise out of the common way, a rather remarkable architect. It seemed to me, therefore, as if it might interest you to-night, if we were to consider together what fairy tales are, in and by architecture, to be told—what there is for you to do in this severe art of yours "out of your heads," as well as by your hands.

Perhaps the first idea which a young architect is apt to be allured by, as a head-problem in these experimental days, is its being incumbent upon him to invent a "new style" worthy of modern civilization in general, and of England in particular; a style worthy of our engines and telegraphs; as expansive as steam, and as sparkling as electricity.

But, if there are any of my hearers who have been im-pressed [115] with this sense of inventive duty, may I ask them, first, whether their plan is that every inventive architect among us shall invent a new style for himself, and have a county set aside for his conceptions, or a province for his practice? Or, must every architect invent a little piece of the new style, and all put it together at last like a dissected map? And if so, when the new style is invented, what is to be done next? I will grant you this Eldorado of imagination—but can you have more than one Columbus? Or, if you sail in company, and divide the prize of your discovery and the honour thereof, who is to come after your clustered Columbuses? to what fortunate islands of style are your architectural descendants to sail, avaricious of new lands? When our desired style is invented, will not the best we can all do be simply—to build in it?—and cannot you now do that in styles that are known? Observe, I grant, for the sake of your argument, what perhaps many of you know that I would not grant otherwise—that a new style *can* be invented. I grant you not only this, but that it shall be wholly different from any that was ever practised before. We will suppose that capitals are to be at the bottom of pillars instead of the top; and that buttresses shall be on the tops of pinnacles instead of at the bottom; that you roof your apertures with stones which shall neither be arched nor horizontal; and that you compose your decoration of lines which shall neither be crooked nor straight. The furnace and the forge shall be at your service: you [116] shall draw out your plates of glass and beat out your bars of iron till you have encompassed us all,—if your style is of the practical kind,—with endless perspective of black skeleton and blinding square,—or if your style is to be of the ideal kind,—you shall wreathe your streets with ductile leafage, and roof them with variegated crystal —you shall put, if you will, all London under one blazing dome of many colours that shall light the clouds round it with its flashing, as far as to the sea. And still, I ask you, What after this? Do you suppose those imaginations of yours will ever lie down there asleep beneath the shade of your iron leafage, or within the coloured light of your enchanted dome? Not so. Those souls, and fancies, and ambitions of yours, are wholly infinite; and, whatever may be done by others, you will still want to do something for yourselves; if you cannot rest content with Palladio, neither will you with Paxton: all the metal and glass that ever were melted have not so much weight in them as will clog the wings of one human spirit's aspiration.

If you will think over this quietly by yourselves, and can get the noise out of your ears of the perpetual, empty, idle, incomparably idiotic talk about the necessity of some novelty in architecture, you will soon see that the very essence of a Style, properly so called, is that it should be practised *for ages*, and applied to all purposes; and that so long as any given style is in practice, all that is left for individual imagination to accomplish must be within the [117] scope of that style, not in the invention of a new one. If there are any here, therefore, who hope to obtain celebrity by the invention of some strange way of building which must convince all Europe into its adoption, to them, for the moment, I must not be understood to address myself, but only to those who would be content with that degree of celebrity which an artist may enjoy who works in the manner of his forefathers;—

which the builder of Salisbury Cathedral might enjoy in England, though he did not invent Gothic; and which Titian might enjoy at Venice, though he did not invent oil painting. Addressing myself then to those humbler, but wiser, or rather, only wise students who are content to avail themselves of some system of building already understood, let us consider together what room for the exercise of the imagination may be left to us under such conditions. And, first, I suppose it will be said, or thought, that the architect's principal field for exercise of his invention must be in the disposition of lines, mouldings, and masses, in agreeable proportions. Indeed, if you adopt some styles of architecture, you cannot exercise invention in any other way. And I admit that it requires genius and special gift to do this rightly. Not by rule, nor by study, can the gift of graceful proportionate design be obtained; only by the intuition of genius can so much as a single tier of facade be beautifully arranged; and the man has just cause for pride, as far as our gifts can ever be a cause for pride, who finds himself [118] able, in a design of his own, to rival even the simplest arrangement of parts in one by Sanmicheli, Inigo Jones, or Christopher Wren.[119]

JOHN RUSKIN

The Stones of Venice

John Ruskin, *The Stones of Venice* (London, Smith, Elder, and Co., 1853), III.

If . . . any of my readers should determine, according to their means, to set themselves to [193] the revival of a healthy school of architecture in England, and wish to know in few words how this may be done, the answer is clear and simple. First, let us cast out utterly whatever is connected with the Greek, the Roman, or Renaissance architecture, in principle or in form. We have seen above, that the whole mass of the architecture, founded on Greek and Roman models, which we have been in the habit of building for the last three centuries, is utterly devoid of all life, virtue, honourableness, or power of doing good. It is base, unnatural, unfruitful, unenjoyable, and impious. Pagan in its origin, proud and unholy in its revival, paralyzed in its old age, yet making prey in its dotage of all the good and living things that were springing around it in their youth, as the dying and desperate king, who had long fenced himself so strongly with the towers of it, is said to have filled his failing veins with the blood of children [Louis XI of France]; an architecture invented, as it seems, to make plagiarists of its architects, slaves of its workmen, and Sybarites of its inhabitants; an architecture in which intellect is idle, invention impossible, but in which all luxury is gratified, and all insolence fortified;—the first thing we have to do is to cast it out, and shake the dust of it from our feet for ever. Whatever has any connexion with the five orders, or with any one of the orders,—whatever is Doric, or Ionic, or Tuscan, or Corinthian, or Composite, or in any wise Grecized or Romanized; whatever betrays the smallest respect for Vitruvian laws, or conformity with Palladian work,—that we are to endure no more. To cleanse ourselves of these "cast clouts and rotten rags" is the first thing to be done in the court of our prison.[194]

HENRY JAMES

A Small Boy and Others

Henry James, A Small Boy and Others (New York, Charles Scribner's Sons, 1913).*

We were not yet aware of style, though on the way to become so, but were aware of mystery, which indeed was one of its forms—while we saw all the others, without exception, exhibited at the Louvre, where at first they simply overwhelmed and bewildered me.

It was as if they had gathered there into a vast deafening chorus; I shall never forget how—speaking, that is, for my own

* Reprinted with the permission of John Farquharson, Ltd.

sense—they filled [345] those vast halls with the influence rather
of some complicated sound, diffused and reverberant, than of
such visibilities as one could directly deal with. To distinguish
among these, in the charged and coloured and confounding air,
was difficult—it discouraged and defied; which was doubtless why
my impression originally best entertained was that of those magnificent parts of the great gallery simply not inviting us to distinguish. They only arched over us in the wonder of their endless
golden riot and relief, figured and flourished in perpetual revolution, breaking into great high-hung circles and symmetries of
squandered picture, opening into deep outward embrasures that
threw off the rest of monumental Paris somehow as a told story,
a sort of wrought effect or bold ambiguity for a vista, and yet
held it there, at every point, as a vast bright gage, even at moments a felt adventure, of experience. This comes to saying that
in those beginnings I felt myself most happily cross that bridge
over to Style constituted by the wondrous Galerie d'Apollon,
drawn out for me as a long but assured initiation and seeming
to form with its supreme coved ceiling and inordinately shining
parquet a prodigious tube or tunnel through which I inhaled
little by little, that is again and again, a general sense of *glory*.
The glory meant ever so many things at once, not only beauty
and art and supreme design,[346] but history and fame and power,
the world in fine raised to the richest and noblest expression. . . .†
[347]

† The experience here recounted took place in 1856 when Henry James
was thirteen years old. (Ed.)

HENRY VAN BRUNT

Introduction to Eugène-Emmanuel
Viollet-le-Duc's *Discourses*

Eugène-Emmanuel Viollet-le-Duc, *Discourses*, trans. by Henry Van Brunt (Boston, James R. Osgood & Co., 1875).

INTRODUCTION BY THE TRANSLATOR

The French Academy of Painting and Sculpture was founded in 1648; that of Architecture, in 1671. The modern *École des Beaux Arts* is a direct descendant from these official schools; it has inherited all their collections, and in it are merged all their traditions of theory and practice. It is in the department of the Minister of Fine Arts, and is governed by a director appointed by the minister for five years; the administration includes a secretary, a treasurer, a librarian, and a custodian of the museum. This bureau is assisted by a council of instruction, composed of certain officials of state, two painters, two sculptors, two architects, an engraver or medallist, and five others. New members are elected to this council every year, replacing old members, who retire in turn. But old members are eligible for re-election, and practically the council has the power of filling its own vacancies. This important council has thus for a century been adapted naturally to the preservation of whatever inheritance of style and practice should be perpetuated for use in the great monuments of state, according to the traditions and prejudices of the school. The curriculum undertakes to embrace all branches of theory and practice. The theoretical studies comprehend aesthetics, the history of art, the elements of anatomy, perspective, geometry, mathematics, geology, physics, chemistry, archaeology, construction, and the administration of works. Practical instruction in drawing and design is given in the seven official *ateliers* of the school, three of these being devoted to architecture, and each being under the charge of a director. The whole is enshrined in a superb Palace, constructed for the accommodation of the school, and filled with precious objects of art and every appliance which can inform and inspire the mind.

Public interest is periodically attracted to the school by the annual competition for the "grand prize of Rome." This is open to any Frenchman under twenty-five years of age, whether a member of the school or not, who shall have been successful in two preliminary and stated competitions. For architects, sculptors, and painters, the grand competition is annual; for engravers on copper, every second year; for engravers on precious stones, every third year. One grand prize is given to each branch of art. The successful competitors (*lauréats*) are maintained at the public expense for four years, at least two of which must be spent at the Academy of France at Rome (in the Villa Medici, purchased for the purpose by Louis XIV.), under the control of a director, who is responsible to government for the progress of their studies. In witness of this progress, each *lauréat*, during his stay at Rome, sends to the school at Paris a work of sculpture,[v] painting, or an architectural composition. The remaining two years may be spent in travel, at the discretion of each *lauréat*, he previously having reported his intentions to the authorities. At Rome the architectural student usually devotes himself to measuring and restoring the antique.

Outside of the school proper, the principal architects of Paris, assuming functions as *patrons,* have their *ateliers* filled with students, who, with more or less regularity, attend the lectures of the school, but have their greatest interest engaged in a series of stated competitions (*concours*) based upon programmes officially prepared and announced. These competitions are decided by juries largely composed of architects not officially connected with the faculty of instruction, and culminate in the two great annual competitions preliminary to the final struggle for the grand prize of Rome.

All this machinery tends directly to the creation and prevalence of a style of architecture peculiarly academical, and which, considering the atmosphere of emulation in which it has grown and its extraordinary fidelity to a comparatively narrow range of precedent and study, must necessarily be carried to the highest degree of technical perfection. This style, first made national by the châteaux of Pierre Lescot, Philibert Delorme, Jean Bullant, and the other French architects of the sixteenth and seventeenth centuries, and afterwards giving expression, with peculiar felicity, to the pomp of that great builder, Louis XIV., is of course a form of the Renaissance.

The council of the school, loyal to the exclusive traditions of the place, is content to keep this national inheritance pure from foreign alloy and free from any rivalry or distractions of mediævalism. The architects of Paris, who desire official patronage and decoration; the students, who rejoice in the superb emulation and national distinction of the grand prize; the multitude, who are proud of their great historical monuments,—all, under these inspirations, cling to the academic style, and recognize no other. Within the shadow of Notre Dame and of the Sainte Chapelle, they are intolerant of any nearer approach to the pointed arch than the conventional use in their ecclesiastical buildings of the round-arched Romanesque of the twelfth century and of such other Byzantine elements as can be adapted to modern means and necessities.

Until lately even Greek influences have been admitted with jealousy. M. Henri Labrouste, a *lauréat* of Rome in the year 1824, studied the monuments of the Greek colonies, and sent home, as his official contribution to the school, a correct restoration of a Greek Doric temple. M. Joseph Louis Duc, a *lauréat* of the following year, and immediately afterwards M. Duban and M. Vaudoyer, pursued their studies in Italy in the same direction with intelligent [vi] enthusiasm, and brought back to France prolific seeds of Greek sentiment. This sentiment afterwards took form in what was known a few years ago in Paris as "the Romantic School," which consisted in the admission of a larger scope of invention and in the refinement of architectural forms by somewhat of the Greek feeling for purity and elegance of line. It was rather a Renaissance of Greek *expressions* than of Greek *principles,* and, owing to the facility with which even caprices could assume an air of studious elegance under this treatment, it became so popular and so well suited to French taste, that, after the construction of the Library of St. Genevieve

Photo John Barrington Bayle

The Arch of Constantine, 312 A.D., Rome, a triumphal arch. Built to commemorate great events, such arches told a story by means of sculpture, both statuary and bas-relief.

by M. Labrouste, the prejudices of the Academy were overcome, and it became an essential element of French architecture.

Meanwhile, in this uncongenial atmosphere, the Gothic or mediæval school received its chief encouragement from the archæological spirit; and M. Lassus and M. Viollet-le-Duc became engaged, not in the legitimate and practical development of their theories of art, but in the restoration of the Gothic monuments of France.

The academic style of Paris has thus enjoyed the unprecedented advantage of an undisturbed growth of four hundred years in the hands of the wealthiest and most artistic people in the world. They have lavished upon the Roman orders and upon their Italian derivatives of the fifteenth century—a basis of a few simple architectural *motifs*—all the decoration and refinement of nearly four centuries of industrious and consistent culture. What wonder if the civilized world accepts the extraordinary result with admiration? Elsewhere, it may be said, architecture has suffered from anarchy; here is what may be accomplished by the vigorous administration of art. Why ask for it the blessing of perfect freedom, when discipline can achieve such triumphs? If all this is wrong, where shall we look for the right? Who shall tell us how we can develop good architecture? Who, in short, shall interpret for us the architectural myth? . . .[vii]

We Americans occupy a new country, having no inheritance of ruins and no embarrassments of tradition in matters of architecture; we are absolutely free from historical prejudice; and yet with our great future we have a constant and growing necessity to make of architecture a living and growing art; we may therefore be in a position peculiarly well adapted to appreciate at its just value any honest and earnest effort to give this art true development according to modern necessities. . . .

But why, it may be asked, being so free and untrammelled, may we not break off from the past entirely and create a new American architecture,—why not begin afresh? To this, of course, there can be but one intelligent reply. All the past is ours; books, engravings, photographs, have so multiplied, that at any moment we can turn to and examine the architectural achievements of any age or nation. These suggestions of beauty and use are always with us. It must not be forgotten that the most essential

distinction between the arts of primitive barbarism and those of
civilization is that, while the former are original and independent,
and consequently simple, the latter must be retrospective, naturally turning to tradition and precedent, and are therefore
complex. A beginning once made by primitive discovery [x] and
experiment, art, like nature, must thenceforward proceed by deri-
vation and development; and where architectural monuments
and traditions have accumulated to the vast extent that they
have in modern times, the question is not whether we shall use
them at all, but how shall we choose among them, and to what
extent shall such choice be allowed to influence our modern practice.[xi]

. . . In the beginning of things, when the needs of mankind
were simple and their resources of knowledge and experience
comparatively small, the master-workman had his day. He developed his primitive forms directly and honestly from practical
necessity;

> "He builded better than he knew,
> The conscious stone to beauty grew."

His successors, unembarrassed by knowledge of other styles,
avoided his obvious errors, profited by his experience, learned
economy of materials, and, in a succession of tentative structures,
gradually and innocently evolved monuments exhibiting the results of well-concentrated thought and of fidelity to a few simple
conditions. The master-workman, however, laid aside his functions as an originator, and the architect was born, when precedent began so to accumulate, when civilization became so complex and exacting, the wants of mankind so various and conflicting, that, to meet the more elaborate emergencies of building,
there came to be needed a larger and more exact knowledge, a
more careful study of plans and details, and a more deliberate
and scientific method of construction. These conditions began to
render essential the organization of some processes and appliances, by means of which the system of structure in each case,
embracing all the details of the building, could be more exactly
and completely set forth long before the first stone was laid.
They implied, in short, draughtsmen, instruments of mathematical precision, a library of reference, and all the other appoint-

ments and conveniences of an office, that is, both of a studio and of a place of business. They implied, moreover, not only the unwritten experience of the builder, but the training and observation of the scholar, by means of which the most remote results could be foreseen and provided for; and more especially, they called for the feeling, the inspiration, the patience, self-denial, and tempered zeal of the artist. Uncultured genius may be eloquent, but its eloquence is ungrammatical; and although in architecture as in literature we may sometimes pardon the awkwardness of the phrase for the sake of the preciousness of the thought, in neither—and more especially in architecture, whose highest duty it is to embody history and civilization in durable monuments, and whose processes are so artificial and scientific— can the preciousness of the thought render less necessary purity of language, elegance of expression, and exactness of knowledge. Uncultured genius may in a moment of heaven-sent [xii] inspiration invent a great architectural thought, but plodding culture is needed to give it such expression as to render it worthy of place in the records of time and capable of doing duty as a new starting-point of architectural style. This is the plain *raison d'être* of the architect. He exists because civilization demands him. It is our present duty to see that he is worthy of his mission. [xiii]

ARTHUR SCHOPENHAUER

The World as Will and Idea

Arthur Schopenhauer, *The World as Will and Idea*, trans. by R. B. Haldane and
J. Kemp from the second German edition (London, Routledge and Kegan Paul, Ltd.,
1957), 10th impression.*

. . . THE OBJECT OF ART
(Book Three, Section 43; 1818)

If now we consider *architecture* simply as a fine art and
apart from its application to useful ends, . . . we can assign to
it no other aim than that of bringing to greater distinctness [I,276]
some of those ideas, which are the lowest grades of the objectivity of will; such as gravity, cohesion, rigidity, hardness,
those universal qualities of stone, those first, simplest, most inarticulate manifestations of will; the bass notes of nature; and
after these light, which in many respects is their opposite. Even
at these low grades of the objectivity of will we see its nature
revealing itself in discord; for properly speaking the conflict between gravity and rigidity is the sole aesthetic material of architecture; its problem is to make this conflict appear with perfect
distinctness in a multitude of different ways. It solves it by
depriving these indestructible forces of the shortest way to their
satisfaction, and conducting them to it by a circuitous route, so
that the conflict is lengthened and the inexhaustible efforts of
both forces become visible in many different ways. The whole
mass of the building, if left to its original tendency, would exhibit a mere heap or clump, bound as closely as possible to the
earth, to which gravity, the form in which the will appears here,
continually presses, while rigidity, also objectivity of will, resists.
But this very tendency, this effort, is hindered by architecture

* [The Haldane and Kemp translation of Schopenhauer's *Die Welt als
Wille und Vorstellung* first appeared in 1883]. (Eds.)

from obtaining direct satisfaction, and only allowed to reach it indirectly and by roundabout ways. The roof, for example, can only press the earth through columns, the arch must support itself, and can only satisfy its tendency towards the earth through the medium of the pillars, and so forth. But just by these enforced digressions, just by these restrictions, the forces which reside in the crude mass of stone unfold themselves in the most distinct and multifarious ways; and the purely aesthetic aim of architecture can go no further than this. Therefore the beauty, at any rate, of a building lies in the obvious adaption of every part, not to the outward arbitrary end of man (so far the work belongs to practical architecture), but directly to the stability of the whole, to which the position, dimensions, and form of every part must have so [I, 277] necessary a relation that, where it is possible, if any one part were taken away, the whole would fall to pieces. For just because each part bears just as much as it conveniently can, and each is supported just where it requires to be and just to the necessary extent, this opposition unfolds itself, this conflict between rigidity and gravity, which constitutes the life, the manifestation of will, in the stone, becomes completely visible, and these lowest grades of the objectivity of will reveal themselves distinctly. In the same way the form of each part must not be determined arbitrarily, but by its end, and its relation to the whole. The column is the simplest form of support, determined simply by its end: the twisted column is tasteless; the four-cornered pillar is in fact not so simple as the round column, though it happens that it is easier to make it. The forms also of frieze, rafter, roof, and dome are entirely determined by their immediate end, and explain themselves from it. The decoration of capitals, &c., belongs to sculpture, not to architecture, which admits it merely as extraneous ornament, and could dispense with it. According to what has been said, it is absolutely necessary, in order to understand the aesthetic satisfaction afforded by a work of architecture, to have immediate knowledge through perception of its matter as regards its weight, rigidity, and cohesion, and our pleasure in such a work would suddenly be very much diminished by the discovery that the material used was pumice-stone; for then it would appear to us as a kind of sham building. We would be affected in almost the same way if we were told that it was made of wood, when we had supposed it to be of stone, just because this alters and destroys the relations between rigidity and gravity, and consequently the significance and necessity of all the parts, for these natural forces reveal themselves in a far weaker degree in a wooden building. Therefore no real work of architecture as a fine art can be made of wood, although it assumes all forms so easily; this can only be [I,278] explained by our theory. If we were distinctly told that a building, the sight of which gave us pleasure, was made of different kinds of material of very unequal weight and consistency, but not distinguishable to the eye, the whole building would become as utterly incapable of affording us pleasure as a poem in an unknown language. All this proves that architecture does not affect us mathematically, but also dynamically, and that what speaks to us through it, is not mere form and symmetry, but rather those fundamental forces of nature, those first Ideas, those lowest grades of the objectivity of will. The regularity of the building and its parts is partly produced by the direct adaptation of each member to the stability of the whole, partly it serves to facilitate the survey and comprehension of the whole, and finally, regular figures to some extent enhance the beauty because they reveal the constitution of space as such. But all this is of subordinate value and necessity, and by no means the chief concern; indeed, symmetry is not invariably demanded, as ruins are still beautiful.

Works of architecture have further quite a special relation to light; they gain a double beauty in the full sunshine, with the blue sky as a background, and again they have quite a different effect by moonlight. Therefore, when a beautiful work of architecture is to be erected, special attention is always paid to the effects of the light and to the climate. The reason of all this is, indeed, principally that all the parts and their relations are only made clearly visible by a bright, strong light; but besides this I am of opinion that it is the function of architecture to reveal the nature of light just as it reveals that of things so opposite to it as gravity and rigidity. For the light is intercepted, confined, and reflected by the great opaque, sharply outlined, and variously formed masses of stone, and thus it unfolds its nature and qualities in the purest and clearest way, to the great pleasure of the beholders, for light is the [I,279] most joy-giving of things, as the condition and the objective correlative of the most perfect kind of knowledge of perception. . . .

Architecture has this distinction from plastic art and poetry: it does not give us a copy but the thing itself. It does not repeat, as they do, the known Idea, so that the artist lends his eyes to the beholder, but in it the artist merely presents the object to the beholder, and facilitates for him the comprehension of the Idea by bringing the actual, individual object to a distinct and complete expression of its nature.

Unlike the works of the other arts, those of architecture are very seldom executed for purely aesthetic ends. These are generally subordinated to other useful ends which are foreign to art itself. Thus the great merit of the architect consists in achieving and attaining the pure aesthetic ends, in spite of their subordination to other [I,280] ends which are foreign to them. This he does by cleverly adapting them in a variety of ways to the arbitrary ends in view, and by rightly judging which form of aesthetical architectonic beauty is compatible and may be associated with a temple, which with a palace, which with a prison, and so forth. The more a harsh climate increases these demands of necessity and utility, determines them definitely, and prescribes them more inevitably, the less free play has beauty in architecture. In the mild climate of India, Egypt, Greece, and Rome where the demands of necessity were fewer and less definite, architecture could follow its aesthetic ends with the greatest freedom. But under a northern sky this was sorely hindered. Here, when caissons, pointed roofs and towers were what was demanded, architecture could only unfold its own beauty within very narrow limits, and therefore it was obliged to make amends by resorting all the more to the borrowed ornaments of sculpture, as is seen in Gothic architecture.

We thus see that architecture is greatly restricted by the demands of necessity and utility; but on the other hand it has in them a very powerful support, for, on account of the magnitude and costliness of its works, and the narrow sphere of its aesthetic effect, it could not continue to exist merely as a fine art, if it had not also, as a useful and necessary profession, a firm and honourable place among the occupations of men. It is the want of this that prevents another art from taking its place beside architecture as a sister art, although in an aesthetical point of view it is quite properly to be classed along with it as its counterpart; I mean artistic arrangements of water. For what architecture accomplishes for the Idea of gravity when it appears in connection with that of rigidity, hydraulics accomplishes for the same Idea, when it is connected with fluidity, *i.e.*, formlessness, the greatest mobility and transparency. Leaping waterfalls foaming and tumbling over rocks,[I,281] cataracts dispersed into floating spray, springs gushing up as high columns of water, and clear reflecting lakes, reveal the Ideas of fluid and heavy matter, in precisely the same way as the works of architecture unfold the Ideas of rigid matter. Artistic hydraulics, however, obtains no support from practical hydraulics, for, as a rule, their ends cannot be combined; yet, in exceptional cases, this happens; for example, in the Cascata di Trevi at Rome.[1] . . .[I,282]

ON THE AESTHETICS OF ARCHITECTURE
(Supplement to Book Three; 1844)

In accordance with the deduction given in the text of the pure aesthetics of architecture from the lowest grades of the objectification of the will or of nature, the Ideas of which it seeks to bring to distinct perception, its one constant theme is *support and burden,* and its fundamental law is that no burden shall be without sufficient support, and no support without a suitable burden; consequently that the relation of these two shall be exactly the fitting one. The purest example of the carrying out of this theme is the column and entablature. Therefore the order or columnar arrangement has become, as it were, the thorough bass of the whole of architecture. In column and entablature the support and the burden are *completely separated;* whereby the reciprocal action of the two and their relation to each other becomes apparent. For certainly even every plain wall contains support and burden; but here the two are still fused together. All

---

[1] [The water of the Trevi Fountain affords not only pleasing cascades in a populous quarter of Rome to this day, but, at least before the introduction of modern plumbing, also served as the source from which the neighborhood drew water for household needs.] *Eds.*

is here support and all is burden; hence there is no aesthetic effect. This first appears through the separation, and takes place in proportion to its degree. For between the row of columns and the plain wall there are many intermediate degrees. Even in the mere breaking up of the wall of a house by windows and doors one seeks at least to indicate that separation by flat projecting pilasters (*antoe*) with capitals, which are inserted under the mouldings, nay, in case of need, are represented by mere painting, in order to indicate [III,182] in some way the entablature and an order. Real pillars, and also consoles and supports of various kinds, realise more that pure separation of support and burden which is striven after throughout by architecture. In this respect, next to the column with the entablature, but as a special construction not imitating it, stands the vault with the pillar. The latter certainly is far from attaining to the aesthetic effect of the former, because here the support and the burden are not *purely separated*, but are fused, passing over into each other. In the vault itself every stone is at once burden and support, and even the pillars, especially in groined vaulting, are, at least apparently, held in position by the pressure of opposite arches; and also just on account of this lateral pressure not only vaults but even mere arches ought not to rest upon columns, but require the massive four-cornered pillars. In the row of columns alone is the separation complete, for here the entablature appears as pure burden, the column as pure support. . . .

Moreover, the support is not adapted to the burden when it is only sufficient to bear it, but when it can do this so conveniently and amply that at the first glance we are quite at ease about it. Yet this superfluity of support must not exceed a certain degree; for otherwise we will perceive support without burden, which is opposed to the aesthetic end. . . . [III,183]

Indeed *ceteris paribus** the aesthetic effect is in exact proportion to the size of the building, because [III,186] only great masses make the action of gravitation apparent and impressive in a high degree. But this confirms my view that the tendency and antagonism of those fundamental forces of nature constitute the special aesthetical material of architecture, which, according

* [other things being equal.] *Eds.*

to its nature, requires large masses in order to become visible, and indeed capable of being felt. The forms in architecture, as was shown above in the case of the column, are primarily determined by the immediate structural end of each part. But so far as this leaves anything undetermined, the law of the most perfect clearness to perception, thus also of the easiest comprehensibility, comes in; for architecture has its existence primarily in our spatial perception, and accordingly appeals to our *a priori* faculty for this. But these qualities always result from the greatest regularity of the forms and rationality of their relations. Therefore beautiful architecture selects only regular figures composed of straight lines or regular curves, and also the bodies which result from these, such as cubes, parallelopipeda, cylinders, spheres, pyramids, and cones; . . . The same principle of perceptibility and easy comprehension demands also that a building should be easily surveyed. This introduces symmetry, which is further necessary to mark out the work as a whole, and to distinguish its essential from its [III, 187] accidental limitations; for sometimes, for example, it is only under the guidance of symmetry that one knows whether one has before one three buildings standing beside each other or only one. Thus only by means of symmetry does a work of architecture at once announce itself as individual unity, and as the development of a central thought.

Now although . . . architecture has by no means to imitate the forms of nature, such as the stems of trees or even the human figure, yet it ought to work in the spirit of nature, for it makes the law its own, *natura nihil agit frustra, nihilque supervacaneum, et quod commodissimum in omnibus suis operationibus sequitur*,* and accordingly avoids everything which is even only apparently aimless, and always attains the end in view in each case, whether this is purely architectonic, *i.e.*, structural, or an end connected with usefulness, by the shortest and most natural path, and thus openly exhibits the end through the work itself. Thus it attains a certain grace, analogous to that which in living creatures consists in the ease and suitableness of every movement and position to its end. Accordingly we see in the good antique

* [Nature does nothing in vain, nothing unnecessary, and follows what(ever) is most fitting in all her works. (Aristotle, *Politics,* Book I, Chap. 1, Section 10.)] Eds.

style of architecture every part, whether pillar, column, arch, entablature, or door, window, stair, or balcony, attain its end in the directest and simplest manner, at the same time displaying it openly and naively; just as organised nature also does in its works. The tasteless style of architecture, on the contrary, seeks in everything useless roundabout ways, and delights in caprices, thereby hits upon aimlessly broken and irregular entablatures, grouped columns, fragmentary cornices on door arches and gables, meaningless volutes, scrolls, and such like. It plays with the means of the art without understanding its aims, as children play with the tools of grown-up people. This was given above as the character of the bungler. Of this kind is every interruption of a straight line, every alteration [III, 188] in the sweep of a curve, without apparent end. On the other hand, it is also just that naive simplicity in the disclosure and attainment of the end, corresponding to the spirit in which nature works and fashions, that imparts such beauty and grace of form to antique pottery that it ever anew excites our wonder, because it contrasts so advantageously in original taste with our modern pottery, which bears the stamp of vulgarity, whether it is made of porcelain or common potter's clay. At the sight of the pottery and implements of the ancients we feel that if nature had wished to produce such things it would have done so in these forms. . . .

The sole theme of architecture here set forth—support and burden—is so very simple, that just on this account this art, so far as it is a fine art (but not so far as it serves useful ends), is perfect and complete in essential matters, since the best Greek period, at least, is not susceptible of any important enrichment. On the other hand, the modern architect cannot noticeably depart from the rules and patterns of the ancients without already being on the path of deterioration. Therefore there remains nothing for him to do but to apply the art transmitted to him by the ancients, and carry out the rules so far as is possible under the limitations which are inevitably laid down for him by wants, climate, age, and country. For in this art, as in sculpture, the effort after the ideal unites with the imitation of the ancients.

I scarcely need to remind the reader that in all these considerations I have had in view antique architecture alone, and not the so-called Gothic style, which is of Saracen origin, and was introduced by the Goths [III,189] in Spain to the rest of Europe. Perhaps a certain beauty of its own kind is not altogether to be denied to this style, but yet if it attempts to oppose itself to the former as its equal, then this is a barbarous presumption which must not be allowed for a moment. How beneficently, after contemplating such Gothic magnificence, does the sight of a building correctly carried out in the antique style act upon our mind! We feel at once that this alone is right and true. If one could bring an ancient Greek before our most celebrated Gothic cathedrals, what would he say to them?—. . . [Barbarians!*] Our pleasure in Gothic works certainly depends for the most part upon the association of ideas and historical reminiscences, thus upon a feeling which is foreign to art. All that I have said of the true aesthetic end, of the spirit and the theme of architecture, loses in the case of these works its validity. For the freely lying entablature has vanished, and with it the columns: support and burden, arranged and distributed in order to give visible form to the conflict between rigidity and gravity, are here no longer the theme. Moreover, that thorough, pure rationality by virtue of which everything admits of strict account, nay, already presents it of its own accord to the thoughtful beholder, and which belongs to the character of antique architecture, can here no longer be found; we soon become conscious that here, instead of it, a will guided by other conceptions has moved; therefore much remains unexplained to us. For only the antique style of architecture is conceived in a purely *objective* spirit; the Gothic style is more in the subjective spirit. Yet as we have recognised the peculiar aesthetic fundamental thought of antique architecture in the unfolding of the conflict between rigidity and gravity, if we wish to discover in Gothic architecture also an analogous fundamental thought, it will be this, that here the entire overcoming and conquest of gravity by rigidity is supposed to be exhibited. For in accordance with this the horizontal line which is that of burden has entirely [III,190] vanished, and the action of gravity only appears indirectly, disguised in arches and vaults, while the vertical line which is that of support, alone prevails, and makes palpable to the senses the victorious action of rigidity,

* [i.e., how outlandish!] *Eds.*

Courtesy French Government Tourist Office

The Cathedral of Notre Dame de Paris, 1163-1235, one of the best known Gothic buildings in Europe. Eugène-Emmanuel Viollet-le-Duc, father of the Modern Style of architecture, restored the Cathedral a hundred years ago.

in excessively high buttresses, towers, turrets, and pinnacles
without number which rise unencumbered on high. While in
antique architecture the tendency and pressure from above
downwards is just as well represented and exhibited as that from
below upwards, here the latter decidedly predominates; whence
that analogy often observed with the crystal, whose crystallisation
also takes place with the overcoming of gravity. If now we at-
tribute this spirit and fundamental thought to Gothic architecture, and would like thereby to set it up as the equally justified
antithesis of antique architecture, we must remember that the
conflict between rigidity and gravity, which the antique architecture so openly and naively expresses, is an actual and true
conflict founded in nature; the entire overcoming of gravity by
rigidity, on the contrary, remains a mere appearance, a fiction
accredited by illusion. Every one will easily be able to see clearly
how from the fundamental thought given here, and the peculiari-
ties of Gothic architecture noticed above, there arises that mysterious and hyperphysical character which is attributed to it. It
principally arises, as was already mentioned, from the fact that
here the arbitrary has taken the place of the purely rational,
which makes itself known as the thorough adaption of the means
to the end. The many things that are really aimless, but yet are so
carefully perfected, raise the assumption of unknown, unfath-
omed, and secret ends, i.e., give the appearance of mystery. On
the other hand, the brilliant side of Gothic churches is the interior; because here the effect of the groined vaulting borne by
slender, crystalline, aspiring pillars, raised high aloft, and, all
burden having disappeared, promising eternal security, impresses
the mind; while most of the faults which have been mentioned
lie [III, 191] upon the outside. In antique buildings the external
side is the most advantageous, because there we see better the
support and the burden; in the interior, on the other hand, the
flat roof always retains something depressing and prosaic. For
the most part, also, in the temples of the ancients, while the
outworks were many and great, the interior proper was small.
An appearance of sublimity is gained from the hemispherical
vault of a cupola, as in the Pantheon, of which, therefore, the
Italians also, building in this style, have made a most extensive
use. What determines this is, that the ancients, as southern

peoples, lived more in the open air than the northern nations who have produced the Gothic style of architecture. Whoever, then, absolutely insists upon Gothic architecture being accepted as an essential and authorised style may, if he is also fond of analogies, regard it as the negative pole of architecture, or, again, as its minor key. In the interest of good taste I must wish that great wealth will be devoted to that which is objectively, *i.e.,* actually, good and right, to what in itself is beautiful, but not to that whose value depends merely upon the association of ideas. Now when I see how this unbelieving age so diligently finishes the Gothic churches left incomplete by the believing Middle Ages, it looks to me as if it were desired to embalm a dead Christianity.[III, 192]

THORSTEIN VEBLEN

The Theory of the Leisure Class

Thorstein Veblen, *The Theory of the Leisure Class* (New York, The Macmillan Company, 1899).

This process of selective adaptation of designs to the end of conspicuous waste, and the substitution of pecuniary [153] beauty for aesthetic beauty, has been especially effective in the development of architecture. It would be extremely difficult to find a modern civilized residence or public building which can claim anything better than relative inoffensiveness in the eyes of anyone who will dissociate the elements of beauty from those of honorific waste. The endless variety of fronts presented by the better class of tenements and apartment houses in our cities is an endless variety of architectural distress and of suggestions of expensive discomfort. Considered as objects of beauty, the dead walls of the sides and back of these structures, left untouched by the hands of the artist, are commonly the best feature of the building.[154]

LOUIS H. SULLIVAN

The Tall Office Building
Artistically Considered

Louis H. Sullivan, "The Tall Office Building Artistically Considered," *Lippincott's Monthly Magazine*, LVII (March, 1896).

Certain critics, and very thoughtful ones, have advanced the theory that the true prototype of the tall office building is the classical column, consisting of base, shaft, and capital,—the moulded base of the column typical of the lower stories of our building, the plain or fluted shaft suggesting the monotonous uninterrupted series of office-tiers, and the capital the completing power and luxuriance of the attic.

Other theorizers, assuming a mystical symbolism as a guide, quote the many trinities in nature and in art, and the beauty and conclusiveness of such trinity in unity. They aver the beauty of prime numbers, the mysticism of the number three, the beauty of all things that are in three parts,—to wit, the day, subdividing into morning, noon, and night; the limbs, the thorax, and the head, constituting the body. So, they say, should the building be in three parts vertically, substantially as before, but for different motives.

Others, of purely intellectual temperament, hold that such a design should be in the nature of a logical statement; it should have a beginning, a middle, and an ending, each clearly defined, —therefore again a building, as above, in three parts vertically.

Others, seeking their examples and justification in the vegetable kingdom, urge that such a design shall above all things be organic. They quote the suitable flower with its bunch of leaves at the earth, its long graceful stem, carrying the gorgeous single flower. They point to the pine-tree,—its massy roots, its lithe, uninterrupted trunk,[406] its tuft of green high in the air.

Thus, they say, should be the design of the tall office building: again in three parts vertically.

Others still, more susceptible to the power of a unit than to the grace of a trinity, say that such a design should be struck out at a blow, as though by a blacksmith, or by mighty Jove, or should be thought-born, as was Minerva, full-grown. They accept the notion of a triple division as permissible and welcome, but non-essential. With them it is a subdivision of their unit: the unit does not come from the alliance of the three; they accept it without murmur, provided the subdivision does not disturb the sense of singleness and repose.

All of these critics and theorists agree, however, positively, unequivocally, in this, that the tall office building should not, must not, be made a field for the display of architectural knowledge in the encyclopædic sense; that too much learning in this instance is fully as dangerous, as obnoxious, as too little learning; that miscellany is abhorrent to their sense; that the sixteen-story building must not consist of sixteen separate, distinct, and unrelated buildings piled one upon the other until the top of the pile is reached.

To this latter folly I would not refer were it not the fact that nine out of every ten tall office buildings are designed in precisely this way in effect, not by the ignorant, but by the educated. It would seem, indeed, as though the "trained" architect, when facing this problem, were beset at every story, or, at most, every third or fourth story, by the hysterical dread lest he be in "bad form;" lest he be not bedecking his building with sufficiency of quotation from this, that, or the other "correct" building in some other land and some other time; lest he be not copious enough in his display of wares; lest he betray, in short, a lack of resource. To loosen up the touch of this cramped and fidgety hand, to allow the nerves to calm, the brain to cool, to reflect equably, to reason naturally, seems beyond him; he lives, as it were, in a waking nightmare filled with the *disjecta membra* of architecture. The spectacle is not inspiriting.

As to the former and serious views held by discerning and thoughtful critics, I shall, with however much of regret, dissent from them for the purposes of this demonstration, for I regard them as secondary only, non-essential, and as touching not at all upon the vital spot, upon the quick of the entire matter, upon the true, the immovable philosophy of the architectural art.

This view let me now state, for it brings to the solution of the problem a final, comprehensive formula:

All things in nature have a shape, that is to say, a form, an outward semblance, that tells us what they are, that distinguishes them from ourselves and from each other.

Unfailingly in nature these shapes express the inner life, the native quality, of the animal, tree, bird, fish, that they present to us; they are so characteristic, so recognizable, that we say, simply, it is "natural" it should be so. Yet the moment we peer beneath this surface of things, the moment we look through the tranquil reflection of ourselves and the clouds above us, down into the clear, fluent, unfathomable depths of nature, how startling is the silence of it, how amazing [407] the flow of life, how absorbing the mystery! Unceasingly the essence of things is taking shape in the matter of things, and this unspeakable process we call birth and growth. Awhile the spirit and the matter fade away together, and it is this that we call decadence, death. These two happenings seem joined and interdependent, blended into one like a bubble and its iredescence, and they seem borne along upon a slowly moving air. This air is wonderful past all understanding.

Yet to the steadfast eye of one standing upon the shore of things, looking chiefly and most lovingly upon that side on which the sun shines and that we feel joyously to be life, the heart is ever gladdened by the beauty, the exquisite spontaneity, with which life seeks and takes on its forms in an accord perfectly responsive to its needs. It seems ever as though the life and the form were absolutely one and inseparable, so adequate is the sense of fulfilment.

Whether it be the sweeping eagle in his flight, or the open apple-blossom, the toiling work-horse, the blithe swan, the branching oak, the winding stream at its base, the drifting clouds, over all the coursing sun, *form ever follows function,* and this is the law. Where function does not change, form does not change. The granite rocks, the ever-brooding hills, remain for ages; the lightning lives, comes into shape, and dies, in a twinkling.

It is the pervading law of all things organic and inorganic, of all things physical and metaphysical, of all things human and all things superhuman, of all true manifestations of the head, of the heart, of the soul, that the life is recognizable in its expression, that form ever follows function. *This is the law.*

Shall we, then, daily violate this law in our art? Are we so decadent, so imbecile, so utterly weak of eyesight, that we cannot perceive this truth so simple, so very simple? Is it indeed a truth so transparent that we see through it but do not see it? Is it really, then, a very marvellous thing, or is it rather so common-place, so everyday, so near a thing to us, that we cannot perceive that the shape, form, outward expression, design, or whatever we may choose, of the tall office building, should in the very nature of things follow the functions of the building, and that where the function does not change, the form is not to change?

Does not this readily, clearly, and conclusively show that the lower one or two stories will take on a special character suited to the special needs, that the tiers of typical offices, having the same unchanging function, shall continue in the same unchanging form, and that as to the attic, specific and conclusive as it is in its very nature, its function shall equally be so in force, in signifi-cance, in continuity, in conclusiveness of outward expression? From this results, naturally, spontaneously, unwittingly, a three-part division,—not from any theory, symbol, or fancied logic.

And thus the design of the tall office building takes its place with all other architectural types made when architecture, as has happened once in many years, was a living art. Witness the Greek temple, the Gothic cathedral, the mediæval fortress.

And thus, when native instinct and sensibility shall govern the [408] exercise of our beloved art; when the known law, the respected law, shall be that form ever follows function; when our architects shall cease strutting and prattling handcuffed and vainglorious in the asylum of a foreign school; when it is truly felt, cheerfully accepted, that this law opens up the airy sunshine of green fields, and gives to us a freedom that the very beauty and sumptuousness of the outworking of the law itself as ex-hibited in nature will deter any sane, any sensitive man from changing into license; when it becomes evident that we are merely speaking a foreign language with a noticeable American accent, whereas each and every architect in the land might, under the benign influence of this law, express in the simplest, most modest, most natural way that which it is in him to say: that he might really and would surely develop his own characteristic individuality, and that the architectural art with him would certainly become a living form of speech, a natural form of utterance, giving surcease to him and adding treasures small and great to the growing art of his land; when we know and feel that Nature is our friend, not our implacable enemy,—that an afternoon in the country, an hour by the sea, a full open view of one single day, through dawn, high noon, and twilight, will suggest to us so much that is rhythmical, deep, and eternal in the vast art of architecture, something so deep, so true, that all the narrow formalities, hard-and-fast rules, and strangling bonds of the schools cannot stifle it in us,—then it may be proclaimed that we are on the high-road to a natural and satisfying art, an architecture that will soon become a fine art in the true, the best sense of the word, an art that will live because it will be of the people, for the people, and by the people.[409]

LOUIS H. SULLIVAN

On the Historic Styles

Louis H. Sullivan, "Kindergarten Chat: A Sketch Analysis of Contemporaneous American Architecture," The Interstate Architect and Builder, III (November 9, 1901).*

It is a not uncommon happening to hear the inquiry made: "In what style is this building?" And, if a categorical answer is given even though it be: "This structure is in the Louis XIV style, with Gothic details, and Celtic ornaments, with adaptations to modern requirements," the questioner is satisfied; for the answer dove-tails into his preconception of architecture; namely, that it is a thing of "styles."

Now suppose the answer to be not categorical, and to run

    * The series is available in a paperback edition published in 1947 by George Wittenborn, New York.

something like this:—The structure is a serious attempt, by a serious architect, to make a building grow naturally, out of all its conditions, logically and poetically, I doubt if the questioner would be satisfied; for the answer will not dove-tail with his preconception;—and a man's preconception always governs unless he possess genuine culture.

Should he demur, and an argument follow, he is pretty sure to close it, to his satisfaction, in saying: "Well, a good copy is the best that can be done:—My friend, Mr. Blank, Architect, in whom I have great confidence, has told me so, repeatedly."

You will find it pretty difficult to convince such a man that there may now, as ever, exist a plastic and organic quality in the architectural art, ready at the hand of the Architect who has these qualities in his own mind. For his knowledge, such as it is, is ready-made, precisely as he believes architecture to be ready-made. It is needless to say that a genuine art cannot flourish within the range of such a man's influence. For such influence is ever a blight, not a nourishment. . . .

. . . If , for the word "style" we substitute the word, civilization, we make at once a pronounced stride in advance toward an intelligent understanding of the "values" of the historical monuments of architecture.

Hereafter, when you look on one of your contemporary "good copies" of historical remains ask yourself the question: not in what "style," but in what "civilization" is this building? and the absurdity, vulgarity, anachronism and solecism of the modern structure will be revealed to you in a most startling fashion. Of such and such a structure of the sort, for instance, manifestly we cannot say: this is a serious attempt, by a seriously minded architect, to make a building grow naturally, logically and poetically out of all its conditions, but no, this is an attempt, by a feeble-minded architect, living on the charity of modern American civilization, to reconstruct a part of the civilization of, say, Francis Ist, namely one of its buildings—a past and gone civilization, dead forever; and of which, he, this architect, can have no real knowledge, no true sense of its reality, not having lived as a part of it. Yet such is architecture, . . . today, as endorsed by people of "culture" or no culture, who believe, or affect to believe that "a good copy is the best that can be done." For shame!

How can culture, so-called, show itself more utterly shallow, than in this aspect of it? [6]

THOMAS E. TALLMADGE

Louis Sullivan and the Lost Cause

Thomas E. Tallmadge, The Story of Architecture in America (New York, W. W. Norton & Co., 1927).*

The ideal of an "American style" was not born in 1893. We find it mentioned, discussed, and prophesied now and again in the pages of architectural magazines. I find as far back as 1879 in the "American Architect" an article [214] entitled, "Originality in American Architecture: Combating the Prevailing Demand for an American Style."

The arguments for an American style seem cogent and reasonable; to some they are unanswerable. They are in effect this: here we are in a new country, favored physically as is no other country in the world; we live under the aegis of a most enlightened and beneficent democracy; our culture has been signalized by great and original discoveries in the sciences and in the mechanical arts; we stand as a nation for ideals of altruism and non-aggression that were unheard-of in the chancelleries of Europe until we practised them; the sun has never shone on a nation so abundantly blessed in material prosperity. Why, then, in Heaven's name, should we go to ancient Greece and Rome, extinct for two thousand years? Why should we go to mediaeval France or Renaissance Italy or modern Europe, whose policies we condemn and whose culture we think we excel, for our architectural styles and motives? The naval architect who built the Leviathan did not go to a Roman trireme for his model, nor does the manufacturer of a new stream-line model of his super-eight automobile fashion his chassis on the lines of a Roman chariot, nor does the modern engineer reinforce his concrete with slabs

* Reprinted with the permission of W. W. Norton & Company, Inc.

of tile after the fashion of Vitruvius. Why should the architects alone be reactionaries? Why should they alone wear the shackles of the past when all the world walks free?

Let it be said here, before we go on with the argument, that the task of the structural or naval or automotive engineer is a much simpler one than that of the architect. The public pretends to know nothing of these matters. The engineer, the scientist, speaks *ex cathedra*. It would be not only presumptuous but even dangerous for *vox populi* to be raised in matters as technical as these, but in [215] questions of art, of taste, of appearance—that is an entirely different matter. The public knows what it likes and says so in unmistakable terms.

I believe the arguments stated above are fallacious, and that the contention for an American style is the pursuit of a will-o'-the-wisp. The fallacy lies in the definition. What is or should be "the American style"? Surely, the style of architecture that best reflects the culture and genius of America. But what is the culture and genius of America? It is European. We are not aborigines. We are nearly or remotely Europeans, and we are not only Europeans, but we are ancients as well. "We are all Greeks. Our laws, our literature, our religion, our art, have their roots in Greece," said Shelley. "The point to which all paths lead and the point from which all paths start again is to be found in Rome and her abiding power."

If, then, it is true that we are co-heirs with our brothers who have not yet emigrated of the glory and the grandeur that were Greece and Rome; if the same blood that joined thrust to thrust in the dizzy groins of Amiens, that hung the vault of St. Peter's so little below the firmament, that flecked the streets of London with the white fingers of Wren's churches—if this same blood flows in our veins, why should we give up this royal heritage? It is ours as much as it is theirs across the seas.

The disciples of Sullivan—if not the master himself—regarded architecture not as a language, but as an habiliment. "Throw off the ancient tunic and the shabby surplice, the long-tail coat and the cocked hat," said they, "and we will give you a garment the like of which was never seen before, but which we tell you is really American and truly modern." But the people, like the

innocent child in the fairy tale, saw and cried, "The king is
naked." [216]

    . . . A third corollary . . . [that Louis Sullivan] attached to
his law [that the form should express the function] . . . which
became in the eyes of his followers more important than the law
itself—was complete originality. Nothing of ancient, mediaeval
or Renaissance Europe, nor, in fact, of any of our own previous
styles—for they in a sense were European—should enter into the
building. The ornament and the lines must be original, indigenous, of "pure design." Originality, however, has nothing to
do with the relations between form and function, and this corollary proved to be a tail heavier than the kite and in the end
turned a magnificent flight into a disastrous crash. . . .[217]

FRANK LLOYD WRIGHT

Louis Sullivan—His Work

Frank Lloyd Wright, "Louis H. Sullivan—His Work," The Architectural Record, LVI
(July, 1924).*

Is it not true that *individuality* is the supreme entertainment
of life? Surely it is the quality most precious in it and most
worthy of conservation; veritably the visible hand of the Creator!
Here in Louis Sullivan was an example as clear and convincing
as any, anywhere, at any time, under conditions as unpromising
to fulfilment as ever existed.

    Is it not probable that the social solidarity that produced
the great "styles" exists no longer in the same sense and that
never more will such a manifestation appear, especially in a
nation composed of nationalities like ours? But, as free opportunity offers, when America awakens spiritually or is awakened
by Spirit, individuality will come to flower in almost as many
styles as there are individuals capable of style. And there will

*Reprinted with the permission of The Architectural Record.

arise more and more men who are capable of it. Until we have a wealth of vital expression. We will then only need order in the aggregate—an "order" which will be established eventually by the nature of the individual intelligence capable of style—*itself* perceiving the necessity for it and making it therefore a veritable condition of every such individual expression. The nature capable of style is more capable than any other of the appropriate conduct of that power when and wherever need be.

Is not that a more desirable and logical conclusion to draw from the principle upon which this country was founded than that the dead level of a mongrelized version of the "Classic," a renaissance of Renaissance, should be allowed to characterize the mongrel as mongrel—and nothing more? [31]

FRANK LLOYD WRIGHT

The Art and Craft of the Machine

Frank Lloyd Wright, "The Art and Craft of the Machine," an address by Frank Lloyd Wright to the Chicago Arts and Crafts Society, at Hull House, March six, and to the Western Society of Engineers, March twenty, nineteen hundred and one. See *Catalogue* of the Fourteenth Exhibition of the Chicago Architectural Club (Chicago, 1901).

As we work along our various ways, there takes shape within us, in some sort, an ideal—something we are to become—some work to be done. This, I think, is denied to very few, and we begin really to live only when the thrill of this ideality moves us in what we will to accomplish. In the years which have been devoted in my own life to working out in stubborn materials a feeling for the beautiful, in the vortex of distorted complex conditions, a hope has grown stronger with the experience of each year, amounting now to a gradually deepening conviction that in the Machine lies the only future of art and craft—as I believe, a glorious future; that the Machine is, in fact, the metamorphosis of ancient art and craft; that we are at last face to face with the

machine—the modern Sphinx—whose riddle the artist must solve
if he would that art live—for his nature holds the key. For one,
I promise "whatever gods may be" to lend such energy and purpose as I may possess to help make that meaning plain; to return
again and again to the task whenever and wherever need be; for
this plain duty is thus relentlessly marked out for the artist in
this, the Machine Age, although there is involved an adjustment
to cherished gods, perplexing and painful in the extreme; the fire
of many long-honored ideals shall go down to ashes to reappear,
phœnix like, with new purposes.

The great ethics of the Machine are as yet, in the main, beyond the ken of the artist or student of sociology; but the artist
mind may now approach the nature of this thing from experience,
which has become the commonplace of his field, to suggest, in
time, I hope, to prove, that the machine is capable of carrying
to fruition high ideals in art—higher than the world has /yet
seen! . . .[1]

That the Machine has dealt Art in the grand old sense a
death-blow, none will deny.

The evidence is too substantial.

Art in the grand old sense—meaning Art in the sense of
structural tradition, whose craft is fashioned upon the handicraft
ideal, ancient or modern; an art wherein this form and that form
as structural parts were laboriously joined in such a way as to
beautifully emphasize the manner of the joining: the million and
one ways of beautifully satisfying bare structural necessities,
which have come down to us chiefly through the books as
"Art.". . .[3]

The artist's present plight is a sad one, but may he truthfully
say that society is less well off because Architecture, or even Art,
as it was, is dead, and printing, or the Machine, lives? Every age
has done its work, produced its art with the best tools or contrivances it knew, the tools most successful in saving the most
precious thing in the world—human effort. Greece used the
chattel slave as the essential tool of its art and civilization. This
tool we have discarded, and we would refuse the return of Greek
art upon the terms of its restoration, because we insist now upon
a basis of Democracy.

Is it not more likely that the medium of artistic expression itself has broadened and changed until a new definition and new direction must be given the art activity of the future, and that the Machine has finally made for the artist, whether he will yet own it or not, a splendid distinction between the Art of old and the Art to come? A distinction made by the tool which frees human labor, lengthens and broadens the life of the simplest man, thereby the basis of the Democracy upon which we insist. . . .[7]

We must walk blindfolded not to see that all that this magnificent resource of machine and material has brought us so far is a complete, broadcast degradation of every type and form sacred to the art of old; a pandemonium of tin masks, huddled deformities, and decayed methods; quarreling, lying, and cheating, with hands at each other's throats—or in each other's pockets; and none of the people who do these things, who pay for them or use them, know what they mean, feeling only—when they feel at all—that what is most truly like the past is the safest and therefore the best; as typical Marshall Field, speaking of his new building, has frankly said: "A good copy is the best we can do."

A pitiful insult, art and craft!

With this mine of industrial wealth at our feet we have no power to use it except to the perversion of our natural resources? A confession of shame which the merciful ignorance of the yet material frame of things mistakes for glorious achievement.

We half believe in our artistic greatness ourselves when we toss up a pantheon to the god of money in a night or two, or pile up a mammoth aggregation of Roman monuments, sarcophagi and Greek temples for a postoffice in a year or two—the patient retinue of the machine pitching in with terrible effectiveness to consummate this unhallowed ambition—this insult to ancient gods. The delicate, impressionable facilities of terra cotta becoming imitative blocks and voussoirs of tool-marked stone, badgered into all manner of structural gymnastics, or else ignored in vain endeavor to be honest; and granite blocks, cut in the fashion of the followers of Phidias, cunningly arranged about the steel beams and shafts, to look "real"—leaning heavily upon an inner skeleton of steel for support from floor to floor, which strains beneath the "reality" and would fain, I think, lie down to die of shame.

Courtesy French Government Tourist Office

The Cathedral of Notre Dame de Paris, 1163-1235; a view of the Cathedral from the east along the River Seine. Flying buttresses, supports devised by Gothic architects to reinforce thin, high-rising walls, are clearly visible around the apse.

The "masters"—ergo, the fashionable followers of Phidias—have been trying to make this wily skeleton of steel seem seventeen sorts of "architecture" at once, when all the world knows—except the "masters"—that it is not one of them.

See now, how an element—the vanguard of the new art—has entered here, which the structural-art equation cannot satisfy without downright lying and ignoble cheating.[8]

This element is the structural necessity reduced to a skeleton, complete in itself without the craftsman's touch. At once the million and one little ways of satisfying this necessity beautifully, coming to us chiefly through the books as the traditional art of building, vanish away—become history.

The artist is emancipated to work his will with a rational freedom unknown to the laborious art of structural tradition—no longer tied to the meagre unit of brick arch and stone lintel, nor hampered by the grammatical phrase of their making—but he cannot use his freedom.

His tradition cannot think.

He will not think.

His scientific brother has put it to him before he is ready.

The Art of old idealized a Structural Necessity—now rendered obsolete and unnatural by the Machine—and accomplished it through man's joy in the labor of his hands.

The new will weave for the necessities of mankind, which his Machine will have mastered, a robe [9] of ideality no less truthful, but more poetical, with a rational freedom made possible by the machine, beside which the art of old will be as the sweet, plaintive wail of the pipe to the outpouring of full orchestra.

It will clothe Necessity with the living flesh of virile imagination, as the living flesh lends living grace to the hard and bony human skeleton.

The new will pass from the possession of kings and classes to the every-day lives of all—from duration in point of time to immortality. . . .[10]

If the artist will only open his eyes he will see that the machine he dreads has made it possible to wipe out the mass of meaningless torture to which mankind, in the name of the artistic, has been more or less subjected since time began; for that matter, has made possible a cleanly strength, an ideality and a poetic fire that the art of the world has not yet seen; for the machine, the process now smooths away the necessity for petty structural deceits, soothes this wearisome struggle to make things seem what they are not, and can never be; satisfies the simple term of the modern art equation as the ball of clay in the sculptor's hand yields to his desire—comforting forever this realistic, brain-sick masquerade we are wont to suppose art. . . .

William Morris pleaded well for simplicity as the basis of all true art. Let us understand the significance to art of that word—SIMPLICITY—for it is vital to the Art of the Machine. . . .

Simplicity in art, rightly understood, is a synthetic, positive quality, in which we may see evidence of mind, breadth of scheme, wealth of detail, and withal a sense of completeness found in a tree or a flower.[12] A work may have the delicacies of a rare orchid or the stanch fortitude of the oak, and still be simple. A thing to be simple needs only to be true to itself in organic sense. . . .

Now let us learn from the Machine.

It teaches us that the beauty of wood lies first in its qualities as wood; no treatment that did not bring out these qualities all the time could be plastic, and therefore not appropriate—so not beautiful, the machine teaches us, if we have left it to the machine that certain simple forms and handling are suitable to bring out the beauty of wood and certain forms are not; that all wood-carving is apt to be a forcing of the material, an insult to its finer possibilities as a material having in itself intrinsically artistic properties, of which its beautiful markings is one, its texture another, its color a third.[13]

The machine, by its wonderful cutting, shaping, smoothing, and repetitive capacity, has made it possible to so use it without waste that the poor as well as the rich may enjoy to-day beautiful surface treatments of clean, strong forms that the branch veneers of Sheraton and Chippendale only hinted at, with dire extravagance, and which the middle ages utterly ignored.

The machine has emancipated these beauties of nature in wood; made it possible to wipe out the mass of meaningless torture to which wood has been subjected since the world began, for it has been universally abused and maltreated by all peoples but the Japanese.

Rightly appreciated, is not this the very process of elimination for which Morris pleaded?

Not alone a protest, moreover, for the machine, considered only technically, if you please, has placed in artist hands the means of idealizing the true nature of wood harmoniously with man's spiritual and material needs, without waste, within reach of all.

And how fares the troop of old materials galvanized into new life by the Machine?

Our modern materials are these old materials in more plastic guise, rendered so by the Machine, itself creating the very quality needed in material to satisfy its own art equation.

We have seen in glancing at modern architecture how they fare at the hands of Art and Craft; divided and sub-divided in orderly sequence with rank and file of obedient retainers awaiting the master's behest.

Steel and iron, plastic cement and terra-cotta.

Who can sound the possibilities of this old material, burned clay, which the modern machine has rendered as sensitive to the creative brain as a dry plate to the lens—a marvelous simplifier? And this plastic covering material, cement, another simplifier, enabling the artist to clothe the structural frame with a simple, modestly beautiful robe where before he dragged in, as he does still drag, five different kinds of material to compose one little cottage, pettily arranging it in an aggregation supposed to be picturesque—as a matter of fact, millinery, to be warped and beaten by sun, wind, and rain into a variegated heap of trash.[14]

FRANK LLOYD WRIGHT

An Organic Architecture:
The Architecture of Democracy

Frank Lloyd Wright, An Organic Architecture: The Architecture of Democracy; The
Sir George Watson Lectures of the Sulgrave Manor Board for 1939 (London, Lund
Humphries & Co., Ltd., 1939).*

An Organic Architecture means more or less organic society.
Organic ideals of integral building reject rules imposed by exterior æestheticism or mere taste, and so would the people to
whom such architecture would belong reject such external im-
positions upon life as were not in accord with the nature and
character of the man who had found his work and the place
where he could be happy and useful because of it in some scheme
of livelihood fair to him.[vii]

　. . . Modern architecture—let us now say *organic* architecture
—is a natural architecture—the architecture of nature, for Nature.

　To go back now for a moment to the central thought of
organic architecture, it was Lao Tze, five hundred years before
Jesus, who, so far as I know, first declared that the reality of the
building consisted not in the four walls and the roof but inhered
in the space within, the space to be lived in. That idea is entire
reversal of all pagan—"Classic"—ideals of building whatsoever. If
you accept that concept of building classical-architecture falls
dead to the ground. An entirely new concept has entered the
mind of the architect and the life of his people. My own recognition of this concept has been instinctive; I did not know of Lao
Tze when I began to build with it in my mind; I discovered him
much later. I came across Lao Tze quite by accident. One day
I came in from the garden where I had been working and picked

* Reprinted with the permission of Lund Humphries & Co., Ltd.

up a little book the Japanese Ambassador to America had sent
me and in it I came upon the concept of building I have just
mentioned to you. It expressed precisely what had been in my
mind and what I had myself been trying to do with a building:
"The reality of the building does not consist of walls and roof
but in the space within to be lived in." There it was! At first I was
[3] inclined to dissemble a little; I had thought myself somewhat
a prophet and felt I was charged with a great message which
humanity needed, only to find after all, that I was an "Also Ran."
The message had been given to the world thousands of years
ago. . . . So what? I could not hide the book nor could I conceal
the fact. For some time I felt as a punctured balloon looks. But
then I began to see that, after all, I had not derived that idea
from Lao Tze; it was a deeper, profound something that survived
in the world, something probably eternal therefore universal,
something that persisted and will persist for ever. Then I began
to feel that I ought to be proud to have perceived it as Lao Tze
had perceived it and to have tried to *build* it! I need not be too
disappointed. As I found, so you may find, that that concept
of architecture alive today as *modern*, is first of all, *organic*.
"Organic" is the word which we should apply to this new architecture. So here I stand before you preaching *organic* architecture; declaring organic architecture to be the modern ideal and
the teaching so much needed if we are to see the whole of life,
and to now serve the whole of life, holding no "traditions" essential to the great TRADITION. Nor cherishing any preconceived
form fixing upon us either past, present or future, but—instead—
exalting the simple laws of common sense—or of super-sense if
you prefer—determining form by way of the nature of materials,
the nature of purpose so well understood that a bank will not
look like a Greek temple, a university will not look like a cathedral, nor a fire-engine house resemble a French château, or
what have you? Form follows Function? Yes, but more important now *Form and Function are One*.[4]

PETER F. R. DONNER

Criticism

Peter F. R. Donner, "Criticism," The Architectural Review, XC (August, 1941).*

The lectures which Mr. Frank Lloyd Wright gave to the R.I.B.A. just before the war were published under the title *An Organic Architecture.* I was not in London at the time, missed the personal impression of the old *charmeur,* and therefore cannot overcome my doubts about the conclusiveness of his arguments. . . .

Mr. Wright's book starts from and keeps paraphrasing the contrast of Classic and Organic, an arbitrary, limping, lop-sided and moreover ugly-sounding contrast. He should at least say Classical. To Mr. Wright organic architecture means an architecture that "loves the ground" on which it stands, classic one that "hates it." Organic includes recognition of "the industrial conditions, the nature of materials, and the purpose of the building"; classic stands for disregard of all these. The organic architect is "the architect of nature": he follows "the nature principle"; all the classic architect can achieve is a "crucifixion of life". Organic is the will "to serve life"; classic "an imposition on it"; organic is "human", "democratic", the happy pursuit of "the suntanned brow"; classic is "monarchic", it is what the "gentleman" chooses to show up his privileges of birth and education; it is "formality". Classic houses present themselves "in military fashion, heels together, eyes front, something on the right, and something on the left". They can never be "buildings to live in", as organic houses are.

Now all this teems with fallacies and bristles with loose verbage. There is, for example, the contention that architecture is the product of purpose, building materials and processes of construction, the old contention launched by Gottfried Semper and then

*Reprinted with the permission of *The Architectural Review.*

immediately taken up by Owen Jones and others, a typical 1850 theory, as blatantly materialistic as Marx's and Darwin's, and yet revived in our days by dogmatic functionalists.[68] . . . Then there is that die-hard fallacy, the accordance with nature. Blondel has it in the seventeenth century, where he tries to derive the Greek temple from the primitive log-hut, and Laugier in the eighteenth, who regards the Gothic cathedral as an imitation of a forest of tall trees. The neo-Classical theorists saw wooden posts reflected in Doric columns, old Hall in 1813 boughs tied together in a pointed arch. In a less superficial way Goethe when he was young praised Gothic because of its "great harmonious masses enlivened by infinite minute parts, as in the works of eternal nature", and when he was older praised Greek because of its harmony with the nobility of human nature, and the beauty of form and proportion of human physique.

To Mr. Wright Greece is, of course, the source of all evil. From Greece via Rome and the Italy of the Renaissance his Classic came to poison the North. But is "the major axis and the minor axis . . . something on the right and something on the left" really anti-organic, unnatural, an "imposition on life"? After all, we are built that way, even Mr. Wright, and so are our horses and our dogs. The "nature principle" is not an undisciplined *élan vital*, but rigid law, cosmos not chaos, symmetry not asymmetry. . . .[69]

JOHN BARRINGTON BAYLEY

Letter to the Editor of LANDSCAPE

Letter of John Barrington Bayley to the Editor of *Landscape*, IV (Summer, 1954).*

. . . [Frank Lloyd] Wright might be described as: one third Elbert Hubbard (the American apostle of the "Arts & Crafts" movement), one third Richard Wagner (in his Teutonic romanticizing of Soil and Earth, and in the great hearths with their

* Reprinted with the permission of *Landscape*.

leaping flames which are the solar plexi of his houses), and one third John Cowper Powys, the Welsh bard. (The [30] metaphysical brio of Wright's philosophy owes much to his Welsh background.) . . .

Why has abstract art become the accepted commercial and academic standard?

In troubled times what could be safer than saying nothing? What could be safer than carving or painting or writing "from within"? What could be more transigent than being safely subjective? The utility of an anesthetized intelligentsia has been recognized and rewarded by the press, and by the eleemosynary institutions, universities, foundations, museums, which are our chief patrons of art through stipends, scholarships, teaching jobs, etc.

The pleasure HE and SHE derive from abstract art has little to do with art. It is the innocent pleasure of feeling a part of an intellectual "corps d'élite." Outsiders are either reactionary, or just plain "dull."

The days of this easy "one-upmanship" are, however, numbered. The trouble is that ANYONE can do abstract art. The professional artist is unnecessary.

This means that the "happy few" are in danger of becoming the anonymous many, and that [31] moment is, in fact, at hand. Professional artists, as distinct from teachers, commercials, etc., are nearly extinct, while department stores from Coast to Coast stock mobiles, driftwood, and the other props of the movement too familiar to mention. (This is not to say, of course, that abstract art will not persist for many years as a kind of occupational therapy.)

Modern architecture is also abstract. First there are the obvious connections with painting and sculpture in the method of composition, of forms, of dependence on pattern, texture, and the like; and second there is the same negation of meaning. For many years architectural books have juxtaposed, say, a gasometer with the Mausoleum of Hadrian, or grain elevators and truncated columns. The purpose of this is to show that what buildings are is not important, but that forms being equal, they are equally beautiful, or rather "important," no matter where they are. Besides the "too familiar syllogism," another form of abstraction is the hailing of power stations as "the cathedrals of our age." What a building *is* has no meaning; it is an abstraction; an abattoir can be as beautiful as a villa.

The pleasures of abstract art have in architecture been joined with those of idealism. Every architect has always felt that the world would be a better place if it could be rebuilt according to his own esthetic preferences. Modern architects, however, differ from their predecessors in one important respect. Whereas the architects of the past dreamt of their Golden Age in terms of architecture, the modern architect (awed and depressed by the strongholds of knowledge inhabited by specialists) has turned to preoccupations with sociology, economics, engineering, and psychology. When the architect is more interested in the relation of a building to various things than in architecture itself, then his design becomes no more than a prose account of this or that situation (a correct answer to a difficult examination question), and architecture as an art ceases to exist. This is precisely what has happened.

Nothing has happened in architectural *art* since the '20's beyond the evolution of mannerisms such as: "natural textures" (always rough), "natural colors" (always blonde), and ever bigger philodendrons, the plant that made modern architecture possible.

The masterpieces of the Modern Style were created in the '20's. Successive operations have not only brought no return upon the Modern's philosophic and theoretical capital, but show an investment so diminished that it seems to have dwindled away completely. The creators of those masterpieces are now the grand panjandrums of the academies; the "modern generation" is in its sixties, and its followers are the "good guys" of Louis Kronenberger's "Company Manners." . . .

John Barrington Bayley

Cambridge, Mass.[32]

LE CORBUSIER

Towards a New Architecture

Le Corbusier, *Towards a New Architecture*, trans. by Frederick Etchells (New York, Payson and Clarke Ltd., 1927).*

EYES WHICH DO NOT SEE

LINERS

A great epoch has begun.

There exists a new spirit.

There exists a mass of work conceived in the new spirit; it is to be met with particularly in industrial production.

Architecture is stifled by custom.

The "styles" are a lie.

Style is a unity of principle animating all the work of an epoch, the result of state of mind which has its own special character.

Our own epoch is determining, day by day, its own style.

Our eyes, unhappily, are unable yet to discern it.[3]

AIRPLANES

The airplane is the product of close selection.

The lesson of the airplane lies in the logic which governed the statement of the problem and its realization.

The problem of the house has not yet been stated.

Nevertheless there also do exist standards for the dwelling house.

Machinery contains in itself the factor of economy, which makes for selection.

The house is a machine for living in. . . .[4]

THE ILLUSION OF PLANS

The Plan proceeds from within to without; the exterior is the result of an interior.

The elements of architecture are light and shade, walls and space.

Arrangement is the gradation of aims, the classification of intentions.

Man looks at the creation of architecture with his eyes, which are 5 feet 6 inches from the ground. One can only deal with aims which the eye can appreciate, and intentions which take into account architectural elements. If there come into play intentions which do not speak the language of architecture, you arrive at the illusion of plans, you transgress the rules of the Plan through an error in conception, or through a leaning toward empty show. . . .[5]

MASS-PRODUCTION HOUSES

A great epoch has begun.

There exists a new spirit.

Industry, overwhelming us like a flood which rolls on toward its destined ends, has furnished us with new tools adapted to this new epoch, animated by the new spirit.

Economic law inevitably governs our acts and our thoughts.

The problem of the house is a problem of the epoch. The equilibrium of society to-day depends upon it. Architecture has for its first duty, in this period of renewal, that of bringing about a revision of values, a revision of the constituent elements of the house.

Mass production is based on analysis and experiment.

Industry on the grand scale must occupy itself with building and establish the elements of the house on a mass-production basis.

We must create the mass-production spirit.

The spirit of constructing mass-production houses.

The spirit of living in mass-production houses.

The spirit of conceiving mass-production houses.

If we eliminate from our hearts and minds all dead concepts

Photo John Barrington Bay

The Church of San Francesco, 1447-1455, Rimini, designed by Leon Battista Alberti. Beneath the arches along the flank of the church are symbolic tombs to commemorate great poets.

in regard to the house, and look at the question from a critical [6] and objective point of view, we shall arrive at the "House-Machine," and the mass-production house, healthy (and morally so too) and beautiful in the same way that the working tools and instruments which accompany our existence are beautiful.

Beautiful also with all the animation that the artist's sensibility can add to severe and pure functioning elements.

ARCHITECTURE OR REVOLUTION

In every field of industry, new problems have presented themselves and new tools have been created capable of resolving them. If this new fact be set against the past, then you have revolution.

In building and construction, mass-production has already been begun; in face of new economic needs, mass-production units have been created both in mass and detail; and definite results have been achieved both in detail and in mass. If this fact be set against the past, then you have revolution, both in the method employed and in the large scale on which it has been carried out.

The history of Architecture unfolds itself slowly across the centuries as a modification of structure and ornament, but in the last fifty years steel and concrete have brought new conquests, which are the index of a greater capacity for construction, and of an architecture in which the old codes have been overturned. If we challenge the past, we shall learn that "styles" no longer exist for us, that a style belonging to our own period has come about; and there has been a Revolution. [7]

Our minds have consciously or unconsciously apprehended these events and new needs have arisen, consciously or unconsciously.

The machinery of Society, profoundly *out of gear*, oscillates between an amelioration, of historical importance, and a catastrophe.

The primordial instinct of every human being is to assure himself of a shelter. The various classes of workers in society today *no longer have dwellings adapted to their needs; neither the artizan nor the intellectual.*

It is a question of building which is at the root of the social unrest of to-day: architecture or revolution.[8]

THREE REMINDERS TO ARCHITECTS

I

MASS

Architecture has nothing to do with the various "styles."

The styles of Louis XIV, XV, XVI or Gothic, are to architecture what a feather is on a woman's head; it is sometimes pretty, though not always, and never anything more.

Architecture has graver ends; capable of the sublime, it [25] impresses the most brutal instincts by its objectivity; it calls into play the highest faculties by its very abstraction. Architectural abstraction has this about it which is magnificently peculiar to itself, that while it is rooted in hard fact it spiritualizes it, because the naked fact is nothing more than the materialization of a possible idea. The naked fact is a medium for ideas only by reason of the "order" that is applied to it. The emotions that architecture arouses spring from physical conditions which are inevitable, irrefutable and to-day forgotten.

Mass and surface are the elements by which architecture manifests itself.

Mass and surface are determined by the plan. The plan is the generator. So much the worse for those who lack imagination! [26]

FIRST REMINDER: MASS

Architecture is the masterly, correct and magnificent play of masses brought together in light. Our eyes are made to see forms in light; light and shade reveal these forms; cubes, cones, spheres, cylinders or pyramids are the great primary forms which light reveals to advantage; the image of these is distinct and tangible within us and without ambiguity. It is for that reason that these are *beautiful forms, the most beautiful forms*. Everybody is agreed as to that, the child, the savage, and the meta-physician. It is of the very nature of the plastic arts. . . .[29]

The *architects* of today, lost in the sterile backwaters of their plans, their foliage, their pilasters and their lead roofs, have never acquired the conception of primary masses. They were never taught that at the Schools.

Not in the pursuit of an architectural idea, but simply guided by the results of calculation (derived from the principles which govern our universe) and the conception of A LIVING ORGANISM, *the* ENGINEERS *of to-day make use of the primary elements and, by co-ordinating them in accordance with the rules, provoke in us architectural emotions and thus make the work of man ring in unison with universal order.*

Thus we have the American grain elevators and factories, the magnificent FIRST-FRUITS *of the new age.* THE AMERICAN ENGINEERS OVERWHELM WITH THEIR CALCULATIONS OUR EXPIRING ARCHITECTURE.[31]

Eyes Which Do Not See

II

AIRPLANES

One commonplace among Architects (the younger ones): *the construction must be shown.*

Another commonplace amongst them: *when a thing responds to a need, it is beautiful.*

But . . . To show the construction is all very well for an Arts and Crafts student who is anxious to prove his ability. The Almighty has clearly shown our wrists and our ankles, but there remains all the rest!

When a thing responds to a need, it is not beautiful; it satisfies all one part of our mind, the primary part, without which there is no possibility of richer satisfactions; let us recover the right order of events.

Architecture has another meaning and other ends to pursue than showing construction and responding to needs (and by "needs" I mean utility, comfort and practical arrangement).

ARCHITECTURE is the art above all others which achieves a state of platonic grandeur, mathematical order, speculation,[110] the perception of the harmony which lies in emotional relationships. This is the AIM of architecture. . . .[111]

WALTER GROPIUS

The New Architecture and the Bauhaus

Walter Gropius, *The New Architecture and the Bauhaus*, trans. by P. Morton Shand (New York, Museum of Modern Art, 1937).*

A breach has been made with the past, which allows us to envisage a new aspect of architecture corresponding to the technical civilization of the age we live in; the morphology of dead styles has been destroyed; and we are returning to honesty of thought and feeling. The general public, formerly profoundly indifferent to [17] everything to do with building, has been shaken out of its torpor; personal interest in architecture as something that concerns every one of us in our daily lives has been very widely aroused; and the broad lines of its future development are already clearly discernible. It is now becoming widely recognized that although the outward forms of the New Architecture differ fundamentally in an organic sense from those of the old, they are not the personal whims of a handful of architects avid for innovation at all cost, but simply the inevitable logical product of the intellectual, social and technical conditions of our age. . . .

But the development of the New Architecture encountered serious obstacles at a very early stage of its development. Conflicting theories and the dogmas enunciated in architects' personal manifestos all helped to confuse the main issue.[18]. . .

That is why the movement must be purged from within if its original aims are to be saved from the straitjacket of materialism and false slogans inspired by plagiarism or misconception. Catch phrases like 'functionalism' . . . and 'fitness for purpose =

* Reprinted with the permission of the Museum of Modern Art.

beauty' have had the effect of deflecting appreciation of the New Architecture into external channels or making it purely one-sided. . . .

For instance, rationalization, which many people imagine to be its cardinal principle, is really only its purifying agency. The liberation of architecture from a welter of ornament, the [19] emphasis on its structural functions, and the concentration on concise and economical solutions, represent the purely material side of that formalizing process on which the *practical* value of the New Architecture depends. The other, the aesthetic satisfaction of the human soul, is just as important as the material. Both find their counterpart in that unity which is life itself. What is far more important than this structural economy and its functional emphasis is the intellectual achievement which has made possible a new spatial vision. For whereas building is merely a matter of methods and materials, architecture implies the mastery of space. . . .[20]

One of the outstanding achievements of the new constructional technique has been the abolition of the separating function of the wall. Instead of making the walls the element of [21] support, as in a brick-built house, our new space-saving construction transfers the whole load of the structure to a steel or concrete framework. Thus the role of the walls becomes restricted to that of mere screens stretched between the upright columns of this framework to keep out rain, cold, and noise. . . . It is, therefore, only logical that the old type of window—a hole that had to be hollowed out of the full thickness of a [22] supporting wall—should be giving place more and more to the continuous horizontal casement, subdivided by thin steel mullions, characteristic of the New Architecture. And as a direct result of the growing preponderance of voids over solids, glass is assuming an ever greater structural importance. Its sparkling insubstantiality, and the way it seems to float between wall and wall imponderably as the air, adds a note of gaiety to our modern homes.

In the same way the flat roof is superseding the old penthouse roof with its tiled or slated gables. . . .[23]

Our age has initiated a rationalization of industry based on the kind of working partnership between manual and mechanical production we call standardization which is already having direct repercussions on building. . . .[25] A standard may be defined as that simplified practical exemplar of anything in general use which embodies a fusion of the best of its anterior forms — a fusion preceded by the elimination of the personal content of their designers and all otherwise ungeneric or non-essential features. . . . The fear that individuality will be crushed out by the growing 'tyranny' of standardization [26] is the sort of myth which cannot sustain the briefest examination. In all great epochs of history the existence of standards—that is the conscious adoption of type-forms—has been the criterion of a polite and well-ordered society; for it is a commonplace that repetition of the same things for the same purposes exercises a settling and civilizing influence on men's minds. . . .[27]

. . . A prudent limitation of variety to a few standard types of buildings increases their quality and decreases their cost; thereby raising the social level of the population as a whole. Proper respect for tradition will find a truer echo in these than in the miscellaneous solutions of an often arbitrary and aloof individualism because the greater communal utility of the former embodies a deeper architectural significance. . . .[28]

We are approaching a state of technical proficiency when it will become possible to rationalize buildings and mass-produce them in factories by resolving their structure into a number of component parts. Like boxes of toy bricks, these will be assembled in various formal compositions in a dry state: which means that building will definitely cease to be dependent on the weather. Ready-made houses of solid fireproof construction, that can be delivered fully equipped from stock, will ultimately become one of the principal products of industry. Before this is practicable, however, every part of the house—floor-beams, wall-slabs, windows, doors, staircases, and fittings—will have to be normed.[29] The repetition of standardized parts, and the use of identical materials in different buildings, will have the same sort of coordinating and sobering effect on the aspect of our towns as uniformity of type in modern attire has in social life. But that will in no sense restrict the architect's freedom of design. For although every house and block of flats will bear the unmistakable impress of our age, there will always remain, as in the clothes we wear, sufficient scope for the individual to find expression for his own personality. . . .[30]

So much for technique!—But what about beauty?

The New Architecture throws open its walls like curtains to admit a plenitude of fresh air,[31] daylight and sunshine. Instead of anchoring buildings ponderously into the ground with massive foundations, it poises them lightly, yet firmly, upon the face of the earth; and bodies itself forth, not in stylistic imitation or ornamental frippery, but in those simple and sharply modelled designs in which every part merges naturally into the comprehensive volume of the whole. Thus its aesthetic meets our material and psychological requirements alike.

For unless we choose to regard the satisfaction of those conditions which can alone animate, and so humanize, a room—spatial harmony, repose, proportion—as an ideal of some higher order, architecture cannot be limited to the fulfilment of its structural function.

We have had enough and to spare of the arbitrary reproduction of historic styles. In the progress of our advance from the vagaries of mere architectural caprice to the dictates of structural logic, we have learned to seek concrete expression of the life of our epoch in clear and crisply simplified forms.[32]

HENRY-RUSSELL HITCHCOCK, JR.
AND PHILIP JOHNSON

The International Style:
Architecture Since 1922

Henry-Russell Hitchcock, Jr., and Philip Johnson, *The International Style: Architecture Since 1922* (New York, W. W. Norton & Co., 1932).*

PREFACE by Alfred H. Barr, Jr.

The distinguishing aesthetic principles of the International Style as laid down by the authors are three: emphasis upon volume—space enclosed by thin planes or surfaces as opposed to the suggestion of mass and solidity; regularity as opposed to symmetry or other kinds of obvious balance; and, lastly, dependence upon the intrinsic elegance of materials, technical perfection, and fine proportions, as opposed to applied ornament.[13]

A FIRST PRINCIPLE: ARCHITECTURE AS VOLUME

Contemporary methods of construction provide a cage or skeleton of supports. This skeleton as it appears before the building is enclosed is familiar to everyone. Whether the supports are of metal or of reinforced concrete, the effect from a distance is of a grille of verticals and horizontals. For protection against the weather it is necessary that this skeleton should be in some way enclosed by walls. In traditional masonry construction the walls were themselves the supports. Now the walls are merely subordinate elements fitted like screens between the supports or carried like a shell outside of them. . . .[40]

* Reprinted by permission of W. W. Norton & Company, Inc.

. . . Entire façades are frequently cantilevered and the screen walls set some distance outside the supports. . . .

The effect of mass, of static solidity, hitherto the prime quality of architecture, has all but disappeared; in its place there is an effect of volume, or more accurately, of plane surfaces bounding a volume. The prime architectural symbol is no longer the dense brick but the open box. . . .[41]

. . . Style is character, style is expression; but even character must be displayed and expression may be conscious and clear, or muddled and deceptive. The architect who builds in the international style seeks to display the true character of his construction and to express clearly his provision for function. He prefers such an organization of his general composition, such a use of available surface materials, and such a handling of detail as will increase rather than contradict the prime effect of surface of volume.

In giving this effect the flat roofs normal with modern methods of construction have an essential aesthetic significance. . . .

The clarity of the impression of volume is diminished by any sort of complication. Volume is felt as immaterial and weightless, a geometrically bounded space. Subsidiary projecting parts of a building are likely to appear solid. Hence a compact and unified solution of a complex problem will be best aesthetically as well as economically. . . .[44]

Thus as a corollary of the principle of surface of volume there is the further requirement that the surfaces shall be unbroken in effect, like a skin tightly stretched over the supporting skeleton. The apparent tensions of a masonry wall are directly gravitational, although they are actually modified more or less by the use of lintels and arches. The apparent tensions of screen walls are not thus polarized in a vertical direction, but are felt to exist in all directions, as in a stretched textile. Hence the breaking of the wall surface by placing windows at the inner instead of at the outer edge of the wall is a serious fault of design. For the glass of the windows is now an integral part of the enclosing screen rather than a hole in the wall as it was in masonry construction.[45] . . .

SURFACING MATERIAL

The character of surface of volume is not expressed merely
by the general design of a modern building; the actual materials
of the surface itself are of the utmost importance. . . .[50]

In any sort of plate covering it is important that the plates
be so joined that the surface is as little broken as possible. . . .
It is also important that the surface remain a plane without con-
vexities and concavities. Otherwise the effect becomes picturesque
and the sense of equal tension in all directions is destroyed.[51] . . .

A SECOND PRINCIPLE: CONCERNING REGULARITY

Beside the principle of surface of volume already discussed
there is a second controlling principle, evident in the productions
of the international style including the work of the European
functionalists.

This second principle of contemporary style in architecture
has to do with regularity. The supports in skeleton construction
are normally and typically spaced at equal distances [56] in order
that strains may be equalized. . . . Good modern architecture expresses in its design this characteristic orderliness of structure
and this similarity of parts by an aesthetic ordering which emphasizes the underlying regularity. . . .

In most cases, within a structure as regular as possible and
using similar parts the architect must provide for many varying
functions related in various different ways to one another. . . .
Thus technically the prime architectural problem of distribution
is to adjust the irregular and unequal demands of function to
regular construction and the use of standardized parts.[57]

Just as the aesthetic principle of surface of volume has been
derived from the fact that architecture no longer has solid supporting walls, the second principle, that of regularity, depends
on the regularity typical of the underlying skeleton of modern
construction. . . .[58]

Structure today is usually highly regular for economic reasons which either did not apply to masonry structure or were

given less emphasis in the architecture of the past. . . .[60]

Horizontality, which is the most conspicuous characteristic of the international style as judged [65] in terms of effect, is still unacceptable aesthetically to the average American client.

Yet its logic is unescapable. Storeyed construction naturally produces horizontality. Most functions, moreover, require extended development in the horizontal plane—in plan, that is, rather than in elevation. Rooms are usually broader than they are high, and are most evenly illuminated by windows of the same proportion. Structural and functional horizontality is naturally expressed in façade design by architects who seek to obtain consistency in the principle of regularity. . . .[66]

A THIRD PRINCIPLE: THE AVOIDANCE OF APPLIED DECORATION

Absence of ornament serves as much as regular horizontality to differentiate superficially the current style from the styles of the past and from the various manners of the last century and a half. . . .[69]

Architecture, however, has never been without other elements of decoration. For decoration may be considered to include not only applied ornament, but all the incidental features of design which give interest and variety to the whole. Architectural detail, which is required as much by modern structure as by the structure of the past, provides the decoration of contemporary architecture. . . .

The fact that there is so little detail today increases the decorative effect of what there is. Its ordering is one of the chief means by which consistency is achieved in the parts of a design. . . .[70]

Whether from these two different forms of decoration—architectural detail and related works of painting and sculpture—the contemporary style will in time develop an ornament of its own as did the styles of the past, no one can say. The supposedly novel ornament from which architecture is now freeing itself has put us on our guard against innovations which are merely decorative. The force of all self-conscious theory tends to deny the necessity for ornament as such. . . .[74]

PLANS

Thus far there has been only incidental mention of the plan in contemporary architecture. Modern methods of skeleton construction have freed planning from conforming to the rigid lines of masonry structure. Isolated supports interfere hardly at all with free space and circulation. Interior partitions, like exterior walls, are mere screens. Thus planning has become absolutely pliant to the needs of function. New study of function, moreover, has broken down most of the conventions of planning inherited from the past, quite as rapidly as structural advance has made radical changes in plan possible.[85]

GEOFFREY SCOTT

The Architecture of Humanism

Geoffrey Scott, The Architecture of Humanism, 2nd ed. (New York, Charles Scribner's Sons, 1924).* A paperback edition is available in the Anchor Book series of Doubleday & Company, New York.

Introduction

THE ARCHITECTURE OF HUMANISM

'Well-building hath three conditions: Commodity, Firmness, and Delight.' From this phrase of an English humanist[1] a theory of architecture might take its start. Architecture is a focus where three separate purposes have converged. They are blended in a single method; they are fulfilled in a single result; yet in their own nature they are distinguished from each other by a deep and permanent disparity. The criticism of architecture has been confused in its process; it has built up strangely diverse theories of the art, and the verdicts it has pronounced have been contra-

---

* Reprinted with the permission of Constable & Company, Ltd.

1 Sir Henry Wotton, *Elements of Architecture*. He is adapting Vitruvius, Bk. I. chap. iii.

dictory in the extreme. Of the causes which have contributed to its failure, this is the chief: that it has sought to force on architecture an unreal unity of aim. 'Commodity, firmness, and delight'; between these three values the criticism of architecture has insecurely wavered, not always distinguishing very clearly between them,[1] seldom attempting any statement of the relation they bear to one another, never pursuing to their conclusion the consequences which they involve. It has leaned now this way and now that, and struck, between these incommensurable virtues, at different points, its arbitrary balance.

Architecture, the most complex of the arts, offers to its critics many paths of approach, and as many opportunities for avoiding their goal. At the outset of a fresh study in this field, it is well, at the risk of pedantry, to define where these paths lead.

Architecture requires 'firmness.' By this necessity it stands related to science, and to the standards of science. The mechanical bondage of construction has closely circumscribed its growth. Thrust and balance, pressure and its support, are at the root of the language which architecture employs. The inherent characters of marble, brick, wood and iron have moulded its forms, set limits to its achievement, and governed, in a measure, even its decorative detail. On every hand the study of architecture encounters physics, statics, and dynamics, suggesting, controlling, justifying its design. It is open to us, therefore, to look in buildings for the logical expression of material properties and material laws. Without these, architecture is impossible, its history unintelligible. And if, finding these everywhere paramount, we seek, in terms of material properties [2] and material laws, not merely to account for the history of architecture, but to assess its value, then architecture will be judged by the exactness and sincerity with which it expresses constructive facts, and conforms to constructive laws. That will be the scientific standard for architecture: a logical standard so far as architecture is related to science, and no further.

But architecture requires 'commodity.' It is not enough that it should possess its own internal coherence, its abstract logic of construction. It has come into existence to satisfy an external need. That, also, is a fact of its history. Architecture is subservient to the general uses of mankind. And, immediately,

The Farnese Palace, 1534, Rome; the courtyard of the grandest palace in Rome. The Farnese, the work of Antonio da Sangallo and Michelangelo, recalls Alberti's definition of beauty in architecture: "a harmony of all the parts, in whatsoever subject it appears, fitted together with such proportion and connection, that nothing could be added, diminished or altered, but for the worse."

politics and society, religion and liturgy, the large movements of races and their common occupations, become factors in the study. These determine what shall be built, and, up to a point, in what way. The history of civilisation thus leaves in architecture its truest, because its most unconscious record. If, then, it is legitimate to consider architecture as an expression of mechanical laws, it is legitimate, no less, to see in it an expression of human life. This furnishes a standard of value totally distinct from the scientific. Buildings may be judged by the success with which they supply the practical ends they are designed to meet. Or, by a natural extension, we may judge them by the value [3] of those ends themselves; that is to say, by the external purposes which they reflect. These, indeed, are two very different questions. The last makes a moral reference which the first avoids, but both spring, and spring inevitably, from the link which architecture has with life—from that 'condition of well-building' which Wotton calls commodity.

And architecture requires 'delight.' For this reason, interwoven with practical ends and their mechanical solutions, we may trace in architecture a third and different factor—the disinterested desire for beauty. This desire does not, it is true, culminate here in a purely æsthetic *result*, for it has to deal with a concrete basis which is utilitarian. It is, none the less, a purely æsthetic *impulse*, an impulse distinct from all the others which architecture may simultaneously satisfy, an impulse by virtue of which architecture becomes art. It is a separate instinct. Sometimes it will borrow a suggestion from the laws of firmness or commodity; sometimes it will run counter to them, or be offended by the forms they would dictate. It has its own standard, and claims its own authority. It is possible, therefore, to ask how far, and how successfully, in any architectural style, this æsthetic impulse has been embodied; how far, that is to say, the instincts which, in the other arts, exert an obvious and unhampered activity, have succeeded in realising themselves also through [4] this more complicated and more restricted instrument. And we can ask, still further, whether there may not be æsthetic instincts, for which this instrument, restricted as it is, may furnish the sole and peculiar expression. This is to study architecture, in the strict sense, as an art.

The criticism of architecture has been of two kinds. The first of these remains essentially historical. It is content to describe the conditions under which the styles of the past arose. It accepts the confused and partly fortuitous phenomenon which architecture [5] actually is, and estimates the phenomenon by a method as confused and fortuitous as itself. It passes in and out of the three provinces of thought, and relates its subject now to science, now to art, and now to life. It treats of these upon a single plane, judging one building by standards of constructive skill, another by standards of rhythm and proportion, and a third by standards of practical use or by the moral impulse of its builders. This medley of elements, diverse and uncommensurated as they are, can furnish no general estimate or true comparison of style.

Doubtless, *as a matter of history,* architecture has not come into existence in obedience to any *a priori* æsthetic. It has grown up around the practical needs of the race, and in satisfying these it has been deflected, now by the obstinate claims of mechanical laws, now by a wayward search for beauty. But the problem of the architect and that of the critic are here essentially different. The work of the architect is synthetic. He must take into simultaneous account our three 'conditions of well-building,' and find some compromise which keeps a decent peace between their claims. The task of the critic, on the contrary, is one of analysis. He has to discover, define, and maintain the ideal standards of value in each province. Thus the three standards of architecture, united in practice, are separable, and [6] must be separated, in thought. Criticism of the historical type fails to apply an ideal and consistent analysis, for the insufficient reason that the *practice* of architecture has, of necessity, been neither consistent nor ideal. Such criticism is not necessarily misleading. Its fault is more often that it leads nowhere. Its judgments may be individually accurate, but it affords us no general view, for it adopts no fixed position. It is neither simple, nor comprehensive, nor consistent. It cannot, therefore, furnish a theory of style.

The second type of criticism is more dangerous. For the sake of simplicity it lays down some 'law' of architectural taste. Good design in architecture, it will say, should 'express the uses the building is intended to serve'; 'it should faithfully state the facts of its construction,' or again it should 'reflect the life of a noble civilisation.' Then, having made these plausible assumptions, it drives its theory to a conclusion, dwells on the examples that support its case, and is willing, for the sake of consistency, to condemn all architecture in which the theory is not confirmed. Such general anathemas are flattering alike to the author and his reader. They greatly simplify the subject. They have a show of logic. But they fail to explain why the styles of architecture. which they find it necessary to condemn have in fact been created and admired. Fashion consequently [7] betrays these faultless arguments; for whatever has once genuinely pleased is likely to be again found pleasing; art and the enjoyment of art continue in the condemned paths undismayed; and criticism is left to discover a sanction for them, if it can, in some new theory, as simple, as logical, and as insufficient as the first.

The true task of criticism is to understand such æsthetic pleasures as have in fact been felt, and then to draw whatever laws and conclusions it may from that understanding. But no amount of reasoning will create, or can annul, an æsthetic experience; for the aim of the arts has not been logic, but delight. The theory of architecture, then, requires logic; but it requires, not less, an independent sense of beauty. Nature, unfortunately, would seem to unite these qualities with extreme reluctance.

Obviously, there is room for confusion. The 'condition of delight' in architecture—its value as an art—may conceivably be found to *consist in* its firmness, or in its commodity, or in both; or it may consist in something else different from, yet dependent upon these; or it may be independent of them altogether. In any case, these elements are, at first sight, distinct. There is no reason, *prima facie*, to suppose that there exists between them a pre-established harmony, and that in consequence a perfect principle of building can be laid down which should, [8] in full measure, satisfy them all. And, in the absence of such a principle, it is quite arbitrary to pronounce dogmatically on the concessions which art should make to science or utility. Unless it can be proved that these apparently different values are in reality commensurable, there ought to be three separate schemes of criticism : the first based on construction, the second on convenience, the third on æsthetics. Each could be rational, complete, and, within its own province, valid. Thus by degrees might be obtained what at present is certainly lacking—the data for a theory of architecture which should not be contradicted at once by the history of taste.[9]

... The science, and the history, of architecture are studies of which the method is in no dispute. But for the art of architecture, in this strict sense, no agreement exists. The reason has few problems so difficult as those which it has many times resolved. Too many definitions of architectural beauty have proved their case, enjoyed their vogue, provoked their opposition, and left upon the vocabulary of art their legacy of prejudice, ridicule, and confusion. The attempt to reason honestly or to see clearly in architecture has not been very frequent or conspicuous; but, even where it exists, the terms it must employ are hardened with misuse, and the vision it invokes is distorted by all the preconceptions which beset a jaded argument. Not only do we inherit the wreckage of past controversies, but those controversies themselves are clouded with the dust of more heroic combats, and loud with the battle-cries of poetry and morals, philosophy, politics, and science. For it is unluckily the fact that thought about the [12] arts has been for the most part no more than an incident in, or a consequence of, the changes which men's minds have undergone with regard to these more stimulating and insistent interests. Hardly ever, save in matters of mere technique, has architecture been studied sincerely for itself. Thus the simplest estimates of architecture are formed through a distorting atmosphere of unclear thought. Axioms, holding true in provinces other than that of art, and arising historically in these, have successively been extended by a series of false analogies into the province of architecture; and these axioms, unanalysed and mutually inconsistent, confuse our actual experience at the source.

To trace the full measure of that confusion, and if possible to correct it, is therefore the first object of this book. . . .[13]

The Romantic Fallacy

The first fallacy of Romanticism, then, and the [51] gravest, is to regard architecture as *symbolic*. Literature is powerful to invest with fascination any period of history on which its art is imaginatively expended. Under the influence, directly or indirectly, of literature the whole past of the race is coloured for us in attractive or repellent tones. Of some periods inevitably we think with delight; of others with distaste. A new historical perspective, a new literary fashion, may at any time alter the feeling we entertain. Yet the concrete arts which these different periods produced remain always the same, still capable of addressing the same appeal to the physical senses. If, then, we are to attend impartially to that permanent appeal, we must discount these 'literary' preconceptions. But everything which recalls a period of the past may recall, by association, the emotions with which that period is, at the time, poetically regarded. And to these emotions, originally engendered by literature, romanticism makes the other arts subservient. The element in our consciousness which ought to be discounted, it makes paramount. Its interest in the arts is that, like poetry, they should bring the mind within the charmed circle of imaginative *ideas*. But these ideas really belong to the literary imagination whence they sprang, and one result of applying them to architecture, where they are not inherent, is that all permanence and objectivity of judgment is lost. Thus, for example, the Gothic building from being [52] the 'expression' of 'ignorant and monkish barbarians,' came to 'suggest' the idealised Goth—'firm in his faith and noble in his aspirations' —who inspired the enthusiasm of Coleridge; and the forms of an architecture which later came to be admired as the lucid expression of constructive mathematics were about this time commonly praised as the architectural image of primeval forests. Some minds find in the work of the mediæval builders the record of a rude and unresting energy; others value it as the evidence of a dreaming piety. Now, it is an 'expression of infinity made imaginable'; next, the embodiment of 'inspired' democracy. It is clear that there is no limit to this kind of writing, and we have only to follow the romantic criticism through its diverse phases to feel convinced of its total lack of any objective significance. . . . The whole process is purely literary, its charm is in the literary value of the idea itself, or in the act and process of [53] association. Moreover, since literary exercises invite effects of contrast, the architecture of the Renaissance comes to be treated, like the villain in the melodrama, as a mere foil to the mediæval myth.

And because Renaissance life happened to yield no stimulus to the nineteenth century imagination, the architecture which ministered to the uses of that life became *ipso facto* commonplace. A combination of plastic forms has a sensuous value apart from anything we may *know* about them. Romanticism allows what it knows, or conceives itself to know, about the circumstances among which the forms were produced, to divert it from giving unbiassed attention to the purely æsthetic character, the sensuous value, of the concrete arts. If it is a question of architecture, the architectural design is taken as standing for the period which invented and is associated with it, and as suggesting, conventionally, the general imaginative state, the complex feelings of approval or disapproval which the idea of that period happens to evoke. Architecture, in fact, becomes primarily symbolic. It ceases to be an immediate and direct source of enjoyment, and becomes a mediate and indirect one.

Under the romantic influence, then, the interest in architecture is symbolic, and taste becomes capricious. . . .[54]

Such were the consequences of the prepossession which *translates* material forms into terms of 'literary' ideas. Yet it must not be said that literary ideas have no 'legitimate' place in architectural experience. Every experience of art contains, or may contain, two elements, the one direct, the other indirect. The direct element includes our sensuous experience and simple perceptions of form: the immediate apprehension of the work of art in its visible or audible material, with whatever values may, by the laws of our nature, be inherently connected with that. Secondly, and beyond this, there are the associations which the work awakens in the mind—our conscious reflections upon it, the significance we attach to it, the fancies it calls up, and which, in consequence, it is sometimes said to express. This is the indirect, or associative, element.

These two elements are present in nearly every æsthetic experience; but they may be very differently [59] combined. Literature is an art which deals preponderatingly with 'expression.' Its appeal is made through the indirect element. Its emphasis and its value lie chiefly in the significance, the meaning and the associations of the sounds which constitute its direct material. Architecture, conversely, is an art which affects us chiefly by direct appeal. Its emphasis and its value lie chiefly in material and that abstract disposition of material which we call form. . . .[60]

. . . Literature may possess abstract architectural properties —scale, proportion, distribution—independent of its significance; architecture may evoke a poetic dream, independent of its forms; but, fundamentally, the language of the two arts is distinct and even opposite. In the one we await the meaning; in the other we look to an immediate emotion resulting from the substance and the form.

The reason of this difference is obvious. The material of literature is *already* significant. Every particle of it has been organised in order to convey significance, and in order to convey the same significance to all. But for the material of architecture, no system of accepted meanings has been organised. If, therefore, we derive associative values from its forms, those values will be determined wholly by the accidents of our time and personality. . . .[61]

. . . This same habitual preoccupation with 'significance' which has kept literature vital has, in architecture, led us to lay undue weight on what is there the secondary element, and to neglect its direct value, its immediate and typical appeal. This, then, is the 'literary fallacy' in architecture. It neglects the fact that in literature meaning, or fixed association, is the universal term; while in architecture the universal term is the sensuous experience of substance and of form.

The Romantic Movement is a phase, precisely, of this literary preoccupation. It is the most extreme example of the triumph of association over direct experiences which the history of culture contains. . . .[62]

. . . In so far as the Romantic Movement has stimulated our sensibility to such literary values, that also is a clear gain. It would be absurd to demand (as in some of the arts enthusiasts are constantly demanding) that we should *limit* our enjoyment of an art to that delight which it is the peculiar and special function of the art to provide. To sever our experience into such completely isolated departments is to impoverish it at every point. In the last resort, as in the first, we appreciate a work of art not by the single instrument of a specialised taste, but with our whole personality. Our experience is inevitably inclusive and synthetic. It extends far beyond the mere reaction to material form. But its nucleus, at least, should be a right perception of that form, and of its æsthetic function. It is reasonable, then, to claim that the æsthetic enjoyment which is proper and special to a given art should be the first [64] and the necessary consideration, and that in relation to this the quality of a style should primarily be appraised. Whether or not that peculiar enjoyment can be enriched and surrounded with others of a different and more general nature must be a secondary question, and one with which the criticism of a given art, as such, need have no concern. . . .[65]

The Romantic Fallacy (continued)
NATURALISM AND THE PICTURESQUE

Romanticism has another aspect. We have seen that it allows the poetic interest of distant civilisation to supplant the æsthetic interest of form. But the romantic impulse is not attracted to history alone. It is inspired by the distant and the past; but it is inspired, also, by Nature. For, obviously, those qualities which romanticism seeks, these Nature possesses in the highest degree. Nature is strange, fantastic, unexpected, terrible. Like the past, Nature is remote. Indifferent to human preoccupations and disowning human agency, Nature possesses all the more forcibly an imaginative appeal. Thus, in the last century and earlier, together with the ballad-revival and the historical fiction, came, far more powerful than either, a new poetry of Nature. Under the influence of this poetry, Nature's unconsidered variety became the very type and criterion of beauty, and men were led by an inevitable consequence to value what is various, irregular, or wild, and to value [66] it wherever it might be found. As in the cult of the past, so, too, in this cult of the 'natural,' it was literature, the true instrument of the Romantic Movement, that led the way.[67]

. . . Order and subtleties of proportion require an habitual training in the eye. The Greeks, as some of the 'optical' corrections of the Parthenon have revealed, responded here to distinctions of which to-day even a practised taste will be almost in-

Photo Viguier, Courtesy French Government Tourist Office

The Palace of Versailles, 1661-1756; the principal garden façade illuminated at night. Versailles was Louis XIV's proudest monument, the one that most expressed the glories of his reign.

sensible. The Renaissance inherited their ideal, if not their delicacy of sense. . . . A 'natural' architecture, so far from affording such practice to the eye, raises a prejudice against order itself; because whatever qualities a 'natural' architecture may possess are dependent on the negation of order. A taste formed upon this violent and elementary variousness of form, conceives a Renaissance front as a blank monotony because that, by contrast, is all it can discern. What wonder, then, if it accepts the verdict of the poetry of Nature, and declares the Renaissance style to be a weary and contemptible pomp, while it endows its own incompetence with the natural 'dignity' of the fields and woods. . . .[70]

It is of the essence of romantic criticism that it permits literary fashion to control architectural taste. This is the cardinal point to which once more we are brought back, and on which

once more we may [71] insist. That the architectural judgment is
made in unconsciousness of the literary bias is immaterial. A
literary fashion is easily conceived of as an absolute truth, and
the unconsciousness of a prejudice only adds to its force. For
the power of literature extends far beyond its conscious students;
by a swift contagion it determines, even in illiterate minds, the
channels of their thought, the scope of their attention, and the
values to which they will respond. It leads men to say, at a given
epoch, summarily: 'The artificial or the formal is less worthy than
the natural,' without any necessary analysis of what these abstract terms involve. Their æsthetic attention to the concrete case
is obstructed by the phrase; and architecture serves as a mere
symbol of the idea.[72]

. . . But the prejudice against the 'unnatural' style of the
Renaissance was something more than an [74] association of architecture with *poetical* ideas. As that, indeed, it began. But we
shall underrate its force, and falsely analyse its ground, if we do
not recognise in it, also, an association of architecture with
ethical ideas. The poetry of Nature furnished the imagery of
the gospel of freedom. The Romantic Movement, with its theory
of Natural Rights, gave to Nature a democratic tinge. The cult
of Nature had its say on conduct: it was a political creed. It was
more; for, in proportion as orthodoxy waned and romanticism
gathered force, a worship of Nature—for such, in fact, it was—
supplanted the more definite and metaphysical belief. The instinct of reverence, if science dislodged it from the supernatural
world, attached itself to the natural. . . . A vague pantheism was
common ground between the Anglican Wordsworth, the rational-
ist Mill, and the revolutionary Shelley. Nature, unadorned, was
divine herself—or, at the least, was God's [75] garment and His
book; and this, not in the elegant and complimentary sense in
which Addison might have so regarded her, but with a profound
power to satisfy the mystic's adoration. The argument assumed
a different plane. To be 'natural' was no longer a point merely
of poetic charm—it was a point of sanctity. With Ruskin, for
example, the argument from Nature is always final. . . .[76]

On the one side was Nature: the curves of the waves, the
line of the unfolding leaf, the pattern of the crystal. All these
might be studied, and in some way architecturally employed—

no matter how—so long as the knowledge and the love of them were evident. On the other stood the principles of Palladio, and all the pedantry of rule and measure, made barren by the conscious intellect. The choice between them was a moral choice between reverence and vanity. This was the refrain of *The Stones of Venice* and all the criticism 'according to Nature.'

The cult of Nature has a venerable history; but it is interesting to notice the change it has here undergone. For Nature, as the romantic critics conceive it, is something very different from the Nature which their Stoic predecessors set up as an ideal, and very different also from Nature as it actually is. For the element in Nature which most impressed the Stoics was law, and its throne was the human reason. To 'follow reason' and 'to live according to Nature' for Marcus Aurelius were convertible terms. The human intellect, with its inherent, its 'natural' leanings towards order, balance, and proportion, was a part of Nature, and it was the most admirable and important part. But Nature, in the ethical language of her modern æsthetic devotees, stands most often in definite contradistinction to the human reason. They were willing to recognise authority 'in the round [78] ocean and the living air,' but few remembered with Wordsworth to add: 'and in the mind of man.' . . . Even now a discernible taint or moral reproof colours the adverse criticism of formal architecture; and a trace of conscious virtue still attends on crooked planning, quaint design and a preference for Arctic vegetation unsymmetrically disposed. . . .[79]

. . . Naturalism in architecture is partly a poetical taste; partly it is an ethical prejudice, and in each case it has been shown to be fallacious. But naturalism is also frankly æsthetic: a preference not merely of the fancy or the conscience, but of the eye. It may have entered modern architecture by a kind of false analogy, and may still derive from poetry a half-unreal support; but it has a solid footing of its own. For the place of what is unexpected, wild, fantastic, accidental, does not belong to poetry alone. These are the qualities which constitute the *picturesque*—qualities which have always been recognised [81] as possessing a value in the visual arts. And one cause of offence in Renaissance architecture is precisely its lack of this picturesqueness of which Nature is so full. For the sake of this merit to the

eye, how much decay has been endured and awkwardness forgiven! In a theory of architecture, what place then, if any, can
be found for this true merit of the picturesque? What was, in
fact, its place in the architecture of the Renaissance? To these
questions an answer should be given before the romantic criticism
of architecture can be fairly and finally dismissed.

If the wild and the accidental are absent from Renaissance
architecture, it is certainly not because the men of that period
were blind to their attraction. The term *pittoresco* was, after all,
their own invention. It stood, on its own showing, for the qualities which suggest a picture, and are of use in the making of it.
Picturesque elements—elements that are curious, fantastic, accidental, had been sought after in the painting of Italian backgrounds almost from the first. . . .[82]

But their sense of the freedom appropriate to the painted
architecture is in strong contrast to the strictness they imposed
upon themselves in the concrete art. The nearer art approached
to the monumental, the more this self-denying ordinance became
severe. Whatever surrounds us and contains our life; whatever
is insistent and dominating; whatever permits us no escape—that,
they felt, must be formal, coherent, and, in some sense, serene.
Real architecture, by its very scale and function, is such an art.
It is insistent, dominating, and not to be escaped. The wild, the
fantastic, the unexpected in such an art could not therefore be
allowed to capture the design. That, if we may judge from their
work, was the principle in which Renaissance architects put faith.

This principle, like all the principles of Renaissance architecture, rested on a psychological fact. The different effects which
art is able to produce, however various and incommensurable
they may radically be,[83] are commensurable at least in this: that
each in some degree makes a demand on our *attention*. Some
works of art affect us, as it were, by infiltration, and are calculated to produce an impression that is slow, pervasive, and profound. These seek neither to capture the attention nor to retain
it; yet they satisfy it when it is given. Other works arrest us,
and by a sharp attack upon the senses or the curiosity, insist on
our surrender. Their function is to stimulate and excite. But
since, as is well known, we cannot long react to a stimulus of this
type, it is essential that the attention should, in these cases, be

Galerie des Glaces, 1680, in the Palace of Versailles, inspired by, and similar to, the Louvre's Galerie d'Apollon in its use of marble, mirrors, gold and mural paintings. For Henry James, the Galerie d'Apollon seemed "to form with its supreme coved ceiling and inordinately shining parquet a prodigious tube or tunnel through which I inhaled little by little, that is again and again, a general sense of **glory**."

soon enough released. Otherwise, held captive and provoked, we are confronted with an insistent appeal which, since we can no longer respond to it, must become in time fatiguing or contemptible.

Of these two types of æsthetic appeal, each commands its own dominion; neither is essentially superior to the other, although, since men tend to set a higher value on that which satisfies them longest, it is art of the former kind which has most often been called great. But they do both possess an essential fitness to different occasions. Wherever an occasion either refuses or compels a sustained attention, a right choice between the two types will be a first condition of success. Fantastic architecture, architecture that startles and delights the curiosity and is not dominated by a broad repose, may sometimes [84] be appropriate. On a subdued scale, and hidden in a garden, it may be pleasant enough; but then, to be visited and not lived in. At a theatrical moment it will be right. It may be gay; it may be curious. But it is unfitted, æsthetically, for the normal uses of the art, for it fatigues the attention; and architecture once again is insistent, dominating and not to be escaped.[85]

. . . But architecture which aims at the picturesque *need not* be insistent. There is a romanticism of conceits: the romanticism of Chambord, or the poetry of Donne. But there is also a romanticism of natural simplicity: the romanticism of Wordsworth and of a 'rustic' architecture. Architecture, in fact, can be picturesque without affectation, and various without disquiet. Why should not this be favoured? Where is the fault in that domestic type of architecture, in which we see a variety of form conditioned solely by convenience? Here will be repose, because the picturesqueness is unstudied, fitting the house to unselfconscious nature. No insistent appeal is thrust on the attention, for no deliberate appeal exists. This, in our time, is the true rival to the Renaissance style. It is this architecture which has so firm a hold in England, which seems to us so good to paint and good to live in. Poetry and sentiment are in its favour; it indolently provides pleasure to the eye. Leave it to be overgrown and it will be soon 'transformed by the enchantment of Nature to the likeness of her own creations.' Its beauty is secure from fashion, for it is elementary and genuine.

This is true; but how much shall we be willing to forego for the sake of this inoffensive, this sometimes [90] charming, architecture? With what is it contrasted? It is usually implied that the alternative is *mere* formality. Formality, too, has its inherent, its, perhaps equal, charm. But it has more. It is the basis of *design*. Everything in architecture which can hold and interest the intellect; every delight that is complex and sustained;

every subtlety of rhythm and grandeur of conception, is built upon formality. Without formality architecture lacks the syntax of its speech. By means of it, architecture attains, as music attains, to a like rank with thought. Formality furnishes its own theme and makes lucid its own argument. 'Formal' architecture is to the 'picturesque' as the whole body of musical art to the lazy hum and vaguely occupying murmur of the summer fields.

All this is sacrificed; and perhaps even that little merit is not gained. Time and decay, colour and the accidents of use, the new perspective from the unforeseen angle of chance vision, may be trusted to give picturesqueness to the austerest architecture. Confusion will not lose its charm because there once was thought. Design is no implacable enemy of the picturesque; but the picturesque *ideal* is at variance with tradition and repugnant to design.

Our concern is here with one point only. It is not, certainly, that the picturesque is without merit; the merit of it is indeed too obvious. It is that, as an [91] ideal, the picturesque renders taste obtuse, or suffers it to remain so. Like a coarse weed, not unbeautiful in itself, it tends to stifle every opportunity of growth. The modern taste for picturesqueness—as the old painters suffice to prove—brought with it nothing that was new. Nature, and man's work, is full of a picturesque beauty that has never passed unnoticed. But the æsthetic content of the picturesque is not constructive and cannot be extended. Nevertheless, it is upon this quality, so low in the scale, so unhopeful for future creation, and so unhelpful for an understanding of the formal past, that modern taste has been concentrated. This is the novelty and the prejudice.

There is a beauty of art and a beauty of Nature. Construction, when it relaxes the principles of design, does not become Nature; it becomes, more probably, slovenly art. Nature, for a living art, is full of suggestion; but it is none the less a resisting force—something to be conquered, modified, adorned. It is only when the force of art is spent, when its attempt is rounded and complete, that Nature, freed from the conflict, stands apart, a separate ideal. It is thus the last sign of an artificial civilisation when Nature takes the place of art. Not without reason, it was the eighteenth century at its close—that great, finished issue and realised pattern—which began the natural cult. For a single moment, while the past [92] still imposed its habit upon thought, disaster was arrested. The cult of Nature was a convention like the rest, and sought a place within the scheme. But the next step was the suicide of taste. Taken in isolation, made hostile to the formal instincts of the mind, Nature led, and can only lead, to chaos; whence issued a monstrous architecture: *informe ingens, cui lumen ademptum.* Thus it was that by the romantic taste the artificial was scorned, though art, whatever else it is, is necessarily that; and it was scorned simply because it was not natural, which no art can hope, by whatever casuistry, to become. [93]

The Mechanical Fallacy

Such, in broad outline, were the tendencies, and such, for architecture, the results, of the criticism which drew its inspiration from the Romantic Movement. Very different in its origins, more plausible in its reasoning, but in its issue no less misleading, is the school of theory by which this criticism was succeeded. Not poetry but science, not sentiment but calculation, is now the misguiding influence. . . .

Every activity in life, and even the philosophy of life itself, was interpreted by the method which, in one particular field, had proved so fruitful. Every aspect of things which eluded mechanical explanation became disregarded, or was even forced by violence into mechanical terms. For it was an axiom of [94] scientific method that, only in so far as phenomena could so be rendered, might any profitable results be expected from their study. To this rule the arts proved no exception. But they were affected by the prevailing theories in two contrary directions. In many minds, æsthetics, like all philosophy, became subordinated to the categories of materialistic and mechanical science. On the other hand, those who valued art tended more and more to claim for each art its separate consideration. For, since the essence of the scientific procedure had been the isolation of fields of inquiry —the subjection of each to its own hypothetical treatment—it was natural that the fine arts, also, should withdraw into a sphere of autonomy, and demand exemption from any values but their own.

'Art for art's sake,' for all its ring of æstheticism, was thus, in a sense, a motto typical of the scientific age; and Flaubert, who gave it currency, was an essentially scientific artist. But the fine arts employed their autonomy only to demonstrate their complete subservience to the prevailing scientific preoccupation. Each bowed the knee in a different way. Thus Painting, becoming confessedly impressionistic, concerned itself solely with optical facts, with statements about vision instead of efforts after significance. Literature became realistic, statistical, and documentary. Architecture, founded, as it is, on construction, could be rendered, even more [95] readily than the rest, in the terms of a purely scientific description; its aims, moreover, could easily be converted into the ideals of the engineer. Where mechanical elements indisputably formed the basis, it was natural to pretend that mechanical results were the goal; especially at a time when, in every field of thought, the nature of value was being more or less confused with the means by which it is produced.[96]

. . . The relation of construction to design is the fundamental problem of architectural æsthetics. . . .

. . . We must ask, then, what is the true relation of construction to architectural beauty. . . .

Let us begin by attempting, as fairly as we may, to formulate the 'scientific' answer to this question; let us see where it leads us, and if it leads us into difficulties, let us modify it as best we can, in accordance with the scientific point of view.

'Architecture,' such critics are apt to say, 'architecture *is* construction. Its essential characteristic as an art is that it deals, not with mere patterns of light and shade, but with structural laws. In judging architecture, therefore, this peculiarity, which constitutes its uniqueness as an art, must not be overlooked: on the contrary, since every art is primarily to be judged by its own special qualities, it is precisely by reference to these structural laws that architectural standards must be fixed. That architecture, in short, will be beautiful in which the construction is best, and in which it is most truthfully displayed.'. . .[100]

. . . In the modern criticism of architecture, we are habitually asked to take this view for granted, and the untenable assertions as well; and this is accepted without discussion, purely owing to the mechanical preconceptions of the time, which make all criticisms on the score of 'structure' seem peculiarly convincing. Such a view, even in the modified form in which we have stated it, sets up an ideal of architecture. . . . Before accepting this unfortunate conclusion, let us see [108] whether the ideal is as rational and consistent as it sounds.

In the first place, it is clear that the vivid constructive properties of a building, in so far as they are effectively constructive, must exist as *facts*. The security of the building, and hence also of any artistic value it may possess, depends on this; and a support which seemed to be adequate to its load, but actually was not, would, as construction, be wrong. But in so far as they are vivid, they must exist *as appearances*. It is the effect which the constructive properties make on the eye, and not the scientific facts that may be intellectually discoverable about them, which alone can determine their vividness. Construction, it may be granted, is always, or nearly always, in some sense, our concern, but not always in the same sense. The two requirements which architecture so far evidently has are constructive integrity in fact, and constructive vividness in appearance. Now, what our scientific critics have taken for granted, is that because these two requirements have sometimes been satisfied at the same moment, and by the same means, no other way of satisfying them is permissible. But there has been no necessity shown thus far, nor is it easy to imagine one, for insisting that these two qualifications should always be interdependent, and that both must invariably be satisfied at a single stroke. Their value in [109] the building is of a wholly disparate kind: why, then, must they always be achieved by an identical expedient? No doubt when this can be done, it is the simplest and most straightforward way of securing good architectural design. No doubt when we realise that this has been done, there may be a certain intellectual pleasure in the coincidence. But even the Greeks, to whom we are always referred, were far from achieving this coincidence. When they took the primitive Doric construction, and raised it to a perfect æsthetic form, the countless adjustments which they made were all calculated for optical effect. They may not have entailed consequences *contrary* to structural requirements, but at least the optical effect and the structural requirements were distinct. The Renaissance grasped this distinction between the several elements of architectural design with extreme clearness. *It realised that, for certain purposes in architecture, fact counted for everything, and that in certain others, appearance counted for everything. And it took advantage of this distinction to the full.* It did not insist that the necessary fact should itself produce the necessary appearance. It considered the questions separately, and was content to secure them by separate means. It no longer had to dance in fetters. It produced architecture which *looked* vigorous and stable, and it took adequate measures to see that it actually *was* so. . . .[110] Renaissance architecture had to supply the utilitarian needs of a still more varied and more fastidious life. Had it remained tied to the ideal of so-called constructive sincerity, which means no more than an arbitrary insistence that the structural and artistic necessities of architecture should be satisfied by one and the same expedient, its search for structural beauty would have been hampered at every turn. And, since this dilemma was obvious to every one, no one was offended by the means taken to overcome it.[111]

. . . Two senses of 'structure' have been entangled and confused. Structure, in one sense, is the scientific method of 'well-building.' Its aim is *'firmness.'* Its end is achieved when once the stability of architecture is assured. And any means to that end are, scientifically, justified in proportion to their effectiveness. Structure, but now in a different sense, is also the basis of architectural *'delight.'* For architecture, realised æsthetically, is not mere line or pattern. It is an art in three dimensions, with all the consequence of that. It is an art of spaces and of solids, a felt relation between ponderable things, an adjustment to one another of evident forces, a grouping of material bodies subject *like ourselves* to certain elementary [118] laws. Weight and resistance, burden and effort, weakness and power, are elements in our own experience, and inseparable in that experience from feelings of ease, exultation, or distress. But weight and resistance, weakness and power, are manifest elements also in architecture, which enacts through their means a kind of human drama. Through them the mechanical solutions of mechanical problems achieve an æsthetic interest and an ideal value. Structure, then, is, on the one hand, the technique by which the art of architecture is made possible; and, on the other hand, it is part of its artistic content. But in the first case it is subject to mechanical laws purely, in the second to psychological laws. This double function, or double significance, of structure is the cause of our confusion. For the æsthetic efficacy of structure does not develop or vary *pari passu* with structural technique. They stand in relation to one another, but not in a fixed relation. Some structural expedients, though valid technically, are not valid æsthetically, and *vice versa*. Many forces which operate in the mechanical construction of a building are prominently displayed and sharply realisable. They have a mastery over the imagination far in excess, perhaps, of their effective use. Other forces, of equal moment towards stability, remain hidden from the eye. They escape us altogether; or, calculated by the intellect, still find no echo in our physical imagination. They [119] do not express themselves in our terms. They are not powerful over us for delight.

In proportion as these differences became distinguished, the *art* of architecture was bound to detach itself from mechanical science. The art of architecture studies not structure in itself, but the effect of structure on the human spirit. Empirically, by intuition and example, it learns where to discard, where to conceal, where to emphasise, and where to imitate, the facts of construction. It creates, by degrees, a humanised dynamics. For that task, constructive science is a useful slave, and perhaps a natural ally, but certainly a blind master. . . . The Mechanical Fallacy, in its zeal for structure, refuses . . . an art where structure is raised to the ideal. It looks in poetry for the syntax of a naked prose.[120]

The Ethical Fallacy

. . . The ethical tendency in criticism is consequent upon the two we have already discussed. The Romantic Fallacy paved the way for it. The Mechanical Fallacy provoked it.

The essential fallacy of romanticism was, we saw, that it treated architectural form as primarily symbolic. Now there is evidently no reason why an art of form, if it be regarded as significative at all, should have its meaning limited to an *æsthetic* reference.[125] Romanticism, it is true, was concerned with the imaginative or poetic associations of style. But when once this habit of criticism was established—when once it seemed more natural to attend to what architecture indirectly signified than to what it immediately presented—nothing was required but a slight alteration in the predominant temper of men's minds, an increased urgency of interest outside the field of art, to make them seek in architecture for a *moral* reference. Romanticism had made architecture speak a language not its own—a language that could only communicate to the spectator the thoughts he himself might bring. Architecture had become a mirror to literary preferences and literary distastes. Now, therefore, when the pre-occupations inevitable to a time of social change and theological dispute had become predominantly moral, the language of art, reflecting them, was rife with ethical distinctions. The styles of architecture came to symbolise those states of human character in the craftsman, the patron or the public which they could be argued to imply. They were praised or blamed in proportion as those states were morally approved. . . . [126]

The ethical criticism, then, though it claims a different sanction and raises a wider issue, arose from the romantic. It arose, also, as a protest against the mechanical theory. Its motive was to assert the human reference of art against the empty cult of abstract technique. We have already seen that the extreme constructional ideal of architecture was no more than a phase of nineteenth century materialism. It ignored feeling. It neglected alike the æsthetic conscience and the moral. It appealed solely to an intellect which recognised no law but the mechanical. It was an episode in the dehumanisation of thought: a process which, carried to its logical conclusion, renders all values unmeaning. Such a process, however powerful its impulse, could not but provoke in many minds an immediate resistance. But it was a resistance in the field of ethics and theology. For here were the interests which materialism seemed most obviously and immediately to challenge: here, at any rate, were the interests which it was all-important to safeguard. Æsthetic values are a luxury; they are readily forgotten when more vital conflicts become acute. Thus, the necessary counter-attack to the movement of science was consequently ethical in temper. Its concern was with conduct and not [128] primarily with art. It was, in effect, a Puritan revival. The intellectual alternative was strict: either a truculent materialism (with consequences for architecture already analysed) or a moralistic ardour more severe than any that had been dominant since the seventeenth century. . . .[129]

There are those who claim a *direct* perception in architectural forms of moral flavours. They say, for example, of the baroque . . .[146] that it is . . . false. . . .[147]

. . . This is an argument of moral taste. Can we approve a style thus saturated with deceit: a style of false façades, false perspective, false masonry and false gold? For all these, it must be agreed, are found in the baroque as they are found in no other style of architecture. It is an art, not indeed always, but far too often, of 'deceit.'

This is probably the commonest of all the prejudices against the Renaissance style in its full development. But here, too, the facts are sounder than the conclusions.

The harmfulness of deceit lies, it must be supposed, either as a quality in the will of the deceiver, or in the damage inflicted by the deceit. If, in discharge of a debt, a man were to give me instead of a sovereign a gilded farthing, he would fail, no doubt, of his promise, which was to give me the value of twenty shillings. To deceive me was essential to his plan and the desire to do so implied in his attempt. But if, when I have lent him nothing, he were to give me a [151] gilt farthing because I wanted something bright, and because he could not afford the sovereign and must give me the bright farthing or nothing bright at all, then, though the coin might be a false sovereign, there is evidently neither evil will nor injury. There is no failure of promise because no promise has been made. There is a false coin which, incidentally, may 'deceive' me; but there is no damage and no implied determination to deceive, because what I required in this case was not a sovereign but the visible effect of a sovereign, and that he proposed to give—and gave.

I am probably *not* persuaded into believing that the false window of a Renaissance front is a real one, and [152] the more familiar I am with Renaissance architecture, the less likely am I to believe it; but neither do I wish to believe it, nor does it matter to me if, by chance, I am persuaded. I want the window for the sake of the balance which it can give to the design. If the window, in regard to its utilitarian properties, had been wanted at that point, presumably it would have been made. But, on the contrary, it was—very likely—definitely *not* wanted. But its æsthetic properties—a patch of its colour, shape and position—*were* required in the design, and these I have been given. Had it been otherwise there would have been artistic disappointment; as it is, there is no disappointment either practical or artistic. And there is no deceit, for, as the architect is aware, the facts, should I choose to know them, are readily discoverable. True, if I find the apparent stonework of the window is false, there is an element of genuine æsthetic disappointment, for the quality of the material has its own æsthetic beauty. But the baroque architects did not prefer paint to stone. Ruskin was not more disappointed than Palladio that the palaces of Vicenza are of stucco. Few generations realised more clearly the æsthetic quality of rich material; as the bronze and *lapis lazuli* of the altar of S. Ignazio in the Roman *Gesù* may suffice to show. But these architects placed æsthetic values in the scale of their importance, and where economic or other barriers [153] stood in their way, preferred at least, and foremost, to indicate *design*. And, since, in the rich material, part only of the charm resides in the imaginative value of its preciousness—its rarity, the distance it has come, the labours and sacrifices it has cost—and a far greater part in the material beauty, for the sake of which those sacrifices are made, those labours undertaken, the baroque architects, seeing this, sought to secure the last by brilliant imitation, even when, of necessity, they forewent the first. Nor was the imitation, like many that are modern, sordid and commercial — a meticulous forgery. It was a brave impressionism, fit to satisfy the eye. The mind was deluded, if at all, then merrily, and for a moment.[154]

The Biological Fallacy

Of all the currents that have lapped the feet of architecture, since architecture fell to its present ruin, the philosophy of evolution must be held to have been the most powerful in its impulse, the most penetrating in its reach. . . .[165]

The object of 'evolutionary' criticism is, *prima facie,* not to appreciate but to explain. To account for the facts, not to estimate them, is its function. And the light which it brings comes from one great principle: that things are intelligible through a [168] knowledge of their antecedents. *Ex nihilo nihil fit;* the nature of things is latent in their past. The myriad forms of architecture fall, by the compulsion of this principle, into necessary order. The interest of the study shifts from the terms of the sequence to the sequence itself. In such a view there is no place for praise or blame. The most odious characteristics of an art become convenient evidences of heredity and environment, by means of which every object can be duly set in a grand and luminous perspective. This tendency of the mind was a needed corrective to the Ethical Criticism; and the clear light of philosophic calm replaces, in these expositions, the tragic splendour of denunciatory wraths. Nevertheless, the direction of the tendency is unmistakable. It is a *levelling* tendency. The less successful moments of the architectural sequence have an equal place with the greatest. More than this, the minor periods, the transitional and tentative phases, acquire, when our interest is centered in the sequence, a *superior* interest to the outstanding landmarks of achieved style. For the intellectual problem is, precisely, to connect these landmarks with one another and with their obscure origins. . . .[169]

Decadence is a biological metaphor. Within the field of biology it holds true as a fact, and is subject [182] to law; beyond that field it holds true only by analogy. We can judge an organism by one constant standard—its power to survive: a power that varies in a known progression, a power of supreme importance. But even here—where the sequence of immaturity, prime and decay is a fact governed by predictable law—the power to survive is no test of æsthetic quality: the fragile unfolding of a leaf in spring, its red corruption in autumn, are not less beautiful than its strength in summer. And when we have to deal, not with a true and living organism but with a series of works of art, the tests of evolution are even more misleading. For here we ourselves define the unit which we estimate. We have to be sure that our squence is really a sequence and not an accidental group. We have to be sure that there is a permanent thread of quality by which the sequence may at every point be judged, and that this quality is at each point the true centre of the art's intention. The mere power of an architectural tradition to survive—could we estimate it—might be a permanent quality but hardly a relevant one; for the successive moments of an art are self-justified and self-complete. To estimate one by reference to another is a dangerous method of criticism. . . .[183]

The Academic Tradition

'There are in reality,' says architecture's principal historian, 'two styles of Architectural Art—one practised universally before the sixteenth century, and another invented since.' To the former belong 'the true Styles of Architecture,' to the latter 'the Copying or Imitative Styles.'

Renaissance architecture is imitative. It is more imitative than any style of building that preceded it. . . .[186]

. . . While this main fact is undeniable, the deductions which criticism has drawn from it are opposite enough. . . .[187]

. . . It is too often forgotten by those who assail the influence of Vitruvius, how little in the curiously dual nature of the Renaissance architect the zeal of the scholar was allowed to subjugate the promptings of the artist. True, the zeal of scholarship was there, and it was a new force in architecture; but, fortunately for architecture, the conscience of scholarship [197] was lacking. Pedantry, in that astonishing time, was an ideal; it was an inspiration; it was not a method. Vitruvius helped the architect to master the conventions of an art, of which the possibilities were apprehended but not explored. He wrapt it in the pomp and dignity of learning. But in Italy when he was found at variance with the artist's wishes, his laws were reverently ignored. . . .[198]

The value of Vitruvius was relative to a time and place. After three hundred years of exaggerated glory and honest usefulness he became a byword for stupidity. . . .[200]

In this revulsion was born the current prejudice that Renaissance architecture is 'imitative, academic, unalive.' A measure of truth, slight but sufficient to give the prejudice life, underlies the judgment. Fundamentally it is a confusion. An art is academic, in this harmful sense, when its old achievements crush down the energies that press towards the new. But the academic canons of the Renaissance did not represent the past achievements of the Renaissance, but of antiquity. To the Renaissance they were

Saint Paul's Cathedral, 1675-1710, London, designed by Sir Christopher
Wren, who wrote: "Architecture has its political use; public buildings
being the ornament of a country, it establishes a nation, makes people
love their native country." How true this is was observed in the last
war when the area around the cathedral was devastated by enemy
bombs. Saint Paul's itself, though partially damaged, escaped and
became an emblem of British courage and resistance.

the symbol of an unsatisfied endeavour: the source, consequently, not of inertia, but of perpetual fruitfulness. The pedantry was superficial. Beneath this jargon of the 'Orders'—to us so dead, to them so full of inspiration—the Italian architects were solving a vast and necessary problem. They were leading back European style into the main road of European civilisation—the Roman road which stretched forward and back to the horizon, sometimes overlaid, but not for long to be avoided. They were adapting, enlarging, revivifying the forms of the antique to serve the uses of the modern world. The change was deeply natural. Europe no longer recognised [201] itself in the hopes and habits of its immediate past; it did recognise itself, on the contrary, in that remoter and more civilised society in which it had its origin. The mediæval styles had run their course and outlived their usefulness. To have resisted the logic of events, to have clung to the vestiges of local Gothic—vital and 'rational' as in their time they had been, picturesque and romantic as they are in their survival—this in truth would have been an artificial act of style. It would have led, in a few generations, to a state of architecture as unalive, as falsely academic, as were the shams of archæology three hundred years later.

That Renaissance architecture was built up around an academic tradition—that it was, in a measure, imitative—will not, if we understand aright the historical and æsthetic conditions of the case, appear to be a fault. The academic tradition will, on the contrary, be realised as a positive force that was natural, necessary, and alive. The Renaissance architects deviated from the canon whenever their instinctive taste prompted them to do so; they returned to the canon whenever they felt that their creative experiment had overreached its profitable bounds. And it should be realised that a convention of form in architecture has a value *even when it is neglected*. It is present in the spectator's mind, sharpening his perception of what is new in the [202] design; it gives relief and accent to the new intention, just as the common form of a poetical metre enables the poet to give full value to his modulations. So, in Renaissance architecture, a thickening of the diameter of a column, a sudden increase in the projection of a cornice, each subtlest change of ratio and proportion, was sure of its effect. A new æsthetic purpose when it is ready for expression first shows itself and gathers force in a thousand such deviations, all tending in a sole direction. We may mark them, for instance, in the early years of the baroque, and realise how large a factor in their effect lies in the academic canon which they contradicted.[203]

KATHERINE GILBERT

A Study of Architectural Semantics

Katherine Gilbert, *Aesthetic Studies: Architecture and Poetry* (Durham, Duke University Press, 1952).*

A curious reader of the architectural literature of the last few years is struck by the recurrence of certain terms of praise applied to the new forms, for example, the word "clean." "A good word in architecture is clean." Frank Lloyd Wright said this many years ago, and a reader sensitive to words will have noticed how frequently it is his ultimate sign of approval. For instance: "We may now live in prismatic buildings, clean, beautiful and new"; "straight lines . . . severely clean and delicate"; ". . . the clean, significant lines of sculptural contours." And with machines and Shinto in mind he expands into: "Today it seems to me we hear this cry 'Be clean' from the depths of our own need. . . . Clean lines . . . clean surfaces . . . clean purposes. As swift as you like, but clean as the flight of an arrow." In his *Autobiography*, as if hailing a glad day, he writes: "A sense of cleanliness directly related to living in the sunlight is coming." Whatever his divergence from Wright otherwise, Le Corbusier also admires the clean. He testifies that it was the effect of the Acropolis upon him that made him a [25] rebel, the Acropolis with its "clear, clean, intense, economical, violent Parthenon." Frederick Etchells, introducing Le Corbusier's *Towards a New Architecture*, speaks

* Reprinted by courtesy of the Society of Architectural Historians from "Clean and Organic: A Study in Architectural Semantics," *Journal of the Society of Architectural Historians* X-3 (March, 1951), pp. 3-7.

of a house "hard and clean," with "fittings as coldly efficient as those of a ship's cabin." J. M. Richards has spoken of "the triumphs of clean engineering" and "the clean and efficient" new style. Prizes have recently been awarded for designs for churches because they were "cleanly simple and structurally straightforward." Elizabeth Mock, ending her essay *Built in U.S.A., 1932-1944* with appreciation of the unique beauty possible in a bridge —the "spare and muscular beauty" achievable there—comes to a period with the phrase "the clean economy of the essential form."

The frequency of this one "good word" is striking. But others are common, for example, "logical," "economical," "constructive." Indeed, any word-sensitive reader could verify the pervasive presence of the following ten terms as carrying an assumption of positive value in contemporary architectural design: modern, clean, logical, economical, basic, social, honest, organic, constructive, vital.

For observers of the ways of words these terms do not remain in isolation, but dispose themselves in families of terms, and mate with synonyms more or less exact. The groups of terms having thus massed themselves generate families of counterterms. One may envisage an architectural-verbal situation with dynamic interrelations approximating this pattern: (1) A positive group of near-synonyms: *clean,* pure, sharp, trim, hard, bright, tight, stripped, stark, antiseptic, crystalline, uncluttered, naked, crisp, sheer. (2) A sympathetic family of moral terms, cousins to the first set, immediately recognizable both as of frequent occurrence and of cognate intention: *honest,* candid, frank,[26] straightforward, virile, uncompromising, integral, restrained, ascetic, just, chaste, mature, orderly, dignified, right, courageous. (3) Another sympathetic group connoting analytical reduction: *logical,* scientific, rational, true, inevitable, basic, diagrammatic, valid, simple, essential, geometric. (4) A group of terms used for denigration and representing an architectural state of affairs uncongenial to the first, and by implication to the second and third: *ideal,* unreal, romantic, mixed, soft, murky, cluttered, untidy, misty, sentimental, emotional, traditional, subjective.

Though we have here to do with words and not with designs themselves, there can be no doubt that the architects who use the words intend them to apply to real architectural designs, for description and/or appraisal. The words do not compose a "literary" or "subjective" characterization of architectural facts, but are clearly taken to refer to properties that inhere in those facts. Semanticists approaching this double situation of words and shapes would agree that the words are intended to describe and to evaluate architectural facts. They would assume that a verbal design parallel to the visual design was being constructed. Such analysts would also be interested, however, in tracing the terms reflectively to their various contexts and in checking the values associated by the authors with the terms. It would not be strange if they disclosed ambiguities in the employment of identical signs, and tensions buried in apparent verbal agreements, so that the two designs might not fit together after all.

If this occurred, it would seem that suggestions of more than verbal interest might come out of the examination of language habits and preferences in the architectural field. Words, floating like veils over a philosophy of design, may [27] cover up shifts in thinking and attachments to surprising values.

This can be shown in the case of our word "clean." A study of passages, illustrations, and references in which "clean" occurs gradually reveals at least four distinguishable directions of meaning of this favorite adjective. As associated with the triumphs of engineering, and its general economy and efficiency, "clean" architecture would simply signify building involving the minimum expenditure of energy and materials for the end desired. This is, of course, the basic virtue usually attached to "functional" architecture. But when functional architecture becomes self-consciously clean, it assumes a strong negative tone. Its first value involves expulsion: ejecting the irrelevant. All architectural elements are then termed irrelevant that have no basis in actual human need but are lifted out of a bygone culture for sentiment or ornament's sake, through literary allusion, secondary meaning, or inertia; offering what once was fitting form for an epoch's habits after the habits are dead. "This clearing away of the historic debris, this stripping to the skin, was the first essential mark of the new architecture." Architecture that is "pure," then, in deed and intention cuts away the fatty excrescences of the traditional styles, the classical orders, cornices, and embellishments. From inner equipment disappear old carved furniture and heirloom silver and china. The purists of architectural language throw out the moldy rhetoric of Roman banks and Gothic churches. Nuances of color containing the impurities of gray reflect for them a feeble and lingering fancy for dimly remembered shadows and compare poorly with clean heraldic colors.

First of all, then, "clean" as an honorific term in architectural [28] writing means relevance, and it becomes synonymous with "logical." A specific, practical purpose confronts the designer and his business is to build solely for that end. Here the value involved is concrete, practical, and verifiable. All the group of kindred terms that expand the idea of good logic belong with "clean" (1), and dirt, as in the proverb, means something out of place. Close calculation, clear statement of what is wanted, and computation controlled by the limited, tangible, conscious goal sum up the intention.

The second association leaves metaphors for literal significance. It is a direct carry-over from hygiene, antisepsis, good housekeeping. Here may be noticed the conspicuous interest in sun and air, washing machines, bathrooms and kitchen equipment. It is no accident that Dean Hudnut, recounting in a charming fable the conquest of modern design over antiquarianism, points his moral with a washing machine. "The clean round washing-machine" with its "white and restful serenity" drove out, in his parable, attachment to highboys, mirrors, and glass chandeliers. The same overtones of "the surgery and enameled bath" are acknowledged by Kenneth Clark, but from the opposition. "Art," he asserts, "must be slightly septic." He allows that modern functionalism has perhaps been a health-giving interval in the history of European building, as it has applied the cure of starvation and the cold pack. In general, the wholesome character of sun and air is a common theme for the new architect. We have already noted Wright's remark: "A sense of cleanliness directly related to living in the sunlight is coming." [Sigfried] Giedion takes the evolution of the bath as one of the significant aspects of the command taken by the machine;[29] and James Fitch gives a section to "When the Bathroom Comes of Age," in his recent American Building. Le Corbusier calls good planning "healthy." Associated with the overtone of health and sanitation in the term "clean" are allusions to the fit form and function of the athlete. The clean line of modern engineering is, we are told, like the economical cut and curve of a diver's leap. Again, pure building would "show the naked wall in all its sleek beauty," and once more, a modern bridge is "spare and muscular."

"Clean" may also mean for our writers the clean soul as well as the bathed, sunned, and taut body, and this is the third variant. The group of terms denoting moral character, beginning with "honest," has been given above. An example of this sense occurs in the boast that functional architecture is "virginal of lies." What is meant here by lies? "The hollow sham of axial symmetry"; "the multitude of dishonesties—the cornices and the columns, the fake palaces and fortresses . . . the dishonest use of the symbolic function. . . ." More or less consciously, but at any rate commonly, architectural writers fold moral values in with engineering efficiency and sun baths: chastity, integrity, continence, directness. The expansion of meaning from pure and wholesome in the physical sense to pure and wholesome in the moral sense is natural. It may even be inevitable, for our hygiene stands to us, of course, for a kind of morality. But the semanticist is aware, even so, of a change in tone at this point from description to emotive metaphor. Just how appropriate the attachment to architectural design of terms primarily applicable to human character and motive may be is not to be too hastily judged. It is probably only those influenced by [30] contemporary depth psychology and its symbolisms who would not cry "metonymy" and "question-begging" when moral values are allowed to ride in on material fact and shaped space as real aspects of an architectural situation. Certainly both the large class of architectural theorists and of semanticists who are sympathetic to logical positivism would label as nonsense such metaphorical language in architectural description. For how can you verify the virginity of a wall or the sincerity of a stone cylinder? If words referring to moral character in modern construction are not nonsense, they are at least rhetoric requiring scrutiny.

The fourth meaning of "clean" is an intensification of the first sense so high in degree that the whole conception appears to split and shows not only a new but ultimately contrasting meaning. Now "clean" architecture, we know, always involves stripping and purging. But the cleansing process may be directed against irrelevancies in a specific culture, region, individual plan of life, or building requirement, as in Meaning *1*, or it may imply pursuit of purification for its own sake and abstraction carried to the limit. There is a temperament that never rests until it comes to what it takes for ultimate, absolute, or supreme. Both mathematical logician and mystic seek the basic and the simple in this unqualified way, and a strain in recent architectural thinking moves toward the same limit.[31]

. . . Now construction thus committed to the bare essence of abstract mathematical forms and necessary relations sloughs off not only dead styles and unmeaning ornament but approaches the limit of excluding the rich variety of cumulative human experience. At this extreme it yields pure prisms and lonely cubes. A philosophy of nihilism is not far away. . . .[33]

JOHN E. BURCHARD AND ALBERT BUSH-BROWN

The Architect, More Needed Than Pitied

John E. Burchard and Albert Bush-Brown, "The Architect, More Needed Than Pitied," *Harper's Magazine*, CCXIV (May, 1957).*

. . . One of the silliest arguments advanced for Modern architecture was that it would be cheaper. This seemed plausible enough. If moldings were eliminated, for example, this would save money. But what was forgotten was the greater refinement of detail required when rough construction was no longer covered, as well as the careful proportioning and arrangement that austere Modern design would demand. In the end the most Modern building may cost more than a comparable old-fashioned one. The insistence upon persuading a client to build something that is wonderful for his own time—by relying on economic arguments that will not hold water, instead of on the valid basis of aes-

* Reprinted with the permission of *Harper's Magazine*.

thetics—has never done the contemporary architects anything but harm.[38]

HANS SEDLMAYR

The Abolition of Architecture

Hans Sedlmayr, *Art in Crisis*, trans. by Brian Battershaw (Chicago, Henry Regnery Company, 1958).*

The equation of architecture and geometry, on which 'abstract' building reposes, is relegated to the background by the emergence of a new dogma, which really comprehends the older one. That dogma is that every building is a machine. Men no longer see any essential difference between the building of ships, aeroplanes and vehicles on the one hand, and the building of houses on the other. 'Dynamic' construction takes the place of the purely static principle of geometry.

This new dogma, which is sometimes openly proclaimed and on other occasions intrudes in a more veiled form, produces, wherever it is recognized, a number of phenomena that are entirely new. Whole buildings are now given a shape which suggests a machine or part of a machine. The same applies to the various constituent parts of a building, even down to the smallest, to a handle or a door-knob. Ships, aeroplanes and automobiles are treated as formal models on which the new style of living is based, and it is profoundly significant that this new style is shaped by just those things in which man—now a nomad—can have no lasting habitation and in which he can only live for short periods at a time. . . .[109]

Though the house itself still remains something fixed and firm, the accent is nevertheless on what is mechanical and movable, the lifts, the kitchen furnishings and the bathroom. The walls can often be pushed aside—even the outer walls. Doors

* Reprinted with the permission of Henry Regnery Company and Hollis & Carter, Ltd.

and windows generally have some kind of mechanism connected with them. The material of the machine is, more or less out of pure sentiment, applied to objects which till now had been made of stone and wood. There is much advocacy of houses built wholly out of metal.

In most cases these developments lack all rational foundation, for they are anything but practical; indeed, they are simply the results of romanticizing the world of the machine. Unlike the work of those who create real machines, these creations of architects who betray architecture because the idealized engineer has completely destroyed their balance, are, despite all their tall talk of functionalism, not functional at all.

The fact is that the new type of architect has become hopelessly uncertain of himself. He glances over his shoulder at the engineer, he fancies himself in the rôle of inventor and even in that of a reformer of men's lives, but he has forgotten to be an architect. His attitude to purely aesthetic questions is like that of the builder of a car to the designer of the body. The thing is just superstructure.

Meanwhile the actual dogma of the machine, as an artistic canon, however, is expressed quite openly by the theorists who coin such phrases as 'machines for living in' for houses and apply the term 'machine for sitting in' to a chair.

This general philosophy may be said to reach its culminating point in the 1920's when its extreme exponents proclaim the 'Abolition of Architecture' and tend to deny that so narrow a concept has any claim to survive, and in fact they do abolish it by treating architecture as a purely historical category, which, in view of the new state of development reached by the human spirit, is now destined to be absorbed into the general province of the engineer—much as 'superannuated' religion must yield [110] place to science. The great battle of the machine against architecture—and particularly against the older types of architecture—carried on without service to any recognizable concrete purpose of either peace or war, is thus revealed for what it is—an outburst of hate on the part of the machine men against architecture as such. [111]

PAUL VALÉRY

Pièces sur l'Art

Paul Valéry, *Pièces sur l'art* (Paris, Gallimard, 1934).*

Painting and sculpture are foundlings. Their mother architecture is dead. As long as she lived she offered them their place, their occupation and their qualifications. Freedom to wander was denied them. They had their space, their well-defined light, their subject matter, and their federations. . . . As long as she lived, they knew what they wanted. . . .[99]

SIBYL MOHOLY-NAGY

Frank Lloyd Wright and
The Ageing of Modern Architecture

Sibyl Moholy-Nagy, "Frank Lloyd Wright and the Ageing of Modern Architecture," *Progressive Architecture,* XL (May, 1959).†

Frank Lloyd Wright . . . never . . . presented any of his work without a transcendental message, linking it to Christianity, Ethnography, Democracy, Humanism. Anyone even superficially familiar with his multitudinous writing knows these invocations:

"Architecture I know to be a Great Spirit. It can never be something that consists of the buildings which have been built by man on earth. . . . Any building is a by-product of eternal living force. It is in

*Translated from the French by the editors.
† Reprinted with the permission of the author, Sibyl Moholy-Nagy, and *Progressive Architecture.*

architecture that God meets with nature in the sphere of the relative."

"The Kingdom of God is within You—it seemed to me that organic architecture was the only visible evidence of this."

This spiritual substructure of Wright's work forms one of the most conspicuous links between him and his peers, Le Corbusier and Mies van der Rohe. All three transcendentalized their design, and it is doubtful that God has ever been invoked so frequently in any profession outside the church. One only has to recall Mies van der Rohe's intense preoccupation with St. Augustine and his "God is in the details," or Le Corbusier's comment on his low-cost Domino Houses from 1915, ". . . beautiful, thanks to a soul which artistic creativity has given to these austere and pure organisms," and the Cartesian skyscrapers, 60 floors high, ". . . which allow the inhabitants to savor the good things which a bountiful God dispenses to man." [136]

. . . For the Masters of the Modern Movement, technology never lost its spiritually transfiguring impact; they continued to justify themselves against the erring traditions of their youth. Inherent in this approach to industrialization is a violent conflict between personality and formula, between self-expression and manufactured conformity. This conflict can produce extraordinary creative energy. It also can increase the warping effect of verbalization. . . .[140]

HENRY HOPE REED, JR.

The Golden City

Henry Hope Reed, Jr., *The Golden City* (Garden City, New York, Doubleday and Company, Inc., 1959).*

The term "Modern" is hardly satisfactory as a label for the ultimate convulsive phase of an aging movement. In its place we offer the label "Picturesque Secessionism" because it explains and defines. We have seen that functional architecture is an attempted rebellion or secession from historical styles with emphasis on the mechanics of construction and that its dominating goal is to be original, that is, strange, unusual, and accidental but not beautiful or sublime, in a word, "picturesque." Modern being a term applied to any contemporary work in any period, the title of Picturesque Secessionism is far more satisfactory. . . .[55]

A seeming paradox lies in the struggle for originality. Why, if the aim is so important today, do so many Modern buildings look alike? One explanation is simple enough: By denying the past the Secessionist gives undue importance to [57] his contemporaries; knowing only their work, he can do no more than imitate them. (The building on stilts, as in the example of Lever House, was taken directly from Le Corbusier.) A second reason lies in the limitation of the functional theory. With all ornament ruled out architecture has banished freedom. Like a musician satisfied with one note to his piccolo, the Modernist has already exhausted his few themes, and no new techniques or materials can vary the tune. "His work," wrote the novelist François Mauriac recently of a very successful original painter, "extends like a dead sea over a dead world, spiritually dead." [58]

. . . We are told that the disorder of Picturesque Secessionism is nothing more or less than an order we do not perceive. This is sophistry, an attempt to confuse; the functional theory and the aim of originality are nothing less than nihilism, a nihilism radiating a curious *mystique*. At best it is indifference to humanity, at worst perversity to the point of being evil. It is hardly surprising that the fashion will never become taste.

If we once accept the consequence of present fashion as a form of nihilism, then the Modern can no longer be termed "progress." In truth, it is retrogressive because it denies ornament, an essential product of man's instinct, in part a product of his own reason visually embodied. Man must fill a void, make his mark, draw a line across the canvas. It is backward to be at the mercy of techniques and materials; the truly progressive architect bids the engineer work for him and he makes use of engineering devices, not for their own sake, nor as abstractions, but to build a beautiful building. To bar curiosity by erasing the past is to tie one's hands in approaching the future. Man is made up of the community of the past, the present, and the future, and he must have all three to go forward. Further, it is retrogressive to invite disorder. In architecture order and harmony are of the essence; to deny them is to deny beauty, and to deny beauty, a part of life, is to deny true progress. In an ever-changing world man needs the permanence of beauty, that quasi-sacred beauty which only the arts can bring. Hawthorne knew this. Toward the close of *The House of the Seven Gables,* he has the rebellious Holgrave coming to admire stone architecture because "the exterior, through the lapse of years, might have been adding venerableness to its original beauty, and thus giving that impression of permanence which I consider essential to the happiness of any one moment." It is the tragedy of our time that glass, steel, and other much-touted materials will never achieve the patina, texture, and complexion which conveys the passage of time and the sense of permanence.

With the approaching demise of Picturesque Secessionism, it is obvious that we must begin all over again. Taste must be rediscovered and renewed. We must learn [60] its standards, know how to make use of them, and respect the monuments it calls great. We must admit that the word "functional," to have value, must be blessed with a meaning over and above the mechanical, that it includes ornament to please the eye, and that it welcomes the past because man loves grandeur which has meaning in terms of his heritage.

It is then, and only then, that we will have a fashion which has strong roots in our past, a fashion which will be bound by ancient tradition. There is such a quality as American taste, and we will find it by looking to the best of our inheritance. The key to the future lies there. An artistic fashion of abundance and happiness, not of meanness and denial, will be our reward. [61]

THE ARCHITECTURAL FORUM

Editorial

Editorial, *The Architectural Forum*, CVII (August, 1957).*

". . . Crises in architecture occur with singular regularity," wrote the English Critic John Summerson in 1948, "in fact, once in every generation. If the 'functionalism' crisis can be dated at 1927, the next critical year will be round about 1957."

Now 1957 is here, and change is in the air as predicted. What change? It is hard to say. Change from what? The answer is easier.

There is one aspect of modern architecture with which the public is quite definitely tired. That is the slick, smooth, scrubbed-down effect of so many modern buildings, "as like one another and as fundamentally boorish as block upon block of tenement buildings—just blander."—As bland as castor oil and leaving a feeling just as empty.

Of course modern architects have been aware of this long since; and the better ones have been working doubly hard in recent years to extend the "vocabulary" and multiply the varieties of expressiveness in modern architecture, largely by paying renewed attention to lessons of history. What the art is suffering from now, on the street, is the multiplication of work by the inevitable second-raters.

In the face of this situation a small group of fanatics has been getting some attention in general magazines—they advocate the overthrow of modern architecture altogether in behalf of just one revival which they favor, that of Roman Classical.

Unfortunately it is hard to launch a new style by simply learning nothing and forgetting nothing over a period of 30 years.

* Reprinted by permission from the June, 1952, issue of *Architectural Forum*, © 1952, Time, Inc.

The stately virtues of classical architecture cannot be brought into being in the modern world simply by opening the old Pandora's Box of ready-made style, out of which would leap all manner of other ghosts besides the classical one. The magazines that have been playing around with this shallow dillettantism would do better to give their readers a responsible account of the full effort of modern architecture, whose current "crisis" is but an episode in a 100-year development, ranging widely.[103]

BRUNO ZEVI

Fifth Year: Warning to
The Architectural Avant-Garde

Bruno Zevi, "Fifth Year: Warning to the Architectural Avant-garde," An Editorial, L'Architettura, V (May, 1959).* †

Only three months ago, *The Architect's Journal* of London in their issue of February 12th, observed that, thanks to the quality of *L'Architettura*, Italian architectural journalism had become a vital force. That is not enough. If historical-critical thinking in Italy has any value, it should succeed in defeating the inertia, uncertainties, formalistic evasions, and superficialities which presently pollute the Modern Movement and threaten its development. And because the burden of this activity cannot alone weigh on the magazine which identifies itself through its criticism with the shifting activity of the architect, we all must ask ourselves: In what direction are we pointing? Is Modern Architecture moving forward or retreating? Is it imitating itself or is it encouraging new themes? By spreading itself, is it sinking into professionalism or is it rigorously maintaining its search? Is its avant-garde tired and has it lost its initiative?

* Reprinted with the permission of Bruno Zevi and *L'Architettura*.
† Translation by the editors.

This year there was published in the United States a book entitled *The Golden City* by Henry Hope Reed, Jr. It is the most reactionary but also the most skilful attack on Modern architecture written in the last decades. It begins by comparing a series of buildings executed in the Greco-Roman style between 1860 and 1920 with their Modern equivalents and it concludes in favor of the former. It asserts that functionalism is merely a superstition with by now obvious inconsistencies. It suggests that the American contribution to architecture from the Eighteenth Century to the present is displayed in the neo-Roman and the neo-Renaissance, and it affirms that such it should remain. It derides Wright, Le Corbusier, Mies, Saarinen, Kahn, Harrison, Bunshaft, Lescaze, in short all the better architects who have worked in the United States. It even scorns Richardson and Sullivan. It sees the theoretical origins of the Modern Movement in the structural dogmas of Viollet-le-Duc. . . . With a consistency and a display of ideas worthy of a better cause, Reed denies the significance of a century of history and maintains that it is not only necessary to return to false arches, columns with bases and capitals,[6] and pastiche decoration, but that we will inevitably return to these because the language of Modern architecture has gone sterile and its crisis can only end in a return to the neoclassical. . . .

We must consider this book not so much to refute it analytically as to understand how the project could have been conceived, how in the world a scholar with a solid knowledge of history dares to prophesy with tightly argued logic the coming of the neo-Roman and the neo-Renaissance. It is not a question here of dealing with an old man nostalgic for the past, like our late teachers, but with a culturally equipped individual who has followed the development of Modern architecture and still, with an astonishingly anti-historical mode of approach, denies its significance.

If aberrations of this kind appear, who is to blame? The architect or the student of architecture? Both. The functional, structural, and abstract ideology has been discounted; it no longer has even the attraction of the "poetic" that it had at the dawn of the architectural regeneration. Modern architecture is mature, it has tradition, it has by now a substantial past. But architects are hardly aware of it; they refuse to gain an historical perspective on their own work, and they wallow in the repetition of formulae temporarily valid half a century ago. Stunted in its growth, the Modern idiom has become a "style," and to one "style" it is perfectly legitimate to oppose another. In addition, because the distinction between artistic personalities becomes confused without historical and critical light, it is legitimate to compare the stylistic eclecticism of the Nineteenth Century to the Wright-Le Corbusier-Miesian eclecticism. It is therefore the fault of the architects who do not know how to live and express their maturity. . . . If, in the coming years, the avant-garde does not know how to build on history, it will be overturned and defeated by the anti-historical forces of resurgent eclecticism.[7]

EERO SAARINEN

Function, Structure and Beauty

Eero Saarinen, "Function, Structure and Beauty," Architectural Association Journal, LXXIII (July-August, 1957).*

TECHNOLOGY

Modern technology has already had a profound influence on our architecture. Without it we would never have had the towering skyscraper, the disciplines of the Bauhaus, the geodesic dome or the building created primarily out of prefabricated, mass-produced parts. Without it we would never have had the freedom to build the tensile structures which are unique to our time. But, I believe, we have only just begun. Concrete, aluminum and plastic building techniques have hardly been explored. Mass production techniques offer us opportunities of which we have not yet taken full advantage. Modular systems suggest new opportunities, and geometry and physics have many secrets which

* Reprinted with the permission of The Architectural Association Journal.

will some day be at our disposal. All sorts of space frames and systems of climate control have new potentials for architecture. These are not freak notions or crazy science fiction ideas. They are going to be actualities. They are going to be things of which we can take advantage and of which, if we are going to remain in tune with our times, we must take advantage, or time will pass us by.

But what are we going to do with them? Are we going to let them dominate us and lead us into foolish demonstrations? Are we going just to flex our technological muscles? Or are we going to control them? Are we going to learn to endow them with poetry and significance? Are we going to use them as servants for a new, richer, more wonderful architecture? Structural integrity and structural clarity are basic aesthetic tenets of our time. Can we use the new technology well?

These are the challenges of our technology as I see them. I feel privileged to live at a time when there are these expanding possibilities. I realize their dangers, but I try to take advantage of their possibilities. . . .[41]

PLASTIC FORM

The enthusiasm for structural shapes runs very high in American architectural schools. Shell construction, folded slabs, hyperbolic paraboloids and Bucky Fuller domes are sweeping the draughting rooms in the schools, just as the prairie fires swept the plains in the Indian days. One really wonders whether the next generation of architects will have any patience with ordinary space.

As you know, in America and everywhere else, many buildings have been and are being built probing these possibilities, and the MIT auditorium is an example of that. I feel that usually there are no economic reasons for arriving at these structures—and in the end the same space could have been covered more cheaply by some conventional method. Therefore, I think, the reason why these are being built now and why we are interested is really aesthetic and not economic; and we should face that.

What interests me in these structures is when and where to

use them, and why to use them. Probing deeper into the different possibilities of these structures, one finds that they are not necessarily just mathematical formulae that have to be done in such and such a way or they will fall down, but that there are many equally logical and good ways, which go in many directions. Each direction is just as logical, but one looks better than another, and that is the direction in which we choose. . . .[43]

COLOUR, TEXTURE AND ORNAMENT

. . . All other ages or periods of architecture have had ornaments, but we really have had none. All other periods have grown their ornament out of the emphasis of structure and the emphasis of certain parts of structure which they wanted to underline. The moment one decides that one is not a completely functional purist but is also designing for aesthetic ends that can justify themselves, then an opportunity for the gradual emergence of ornament can be established. My feeling is that it is about time that one spent one's time and energy on that as a challenge, although it should be done slowly. It is only something that can grow slowly one thing on top of another. . . .[46]

. . . Modern architecture did go overboard on the 'commodity' or 'functionalist' tack for a while, but it soon found out that function alone could create neither form nor architecture. . . .

. . . Technology; the possibilities of plastic form; the exploration in colour, texture and ornament; the relation of [48] buildings to their environment—can all be thought of together as concerns and interests in enlarging our vocabulary beyond the measly ABC that we have, perhaps too complacently, been using.

EXPRESSION

But why do we want to expand the vocabulary? I think it is because modern architecture is now mature enough to think about the bigger problems of expression. Perhaps expression does not seem too much of a problem for the ordinary buildings that are really just part of what might be called a 'building-scape', a sort of background scenery; but I think we could argue that even these should have an expression—the modest one of being what they are.

The problem of expression, however, is crucial in the so-called 'special building'. A church must have the expression of a church. An airport should be an expression related to flight. It should make one feel the excitement of arrival and departure and the pleasures and adventures of travel; and so on.

Modern architecture has not had very much opportunity in these areas, but they are the most fascinating ones and we are not yet very mature. If we were confronted with the problem of a capitol or a parliament building, we would probably not do very well. . . .[49]

ROBIN BOYD

The Counter-Revolution in Architecture

Robin Boyd, "The Counter-Revolution in Architecture," Harper's Magazine, CCXIX (July, 1959).*

SWIRLS AND FEELING

Much of the new architecture of excitement is so strong and confident that it may delude us for a moment that it is leading to new realms of architectural beauty. But . . . curves can pall at least as quickly as boxes. All the shapes of architecture are of equal importance or insignificance in the cosmic pattern. Only associations of familiar shapes and surprise in unfamiliar shapes affect the immediate reaction of the eye. Ultimate satisfaction is achieved only when the long-term visual reaction is appropriate to the human activities involved—and when the architectural environment engenders a quicker sense of the realities of the situation, a sharpening of each experience.

Appropriateness of expression has been the aim in most of the "exciting shape" buildings. Stubbins' Berlin Congress Hall,

* Reprinted with the permission of *Harper's Magazine*.

with its jaunty saddle roof, clearly sought to express the concept of freedom in the speech which it was built to house. Utzon's opera house caught up the sails of Sydney Harbor. A restaurant by the sea in Puerto Rico by Toro-Ferrer shaped its concrete roof after a magnified sea shell. At TWA Saarinen and Roche let the movement of the crowd lead them.

But all this is symbolism, or somewhat shallow emotionalism, or plain high-class advertising. It has nothing to do with the appropriateness of an enclosure as *experienced by an occupant*. If curves and swirls really do convey a feeling of movement, what has this to do with the emotional state of the average passenger waiting for his flight signal? *Must* he be swept up in a feeling of movement? The mutual adjustment of the spatial expression and the psychological state of a sensitive occupant is more [47] valuable than any ordained symbolism or poetic abstraction. Excitement, in short, should be pertinent.

Architecture is, as most architects will frequently remind you, an expressive art. Frank Lloyd Wright used to insist that no building had a right to exist unless it had poetry. Yet there never have been and never will be enough artists or poets to go round, and the world-wide architectural mess which is the disgrace of the twentieth century is largely caused because we expect plodding, conscientious architectural technicians to act like artists.

Attempts to solve this anomaly sometimes lead to a concept —which has some support—of a frank division in architectural practice: a separation of the technology from the artistry. Thus the repetitive, reasonable curtain-wall grid—the box-like building —might become a universal backdrop silhouetting a foreground of special individual gems. The most likely impediments to this scheme are the commercial need to advertise the importance of unimportant buildings and the egotistical urge of some builders and architects to raise monuments on their own inadequate ability. The only counter to this, and ultimately the only cure for architecture's ills, is a better educated public taste. . . . [48]

JOHN ELY BURCHARD

Architecture in a Restless Age

John Ely Burchard, "Architecture in a Restless Age," *The Architectural Record*, CXXV (May, 1959).*

Architectural historians looking upon the Western scene of mid-1959 will probably call it a time of chaos in which escape from boredom may have been the dominant cry. This may seem to them the more discouraging because of the great and fresh promise offered by the revolution of the first quarter century and because isolated architectural monuments of great quality continued to appear from time to time as the century rolled into its third quarter. But the doctrines which had held designers and critics and prophets together in the earlier days now appeared to have vanished. If there could have been said to be *one* contemporary movement in the twenties, it had fragmented into many by the fifties; and often the one common agreement was nothing more than rejection of the notion that there was any necessity to return to those patterns of Roman imitation which had provoked and sustained the modern revolution in the beginning.

But save for that common determination there now seems to be little else in common. We are told by an increasing number that the classic form which might have been distilled from the Miesian° cage will not emerge because all the possibilities of the cage have been exhausted—in fact, that it is boring. We are told by others that there must be a retreat from the all-glass façade not for the possibly good reason that it is not a satisfactory façade but because there is nothing more that can be done with glass now; that it too is boring. (Parenthetically we may thank

° Reprinted with the permission of John Ely Burchard and *The Architectural Record*.

° Ludwig Mies van der Rohe.

heaven that the designers of the glass of the Sainte Chapelle did not lay a similar stricture after the installation of the windows of Chartres.) We seem to live in an age when very few architects can be permitted to repeat themselves in any significant way. It is even more an age when it is regarded as plagiarism or worse if one architect takes the work of another as a base and sets out to refine it in his own way—yet this is the way in which every great previous architecture has had to develop. More than that, we live in an age when few clients can be found to want something that is merely an improvement on something that has gone before, even something modern, so that there are design patents on every innovation so to speak and about all that seems to remain as interesting in architecture is its novelty.[174]

I scarcely need to remind this audience of the various forms this restlessness is taking but it is perhaps appropriate to suggest that the overpremiation of novelty and innovation has characterized in the past only the most thoughtless and the most foppish periods and those of power and sobriety. Foppishness in dress or poetry is bad enough, foppishness in architecture has a deadly durability. For this restlessness the great Dante might have apportioned the punishment he gave to those who made "the reason thrall to appetence"

> "And as a great flock of starlings on the wing
>   In winter time together trooping go
>   So did that blast the wicked spirits fling
> Now here, now there, now up and down below;
>   Comfort of hope to them is never known
>   Either of rest or even less bitter woe"

Thus these shadows who on the storm blast whirled and surged, moaned in their ceaseless meaningless flight as the black air whistled round them like a scourge.

Do not misunderstand the tenor of these comments. I do not lump every one who abandoned the 19th-century renaissance of the Renaissance in a single company of "picturesque secessionists" spawned together in the manger of Viollet-le-Duc. I still have as great hope that out of the revolution may yet come a great architecture as I am sure nothing will come from a return

Earls Court, 1786-1796, Dublin, designed by Thomas Cooley and James Gandon, overlooks the River Liffey. The building, seat of the Irish Law Courts, is an example of the classical which Ruskin attacked in **The Stones of Venice** as "base, unnatural, unfruitful, unenjoyable and impious."

to the literal emulation of Vignola. But the term "picturesque secessionist" has a useful bite if we apply it only in our own times and to our own friends who, in their determination to be different and to achieve personal styles and to avoid boredom, are rapidly seceding from each other; and perhaps worse still encouraging all their students to be imaginative, even those who have no imagination. Badly as poor designers may do with their versions of any classic form, including the Miesian, it is as nothing to what is let loose on the world when the unimaginative are told to innovate at all costs and encouraged to believe that the search for the novel is the greatest search in architecture, and that in the "new freedom" there may be no rules at all, not even the rules of scale, proportion, rhythm, balance, which have been observed by every competent architect in every day, whether or not he professed them audibly.... [175]

Are the times victims of their own techniques? Today almost any form can be built at some price, almost any material employed, plans can be forced by equipment to almost any function. Does all this richness of resource bring on the madness of innovation as sitting too long in the moon once did or is it merely an abettor of the eagerness to be personal, different, to be an innovator?

Or is it merely that we cannot learn how to design high buildings for air conditioning?

Or is it just the schools with their lack of discipline or the architectural press with their journalistic nose for news asserting that nothing old is news?

Or are we all in the same boat together? Or is the boat not sailing on rough waters anyway? Or is the shore clearly in sight? Or who are the helmsmen?

Have architects finally fallen victims to the malaria of the Renaissance which in permeating the individual set out to make the name and character of the individual actor or artist of greatest importance? Much of the greatest art has not been produced in these circumstances, or by artists of any ilk who offered only private messages. The world as a whole is moving to a greater and greater collectivism and I mean this in the most general terms, not necessarily economic, not necessarily political. More and more things require group efforts to achieve. Leaders are more and more captains of committees and not of armies, conciliators not commanders. But committees cannot write poetry we know. Are the arts then the last final refuge of the Renaissance philosophy of the individual? Is the dignity of man impossible unless each man can make a strange enough face and speak in loud enough words so that he commands the attention if not the admiration of all who pass by? Has contemporary architecture, lagging painting and sculpture as it always has before, finally fallen heir to the malaise of the other arts based on the notion that it is better to do bad personal work than good collective work? Can architecture as a social art afford this fantasy? [177]

BRUNO ZEVI

Architecture as Space.
How to Look at Architecture

Bruno Zevi, *Architecture as Space. How to Look at Architecture*, trans. by Milton Gandel, Joseph A. Barry, ed. (New York, Horizon Press, 1957).*

Professional architects, who, in order to explore the problem of contemporary architecture, must necessarily have a profound [16] passion for architecture in the living sense of the word, are largely lacking today in the specific cultural background which would qualify them for a knowledgeable entry into the arena of historical and critical debate. The culture of modern architects is too often limited by their chronic controversies. In their fight against feebly imitative or falsifying academicism they have more than once, if only unconsciously, declared their lack of interest in the valid works of the past, and in this way have failed to draw from these works the vital, permanent guiding principle without which no avant-garde position might broaden into a whole cultural complex. We are speaking not only of Frank Lloyd Wright and his disparagement of the Italian Renaissance (anything can be forgiven a genius, particularly critical unobjectivity), but also of the cultural inclination of Le Corbusier, whose superficial skimming and impressionistic judgment of various periods in the history of architecture is more an elegant, brilliant intellectual exercise than a fruitful contribution to a critical reevaluation of architecture. *Les yeux qui ne voient pas,** the eyes which do not see the beauty of Purist forms are eyes that today do not see

---

* Reprinted by permission of Bruno Zevi.
* See Le Corbusier.

and do not understand the lessons of traditional architecture.

Much remains to be done. It is the task of the second generation of modern architects, once having overcome the psychological break involved in the birth of the functionalist movement, to reestablish a cultural order. The moment of ostentatious novelty and avant-garde manifestos has passed and modern architecture must now take its place in architectural tradition, aiming above all at a critical revision of this very tradition. It has become evident that an organic culture cannot, in dealing with the past and specifically with architectural history, use two standards of judgment, one for modern and another for traditional architecture, if it is, as it must be, designed to provide modern disoriented and rootless man with a base and a history, to integrate individual and social needs which manifest themselves today as an antithesis between freedom and planning, theory and practice. Once we are able to apply the same criteria in evaluating contemporary architecture and that of previous centuries, we shall be taking a decisive step forward in this direction! [17]

Five Controversies
of Modern
American Architecture

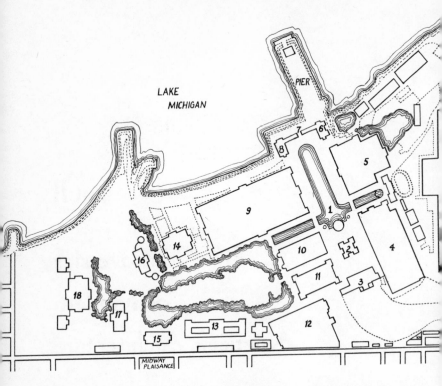

Plan of the World's Columbian Exposition of 1893, Chicago. 1. The Court of Honor. 2. Administration Building by Richard Morris Hunt. 3. Railroad Station. 4. Machinery Hall by Peaboby & Stearns. 5. Agricultural Building by McKim, Mead & White. 6. The Casino by Charles B. Atwood. 7. The Colonnade by Charles B. Atwood. 8. The Music Hall by Charles B. Atwood. 9. Manufactures and Liberal Arts Building by George Brown Post. 10. Electricity Building by Van Brunt & Howe. 11. Mines and Mining Building by Solon S. Beman. 12. Transportation Building by Louis Sullivan. 13. Horticultural Building by William Le Baron Jenney. 14. United States Government. 15. Woman's Building by Miss Sophia G. Hayden. 16. Fisheries Building by Henry Ives Cobb. 17. Illinois Building. 18. Fine Arts Building by Charles B. Atwood.

1

THE WORLD'S COLUMBIAN EXPOSITION

Chicago, 1893

CHARLES MOORE

Lessons of the Chicago World's Fair

Charles Moore, "Lessons of the Chicago World's Fair. An Interview with the Late Daniel H. Burnham," *The Architectural Record*, XXXIII (June, 1913).

[The narrative in Mr. Burnham's own words follows:]

The World's Fair movement began in 1889, when a temporary organization was made—not a legal one; there was no incorporation. The Chicago people went to Congress, and there fought out the question of the location of the fair that was to commemorate the fourth centenary of the discovery of America. Washington, New York and St. Louis, always opposed to Chicago, wanted it; but the commercial conditions in Chicago were sufficient to carry through the location here.

There was a Buildings and Grounds committee consisting of Mayor Cregier, Edward T. Jeffery, Eugene S. Pike, Robert A. Waller, Owen F. Aldis and Charles H. Schwab, as I remember. They asked me in as a sort of unofficial adviser. They incorporated in the spring of 1890. Happily, politics were not in the minds of the committee, and they gave no special attention to that

subject. Along in July, 1890, James Ellsworth, then president of
the South Parks Board (he was very active in artistic matters;
he now lives in New York and has a villa in Florence), happened
to be in the East. He was on one of the committees, [1] and he went
out to Brookline to see Frederick Law Olmsted, whom he asked
to come out here, guaranteeing to pay him $1,000. Olmsted came,
and in August made a report. He brought with him Harry Codman, [2] whom I first saw at a meeting in Chicago. We had already
urged the selection of Jackson Park. Olmsted had figured the
thing out, and on a sheet of foolscap paper he made a rough
sketch—a design of Jackson Park. He recommended this park, and
advised that Wooded Island be left as it was. The latter feature
was not then acted upon, but Jackson Park was definitely
approved as the site.

Then Harry Codman, John Root and I took up the matter. I
have in my records a good many of the drawings made at that
time. We had a cross-section lithograph of the park, on which
we worked. We determined the size of the buildings, and finally
their location; we retained Wooded Island, and, at my suggestion,
placed a fountain in the vista.

Then came the fight. The National Commission [3] demanded
that plans and specifications be submitted for their approval.
We presented the general plan as we had it laid out, on a piece
of brown paper, not rendered at all; and standing up before
the crowd, I made some explanations. In November the National
Commission adopted the plans and specifications submitted as
satisfying the Act of Congress.

In September, 1890, an organization [36] had been formed;
John Root was made consulting architect, Olmsted consulting
landscape architect, and I was named chief of construction. My

[1] James W. Ellsworth was a member of the Committee on Foreign
Exhibits.
[2] Henry Sargent Codman, a partner of Mr. Olmsted. He died January
13, 1893. Tablets for him and Mr. Root were placed on the Fine Arts
building. For the report, see History of the World's Columbian Exposition,
New York, 1897.
[3] Appointed under authority of Act of Congress, approved April 25,
1890, and consisting of two commissioners for each State and Territory and
eight commissioners at large. This commission had important powers. There
were some clashes with the Chicago Directory, but the work was done
mainly by the local body.

commission was drawn by Jeffery, then president of the Illinois
Central, who acted as chairman of the Grounds and Buildings
Committee. He placed everything under my control, and fixed
it so that all others must report to me direct, so that they could
make no communications save through me. It was urged by men
who knew more about organization than I did at that time, that
it was absolutely necessary to have a chief.

We shoved on as fast as we could, without having anything
definite in regard to the various buildings. Then, late in the
year, December, I believe, I grew very impatient, and told the
committee that we must have action—get together a force of
men and begin work. There was further delay, but about the 5th
of January I got orders. It was agreed that I should select five
Chicago architects and five outside architects. I made my selection
and went before the committee of seven members, three of whom
were in political life. The committee could not come to an agreement, the politicians desiring to keep me from making the
selection. Finally Gage put the motion—four voted for and three
against me.

The next morning I had a letter prepared to the men in the
East, asking them to participate in the work. I had written to
them previously, feeling confident that I would carry my point.
My plan was to bring together the men of greatest experience.
I was forty-four and a half years old, and knew who the [38] men
were. I went to New York and met the architects at the Players'
Club; told them they would be expected to design their buildings, and I would guarantee that none of their artistic conceptions
would be interfered with; that Root would give expression, of
course; but that they would be kept in full touch, and whatever
each desired in regard to his own building would be carried out.
I found them in doubt and uncertain whether they would take
part; but they finally decided to come in.[4]

The five Chicago firms [5] selected I called on the morning
after the decision in committee. First Cobb, then Beeman, each

[4] The five firms outside of Chicago were Richard M. Hunt, George B.
Post and McKim, Mead & White of New York; Peabody & Stearns of
Boston; Van Brunt & Howe of Kansas City.
[5] The Chicago firms were Burling & Whitehouse, Jenney & Mundie,
Henry Ives Cobb, Solon S. Beman and Adler & Sullivan.

of whom said he would come in. Next Burling & Whitehouse and Jenney & Mundie consented. Adler & Sullivan "did not know"; later they, too, decided to come in.

The Eastern architects appeared on Saturday, January 10. McKim did not come, but Mead represented that firm; then there was Hunt, Peabody, Van Brunt, George Post and Olmsted. Root, who had been in Georgia for three weeks, got in about nine in the morning. He remained in the office while I drove with the visitors to Jackson Park. It was a cold winter day; the sky was overcast with clouds and the lake covered with foam. We looked the place over. Peabody climbed up on a pier and called out:

"Do you mean to say that you really expect to open a fair here by '93?"

"Yes," I replied, "we intend to."

He said he thought it could not be done; but I told him that point was settled. That night the Grounds and Buildings Committee gave a dinner, the whole crowd being present. Gage presided and made a very beautiful speech. Then Jeffery spoke. Then they asked me to speak. I said that in one sense this was the third great American event, 1776 and 1861 going before; and, that as in both those events men had come to the front and given themselves up to the public, so now the times demanded self-sacrifice. I told them further that the success of this undertaking depended upon team-work. If they worked for the thing as a whole it would be a great success. There was a great deal of response. It was the same old appeal that the Chicago men had been brought up on. From that night on this spirit never failed.

Sunday I did not come into town. Root had asked the visitors to his house on Astor Place, for five o'clock tea. He was in evening dress, ready to go out somewhere. When they were leaving he ran out and saw them into their carriages. The next morning, while the meeting was in progress, Mrs. Root called me up to say that John had a bad cold, but might come in for the afternoon. In the afternoon she called again to say that John had pneumonia. During the next three days I remained with him nearly all the time, night and day. On Thursday Harry Codman went with me to the house, but did not go in. John was breathing rapidly when I entered his room.

"You won't leave me again, will you?" he pleaded.

I promised to stay. Later I went in to see his wife, who was very ill. His aunt came into the room to tell me John was dead; that he had put his hands on the counterpane as if he were running them over a keyboard (he played beautifully), and said:

"Do you hear that? Isn't it wonderful? That is what I call music!" Then he threw up his hand and was dead.

The Eastern men remained for a week working with me. They made one change. Harry Codman's knowledge of formal settings was greater than that of all the others put together. He proposed to carry my fountain back, taking it out of the north and south axis. Then they returned, to meet again in a month. Codman took the plan to Brookline and seriously set to work on exact dimensions, terraces, placing of bridges, and the general laying out of a piece of formal work. We had not given any consideration at all to terraces; but we had [39] agreed that the Italian Renaissance style of architecture should be adopted for the Court of Honor. The buildings were as distinct from one another as could be. Harry Codman was great in his knowledge and in his instincts. He never failed. He liked to come to the business meetings and occasionally he made an excellent suggestion about organization. I loved the man. Nature spoke through him direct.

The men came back I think about the 20th of February. By that time Beeman's building was begun; the design had been made and the foundations were being put in. They came out in a private car. They brought Saint-Gaudens. After they had returned in January I felt I must have Saint-Gaudens. I wrote to ask if he would come out to give general advice; if he would take a fee and his expenses, and go so far as to indicate what sculptors we should use.

The visiting men came to a breakfast. They were filled with enthusiasm. Charles McKim broke out with a good deal of repressed excitement, saying:

"Bob Peabody wants to carry a canal down between our buildings."

I told him I would agree to it and that we would do it even though it would cost something. That was Peabody's contribution to the Fair. At night this canal was wonderfully beautiful.

Next Saint-Gaudens took a hand in the thing. He thought the

east end of the composition should be bound together architecturally. All agreed; and he suggested a statue surrounded by thirteen columns, typifying the thirteen original states. We all hailed this as a bully thing.

We had a meeting a day or two later in my office, the Grounds and Buildings Committee being present. Lyman J. Gage presided. All the fellows, including [41] the Chicago men, were there, each with his sketch or sketches; and one by one they put the drawings on the wall. Hunt, crippled by rheumatism, sat on the edge of a table, and told about his Administration Building, with its dominating dome, expressing the leadership of the Government. The scheme as a whole had begun to take hold of us. Then came Post. George Post had a dome 450 feet high. The moment they all saw that dome you could hear them murmuring. George turned around to the crowd, saying:

"I don't think I shall advocate that dome. Probably I shall modify the building."

Charles McKim had a portico extending out over the terrace and made extremely prominent. He did not wait, as George had done, but explained that the portico had been under consideration; but that he would withdraw it to the face of the building. The feeling for unity thus manifested, and the willingness of those two men to subordinate their individual ideas in order to produce a single harmonious effect, will illustrate the spirit which made possible the artistic success of the Fair. Where they led, others were willing to follow.

So the day went on. We had luncheon brought in. Then came the large committee. The winter afternoon was drawing to an end. In the room it was as still as death, save for the low voices of the speakers commenting on their designs. You could feel the thing as a great magnet. Finally, when the last drawing had been shown, Gage drew a long breath, stood up against the window, shut his eyes and said:

"Oh! gentlemen, this is a dream!" Then, opening his eyes, he smilingly continued, "You have my good wishes, and I hope it can be carried out."

Saint-Gaudens had been in the corner all day, never opening his mouth, and scarcely moving. He came over to me, and taking both my hands, said:

"Look here, old fellow, do you realize that this is the greatest meeting of artists since the Fifteenth Century?"

I had a great deal of private work; not as large a business as I have now, but for that time it was a large business. I had a shanty down at the Fair grounds, where I spent most of my nights. A special metallic-circuit telephone connected with my office. I wanted as great an architect as I could get to help in my own work, and consulted several men, among them Professor Ware. The latter was most emphatic about Atwood,[6] who had been doing beautiful things here and there. I made an appointment with Atwood to meet him in New York. Charles McKim shook his head about him. Atwood did not keep his appointment. I waited an hour at the Brunswick Hotel and then left. As I was crossing the street a man stepped up and asked if I was Mr. Burnham. He said he was Mr. Atwood and asked if I wanted to see him. I told him I was going back to Chicago and would think it over and let him know. Within four hours after I reached my office Atwood came in. He had followed me out. I told him I would like to have him design an art building, and explained what was wanted. He was a very gentle, sweet man, and certainly he was a very great artist. His Art Building is today in design the most beautiful building I have ever seen. He weighed things to a nicety.

I sent a blue print of the Art Building to New York. They took it to the Players' Club, and from there sent back the most enthusiastic telegram you ever read, saying that it was a triumph of art.

I sent a letter to the governor of each of the thirteen original states, asking for a granite column. Atwood promised and promised to prepare a drawing for those columns, but I never could get it out of him. One day I told him I could wait no longer. He then drew out a drawer and showed me the column beautifully drawn. He asked if I had really made up my mind about the scheme. I asked what he meant, catching from his manner that he was [42] holding back something. He said he felt that the screen would be too thin, that something a little more solid

[6] Charles B. Atwood, who, after the Fair, became a member of the firm of D. H. Burnham & Co. He designed more than sixty of the buildings of the Fair, besides various ornamental features.

World's Columbian Exposition of 1893, Chicago. Above, a view of the Basin of the Court of Honor in July, 1891, the central axis of the Exposition. The photograph is taken from the site of the Administration Building (**See** plan) looking eastwards across sand dunes toward Lake Michigan. **Below,** the Court of Honor two years later. The photograph, again looking eastwards, is taken from high on the Administration Building. From left to right are the Manufacturers and Liberal Arts Building by George Brown Post, the Colonnade and the Casino by Charles B. Atwood and the Agricultural Building by McKim, Mead & White, atop whose dome is a statue of Diana by the sculptor Augustus Saint-Gaudens. In the foreground, in the Basin, the fountain by Frederick MacMonnies.

World's Columbian Exposition of 1893, Chicago. Above, the Court of Honor in June, 1892, looking westwards. The skeletons of steel and wood await coverings of staff and plaster. In the center, the Administration Building; in the foreground, piles to support the State of the Republic. **Below,** the same view a year later after the opening of the Exposition, taken from atop the Colonnade. From left to right, the Agricultural Building by McKim, Mead & White, Machinery Hall by Peabody & Stearns, the Administration Building by Richard Morris Hunt, the Electricity Building by Van Brunt & Howe, the Manufactures and Liberal Arts Building by George Brown Post. In the foreground, the golden colossus of the Republic by Daniel Chester French.

and tied-together was needed. He was very gentle, but perceiving that he had in mind a scheme, I asked if he could suggest anything. Thereupon he took out a drawing of the Peristyle drawn exquisitely. It was as if some one had flung open the Golden Gates before me. I told him there was no question about it. I sent a copy of it to New York. There was not even a suggestion of a possible alteration. They telegraphed most emphatically that they were glad of the change.

Charles McKim came out often as did the others. Charles McKim would go into the detail of things with me, and was an inspiration. He spent nearly an entire afternoon looking over Atwood's drawings. He took down the books every little while, looked at them, and then turning to me would say:

"Confound him, he is right every time!"

Saint-Gaudens recommended French, McMonnies and a dozen others. Frank Millet came in about three months after our first meeting. I had chosen a man named Prettyman, largely on account of his great friendship with John Root. He was to have charge of the decorations; and, knowing that staff was going to be used, he had at once begun to work out a general coloring of staff. He concluded that ivory would be the best color. The crowd came out when Beeman's building was nearly finished. I was urging every one on, knowing it was an awful fight against time. We talked about colors, and finally the thought came, "Let us make it all perfectly white." I don't recall who made the suggestion. It might have been one of those things that occurred to all minds at once, as so often happens. At any rate the decision was mine. Prettyman [43] was in the East, and I had Beeman's building made cream white. When Prettyman came back he was outraged. He said that so long as he was in charge I must not interfere. I told him that I did not see it that way; that I had the decision. He then said he would get out; and he did. McKim said Frank Millet would be the man for the place. George Post recommended him and this went far, because I have great faith in Post's judgment of men. So I went down to New York and met Frank at a dinner at Delmonico's—Charles McKim gave the dinner and at the dinner I made Frank a proposition, offering him the largest salary of any one on the staff, $15,000. Frank said it cost him that to live, and I went before the Directors and told them I thought we should pay that. Of course we could not afford to do anything else. Frank organized the whitewash gang. Turner of New York got up a method of blowing paint on buildings; this Frank adopted, and it is now in common use in car shops.

In a sense the Chicago Fair was the first attempt made in this country to connect landscape with architecture, although of course L'Enfant's plan of Washington cannot be ignored. You cannot find an instance of planning an entire city until you come to L'Enfant's plan; and I believe that the plan of Washington exerted a decided influence in Europe.[44]

RICHARD MORRIS HUNT

Address to the Convention of the American Institute of Architects

Address by Richard Morris Hunt, President of the American Institute of Architects, at the convention of 1891; Proceedings of the American Institute of Architects, XXV (1891).

. . . At the first conference, held in Chicago, of the ten architects selected, together with the Chief of Construction and the Consulting Landscape Architects, the duties and responsibilities of all were definitely defined, and the question of compensation, so far as the architects were concerned, agreed on. This latter question was rather an intricate one, principally on account of the limitation of employment, each architect being only required to furnish a general design, one set of full and complete general working drawings, and full details of all work of an artistic character connected therewith,[12] together with such descriptions and instructions as might be necessary to elucidate fully his views as to construction and treatment. Everything relating to the construction and stability of the work was delegated to the Bureau of Construction. . . .[13]

The architects in charge of the buildings about this court, after considerable thought and discussion, decided that it would be wiser to treat the façades on the court in a quiet way rather than attempt to vie with each other in the solution of that vexed problem, "Iron Architecture," a problem never yet altogether satisfactorily solved. The last two French expositions showed great merit in the adaptation of iron to architectural effects, but much yet remains to be accomplished before the artistic mind will be satisfied; and certainly, if Paris, with her multitude of artists and artisans of the highest grade, and having plenty of time for the study and execution of this problem, could not satisfactorily solve it, it would have been foolhardiness to attempt it on this occasion, the time being so restricted; besides which it would be well-nigh impossible to secure harmony in the several designs, whose authors were hundreds of miles distant one from the other. Furthermore, in view of the fact that in all probability examples in every style of architecture would be found in the vast number of structures to be erected, it was deemed advisable that the court should be treated in a dignified way, in the classic style —each one to be left free in regard to his façade; the only restriction being that the main cornice be fixed at a height of 60 feet above the terrace level, not including any prominent features, such as towers, etc. It was further deemed advisable, by introducing a dome or otherwise, to give prominence to the Administration building, located at the west end of the court, and at the intersection of the two main axes of the plan, one extending north and south, the other east and west.

Should the general effect of this court prove to be what its designers [14] intended, I can but believe that it will be of benefit to the public and to the profession, a practical illustration of that dignity and repose so characteristic of classic architecture— features too often nowadays lost sight of in the search for originality, not to say eccentricity. It is useless, perhaps, to add that perfect harmony has reigned at all the conferences, which have demonstrated the great benefit resulting from an interesting and earnest discussion of the many important points naturally presenting themselves. These conferences have also accomplished much in strengthening the bonds of fellowship, not only among ourselves, but also with our co-workers, the sculptors and the decorators, on whom so much depends in the execution of our projects. Thus a precedent has been established in the right direction; the high standing of the profession has been fully recognized, and it is to be hoped that this step will inaugurate a new era in the employment of members of our profession.

When we consider how rarely, in this country, any time can be found for the serious consideration of art matters, we cannot fail to give unstinted praise to those who have directed this great undertaking in such a truly national spirit. Allusion is often made to the difficulties of our position, as compared with those of our confrères in Europe, who are surrounded by ancient examples of our art, and by an appreciative public, trained to admire the monumental glories of the past. On the other hand, our opportunities are far greater than theirs, owing to the rapid increase of our population, to the accumulation of large fortunes, to the great variety of building materials, to the excellency of our mechanics, etc.; besides which, the greatest freedom with us is allowed in design, uncontrolled as we are by precedents. Our individual responsibilities are also correspondingly greater, on account of the rapidity with which our work must be carried on, and the many new and complex problems daily presented for solution, such as high buildings, etc.[15]

EDWIN H. BLASHFIELD

A Painter's Reminiscences of a World's Fair

Edwin H. Blashfield, "A Painter's Reminiscences of a World's Fair," *The New York Times Magazine*, March 18, 1923; an address given at a dinner of the National Society of Mural Painters at the Architectural League of New York, on March 6, 1923.*

THE NEW YORK TIMES MAGAZINE (March 18, 1923)

In the midsummer of 1893 [A mistake for 1892. Eds.] telegrams of a surprising, gratifying and, withal, disconcerting character came to a number of painters. They surprised by their unexpectedness,

* Reprinted with the permission of *The New York Times*.

gratified by their flattering implication, disconcerted by their suggestion of a terra incognita of painting. They were all signed F. D. Millet. Mine was a cablegram: Would I come to Chicago and execute a mural painting for the Columbian exhibition? Would I? Would a duck swim? And we began to move northward, stopping ten days in Venice in the hope that some of Veronese's or Tintoretto's secret would look out on to the inspiration of such a very green hand as I was. We lucky candidates were all green together. Dante's simile of enamel for meadows was not greener than we.

In Chicago Millet met me at the gate of the Fair, Burnham at the door of his office, and in a sort of trotting buggy, an extinct vehicle, he drove me all over the Fair Grounds.

It was awesome. Any one who wanted to see wheels go round could see and hear and go from surprise to surprise. This was America with a vengeance. I had come from classical columns in the Roman Forum, where drum upon drum had been piled by antique enginery and years of labor.

Here on every side were groups of a half dozen men debonairly picking up a colossal fluted thing that looked like a monolith, standing it on end and with light tackle fitting a Corinthian cap to it; white walls were rising as you watched and domes seemed big iridescent bubbles in the vapor of the lagoons. My chin dropped. What was it all? This was staff, they told me—and what was staff? Something light to juggle with and stop out wind and weather long enough for exhibition purposes. . . .

. . . Millet said: ". . . We'll introduce a new child into American art, mural painting, and christen it right here in Chicago." [13]

. . . My companions who were present that day [opening day of the Exposition] must remember how we stood at the refreshment table before the ceremony, eating sandwiches, and realized that the Government of the United States on a large scale had recognized art for the first time and that medals would soon be brought around to the architects and sculptors and painters; brought in baskets, so numerous were we and so lavish was the spirit of reward. . . .

"Well, it all ended, and we hardly realized what a great beginning had been made. For those amazing men of the World's Fair, Burnham and McKim, Olmsted and Hunt, Post and Pea-

body, Millet, Atwood, Saint-Gaudens, had created an object lesson which taught from Portland, Me. to Portland, Ore. . . .

If such a vision could be materialized in '93, what might not
the untried future bring? It looked as iridescent as the sunfilled
vapor of the lagoons. Sympathy, enthusiasm was shared so completely that after a generation has passed those of us who worked
in Chicago can still sigh happily to each other, "I, too, was in
Arcadia." [14]

HENRY VAN BRUNT

Architecture at the
World's Columbian Exposition

Henry Van Brunt, "Architecture at the World's Columbian Exposition," *The Century Magazine*, XLIV (1892).

The basis of operations is explained by the plan of the
grounds herewith presented, which exhibits in outline the result,
not of the latest studies, but of that stage of the work reached at
the time when it was necessary to prepare the map for the purpose of illustrating this paper. In a subsequent paper we hope
to present a more comprehensive plan, indicating the nature of
the modification to which the whole scheme has been subject
from month to month. It will be observed that there are three
grand divisions. Of these the northernmost, which had already
been laid out as a park by the city, is to be occupied centrally
by the Department of Fine Arts, the State pavilions being
grouped north and west of it; while the foreign government buildings will be placed east of it, toward the lake, and, if occasion
requires, in the Plaisance, which is a long reserved tract 600 feet
wide between 59th and 60th streets, forming a boulevard approach to Jackson Park from the west. In this tract also areas
have been granted to foreign enterprise for the establishment of
model villages and groups of pavilions illustrating the character-

istics of domestic and industrial life in remote countries.

The middle division is formed by the lagoon, the most characteristic landscape feature of the grounds. This is an irregular, artificial water-way surrounding several islands, the largest among them being a wooded tract about 1700 feet long and from 200 to 500 feet wide, the natural conditions of which will be enhanced by aquatic shrubbery and flower-beds, with kiosks and rustic pavilions approached by bridges. A part of the northern end of this island has been applied for by, and will probably be granted to, the Japanese commissioners, who propose to lay out a considerable area in a characteristic garden, according to their ancient traditions in this art, and to embellish it with exact reproductions of several of their most venerable temples. The outer margins of the lagoon will be occupied on the west by the Transportation Building, by the Horticultural Building, with its gardens, and by the Woman's Building; on the east, toward the lake, will stand the Palace of Manufactures and Liberal Arts, and the United States Pavilion. The lagoon branches capriciously northward and eastward, giving water-fronts to the Pavilion of Fine Arts, to the Illinois State Building,[84] and to the Fisheries and United States Government buildings. Southward this irregular quadrangle is closed by the north façades of the Mines and Electricity buildings.

The lagoon connects southward with a system of formal stone-bordered canals and basins, where will be symmetrically placed the great plaza, or *cour d'honneur*, of the Exposition, a regular quadrangle 700 by 2000 feet, about equal in size to that of the last Paris Exposition. Water-communication will be provided for at the east end of this court, and the system of railroads will debouch at the west end in a railroad terminus, masked by the Administration Building, which will be treated so as to serve as the monumental porch of the Exposition. From the railroad terminus, through the arches of this porch and beneath its lofty dome, the visitors will enter the court, which is bounded on the right hand (southward) by the Departments of Machinery and Agriculture, on the left (northward) by those devoted to Mines, Electricity, and to Manufactures and the Liberal Arts, and in front (eastward) by Lake Michigan. The center of this court is occupied by a great artificial basin which forms a part of the water-system of the Park. Connecting with this basin, a broad canal, bordered by double terraces and crossed by arched bridges, will run southward into a minor court between the palaces of Agriculture and Machinery.[85] This minor court will be closed toward the south by an architectural screen in the form of an arcade on the first story and a colonnade on the second, with a triumphal arch in the center, through which the visitor will enter the Department of Live Stock, which constitutes the southernmost feature of the Exposition. Opposite this canal, on the same axis, is another of similar character, running northward between the Departments of Electricity and the Liberal Arts, and connecting, as we have already seen, with the waters of the lagoon.

This brief description, aided by the topographical views which we present, may serve to give in outline the general architectural scheme of the Exposition-grounds. The relative positions of the buildings being understood, we may now devote ourselves to a consideration of the architectural motives which underlie the designs of the buildings, and confer upon them character and significance as works of art. In other words, we do not attempt a description of these buildings, still less a criticism,—which would be premature,—but an analysis of the principles according to which they have been severally developed. We purpose, in fact, to put ourselves in the position of the architect when first confronted by his problem, and, as far as possible, to outline some of the processes of investigation and study through which his work gradually grew into its final form. Of course it would be impracticable to indicate the numerous false starts, the erasures, the studies tried and abandoned, and all the long tentative processes which must in every case be labored through before the scheme of a building takes its ultimate shape. The main object of these papers will have been attained if they may serve to show how a work of architecture, like any other work of art, is the result of logical processes studiously followed, and not a mere matter of taste, a following of fashion, or an accident of invention more or less fortuitous.

The highest claim which can be made for modern architecture must rest on those characteristics of ornamented or ordered structure which have grown out of the unprecedented exigencies

of modern buildings. Wherever these exigencies have been met
in such a spirit that a corresponding development of style has
been produced, justly differentiated from all other historic or
contemporary styles not by caprice, but by growth, there exists
a living and progressive art, which, like all other living arts in
history, will stand as the exponent of the civilization under which
it obtained its definite form. Probably the largest, the most deliberate, and the most conspicuous expression of the present condition of architecture in this country will be looked for by foreign
critics on the grounds of the World's Columbian Exposition; but
they will find it rather in the latest commercial, educational, and
domestic structures in and near our larger cities. By these our
architecture should be judged. It is true that the industrial
palaces of our Exposition will be larger in area than any which
have preceded them, and will surpass in this respect even the
imperial villas and baths of the ancient Romans. But they will
be an unsubstantial pageant of which the concrete elements will
be a series of vast covered inclosures, adjusted on architectural
plans to the most lucid classification and the most effective arrangement of the materials of the Exposition, and faced with a
decorative mask of plaster composition on frames of timber and
iron, as the Romans of the Empire clothed their rough structures
of cement and brick with magnificent architectural veneers of
marbles, bronze, and sculpture. Mr. Burnham, the Chief of Construction, rubs his wonderful lamp of Aladdin in his office at
Chicago, and the sudden result is an exhalation, a vast phantasm
of architecture, glittering with domes, towers, and banners, like
the vision of Norumbega, which presently will fade and leave no
trace behind. But these shapes do not make themselves. There
is, it is true, a creative energy, followed by an apparition of
palaces and pavilions; but between the energy and the apparition
are the consultations, the experiments, the studies of a very palpable board of representative architects of the nation, who have
learned that this great architectural improvisation requires as
much of their zeal, labor, knowledge, and professional experience
as if they were planning to build with monumental stone and
marble. However temporary the buildings, the formative motives
behind them will be on trial before the world; for these motives,
disembarrassed as they have been, to a great extent, of the usual

controlling considerations of structure and cost, and concentrated upon the evolution of purely decorative forms, have made demands upon our resources of art such, perhaps, as have been required by no previous emergency in architecture.

The liberality exhibited by the management and by the architects of Chicago toward their brethren summoned from other cities has been more than generous. To the latter were assigned all the buildings around the great court, a compliment which involved the most serious responsibilities, and of which the only adequate recognition could be an especial effort to justify it. In view of the fact that these buildings had a mutual dependence much more marked than any others on the grounds, and that the formal or architectural character of the court absolutely [86] required a perfect harmony of feeling among the five structures which inclose it, it became immediately evident to these gentlemen that they must adopt, not only a uniform and ceremonious style,—a style evolved from, and expressive of, the highest civilizations in history,—in which each one could express himself with fluency, but also a common module of dimension. These considerations seemed to forbid the use of medieval or any other form of romantic, archæological, or picturesque art. The style should be distinctly secular and pompous, restrained from license by historical authority, and organized by academical discipline. It was not difficult, therefore, to agree upon the use of Roman classic forms, correctly and loyally interpreted, but permitting variations suggested not only by the Italians, but by the other masters of the Renaissance. It was considered that a series of pure classic models, in each case contrasting in character according to the personal equation of the architect, and according to the practical conditions to be accommodated in each, but uniform in respect to scale and language of form, all set forth with the utmost amount of luxury and opulence of decoration permitted by the best usage, and on a theater of almost unprecedented magnitude, would present to the profession here an object-lesson so impressive of the practical value of architectural scholarship and of strict subordination to the formulas of the schools, that it would serve as a timely corrective to the national tendency to experiments in design. It is not desired or expected that this display, however successful it may prove to be in execution, should make a new revival or a new school in the architecture of our country, or interfere with any healthy advance on classic or romantic lines which may be evolving here. There are many uneducated and untrained men practising as architects, and still maintaining, especially in the remote regions of the country, an impure and unhealthy vernacular, incapable of progress; men who have never seen a pure classic monument executed on a great scale, and who are ignorant of the emotions which it must excite in any breast accessible to the influences of art. To such it is hoped that these great models, inspired as they have been by a profound respect for the masters of classic art, will prove such a revelation that they will learn at last that true architecture cannot be based on undisciplined invention, illiterate originality, or, indeed, upon any audacity of ignorance.

It was further agreed by the architects of the court that the module of proportion for the composition of their façades should be a bay not exceeding twenty-five feet in width and sixty feet in height to the top of the main cornice, which is about the size of a five-storied façade on an ordinary city lot. In all other respects each of these gentlemen, influenced of course by mutual criticism, and subject to the approval of the executive of the Exposition through its Committee on Grounds and Buildings, has been left perfectly free to develop, within the area prescribed in each case, the design of the building assigned to him, according to his own convictions as to general outlines and details of architectural expression. Under these circumstances, therefore, it may fairly be anticipated that the great palaces of the court will illustrate the vital principle of unity in variety on a scale never before attempted in modern times.

It must be borne in mind, however, that all this is not architecture in its highest sense, but rather a scenic display of architecture, composed (to use a theatrical term) of "practicable" models, executed on a colossal stage, and with a degree of apparent pomp and splendor which, if set forth in marbles and bronze, might recall the era of Augustus or Nero. We have not, it is true, the inexhaustible resources of the museums and schools and gardens of Paris to people this great industrial court with statues and vases, set against rich backgrounds of exotic foliage; but the opportunity will possibly enable us to prove that whatever characteristics of audacious invention or adaptation are exhibited in the best buildings of modern America, it is not because our architects are untrained in the organization of structural forms, ignorant of historical precedent, or wanting in respect for the works of the masters, nor yet because they do not know how on occasion to express themselves in the language of the most venerable traditions of art. But these great Doric, Ionic, Corinthian, and Composite orders, with their arches, porticos, pavilions, attics, domes, and campaniles, do not express actual structure in any sense, as was the case with Paxton's apotheosis of the greenhouse in the great glass and iron building of the first London Exposition; they rather serve as architectural screens, of which only the main divisions and articulations have been suggested by the temporary framework of iron and timber which they mask, and which, in itself, is incapable of expression in any terms of monumental dignity. If each architect of the board had been permitted or encouraged to make his especial screen an unrestricted exhibition of his archæological knowledge or ingenuity in design, we should have had a curious, and in some respects perhaps an interesting and instructive, polyglot or confusion of tongues, such as in the early scriptural times on the plains of Shinar was so detrimental to architectural success. The show might have contained some elements of the great "American Style"; but as a whole it would have been [88] a hazardous experiment, and it certainly would have perplexed the critics. In respect to the architecture of the great court, therefore, it seemed at least safer to proceed according to established formulas, and to let the special use and object of each building, and the personal equation of the architect employed on it, do what they properly could, within these limits, to secure variety and movement.

It is a fashion of the times, following Mr. Ruskin, to stigmatize the marvelous multiplication of mechanical appliances to life in the nineteenth century as degrading to its higher civilization and destructive of its art. Mr. Frederic Harrison agrees with these philosophers of discontent so far as to say that if machinery were really the last word of the century we should all be rushing violently down a steep place, like the herd of swine. But he says:

To decry steam and electricity, inventions and products, is hardly more foolish than to deny the price which civilization itself has to pay for the use of them. There are forces at work now, forces more unwearied than steam, and brighter than the electric arc, to rehumanize the dehumanized members of society; to assert the old, immutable truths; forces yearning for rest, grace, and harmony; rallying all that is organic in men's social nature, and proclaiming the value of spiritual life over material life.

In order, therefore, to present a complete and symmetrical picture of modern civilization, it is necessary that the Columbian Exposition should not only bring together evidences of the amazing material productiveness which, within the century, has effected a complete transformation in the external aspects of life, but should force into equal prominence, if possible, corresponding evidences that the finer instincts of humanity have not suffered complete eclipse in this grosser prosperity, and that, in this headlong race, art has not been left entirely behind. The management of the Exposition is justified in placing machinery, agricultural appliances and products, manufactures and the liberal arts, the wonderful industrial results of scientific investigation, and the other evidences of practical progress, in the midst of a parallel display shaped entirely by sentiment and appealing to a fundamentally different set of emotions. It is the high function of architecture not only to adorn this triumph of materialism, but to condone, explain, and supplement it, so that some elements of "sweetness and light" may be brought forward to counterbalance the boastful Philistinism of our times. Each department of the Exposition must possess more or less capacity for architectural expression, if not by disposition of masses, by style, or by sympathetic treatment of technical detail, at least by the [89] suggestions of sculpture and characteristic decoration. It is true that the vast preponderance of human effort in these closing years of the century has been in favor of practical things; it remains to be seen whether this supreme test of the elastic powers of architecture to develop out of these practical things demonstrations of art will result in furnishing any of that "rest, grace, and harmony" which are needed as a compensation for materialism.

By a remarkable piece of fortune, the architects to whom the five buildings on the great court were assigned constituted a family, by reason of long-established personal relations and of unusually close professional sympathies. Of this family Mr. Hunt was the natural head; two of its members, Post and Van Brunt, were his professional children; Howe, Peabody, and Stearns, having been pupils and assistants of the latter, may be considered the grandchildren of the household; while McKim, who had been brought up under the same academical influences, was, with his partners, of the same blood by right of adoption and practice. Collaboration under such circumstances, and under a species of parental discipline so inspiring, so vigorous, and so affectionate, should hardly fail to confer upon the work resulting from it some portion of the delightful harmony which prevailed in their councils.

By common consent the most monumental of these buildings —that devoted to the Administration—was undertaken by Mr. Hunt. Having all the elements of an academical project of the first class, it was eminently fitting that this important structure should fall into hands so admirably equipped by learning and experience to do it full justice. It was to occupy the western or landward side of the great court, and to stand in its main central axis at the point where this axis was intersected by a transverse axis which ran north and south between the Mines and Electricity buildings. It was designed to be the loftiest and most purely monumental composition in the Park, and to serve not only for the accommodation of the various bureaus of administration, but, more conspicuously, as the great porch of the Exposition. The area assigned was a square measuring about 260 feet on each side, and it was necessary to divide it into four equal parts by two great avenues crossing at right angles on the axial lines which we have described. In fact, the building was in some way to stand on four legs astride this crossing of the ways, like one of the quadrilateral Janus-coaches of the Romans, but on a much greater scale. The whole system of railway communication was to be so connected on the west with this building, that the crowds of visitors, on arriving, should enter and cross this ceremonial vestibule; should there obtain their first impressions; and by the majesty and spacious repose of the interior, should be in a manner introduced into a new world, and forced into sympathy with the highest objects of this latest international exposition of arts. Its function, indeed, was that of an overture.

These conditions suggested to Mr. Hunt the idea of a civic

temple based upon the model of the domical cathedrals of the Renaissance. Following this type, he projected, upon the crossing of the two axial lines, a hall of otagonal plan; but unlike the cathedrals, this hall was designed to form the fundamental basis, the leading motive, of the design, not only on the interior but on the exterior of the structure, there being neither nave nor transepts to interfere with the clear external development of this dominating feature from the ground to the summit. Thus, at the outset, he secured that expression of unity which is essential to the noblest monumental effect in architecture. The expression of repose, at once majestic and graceful, which is no less essential, was to be obtained, not only by a careful subordination of detail to the leading idea, but by such a disposition of masses as would impart an aspect [90] of absolute stability. This implied the necessity of procuring a pyramidal or culminating effect; the whole composition, from bottom to top, preparing for this effect by some process of diminution by stages upward. To this end he enveloped his hall (which the conditions of area permitted him to make 120 feet in interior diameter) with two octagonal shells about 24 feet apart, the space between being occupied by galleries, elevators, vestibules, and staircases. Against the alternate or diagonal sides of the octagon he erected four pavilions in the form of wings 84 feet square, in four stories, in which he accommodated the various offices of administration; the archways, pierced through the four cardinal sides of the octagon, being externally recessed between these pavilions, thus affording two direct, broad passageways through the building at right angles. These pavilions are so treated as to be in scale with the other buildings of the great court, and are carried to the same height of 60 feet, thus securing four wide-spreading abutments with flat, terraced roofs. Above these the outer octagonal shell of the central mass detaches itself, and asserts its outline against the sky through another stage, where it [91] stops in the form of a gallery, decorated with bronze flambeaux, and permits the inner shell in turn to become outwardly manifest in a third stage of diminished diameter, rising in an octagonal drum, the whole mass finishing with the soaring lines of the central dome; which by vertical growth, determined by conditions of proportion, reaches the height of 275 feet from the pavement. Enriched with decorated ribs and sculptured panels, and made splendid with shining gold, this noble dome rises far above the other structures of the Exposition, proclaiming afar the position of its monumental gateway.

But as the inner surface of the outer dome would form a ceiling far too lofty to serve as a proper and effective cover for the hall, it became necessary, in order to give proper proportions to this monumental chamber, to construct an inner and lower dome, 190 feet high from the pavement, with an open eye at the apex, through which from below could be seen the upper structure, like the cope of a mysterious sky beyond. This architectural device is similar to those used by Mansart in the dome of the Invalides at Paris, by Soufflot in the Panthéon, and by Wren in St. Paul's at London, which rank next to St. Peter's as the largest and most important of the great Renaissance temples of Europe. It also appears in the rotunda of the national Capitol at Washington. But, as conceived by Hunt, the exterior dome of the vestibule of the Exposition is 42 feet higher than that of Mansart, 45 feet higher than that of Soufflot, about the same height as that of St. Paul's, and 57 feet higher than that of our national Capitol, exclusive of the lantern in each case. The interior dome has a height from the pavement 15 feet higher than that of the Invalides; it has about the same height as that of the French Panthéon; is 20 feet lower than that of St. Paul's, and 10 feet higher than that of the Capitol at Washington. In diameter it surpasses all these domes, being 38 feet wider than the first, 56 feet wider than the second, 12 feet wider than the third, and 26 feet wider than the Washington example. Indeed, in this regard, it is only 20 feet less than that of St. Peter's at Rome, which, however, in exterior height exceeds the American model by 90 feet, and in interior height by 143. Being thus in dimensions inferior only to the work of Michelangelo, it may be considered, in this respect, at least, an adequate vestibule to the Exposition of 1893.

The method of lighting the interior of this vast domical chamber in a proper and adequate manner was a problem so important that Mr. Hunt considered it one of the primary formative influences controlling the evolution of his architectural scheme. One of the noblest effects of interior illumination known in historical art is in the Roman Pantheon, the area of which

(140 feet in diameter) is lighted only by the circular hypethral opening 25 feet wide at the apex of the dome, 140 feet from the pavement. Inspired by this majestic example, Mr. Hunt proposed in this respect to depend mainly upon such light as could be obtained from the open eye of his lower dome, 50 feet wide and 190 feet from the pavement, which should in turn borrow its light from the illumination of the space between his outer and inner domes through a glazed hypethral opening 38 feet wide, forming the summit of the building, and taking the place of the lantern or belvedere which usually forms the finial of the greater domes of the Renaissance.

In his decorative treatment of the problem thus evolved Mr. Hunt has exercised a fine spirit of scholarly reserve. The architectural language employed is simple and stately, and the composition as a whole is so free from complications, its structural articulations are so frankly accentuated, that it is easy to read, and, being read, cannot fail to surprise the most unaccustomed mind with a distinct and veritable architectural impression. But to obtain this simplicity of result a far greater knowledge of design and far more ingenuity of adaptation have been required than if the building had been sophisticated with all the consciousness and affectations of modern art. In order to bring his design into the family of which, by the adoption of a common module of proportion, the other buildings of the groups around the great court are members, Mr. Hunt's four pavilions of administration, forming the lower story of the façades, are treated externally, like them, with a single order raised upon a basement. He has preferred the Doric in his case, so as to obtain by contrast with its neighbors an effect of severe dignity and what might be called colossal repose, and to provide for a gradual increase of enrichment in the upper parts of his monument. His second story is Ionic, with an open colonnade, or loggia, on each of the cardinal faces of the octagon, showing the inner shell behind, and with domed circular staircase pavilions of the same order on the narrower alternate sides, niched between heavy corner piers, which bear groups of statuary, thus obtaining a certain degree of movement and complication in the outlines of his design, and enhancing its pyramidal effect. On all his exterior he has used conven-

World's Columbian Exposition of 1893, Chicago; the Court of Honor looking southeast. In the foreground, a rostral column. At right, in the middleground, a portion of the MacMonnies fountain. Right background, colonnade leading to Machinery Hall by Peabody & Stearns. Middle background, the Agricultural Building by McKim, Mead & White. On the distant left, the Casino by Charles B. Atwood.

tional ornament with great reserve, depending for richness of effect upon three colossal groups of statuary on each of his administrative pavilions, upon two, flanking each of his main entrances, and upon eight, crowning the gallery below the drum of his dome.

This sculpture, the work of Mr. Karl Bitter of New York, is characterized by great breadth [92] and dignity of treatment, and by that expression of heroic power and fitness which is derived from knowing how to treat colossal subjects in a colossal way, and how to model figures so that they may assist the main architectural thought and not compete with it. Thus the groups which crown the corner piers of the four wings in the lower part of the building are in repose, and are so massed that they serve properly as monumental finials, while those surmounting the gallery above are more strongly accentuated, so as to become intelligible at that great height, and are distinguished by a far greater animation of outline and lightness of movement, by means of gesture, outspread wings, and accessories, so that they may act as foils to the simple and stately architectural lines of the dome, at the base of which they stand, and so that they may aid it in its upward spring. The subjects are apparently intended to typify, in a succession of groups, beginning in the lower parts of the monument, the advance of mankind from barbarism to civilization, and the final triumph of the arts of peace and war.

Unlike the other buildings of the Exposition, Mr. Hunt's has two sets of façades, an exterior and an interior. In the latter he has not repeated his exterior orders, and the same self-denial which has chastened and purified the exterior has left these inner walls large, simple, and spacious, not even the angles of the inclosing [93] octagon being architecturally emphasized at any point. Each of the eight sides of this interior octagon is pierced with an archway occupied by a screen of doors below and bronze grilles above; over these is a series of panels filled with sculpture and inscriptions, and upon the great interior cornice which crowns these walls is a balcony, like the whispering-gallery of St. Paul's, by means of which the scene may be viewed from above. An order of pilasters directly under the inner dome surmounts this gallery, and the dome itself is decorated with panels, the whole interior being enriched with color, so disposed as to complete and perfect the design.

We have already said that this vestibule was intended to introduce the visitors to the Exposition into a new world. As they emerge from its east archway and enter the court, they must, if possible, receive a memorable impression of architectural harmony on a vast scale. To this end the forums, basilicas, and baths of the Roman Empire, the villas and gardens of the princes of the Italian Renaissance, the royal courtyards of the palaces of France and Spain, must yield to the architects, "in that new world which is the old," their rich inheritance of ordered beauty, to make possible the creation of a bright picture of civic splendor such as this great function of modern civilization would seem to require.

At the outset it was considered of the first importance that the people, in circulating around the court and entering or leaving the buildings, should so far as possible be protected from the heat of the midsummer sun. To assist in accomplishing this object the great quadrangle will be closed in by a series of sheltered ambulatories, like the Greek *stoa*, included in and forming a part of the façades of the palaces of Machinery and Agriculture on the right, and of the Liberal Arts and Electricity on the left. The vast fronts of these buildings, far exceeding in dimensions those of any other ancient or modern architectural group, with their monumental colonnaded pavilions, their sculptured enrichments, their statuary, domes, and towers, will appear in mellowed ivory marble, relieved by decorations in color in the shadowy recesses of the porticos. Immediately before him the stranger will behold the great basin 350 feet wide and 1100 feet long, stretching eastward in the middle of the court, bordered with double walled terraces, of which the lower will be decorated with shrubbery and flowers, and the upper, with balustrades, rostral columns, vases, and statuary. Broad stairs descend from the main porticos of the buildings to the water, and the canals, which enter the basin on each side, are crossed by monumental bridges. On the nearer margin of the greater basin, and in the axis of the court, he will see a smaller circular basin 150 feet in diameter, on a level with the upper terrace, flanked by two lofty columns bearing eagles. In the center of this, on an antique galley of bronze 60 feet long, eight colossal rowers, portraying the Arts and Sciences, stand, four on a side, bending to their long sweeps; in the prow is poised the herald Fame, with trump and outspread wings; while aft, Time, the pilot, leans upon his helm; and, high aloft on a throne, supported by cherubs, Columbia sits, a fair, youthful figure, eager and alert, not reposing upon the past, but poised in high expectation. Eight couriers precede the barge, mounted upon marine horses ramping out of the water. The whole triumphal pageant is seen through a mist of interlacing fountain-jets, and from the brimming basin the water falls 14 feet in a series of steps into the greater sheet below, a half-circle of dolphins spouting over the cascade. This pompous allegory is the work of the sculptor Frederick MacMonnies. At the outer end of the basin a colossus of the Republic, by the sculptor Daniel C. French, rises from the water. It is treated somewhat in the Greek archaic manner, with a strong accentuation of vertical lines, but with a simplicity and breadth which give to the figure an aspect of majesty and power. Beyond it, a double open colonnade, or peristyle, 60 feet high, like that of Bernini in front of St. Peter's, forming three sides of a square, closes in the great court toward the lake. Of the two wings of this colonnade one is a concert-hall, and the other a casino or waiting-hall for passengers by boat. Its columns typify the States of the Union. In the center of this architectural screen is a triumphal arch thrown over the canal which connects the basin with the harbor. Through this and through the open screen of the colonnade one may see the wide-spreading lake, the watery horizon, and, still in the axis of the court and a thousand feet from the shore, a lofty pharos with an island-casino at its base. Animating the whole, banners and gonfalons flutter gaily from innumerable staffs; people of all nations walk in the shadow of the porches, linger on the bridges, crowd along the broad pavement of the terraces, and watch from the balustrades the incessant movement of many-colored boats and electric barges upon the water. . . .[94]

It has already been stated that the main object of these papers is to secure for the great buildings of the Exposition, through an analysis of the evolution of their several designs, an intelligent if not a respectful appreciation, because of the extreme importance of the occasion in the history of American art, and also because of the exceptional circumstances under which the buildings have been produced. Without such appreciation, the work of the architect, although it may be eloquent and imposing enough to give even to the most careless observers a certain indefinite impression of order, beauty, or grandeur, fails to convey to them the most essential part of the ideas which he has in mind to set forth. He needs this popular appreciation, not only as an encouragement, but as a corrective, and that he may bring himself into fuller and more perfect sympathy with the civilization which it is his duty to express.

Architecture and music alike have, in their highest developments, clearly defined qualities, which convey a delight of meaning to the capable eye or ear, but which, to the untrained mind, are nothing but inarticulate harmonies of form or sound.

In attempting, in the previous paper, to follow in outline the principles which controlled the designs of the Administration and Machinery buildings, it became evident that, before proceeding with the other buildings, it would be well to state, once for all, that in monumental [385] designs based upon pure classic formulas, the principle of symmetry—that is, of a balanced correspondence of parts on each side of a center line—must govern the disposition of the masses into which, in order to form an articulate composition, each façade should be divided. The greater the dignity and importance of the building, the more absolute and uncompromising must be the application of this principle. The monument must be evident as the orderly result of forethought, and not as a growth from a succession of unexpected contingencies. It must embody the idea of a harmonious development of structure from beginning to end, so exactly adjusted, and so carefully proportioned in respect to its elements, that nothing can be added to or taken from it without sensibly affecting the composite organism as a whole. The test of the completeness of a classic design resides in its sensitiveness to change—a sensitiveness which becomes more delicate as the design approaches perfection. In fact, symmetry is the visible expression of unity. The moment the correspondence of balanced parts on each side of a center line is disturbed by the introduction on one side of a mass or detail which does not appear on the other, at that moment the design begins to lose somewhat of its unity and to enter the domain of the picturesque, in which ceremony and state become secondary to considererations of comfort and convenience.

With the exception of the Administration Building, which is a compact, domical composition, like the front of the Invalides, all the larger structures of the Exposition have a great extension of length in comparison to their average height, the former varying from 700 to 1700 feet, and the latter from 40 to 60. The application of the principle of symmetry to these has resulted uniformly in a central pavilion of some sort, and in a corner pavilion of varying importance on each angle of the façades. This remark does not apply to the Transportation and Fisheries buildings, which are not classic in form or intention. Between these pavilions there are intermediate spaces known as curtain-walls, the architectural character of which depends on a continuous repetition of bays, developed from the interior structure, and constituting the characteristic mass of the frontage, to which the three pavilions serve as points of emphasis and relief. But it will be found that this arrangement of the several buildings is not only the result of the common observance of an abstract principle of design, but follows from an obvious necessity of the plan in each case, from the mutual relations of neighboring structures, and from considerations of the most convenient ingress and egress.

It will be remembered that the architects of the five buildings surrounding the great court, which have the closest architectural relations, agreed, for the sake of securing a harmonious result, to confine themselves to pure classic forms in their designs, to fix upon 60 feet from the ground as the height of their main cornices, to provide for an open portico or shelter along their whole frontage, and to assume about 25 feet as their module or unit of dimension. We have seen also that one of the results of the fundamental conditions of the plan is the division of the façades respectively by a central pavilion and by corner pavilions, with stretches of curtain-wall [386] between. Moreover, each of these compositions has submitted to certain compromises for the sake of harmony with its neighbors. Now this stately uniformity of design would have been too serious for an occasion of festivity, if it were not relieved by a certain luxury of conventional ornament, sculpture, painting, and decoration in metals, and by a profusion of bright and joyful accessories. We shall now see how this uniformity of scheme, apparently working for a monotony which would be fatiguing, is, by the operation of the personal equation of the architect in each case, and by the adjustment of each building to its especial use, entirely consistent with that individuality of technic, of sentiment, and of expression which constitutes the essential difference between a cold academical composition and a work of art having a definite purpose.

By this apparent identity in general outline and language of form the architects have necessarily been invited to a study of detail and expression far more fastidious than would be easily practicable in dealing with a style less accurately formulated. In somewhat similar manner a dozen trained writers, expressing their thoughts on a similar range of subjects in an established literary form,—in that of the sonnet for example,—would commit themselves by their differences in treatment to a comparison more subtle and sensitive than would be possible had they been at liberty to handle their common theme without definite and arbitrary restrictions of form. Whether the test is one of architecture or poetry (and the two are closely analogous), it seems to compel the architect or poet to enter a region, if not of higher thought, then of more delicate study and of finer discrimination in method. Freedom of style, though it is the natural and healthy condition of architecture in our country, and adapts itself more readily to our inventiveness in structure and to the practical exigencies of building, is also a temptation to crude experiments, to *tours de force,* and to surprises of design, such as form the characteristic features of an American city. Under these circumstances, personal idiosyncrasies and accidents of mood or temperament are apt to have an undue influence upon current architecture, and to perpetuate, in monumental form, the caprice of a moment or a passing fashion of design, which, in a year's time, the author himself may be the first to repudiate. It is the aim of our architectural schools not to kill but to correct this abundant vitality, and to direct it into channels of fruitful and rational progress.

A glance at the general plan of the grounds will show that the buildings are separated one from the other by avenues of water or land [389] sufficiently wide to furnish noble vistas penetrating to the remoter regions of the Park, and to isolate each structure, so that its characteristic mass and details may not be confused by those of its neighbors, but not so wide as to prevent their mutual architectural relations from being clearly evident in a common alignment, and in a common observance of the system of axial lines which controls the location and arrangement of the group as a whole.

The general disposition of masses in these façades being thus defined, the way seems to be prepared for a more intelligent examination of the processes by which the especial architectural character of each building has been evolved. . . .[390]

That department of the Exposition classified as "Manufactures and the Liberal Arts" embraces so many and such varied industrial interests, that the building to accommodate it must be by far the most spacious in Jackson Park. The thirty acres which were assigned to it, though including an area much larger than that assigned to a single department in any previous Exposition, will need to be carefully husbanded to meet the requirements for space under this head. The site admitted of a building, in exterior dimensions, 1687 feet long, north and south, and 787 feet in width. Its southern end, forming a part of the inclosure of the great court, was necessarily subjected to the same conditions regarding architectural style and scale as were agreed upon for the other structures around the quadrangle, and these conditions were extended so as to control the other façades. The interposition of an architectural wall nearly 1700 feet long, and but little over 60 feet high, between the lake and the flat district known as the lagoon would have the effect of transforming the whole aspect of the Park as viewed from any point on land or water. The importance of an adequate treatment of this vast scheme was obvious.

Mr. George B. Post of New York, the architect of the building, in considering its general plan, promptly fell upon the scheme of converting its area into a court by surrounding it with a continuous building, and of cutting this court in twain with a central circular structure; thus recalling, but on an immensely larger scale, a much admired disposition of Philibert Delorme in his first project for the palace of the Tuileries as a residence for Catherine de Médicis. But even with such subdivisions the scheme was still so heroic in dimension that no such correspondence as this could be of the slightest avail in furnishing him with types of architectural treatment. He found that he must work in regions quite removed from historical experience. With his assumed module of 25 feet, he found that he could carry around the four sides of his area of thirty acres a building composed of a nave 107 feet 9 inches wide and 114 feet high, covered with a pitched roof with clearstories, and supported on each side by two-storied aisles, or lean-tos, 45 feet wide. This arrangement of plan permitted ready illumination, easy classification, and convenient communication. It left an interior quadrangle 1237 feet long and 337 feet wide. The domical hall in the center of this space was planned to be 260 feet in clear diameter and 160 feet high, surrounded, like the other parts of the building, with two-storied aisles, or lean-tos, 45 feet wide. These circular aisles, compared with the seating space of the Roman Colosseum, would have inclosed an area largely in excess of that great arena. The two courts thus obtained Mr. Post proposed to treat as gardens with fountains and kiosks, or, if more space should be needed for exhibition purposes, to occupy them with a series of covered sheds.

But as the practical needs of this important and comprehensive part of the Exposition became more evident, it was finally concluded to abandon the central dome, and to convert the whole interior court into the largest unencumbered hall ever constructed, by covering it with [394] a glazed semicircular roof without columns, supported by arched steel trusses of 387 feet clear span, 50 feet apart, and with a radius of 190 feet, giving an extreme height of 210 feet. This roof was arranged to be hipped at the ends. The much admired truss of Machinery Hall in the last Paris Exposition (the largest constructed for roofing purposes up to that time) is inferior to this in span and is 58 feet lower. It has been proposed to equip this vast hall, containing nearly 500,000 square feet of clear floor-space inside the enveloping building, with seats and a stage for the ceremonies of the inauguration, before adjusting it to its legitimate objects. It was sufficiently evident that the mountainous roof which covered the hall could not fail, from the mere power and weight of its enormous structural mass, to impose upon the scheme of the building, as a work of art, an element unknown in the precedents of monumental architecture.

In studying the most effective architectural treatment of a

symmetrical building more than a third of a mile long and almost a sixth of a mile wide, with a height of cornice limited to 60 feet, the architect was confronted by conditions of composition such as perhaps had not occurred before. The natural dispositions of any extended building, which is to be adapted, not to various and different services, like a royal château, with its halls of ceremony, its wings for household convenience, its chapels and galleries, its provisions for dignity and its provisions for comfort, but to a single and well-understood purpose, must be guided by the most convenient and economical structure, and show a distinct unity of thought throughout. This unity is expressed by a mutual dependence of parts. We must at least have some feature of emphasis on the corners, against which the long fronts may stop —a period, as it were, and place of rest; and there is even [396] greater necessity for pavilions of sufficient importance to give dignity to the entrances. The natural place for these is in the middle of each front, where the visitors may be introduced most conveniently to the great interior space, and receive their first impressions of its grandeur. We have seen how the architects of the Agricultural Building on the opposite side of the court,— where it was understood that everything must be in full dress and on parade, so to speak,—in adopting this natural treatment in their façade, found it necessary, for the sake of variety and movement, to provide between the center and the ends certain regularly disposed, intermediate accentuations, which the eye, in surveying the whole façade, could readily grasp and justify by an instinctive balancing of the masses on each side of the center line. The mind of the observer is flattered by this evidence of art.

Architecture, as compared with nature, has been called a creation of the second order; but this secondary creation must be fundamentally controlled by conditions of structure which, to a greater or less degree, must impose regularity or repetition of parts, as contrasted with the irregularity or picturesqueness which results from the infinite resources and the accidental conditions in nature. Medieval art, though often picturesque in its effects, is subject to these human conditions no less than classic art.

On the one hand the author of these almost interminable

façades felt that he could not treat them picturesquely or accidentally without sacrifice of truth and dignity, and, on the other hand, that to break them with frequent pavilions, however subordinate to a preëminent central feature, would fail to procure for them all the advantages of symmetry; because, in a length so great, the mind could not readily discover and, at a glance, compare that correspondence of parts on each side of the center which is essential to effects of this sort. The rule of composition which properly governs a building 500 to 800 feet long and 60 feet high cannot be applied successfully to one two or three times as long and no higher. The architect, therefore, remembering the imposing effects of certain long porticos and aqueducts of Roman structure, had the courage, in this case, to withstand the temptations furnished by the customs of the Renaissance architects in their palaces and other public monuments, and to leave his skyline and his frontage unbroken by any competition of pavilions save the one in the center and that on each angle of each front. By this severe measure he hoped to make the unity of his design clear to the most casual observer.

The module or unit of measurement, of 25 feet, with which the architect found it convenient to lay out his plan, communicated to his elevations a corresponding division of bays, of which 29 occur on each half of the long fronts and 11 on each half of the short fronts. These bays are treated with arches, springing from piers, and each archway embraces two stories. It was anticipated that these long, monotonous, and mechanical perspectives of equal and similar arches would affect the eye like the arcades of the Campagna, and would rather increase than diminish the apparent length of the building; for repetition, even if mechanical, is, humanly speaking, a suggestion of the infinite, and the architect who has the opportunity and self-denial to adopt it frankly, and on a scale so vast, would give even to the most thoughtless and most uncritical minds a memorable impression of architectural majesty and repose.

Now the covered ambulatory, or stoa, which is made a feature of all the court fronts, should, on account of the great length of these long façades, where there is no other natural refuge from the sun, be extended all around the building, but within its lines. The lintel course or decorated belt, which is the exterior development of the floor of the second story in each bay, is supported by an open, flat, segmental arch springing from pier to pier; behind these arches this continuous ambulatory obtains spacious shade. Frequent doors open upon it from the interior. No subordinate architectural order of columns was placed under this lintel course, as was done with singularly happy results in the Agricultural Building, because it was apparent that such an order would not have been in scale with the rest of the design, and would have introduced an element which would have complicated with unnecessary details the careful simplicity of its lines and the studied breadth of its general treatment.

The adoption of a severe classical formula for the building naturally led to the adoption of a common *motif* for the four central pavilions, and another, adapted to its situation, for each of the corner pavilions. These repetitions were encouraged by the fact that all the façades were of equal importance. As these pavilions must be distinctly recognized as the main porches, they must break the monotony with emphasis, or they will not be adequate. Consequently at these points there should be a sudden change in the architectural scheme of the fronts. But the strictly classic ideal does not seem to be favorable to the absolute interruption of all the horizontal lines of frontage by the pavilions; there must be some connection by continuity of lines between them.[1] The Greek [397] idea of a monumental entrance is a columned propylæum; that of the Romans, who better understood pomp and ceremony, is an arch. The former would be appropriate if the general architectural character of the façades were based upon an order of columns or pilasters; in the present case the latter would more naturally follow.

Thus the architect, by logical process, encountered the idea of inserting in the midst of his arcades the triple triumphal

[1] The solution of this continuity, boldly attempted by the architects of the Machinery Building in their central towers, which, as we have noted, interrupt all the lines, constitutes the most remarkable feature of their design. This, as we have said, is contrary to the strict classic idea, but in so far as this interruption does not destroy the unity of the composition, it is the successful stroke of one who dares to put his fate to the touch, "to gain or lose it all."

arches of Constantine or Septimius Severus, and of stopping his arcade at the corners with the single arch of Titus or Trajan, the *motif* in both cases being very greatly enlarged from the original in order to fit the greater scale of the building. The architectural connection of the central pavilions with the mass of the structure is established by bringing their two side arches into the same scale as those of the curtain-walls, and by causing the main cornice line to be continued across the central pavilion or pylon as a string-course over its two side arches, and as an impost, from which springs its great central arch. Over the whole is carried a horizontal entablature with a high attic, and in front of the four piers are lofty pedestaled columns, after the manner of buttresses, supporting figures against the attic, thus closely following the characteristics of the Roman prototypes. The order employed for these columns is the sumptuous Corinthian of the temple of Jupiter Stator, the columns being 65 feet high with a lower diameter of more than 6 feet. We have already intimated that the architect turned the four corners of this building with a single arch on each adjacent face of the angles; these also are decorated with magnificent coupled Corinthian columns, as in some of the Roman examples. The width of the corner pavilions is adjusted to the width of the ambulatory which enters them on each side. The esthetic function of these boldly accentuated buttress-columns, which are clearly [398] detached from the mass of the building, is sufficiently evident in the perspective views of the long fronts. They furnish the only strongly marked vertical lines in the composition, and by contrast suffice to relieve the design from the excessive predominance of its horizontal lines.

It is to be noted that as yet the architectural expression of this building, the development of which we have been following in the natural order of design, has been confined to the exterior closure of a vast interior space. Before it had been happily determined to cover the interior court with a great glazed roof, it was the professional instinct of Mr. Post to indicate externally that the area enveloped by his façades was not empty, but had a magnificent interior central feature in his original circular hall. To this end, and in order that this feature might become evident from afar as an essential element of design, it became necessary to cover it with a dome sufficiently lofty to be seen over the sky-lines of the inclosing galleries from usual points of view, and to form a crown and finish to the long, low mass of his building. This feature, if executed, would have exceeded any similar structure yet erected; but as it challenged comparison with the dome of the porch of the Exposition, the preëminence of which it was considered desirable to maintain, it was reluctantly abandoned. But the final treatment of the central court as a hall, 1287 x 387 feet in floor area, covered with a semicircular roof, whose longitudinal ridge rises far above the cornice of the façades, at once suggested an entirely different architectural aspect for the building. By the upward succession of cornice-line, 60 feet high, and clearstory-line, 108 feet high, culminating in a central ridge-line, 210 feet high, a pyramidal effect was secured; the low-lying mass at once obtained adequate height; its vast extent was condoned and explained; a dominant expression of unity was conferred upon the composition; the upper outlines of the façades were projected against a colossal roof instead of the empty sky; and the roof itself, wisely left to the majesty of its dimensions and to the simplicity of its structure for architectural effect, enhanced the refinement and purity of the architectural screens below.

Indeed, this design as a whole admirably illustrates the fact that reservation rather than expenditure of force is the secret of noble art. The modern architectural mind is an archæological chaos of ideas inherited from Egypt, from the far East, from Greece and Rome, from the middle ages, and from the Renaissance. Under these circumstances the highest virtue which can be exercised by the educated architect of to-day is self-denial in the use of his treasures. He who squanders them in his work betrays his trust, and depraves the art of his time. He who can be refined in the use of the splendid resources furnished by his knowledge of the past, who can be simple in the midst of the temptations to display his wealth, is rendering high service to a civilization which, in the midst of its complications and sophistications, needs the refreshment and chastisement of pure types.

It is evident that within his classic Roman frame Mr. Post has desired, in his detail of decoration, to bring his design into sympathy with modern civilizations; for we shall see that the luxury of Napoleon III. affects the sculpture of his spandrels and panels, and that nearly all the ornament bears traces of the influence of the latest French Renaissance and the last Paris Exposition. Moreover, in order to relieve his design from the serious expression imposed upon it by the grandeur of his leading motives, he makes a very proper concession to the festive and holiday aspect which should pervade the place by planting permanent standards and gonfalons on his triumphal arches, and by decorating his battlements with banner-staffs and bunting.

We have repeatedly stated that these papers do not embody either a description or a criticism, nor yet an apology, but constitute an attempt to explain the architectural development of the Exposition buildings. But it may be proper, before leaving the consideration of the largest of these buildings, to look back upon Mr. Post's immense façades, and to ask whether, if they had been treated with the variety, contrast, and balance of motives customary in the works of the Renaissance, if they had been broken by towers and campaniles, or tormented by gabled pavilions, they would not have presented a somewhat confused and incoherent aspect, wanting in apparent unity of thought, and resembling rather a combination of many buildings of various use than a single building of one use; and further, whether the simplicity of treatment which he has preferred (and which some, not considering its detail and the unusual difficulties of the problem, might call poverty) has not resulted in a composition having architectural qualities which, instead of confusing and puzzling the mind, can be read, understood, and remembered with pleasure. The civilization of our time owes a debt of gratitude to any architect, or to any writer, who, in the midst of the temptations which beset us to force effects of beauty by affectations and mannerisms, dares to make his work at once strong, simple, and elegant.[399]

HAMLIN GARLAND

A Son of the Middle Border

Hamlin Garland, A Son of the Middle Border (New York, The Macmillan Company, 1917).*

I packed my books ready for shipment and returned to Chicago in May just as the Exposition was about to open its doors.

Like everyone else who saw it at this time I was amazed at the grandeur of "The White City," and impatiently anxious to have all my friends and relations share in my enjoyment of it. My father was back on the farm in Dakota and I wrote to him at once urging him to come down. "Frank will be here in June and we will take charge of you. Sell the cook stove if necessary and come. You *must* see this fair. On the way back I will go [458] as far as West Salem and we'll buy that homestead I've been talking about."

My brother whose season closed about the twenty-fifth of May, joined me in urging them not to miss the fair and a few days later we were both delighted and a little surprised to get a letter from mother telling us when to expect them. "I can't walk very well," she explained, "but I'm coming. I am so hungry to see my boys that I don't mind the long journey."

Having secured rooms for them at a small hotel near the west gate of the exposition grounds, we were at the station to receive them as they came from the train surrounded by other tired and dusty pilgrims of the plains. Father was in high spirits and mother was looking very well considering the tiresome ride of nearly seven hundred miles. "Give us a chance to wash up and we'll be ready for anything," she said with brave intonation.

We took her at her word. With merciless enthusiasm we hurried them to their hotel and as soon as they had bathed and

* Reprinted with the permission of The Macmillan Company.

eaten a hasty lunch, we started out with intent to astonish and delight them. Here was another table at "the feast of life" from which we did not intend they should rise unsatisfied. "This shall be the richest experience of their lives," we said.

With a wheeled chair to save mother from the fatigue of walking we started down the line and so rapidly did we pass from one stupendous vista to another that we saw in a few hours many of the inside exhibits and all of the finest exteriors—not to mention a glimpse of the polyglot amazements of the Midway.

In pursuance of our plan to watch the lights come on, we ate our supper in one of the big restaurants on the grounds and at eight o'clock entered the Court of Honor. It chanced to be a moonlit night, and as lamps were lit and the waters of the lagoon began to reflect the gleaming[459] walls of the great palaces with their sculptured ornaments, and boats of quaint shape filled with singers came and went beneath the arching bridges, the wonder and the beauty of it all moved these dwellers of the level lands to tears of joy which was almost as poignant as pain. In addition to its grandeur the scene had for them the transitory quality of an autumn sunset, a splendor which they would never see again.

Stunned by the majesty of the vision, my mother sat in her chair, visioning it all yet comprehending little of its meaning. Her life had been spent among homely small things, and these gorgeous scenes dazzled her, overwhelmed her, letting in upon her in one mighty flood a thousand stupefying suggestions of the art and history and poetry of the world. She was old and she was ill, and her brain ached with the weight of its new conceptions. Her face grew troubled and wistful, and her eyes as big and dark as those of a child.

At last utterly overcome she leaned her head against my arm, closed her eyes and said, "Take me home. I can't stand any more of it."

Sadly I took her away, back to her room, realizing that we had been too eager. We had oppressed her with the exotic, the magnificent. She was too old and too feeble to enjoy as we had hoped she would enjoy, the color and music and thronging streets of The Magic City.

At the end of the third day father said, "Well, I've had enough." He too, began to long for the repose of the country, the solace of familiar scenes. In truth they were both surfeited with the alien, sick of the picturesque. Their ears suffered from the clamor of strange sounds as their eyes ached with the clash of unaccustomed color. My insistent haste, my desire to make up in a few hours for all their past deprivations seemed at the moment to have been a mistake.[460]

Seeing this, knowing that all the splendors of the Orient could not compensate them for another sleepless night, I decided to cut their visit short and hurry them back to quietude. Early on the fourth morning we started for the LaCrosse Valley by way of Madison—they with a sense of relief, I with a feeling of disappointment. "The feast was too rich, too highly-spiced for their simple tastes," I now admitted.

However, a certain amount of comfort came to me as I observed that the farther they got from the Fair the keener their enjoyment of it became!—With bodies at ease and minds untroubled, they now relived in pleasant retrospect all the excitement and bustle of the crowds, all the bewildering sights and sounds of the Midway. Scenes which had worried as well as amazed them were now recalled with growing enthusiasm, as our train, filled with other returning sight-seers of like condition, rushed steadily northward into the green abundance of the land they knew so well, and when at six o'clock of a lovely afternoon, they stepped down upon the platform of the weatherbeaten little station at West Salem, both were restored to their serene and buoyant selves. The leafy village, so green, so muddy, so lush with grass, seemed the perfection of restful security. The chuckle of robins on the lawns, the songs of catbirds in the plum trees and the whistle of larks in the pasture appealed to them as parts of a familiar sweet and homely hymn.[461]

WILLIAM DEAN HOWELLS

Letters of an Altrurian Traveller

William Dean Howells, "Letters of an Altrurian Traveller," *The Cosmopolitan*, XVI (December, 1893).

Chicago, Sept. 28, 1893.

My dear Cyril:

After seeing the World's Fair City here, I feel as if I had caught a glimpse of the glorious capitals which will whiten the hills and shores of the east and the borderless plains of the west, when the New York and the Newer York of today shall seem to all the future Americans as impossible as they would seem to any Altrurian now.[218]

. . . It would be useless trying to persuade most Americans that the World's Fair City was not the effect, the fine flower, of the competition which underlies their economy, but was the first fruits of the principle of emulation which animates our happy commonwealth, and gives men, as no where else on earth, a foretaste of heaven.

. . . From the beginning it was believed that there could be no profit in the Fair; money loss was expected and accepted as a necessary part of the greater gain; and when the question passed from how much to how, in the discussion of the ways and means of creating that beauty which is the supreme use, the capitalists put themselves into the hands of the artists. They did not do it at once, and they did not all do it willingly. It is a curious trait of the American who has made money that he thinks he can make anything; and the Chicago millionaires who found themselves authorized by the nation to spend their money in the creation of the greatest marvel of the competitive world, thought themselves fully competent to work the miracle, or to choose the men who would work it according to their ideals. But their clari-

World's Columbian Exposition of 1893, Chicago; the Fine Arts Building by Charles B. Atwood which stood at the northern end of the Exposition grounds. The statue, a plaster cast of the Emperor Augustus, was copied from an original in the Vatican Museum. This building, originally of staff and plaster, was reconstructed in granite in 1931; it now houses the Rosenwald Museum of Science and Industry. The costumes of the day offer an entertaining contrast to the architecture.

fication, if it was not as swift as the passage of light was thorough, and I do not suppose there is now any group of rich men in Europe or America who have so luminous a sense of the true relations of the arts and the interests as they. The notion of a competition among the artists, which is the practical American's notion of the way to get the best art, was at length rejected by these most practical Americans, and one mind large enough to conceive the true means and strong enough to give its conception effect was empowered to invite the free coöperation of the arts through [219] the foremost artists of the country. As yet the governmental function is so weak here that the national part in the work was chiefly obstructive, and finally null; and when it came to this there remained an opportunity for the arts, unlimited as to means and unhampered by conditions.

For the different buildings to be erected, different architects were chosen; and for the first time since the great ages, since the beauty of antiquity and the elegance of the renaissance, the arts were reunited. The greatest landscape gardeners, architects, sculptors and painters, gathered at Chicago for a joyous interchange of ideas and criticisms; and the miracle of beauty which they have wrought grew openly in their breath and under their hands. Each did his work and had his way with it, but in this congress of gifted minds, of sensitive spirits, each profited by the censure of all, and there were certain features of the work—as for instance, the exquisite peristyle dividing the city from the lake—which were the result of successive impulses and suggestions from so many different artists that it would be hard to divide the honor among them with exactness. No one, however, seems to have been envious of another's share, and each one gave his talent as freely as the millionaires gave their money. These great artists willingly accepted a fifth, a tenth, of the gain which they could have commanded in a private enterprise, and lavished their time upon the opportunity afforded them, for the pleasure of it, the pride of it, the pure good of it.

Of the effect, of the visible, tangible result, what better can I say, than that in its presence I felt myself again in Altruria? The tears came, and the pillared porches swam against my vision; through the hard nasal American tones, the liquid notes of our own speech stole to my inner ear; I saw under the careworn masks of the competitive crowds, the peace, the *rest* of the dear Altrurian face; the gay tints of our own simple costumes eclipsed the different versions of the Paris fashions about me. I was at home once more, and my heart overflowed with patriotic rapture in this strange land, so remote from ours in everything, that at times Altruria really seems to me the dream which the Americans think it.

I first saw the Fair City by night, from one of the electric launches which ply upon the lagoon; and under the dimmed heaven, in the splendor of the hundred moony arc-lamps of the esplanades, and the myriad incandescent bubbles that beaded the white quays, and defined the structural lines of dome and porch and pediment, I found myself in the midst of the Court of Honor, which you will recognize on the general plan and the photographs I enclose. We fronted the beautiful Agricultural building, which I think fitly the finest in the city, though many prefer the perfect Greek of the Art building; and on our right was the Administration building with its coroneted dome, and the magnificent sculptured fountain before it, turned silver in the radiance of the clustered electric jets at either side. On our right* was the glorious peristyle, serene, pure, silent, lifting a population of statues against the night, and dividing the lagoon from the lake, whose soft moan came appealingly through the pillared spaces, and added a divine heartache to my ecstacy. Here a group of statuary showed itself prominently on quay or cornice; we caught the flamy curve of a bridge's arch; a pale column lifted its jutting prores † into the light; but nothing insisted; all was harmonized to one effect of beauty, as if in symbol of the concentered impulses which had created it. For the moment I could not believe that so foul a thing as money could have been even the means of its creation. I call the effect creation because it is divinely beautiful, but no doubt suggestion would be a better word, since they have here merely sketched in stucco what we have executed in marble in each of our Regionic capitals.[220]

"... The Americans came into the world too late to have inherited that influence from the antique world which was lost even in Europe, when in mediæval times the picturesque barbarously substituted itself for the beautiful, and a feeling for the quaint grew up in place of love for the perfect. . . ."

"Why," I went on, "I have heard people rave over the beauty of the Fair City, and then go and rave over the beauty of the German village, or of Old Vienna, in the Plaisance. They were cultivated people, too; but they did not seem to know that the

---

* [A mistake for "on our left." Eds.]
† ["Prora" = prow in Latin.]

reproduction of a feudal castle or of a street in the taste of the middle ages, could not be beautiful, and could at the best be only picturesque. Old Vienna is no more beautiful than the Javanese village, and the German village outrivals the Samoan village only in its greater adaptability to the purposes of the painter. There is in your modern competitive world very little beauty anywhere, but there is an abundance of picturesqueness, of forms that may be reflected upon canvas, and impart the charm of their wild irregularity to all who look at the picture, though many who enjoy it there would fail of it in a study of the original. . . ."

. . . We had in fact got to the Court of Honor . . .[230]

"This beauty that we see here is not at all picturesque. If a painter were to attempt to treat it picturesquely, he must abandon it in despair, because the charm of the picturesque is in irregularity, and the charm of the beautiful is in symmetry, in just proportion, in equality. You Americans do not see that the work of man, who is the crown of animate life, can only be beautiful as it approaches the regularity expressive of beauty in that life. . . . Nature is picturesque, but what man creates should be beautiful, or else it is inferior. . . ." [231]

PAUL BOURGET

A Farewell to the White City

Paul Bourget, "A Farewell to the White City," trans. by Walter Learned, The Cosmopolitan, XVI (December, 1893).

The White City of Jackson Park, with its palatial monuments of human achievement lacking only in stability, standing at the gates of a city still incomplete, is not an apotheosis, it is a hope. It is not an end, it is a commencement. It is not a result, it is a promise. . . .[135]

. . . But what form shall this civilization [136] take? Shall it be a mere copy of things European? The national conscience rebels against this thought. It feels its work to be the creation of a personal ideal. That is why, side by side with a passionate craving for French, German and English culture, we find spiteful resentment against those who instead of studying, merely imitate. Emerson understood this when he wrote: "Why need we copy the Doric or the Gothic model? Beauty, convenience, grandeur of thought are as near to us as to any."

That is the promise the White City leaves. Coming after so many others, this exposition is indisputable evidence that the off-shoots of antiquarianism transplanted here by three centuries of immigration will, when given leisure blossom, in this virgin soil, into beautiful flowers. These enormous, splendid palaces of a day, simply and ingeniously constructed, reared with Aladdin-like magic by the shores of this free inland sea, and announcing, as they do, the birth of a new art, do not realize the absolute originality of Emerson's dream, but they prove that the merely colossal, unaccompanied by grace and symmetry, can no longer satisfy the taste of their builders. To the innumerable spectators, gathered from the four corners of their stupendous country those buildings have given, one might say, an indelible object lesson. Speaking of exposition crowds, some one suggested to me that "the people were so anxious to see everything that they forgot to be amused." That is not entirely true. There were many merry faces there, but everywhere was the serious attention of minds imperfectly grasping new ideas. In the gaze of those rustics there was less pride than curiosity—or shall I call it the awakening of a dormant mind, first learning how to comprehend? They saw before them the work of their own countrymen, who can repeat it. Those buildings must vanish tomorrow; but why should their durable counterparts not be reared? What else were the births of the great schools of antiquity and mediævalism, what else the enchanting renaissance? . . . [137]

. . . Too many signs prove that a democracy cannot easily sever the manacles of utility, and attain the ideal. That is demonstrated too clearly by the rude American cities, so barren of monuments, so scanty in structures of delicate and simple style, or any style whatever. But the delightful grace of the White City proves that democracy is not incapable of conceiving, loving, creating an ideal. [140]

MARGARET G. VAN RENSSELAER

The Artistic Triumph of the Fair-Builders

Margaret G. Van Rensselaer, "The Artistic Triumph of the Fair-Builders," *The Forum,* XIV (December, 1892).

This Fair of ours, in its general aspect and judged from the artistic point of view, is not only much more successful than, two years ago, we believed it could be; it is much more successful than any that has ever been created in this or another land. It is not only comparable [527] to the beautiful Paris Exhibition of 1889, and not only equal to it; it is greatly superior. And its excellence is not an imitation or even an adaptation of any precedent, but has been achieved upon entirely new and original lines. It is perfectly certain that every one who goes to Chicago next summer will be astonished, no matter how much he may have heard and believed in advance; and it is just as certain that he will be charmed, no matter how good or how captious his taste may be. Indeed, the more intelligent he is, and the more intimate is his acquaintance with general questions of art and with the character of previous international exhibitions, the more he will be amazed and delighted. Only those who know how hard it is to produce a high degree of beauty on a vast scale and in complicated ways will fully appreciate what they see at Chicago, realizing that the difficulties which always exist were in this case increased by the necessity of absolutely creating an appropriate site for the buildings. They, and only they, will fully understand that they are beholding one of the most beautiful of sights and, considering its genesis, distinctly the most wonderful sight, in the world—a sight the character of which, I am unafraid to say, has not been paralleled since the Rome of the Emperors stood intact with marble palace, statue, terrace, bridge, and temple, under an Italian sky no bluer than our own. . . . [528]

. . . Perhaps, had each of the great Fair buildings been built in independence of all the others, each would have been in itself as majestic, as scholarly, as beautiful as most of them are to-day. But they would not have been by any means the same buildings that we see to-day; and their general effect would have been the effect of the typical American street or square where good buildings chance to stand, only greatly magnified and therefore with all faults of awkward contrast and inharmonious association greatly emphasized. Any one of us can point to good and beautiful buildings in American towns; but can any one think of a single satisfactory large group or long perspective? Beautiful groups, beautiful perspectives, a stupendously beautiful architectural panorama is what the Fair will show us. It will be the first real object-lesson America has had in the art of building well on a great scale; and it will show us how, on a smaller but still sometimes a very large scale, our permanent streets and squares ought to be designed. The most careless eye will understand why this vast architectural panorama looks so well. Every one will see that it is because, although many architects were at work, they worked together in brotherly accord—by no means crushing out their artistic personalities, but basing the expression of individual tastes upon a broad fundamental agreement with regard to the placing, the general style, and the dimensions of the structures, and the scale of their major features. Every one will understand that this was the only way in which harmonious variety of effect could have been secured, and that no kind of inharmonious diversity could have been so agreeable or impressive, however admirable the individual structures might have been. And he will see that while the panorama as a whole is so magnificent because of its unity, the beauty of each structure is enhanced because the beauty of its neighbors agrees with it.

I think also that intelligent observers will feel that for the chief group of buildings the best possible architectural scheme was chosen. No other styles could have served so well as these allied yet not identical Renaissance styles in giving the architects a chance to build in agreement with each other and yet to meet special practical needs and express individual tastes. The essential dignity, the truly modern [531] spirit, and the practical as well as æsthetic plasticity of Renaissance architecture will be convincingly displayed; and, despite the fact that these buildings are not just like the ones we need to shelter our daily lives and works, their aspect ought to prove that Renaissance forms of art are the best for current use. If this be proved, then one great step will have been taken toward the achievement in our towns of that harmony in variety which alone can make them beautiful. Modern English architecture has been hampered by a strong leaning, sentimental rather than reasonable, toward Gothic fashions, inappropriate alike to the intellectual temper and to the practical needs of our time. American architecture has been hampered by an unbridled wilfulness of effort, a perpetual seeking for novelties in the shape of crude inventions or of revivals of unfamiliar ancient architectural types. The sooner our profession agrees upon some broad general basis for the exercise of its exceptionally strong powers of invention, the sooner we are likely to achieve a well-developed coherent national form of art. The establishment of such a basis would, of course, be greatly hastened by a general inclination of popular taste toward some one broad and plastic form of art. And I think the Fair, by bringing Renaissance art into popular favor, will thus do the country a very valuable service. . . .[532]

The longer we look at it the more impressed we shall be by the fact that we have done it—we ourselves, the American people, without foreign help or counsel; and thus we shall learn not only to appreciate American artists and firmly and fruitfully to believe in American art, but to think with new faith and reverence of the institutions which have developed the American citizen of to-day. We ought never again to be tempted to commit the unpardonable sin—to "despair of the Republic"—having seen that the Republic is capable of supremely successful effort in intellectual as well as in political paths.[539]

HENRY ADAMS

The Education of Henry Adams.
An Autobiography

Henry Adams, The Education of Henry Adams. An Autobiography (Boston and New York, Houghton Mifflin Company, 1918).*

By the time he† got back to Washington on September 19, the storm having partly blown over, life had taken on a new face, and one so interesting that he set off to Chicago to study the Exposition again, and stayed there a fortnight absorbed in it. He found matter of study to fill a hundred years, and his education spread over chaos. Indeed, it seemed to him as though, this year, education went mad. The silver question, thorny as it was, fell into relations as simple as words of one syllable, compared with the problems of credit and exchange that came to complicate it; and when one sought rest at Chicago, educational game started like rabbits from every building, and ran out of sight among thousands of its kind before one could mark its burrow. The Exposition itself defied philosophy. One might find fault till the last gate closed, one could still explain nothing that needed explanation. As a scenic display, Paris had never approached it, but the inconceivable scenic display consisted in its being there at all—more surprising, as it was, than anything else on the continent, Niagara Falls, the Yellowstone Geysers, and the whole railway [339] system thrown in, since these were all natural products in their place; while, since Noah's Ark, no such Babel of loose and ill-joined, such vague and ill-defined and unrelated thoughts and half-thoughts and experimental outcries as the Exposition, had ever ruffled the surface of the Lakes.

° Reprinted with the permission of Houghton Mifflin Company.
† [Henry Adams]

The first astonishment became greater every day. That the Exposition should be a natural growth and product of the Northwest offered a step in evolution to startle Darwin; but that it should be anything else seemed an idea more startling still; and even granting it were not—admitting it to be a sort of industrial, speculative growth and product of the Beaux Arts artistically induced to pass the summer on the shore of Lake Michigan—could it be made to seem at home there? Was the American made to seem at home in it? Honestly, he had the air of enjoying it as though it were all his own; he felt it was good; he was proud of it; for the most part, he acted as though he had passed his life in landscape gardening and architectural decoration. If he had not done it himself, he had known how to get it done to suit him, as he knew how to get his wives and daughters dressed at Worth's or Paquin's. Perhaps he could not do it again; the next time he would want to do it himself and would show his own faults; but for the moment he seemed to have leaped directly from Corinth and Syracuse and Venice, over the heads of London and New York, to impose classical standards on plastic Chicago. Critics had no trouble in criticising the classicism, but all trading cities had always shown traders' taste, and, to the stern purist of religious faith, no art was thinner than Venetian Gothic. All trader's taste smelt of bric-à-brac; Chicago tried at least to give her taste a look of unity.

One sat down to ponder on the steps beneath Richard Hunt's dome almost as deeply as on the steps of Ara Coeli, and much to the same purpose. Here was a breach of continuity—a rupture in historical sequence! Was it real, or only apparent? One's personal universe hung on the answer, for, if the rupture was real and the [340] new American world could take this sharp and conscious twist towards ideals, one's personal friends would come in, at last, as winners in the great American chariot-race for fame. If the people of the Northwest actually knew what was good when they saw it, they would some day talk about Hunt and Richardson, La Farge and St. Gaudens, Burnham and McKim, and Stanford White when their politicians and millionaires were otherwise forgotten. The artists and architects who had done the work offered little encouragement to hope it; they talked freely enough, but not in terms that one cared to quote; and to them the Northwest refused to look artistic. They talked as though they worked only for themselves; as though art, to the Western people, was a stage decoration; a diamond shirt-stud; a paper collar; but possibly the architects of Pæstum and Girgenti had talked in the same way, and the Greek had said the same thing of Semitic Carthage two thousand years ago. . . .[341]

Education ran riot at Chicago, at least for retarded minds which had never faced in concrete form so many matters of which they were ignorant. Men who knew nothing whatever . . . had no choice but to sit down on the steps and brood as they had never brooded on the benches of Harvard College, either as student or professor, aghast at what they had said and done in all these years, and still more ashamed of the childlike ignorance and babbling futility of the society that let them say and do it. The historical mind can think only in historical processes, and probably this was the first time since historians existed, that any of them had sat down helpless before a mechanical sequence. Before a metaphysical or a theological or a political sequence, most historians had felt helpless, but the single clue to which they had hitherto trusted was the unity of natural force.[342]

Did he himself quite know what he meant? Certainly not! If he had known enough to state his problem, his education would have been complete at once. Chicago asked in 1893 for the first time the question whether the American people knew where they were driving. Adams answered, for one, that he did not know, but would try to find out. On reflecting sufficiently deeply, under the shadow of Richard Hunt's architecture, he decided that the American people probably knew no more than he did; but that they might still be driving or drifting unconsciously to some point in thought, as their solar system was said to be drifting towards some point in space; and that, possibly, if relations enough could be observed, this point might be fixed. Chicago was the first expression of American thought as a unity; one must start there.[343]

OLIVER W. LARKIN

Art and Life in America

Oliver W. Larkin, *Art and Life in America* (New York, Rinehart & Company, 1949).*

Only a few eyes looked beneath the plaster surface of the Columbian Exposition. When Harry Thurston Peck described it fourteen years later he spoke for the majority: "It revealed to millions of Americans whose lives were necessarily colorless and narrow, the splendid possibilities of art, and the compelling power of the beautiful."

Henry Adams sat on the steps of Hunt's building and reflected more soberly that "since Noah's Ark, no such Babel of loose and ill-joined, such vague and ill-defined and unrelated thoughts and half-thoughts and experimental outcries . . . had ever ruffled the surface of the Lakes." Did the American people know where they were driving? Not by the evidence around him; nor did Henry know, though he would keep on trying. The McKim classicism yielded no answer to him: he dismissed it as "the Beaux-Arts artistically induced to pass the summer on the shore of Lake Michigan." [316]

* Reprinted with the permission of Rinehart & Company, Inc.

FISKE KIMBALL

American Architecture

Fiske Kimball, *American Architecture* (Indianapolis and New York, The Bobbs-Merrill Co., 1928).*

The cumulative impression of the classic phantasm was over-whelming. The throng of visitors, many of whom were seeing large buildings for the first time, was deeply stirred by the ordered magnificance and harmony of the Court of Honor. The example of united effort and effect, associated with the classic forms in which it had been achieved, was stamped on the memory of the whole nation.

The issue, whether function should determine form from within or whether an ideal form might be imposed from without, had been decided for a generation by a sweeping victory for the formal ideal.[168]

HENRY VAN BRUNT

The Columbian Exposition and American Civilization

Henry Van Brunt, "The Columbian Exposition and American Civilization," *The Atlantic Monthly*, LXXI (May, 1893).

"There is a solidarity in the arts," said Mr. Norton; "they do not flourish in isolated independence." Painting and sculpture, in the highest sense, cannot flourish when architecture is in a state

* Reprinted with the permission of the Philadelphia Museum of Art.

of depression. Architecture cannot succeed when it is not sustained and completed by its sister arts. To decorate architecture has ever been, and must ever be, the highest function of sculptor or painter. To make architecture fit to receive such decoration is the noblest impulse of that art. Painting, sculpture, and architecture are in their best estate and are enjoying their highest opportunities when they are working together. . . .[584]

We are already hearing loud and frequent expressions of regret that, after the brilliant six months of pageantry are over, the vast collections of the Exposition will be scattered to the four winds; the great arches and trusses of steel, and the other merchantable portions of the structures of these palaces of art, will be sold to the highest bidder; the majestic ordonnances of columns and arches, pavilions, domes, and towers, with their statuary, their bas-reliefs and paintings, will disappear from the face of the earth; the fountains will be dried up, the bridges destroyed, the gardens absorbed; the Indians, the Algerians, the Japanese, the Egyptians, and the Esquimaux will "fold their tents like the Arabs, and as silently steal away;" and in a few short months nothing will be left but a vacant area of land, and the memory of the greatest function of the century. The productions of the photographer, the medals of award, and whatever of new life and higher endeavor may follow in the practice of all the arts will perhaps be needed to assure ourselves that the Exposition of 1893 was not a dream.

So far as the architectural designs of the buildings are concerned, as much thought and study have been bestowed upon them as if they were intended for all time. The sculptors and painters have embellished them as they would have [586] embellished permanent monuments. Yet it is not difficult to prove that all this will be no waste of treasure or effort, and that even the ephemeral character of the pageant will make it all the more precious to those who read its purpose aright. . . .

. . .Every great work of art, whether it presents itself merely as an incident of travel, or whether it is staled by daily contact, has its influence, more or less undefined and unsuspected, upon mind and character. But if the stranger is conscious that to-morrow he must leave it behind forever, it makes upon his intelligence an ineffaceable image. He analyzes it with eager eyes and senses all alert. He instinctively desires to make it his own, a part of himself. The slow work of years is for him done in a day, and for him the conquest of art over the imagination is at once completed. If it is a work of architecture, this conquest is accomplished by the unity of its organism, by its simplicity and wholeness of scheme in general outline, and by the harmonious subordination of its details. This unity impresses the object upon the mind at first view, and engages the attention and interest of the spectator, who is flattered by his ability to comprehend it. Its complications charm him as he is charmed by a strain of music, though in each case the technique may be far beyond his reach. This interest is confirmed if the monument of art is so devised that its finer meanings unfold themselves to his intelligence gradually, its details presenting themselves in the order of their importance to the general scheme. A less harmonious and less symmetrical organism perplexes his mind by the disorder of its composition; its parts are not so subordinated as to appeal to his eye in proper succession. He sees details before he sees the general idea; and the mental impression conveyed to him is blurred and indistinct, if in this way he is constrained to make an effort to understand its motive of design and the message which it brings,—if indeed it has any message except one of warning against false art.

It would seem, therefore, that, in view of the ephemeral character of the Exposition, nothing has been really wasted, and everything has been gained, by that expenditure of means and effort which has been necessary to make it beautiful. Its great function would have been but poorly fulfilled if the spirit of mere utility and common sense had controlled the enterprise, had cheapened it as a demonstration of art, and, because it was to be merely temporary, had made it palpably economical. "A thing of beauty is a joy" not only while you look at it, but "forever." The collections of the Exposition would have been installed as safely and as conveniently in buildings which cost five or six millions as in buildings which cost ten or twelve; but the work of civilization possible to it at the larger [587] price would have been but half done at the lower. The alabaster box of precious ointment was not broken in vain at the feet of our Saviour, though it might have been sold for three hundred pence, and the money given to the poor.

Not only to the practice of all the industrial and liberal arts, but to that of the fine arts, the Exposition will have a bequest of the utmost value; a bequest which could come from no source less exalted; a bequest which, as regards the fine arts in especial, will ever be associated with the assurance of the triumphs to be achieved in the future by their cooperation in a spirit of cordial unity. Whatever may have been the causes which finally culminated in the brilliant solidarity of the arts in the Italian Renaissance of the fifteenth and sixteenth centuries, from which has developed all the best that has been done in art since that time, it can hardly be doubted that, if a new and equally brilliant era shall presently be begun in the New World of Columbus, upon a far larger field, with nobler opportunities and without embarrassment of traditions and prejudices, it will date its initial movement and inspiration in the last decade of the nineteenth century, when the Exposition at Chicago taught its great lessons of civilization.[588]

MONTGOMERY SCHUYLER

Last Words about the Fair

Montgomery Schuyler, "Last Words About the Fair," *The Architectural Record*, III (1893).

Whether the cloud-capped towers and the gorgeous palaces of the World's Fair are to dissolve, now that the insubstantial pageant of the Fair itself has faded, and to leave not a rack behind, is a question that is reported to agitate Chicago. There is much to be said, doubtless, on both sides of it. While it is still unsettled seems to be a good time to consider the architecture which it is proposed to preserve for yet awhile longer, in order to determine, so far as may be, what influence the display at Chicago is likely to have upon the development of American architecture, and how far that influence is likely to be good and how far to be bad. . . . [291]

Doubtless the influence of the most admired group of buildings ever erected in this country, the public buildings at Washington not excepted, must be great. What it is likely to be has been expressed by Mr. Burnham, the Director of Works of the Columbian Exposition, in some remarks, published in a Chicago newspaper, which crystallize into a lucid and specific form a general hazy expectation, and which may well serve us for a text:

"The influence of the Exposition on architecture will be to inspire a reversion toward the pure ideal of the ancients. We have been in an inventive period, and have had rather contempt for the classics. Men evolved new ideas and imagined they could start a new school without much reference to the past. But action and reaction are equal, and the exterior and obvious result will be that men will strive to do classic architecture. In this effort there will be many failures. It requires long and fine training to design on classic lines. The simpler the expression of true art the more difficult it is to obtain.

"The intellectual reflex of the Exposition will be shown in a demand for better architecture, and designers will be obliged to abandon their incoherent originalities and study the ancient masters of building. There is shown so much of fine architecture here that people have seen and appreciated this. It will be unavailing hereafter to say that great classic forms are undesirable. The people have the vision before them here, and words cannot efface it."

Doubtless the architecture of the Exposition will inspire a great many classic buildings, which will be better or worse done according to the training of the designers, but it is not likely that any of these will even dimly recall, and quite impossible that they should equal the architectural triumph of the Fair. The influence of the Exposition, so far as it leads to direct imitation, seems to us an unhopeful rather than a hopeful sign, not a promise so much as a threat. Such an imitation will so ignore the conditions that have made the architectural success of the Fair that it is worth while to try to discern and to state these conditions, and that is the purpose of this paper.

In the first place the success is first of all a success of unity, a triumph of *ensemble*. The whole is better than any of its parts and greater than all its parts, and its effect is one and indivisible. We are speaking now of the Court of Honor, which alone it is proposed to preserve, and which forms an architectural whole. The proposal to remove the largest building of the group, that of Manufactures, and to set it up by itself in a permanent form on the lake front in Chicago, though the proposition was not made by an architect, is an excellent illustration how easy it is to mistake the significance of the architecture and the causes of its success. It is a masterpiece of misappreciation. The landscape plan of the Fair, with the great basin, open at one end to the lake and cut midway by canals, may be said to have generated the architecture of the Court of Honor. Any group of educated architects who had assembled to consider the problem presented by the plan must have taken much the same course that was in fact taken. The solution of the problem presented by the plan was in outline given by the plan. That the treatment of the border of this symmetrical basin should be symmetrical, that the confronting buildings should balance each other, these were requirements obviously in the interest of unity and a general unity was obviously [292] the result to be sought and the best result that could be attained. The conditions of this unity were all that it was necessary to stipulate for. Variety enough had been secured by the selection of an individual designer for each of the great buildings, and the danger was that this variety would be excessive, that it would degenerate into a miscellany. Against this danger it was necessary to guard if the buildings should appear as the work of collaborators rather than of competitors, and it was guarded against by two very simple but quite sufficient conditions. One was that there should be a uniform cornice-line of sixty feet, the other that the architecture should be classic. The first requirement, keeping a virtually continuous sky-line all around the Court of Honor, and preventing that line from becoming an irregular serration, was so plainly necessary that it is not necessary to spend any words in justifying it. The second may seem more disputable, but in reality it was almost as much a matter of course as the first. Uniformity in size is no more necessary to unity than uniformity in treatment, and classic architecture was more eligible than any other for many tolerably obvious reasons. There are perhaps no effects attained in the exhibition that could not have been attained in other architecture. . . .

Nevertheless, the choice of classic architecture was almost

as distinctly imposed upon the associated architects as the choice
of a uniform cornice line. In the first place, the study of classic
architecture is a usual, almost an invariable part of the professional training of the architects of our time. . . .[293]

That would be one good reason for the adoption of a given
style—that all the persons concerned knew how to work in it.
Another is that the classic forms, although originally developed
from the conditions of masonic structure, have long since, and
perhaps ever since they became "orders," been losing touch with
their origin, until now they have become simply forms, which
can be used without a suggestion of any real structure or any
particular material. We know them in wood and metal, as well
as in stone. They may be used, as they are used in Jackson Park,
as a decorative envelope of any construction whatever without
exciting in most observers any sense of incongruity, much less
any sense of meanness such as is at once aroused by the sight of
"carpenter's Gothic." A four-foot column, apparently of marble,
may have aroused such a sentiment during the process of construction, when it might have been seen without a base and
supported upon little sticks, with its apparent weight thus
emphatically denied. Such a sentiment may have been aroused
again in the closing days of the Fair, when it was no longer
thought necessary to repair defects as fast as they showed themselves, and where the apparent masonry disclosed in places the
lath-backing. But when the buildings were ready for the public
no such incongruity was forced upon the observer, as it would
have been forced upon him if the forms that were used had been
such as are still associated with the structure that gave rise to
them. The alternative to the use of classic architecture was the
development in a few months of an architecture of plaster, or
"staff." For this there are no precedents completely available in
the world, while the world is full of precedents for the employment of the orders, and precedents which do not imply that the
orders are real and efficient constructions, as indeed they have
never been since the Romans began to use columnar architecture
as the decoration of an arched construction.

It is not to be supposed for a moment that the architects of
the Fair would have attained anything like the success they did
attain, if instead of working in a style with which all of them

were presumably familiar, they had undertaken the Herculean task of creating a style out of these novel conditions. In fact the architects of the Court of Honor might "point with pride" to the result of such efforts as were made in that direction by other architects as a sufficient justification for their own course, if such a justification were needed. . . . [294]

But, perhaps, the strongest proof of the good judgment of the architects of the Court of Honor is that the effect of unity is not disturbed by those buildings that are in themselves the least successful. "Classic" is a very comprehensive term, if one include under it, as one must, everything that owes its origin to the Greeks, from their own work to the latest developments of the Renaissance, and yet a certain family-likeness is traceable in all these things. The trail of "the orders" is over them all. There is indeed, and rather curiously, no example of Grecian architecture in the Court of Honor. . . .

There have been critics who insist that, comprehensive as it is, the epithet "classic" is not comprehensive enough to take in all the architecture of the Court of Honor. One of these critics, a Frenchman, found himself unable to reconcile the more fantastic erections with the rest of the architecture of the Court. . . . But the great advantage of adopting a uniform treatment, even when the uniformity is so very general as is denoted by the term classic, and even when the term has been so loosely [296] interpreted, as it has been by some of the associated designers in Jackson Park, is that the less successful designs do not hinder an appreciation of the more successful, nor disturb the general sense of unity in an extensive scheme, which is so much more valuable and impressive than the merits of the best of the designs taken singly. . . . It is a scheme and it has been carried out not only in the huge buildings of unequal merit that we have been considering, but in all the accessories of a monumental composition. This has been done with noteworthy skill and discretion in the peristyle and its flanking buildings, and in the terminal station, any one of which, if done without reference to the rest, under the inspiration of what Mr. Burnham calls an "incoherent originality" or even a coherent originality might have gone for*

* ["far," Eds.]

to spoil the whole. It has been carried out also in the minor details that are scarcely noticeable in their places, but that would have been painfully noticeable if they had been out of place, in the plazas and the bridges and the promenades that are the accessories of a pompous architectural composition. . . . The condition upon which the effectiveness of the whole depends is that there shall be a whole, that there shall be a general plan to the execution of which every architect and every sculptor and every decorator concerned shall contribute. That condition has been fulfilled in the architecture of the Exposition, at least in the architecture of the "Court of Honor," which is what everybody means when he speaks of the architecture of the Exposition, and it is by the fulfillment of this condition that the success of the Fair has been attained. That success is, first of all, a success of unity.

Next after unity, as a source and explanation of the unique impression made by the World's Fair buildings, comes magnitude. It may even be questioned whether it should not come first in an endeavor to account for that impression. If it be put second, it is only because unity, from an artistic point of view, is an achievement, while magnitude from that point of view, is merely an advantage. The buildings are impressive by their size, and this impressiveness is enhanced by their number. Mere bigness is the easiest, speaking æsthetically, though practically it may be the most difficult to attain, of all the means to an effect. It constitutes an opportunity, and one's judgment upon the result, as a work of art, depends upon the skill with which the opportunity has been embraced and employed. But bigness tells all the same, and the critical observer can no more emancipate himself from the effect of it than the uncritical, though he is the better able to allow for it. . . . [297]

The devices by which these inordinate dimensions are brought home to the comprehension of the spectator are various, but they consist, in most cases, at least of a plinth and a parapet in which the height of a man is recalled, as in an architectural drawing the draughtsman puts in a human figure "to give the scale." While the Fair was in progress the moving crowds supplied the scale, but this was given also by all the architectural appurtenances, the parapets of the bridges and the railings of the wharves, so that the magnitude of the buildings was everywhere forced upon the sense. To give scale is also the chief contribution to the effect of a general survey that is made by the accessory and decorative sculpture of the buildings and of the grounds. In this respect, and without reference to their merits strictly as sculpture, the statuary that surmounts the piers and cupolas of the Agricultural building and that with which the angles of the Administration building bristle are particularly fortunate. On the other hand the figures of the peristyle were unfortunate, being too big and insistent for [298] their architectural function of mere finials. . . . It is only with the influence of what has been done in Jackson Park upon the architecture of the country that we are now concerned; with the suitableness of it for general reproduction or imitation, and with the results that are likely to follow that process, if pursued in the customary manner of the American architect. The danger is that that designer, failing to analyze the sources of the success of the Fair, will miss the point. The most obvious way in which he can miss it is by expecting a reproduction of the success of one of the big buildings by reproducing it in a building of ordinary dimensions. It is necessary, if he is to avoid this, that he should bear in mind how much of the effect of one of the big buildings comes from its very bigness, and would disappear from a reproduction in miniature.

There is still another cause for the success of the World's Fair buildings, a cause that contributes more to the effect of them, perhaps, than both the causes we have already set down put together. It is this which at once most completely justifies the architects of the Exposition in the course they have adopted, and goes furthest to render the results of that course ineligible for reproduction or for imitation in the solution of the more ordinary problems of the American architect. The success of the architecture at the World's Fair is not only a success of unity, and a success of magnitude. It is also and very eminently a success of illusion.

What the World's Fair buildings have first of all to tell us, and what they tell equally to a casual glimpse and to a prolonged survey is that they are examples not of work-a-day building, but of holiday building, that the purpose of their erection is festal and temporary, in a word that the display is a display and a triumph of occasional architecture. . . . They have realized in plaster that gives us the illusion of monumental masonry a painter's dream of Roman architecture. . . . It is the province and privilege of the painter to see visions and of the poet to dream dreams. They are unhampered by material considerations of structure of material or of cost. They can imagine unrealizable centaurs and dragons, gorgons, hydras and chimeras dire and in turn affect our imaginations with these. The question how the centaur can subsist, with two sets of respiratory and digestive organs superposed, does not disturb them nor us while we remain under their spell. To quarrel with the incredibilities they ask us to accept is to show not only a hopelessly prosaic but a hopelessly pedantic spirit. . . .

The poet's or the painter's spell or the spell of the architect of an "unsubstantial pageant" cannot be wrought upon the spectator who refuses to [299] take the wonder-worker's point of view, and instead of yielding himself to the influence of the spectacle insists upon analyzing its parts and exposing its incongruities. There would be a want of sense as well as a want of imagination in pursuing this course and criticising a passing show as a permanent and serious piece of building.

It is the part of the spectator who would derive the utmost pleasure from the spectacle to ignore the little incongruities that he might detect, and loyally to assist the scenic artist in his make-believe. Nay, the consciousness of illusion is a part of the pleasure of the illusion. It is not a diminution but an increase of our delight to know that the cloud-capped towers, the gorgeous palaces, and the solemn temples, the images of which scenic art summons before us are in sober reality "the baseless fabric of a vision."

Such a pleasure and such an illusion the architects of Jackson Park have given us. The White City is the most integral, the most extensive, the most illusive piece of scenic architecture that has ever been seen. That is praise enough for its builders, without demanding for them the further praise of having made a useful and important contribution to the development of the architecture of the present, to the preparation of the architecture of the future. . . . Those of us who believe that architecture is the correlation of structure and function, that if it is to be real and living and progressive, its forms must be the results of material and construction, sometimes find ourselves reproached with our admiration for these palaces in which this belief is so conspicuously ignored and set at naught. But there is no inconsistency in entertaining at the same time a hearty admiration for the Fair and its builders and the hope of an architecture which in form and detail shall be so widely different from it as superficially to have nothing in common with it. Arcadian architecture is one thing and American architecture is another. The value of unity, the value of magnitude are common to the two, but for the value of illusion in the one there must be substituted in the other, if it is to come to its fruition, the value of reality. . . .[300] Above all, who would care to have the buildings reproduced without the atmosphere of illusion that enveloped them at Jackson Park and vulgarized by being brought into the light of common day? "This same truth is a naked and open daylight that doth not show the masques and mummeries and triumphs of the world half so stately and daintily as candle lights."

It was a common remark among visitors who saw the Fair for the first time that nothing they had read or seen pictured had given them an idea of it, or prepared them for what they saw. The impression thus expressed is the impression we have been trying to analyze, of which the sources seem to be unity, magnitude and illusion, and the greatest of these is illusion. To reproduce or to imitate the buildings deprived of these irreproducible and inimitable advantages, would be an impossible task, and if it were possible it would not be desirable. For the art of architecture is not to produce illusions or imitations, but realities, organisms like those of nature. It is in the "naked and open daylight" that our architects must work, and they can only be diverted from their task of production by reproduction. It is not theirs to realize the dreams of painters, but to do such work as future painters may delight to dream of and to draw. If they work for their purposes as well as the classic builders wrought for theirs, then when they, in their turn, have become remote and mythical and classic, their work may become the material of an illusion, "such stuff as dreams are made of." But its very fitness for this purpose will depend upon its remoteness from current needs and current ideas, upon its irrelevancy to what will then be contemporary life.[301]

ERNEST FLAGG

Influence of the French School on Architecture in the United States

Ernest Flagg, "Influence of the French School on Architecture in the United States," *The Architectural Record*, IV (Demember, 1894).

. . .The fact that so little of French feeling is to be seen in the work of Americans who have been at the school [the Ecole des Beaux Arts] has often been commented upon and has generally been ascribed to the different conditions which confront them when they return. . . .[211]

. . . We have no structures which resemble the modern buildings of France. Even in the work of those of our men who have received training in France, one can find but little trace of French influence so far as style is concerned. In general the work of these men shows perhaps more refinement and sobriety, a greater facility and more careful study, than that of those who have not received similar advantages, but in other respects there is little difference. Their designs sometimes indicate a leaning towards archaeology and again often bear a striking resemblance to modern English, Italian and Austrian work, but not to that of the French, which is the more strange as almost all of these men profess great fondness and admiration for French architecture of the present day. The explanation of this seeming inconsistency doubtless lies in the fact that French architecture of today is more distinctly national than any other, and not so easy to acquire as the Vignolesque styles of Austria and Italy and the semi-Dutch architecture of England. . . .[215]

LOUIS H. SULLIVAN

The Autobiography of an Idea

Louis H. Sullivan, *The Autobiography of an Idea* (New York, Press of the American Institute of Architects, 1926).* †

Chicago was booming. It had become a powerful magnet. Its people had one dream in common: That their city should become the world's metropolis. There was great enthusiasm and public spirit. . . .[316]

. . . It was deemed fitting by all the people that the four hundredth anniversary of the discovery of America by one Christopher Columbus, should be celebrated by a great World Exposition, which should spaciously reveal to the last word the cultural status of the peoples of the Earth; and that the setting for such display should be one of splendor, worthy of its subject.

Chicago was ripe and ready for such an undertaking. It had the required enthusiasm and the will. It won out in a contest between the cities. The prize was now in hand. It was to be the city's crowning glory. A superb site on the lake adjoined the southern section of the city. This site was so to be transformed and embellished by the magic of American prowess, particularly in its architectural aspects, as to set forth the genius of the land in that great creative art. It was [317] to be a dream city, where one might revel in beauty. It was to be called The White City by the Lake.

Now arose above the horizon the small white cloud. It came from eastward. It came borne upon the winds of predestination. Who could fancy that a harmless white cloud might cast a white shadow? Who could forecast the shape of that shadow? It was here that one man's unbalanced mind spread a gauze-like pall

---

* Reprinted with the permission of the American Institute of Architects.
† Paperback edition, 1957, by Dover Publications, Inc., New York.

of fatality. That one man's unconscious stupor in bigness, and in the droll phantasy of hero-worship, did his best and his worst, according to his lights, which were dim except the one projector by the harsh light of which he saw all things illuminated and grown bombastically big in Chauvinistic outlines. Here was to be the test of American culture, and here it failed. Dreamers may dream; but of what avail the dream if it be but a dream of misinterpretation? If the dream, in such a case, rise not in vision far above the general level of intelligence, and prophesy through the medium of clear thinking, true interpretation—why dream at all? Why not rest content as children of Barnum, easy in the faith that one of "them" is born every minute. Such in effect was the method adopted in practice while the phrase-makers tossed their slogans to and fro.

At the beginning it was tentatively assumed that the firm of Burnham & Root might undertake the work in its entirety. The idea was sound in principle—one hand, one great work—a superb revelation of America's potency—an oration, a portrayal, to arouse that which was hidden, to call it forth into the light. But the work of ten years cannot be done in two. It would require two years to grasp and analyze the problem [318] and effect a synthesis. Less than three years were available for the initiation and completion of the work entire, ready for the installation of exhibits. The idea was in consequence dismissed. As a matter of fact there was not an architect in the land equal to the undertaking. No veteran mind seasoned to the strategy and tactics involved in a wholly successful issue. Otherwise there might have arisen a gorgeous Garden City, reflex of one mind, truly interpreting the aspirations and the heart's desire of the many, every detail carefully considered, every function given its due form, with the sense of humanity at its best, a suffusing atmosphere; and within the Garden City might be built another city to remain and endure as a memorial, within the parkland by the blue waters, oriented toward the rising sun, a token of a covenant of things to be, a symbol of the city's basic significance as offspring of the prairie, the lake and the portage.

But "hustle" was the word. Make it big, make it stunning, knock 'em down! The cry was well meant as things go.

So in the fall of 1890 John Root was officially appointed

consulting architect, and Daniel Burnham, Chief of Construction.

Later, with the kindly assistance of Edward T. Jefferey, Chairman of the Committee on Buildings and Grounds, Burnham selected five architects from the East and five from the West, ten in all. Burnham and Jefferey loved each other dearly. The thought of one was the thought of both, as it were—sometimes. Burnham had believed that he might best serve his country by placing all of the work exclusively with Eastern architects; solely, he averred, on account of [319] their surpassing culture. With exquisite delicacy and tact, Jefferey, at a meeting of the Committee, persuaded Daniel, come to Judgment, to add the Western men to the list of his nominations.

A gathering of these architects took place in February, 1891. After an examination of the site, which by this time was dreary enough in its state of raw upheaval, the company retired for active conference. John Root was not there. In faith he could not come. He had made his rendezvous the month before. Graceland was now his home. Soon above him would be reared a Celtic cross. Louis missed him sadly. Who now would take up the foils he had dropped on his way, from hands that were once so strong? There was none! The shadow of the white cloud had already fallen.

The meeting came to order. Richard Hunt, acknowledged dean of his profession, in the chair, Louis Sullivan acting as secretary. Burnham arose to make his address of welcome. He was not facile on his feet, but it soon became noticeable that he was progressively and grossly apologizing to the Eastern men for the presence of their benighted brethren of the West.

Dick Hunt interrupted: "Hell, we haven't come out here on a missionary expedition. Let's get to work." Everyone agreed. Burnham came out of his somnambulistic vagary and joined in. He was keen enough to understand that "Uncle Dick" had done him a needed favor. For Burnham learned slowly but surely, within the limits of his understanding.

A layout was submitted to the Board as a basis for discussion. It was rearranged on two axes at right angles. The buildings were disposed accordingly. By [320] an amicable arrangement each architect was given such building as he preferred, after consultation. The meeting then adjourned.

The story of the building of the Fair is foreign to the purpose of this narrative, which is to deal with its more serious aspects, implications and results. Suffice it that Burnham performed in a masterful way, displaying remarkable executive capacity. He became open-minded, just, magnanimous. He did his great share.

The work completed, the gates thrown open 1 May, 1893, the crowds flowed in from every quarter, continued to flow throughout a fair-weather summer and a serenely beautiful October. Then came the end. The gates were closed.

These crowds were astonished. They beheld what was for them an amazing revelation of the architectural art, of which previously they in comparison had known nothing. To them it was a veritable Apocalypse, a message inspired from on high. Upon it their imagination shaped new ideals. They went away, spreading again over the land, returning to their homes, each one of them carrying in the soul the shadow of the white cloud, each of them permeated by the most subtle and slow-acting of poisons; an imperceptible miasm within the white shadow of a higher culture. A vast multitude, exposed, unprepared, they had not had time nor occasion to become immune to forms of sophistication not their own, to a higher and more dexterously insidious plausibility. Thus they departed joyously, carriers of contagion, unaware that what they had beheld and believed to be truth was to prove, in historic fact, an appalling calamity. For what they [321] saw was not at all what they believed they saw, but an imposition of the spurious upon their eyesight, a naked exhibitionism of charlatanry in the higher feudal and domineering culture, enjoined with expert salesmanship of the materials of decay. . . . [322]

. . .The virus of the World's Fair, after a period of incubation in the architectural profession and in the population at large, especially the influential, began to show unmistakable signs of the nature of the contagion. There came a violent outbreak of the Classic and the Renaissance in the East, which slowly spread westward, contaminating all that it touched, both at its source and outward. The selling campaign of the bogus antique was remarkably well managed through skillful publicity and propaganda, by those who were first to see its commercial possibilities. The market was ripe, made so through the hebetude of the populace, big business men, and eminent educators alike. By the time the market had been saturated, all sense of reality was gone. In its place had come deep-seated illusions, hallucinations, absence of pupillary reaction [324] to light, absence of knee-reaction—symptoms all of progressive cerebral meningitis: The blanketing of the brain. Thus Architecture died in the land of the free and the home of the brave,—in a land declaring its fervid democracy, its inventiveness, its resourcefulness, its unique daring, enterprise and progress. Thus did the virus of a culture, snobbish and alien to the land, perform its work of disintegration; and thus ever works the pallid academic mind, denying the real, exalting the fictitious and the false, incapable of adjusting itself to the flow of living things, to the reality and the pathos of man's follies, to the valiant hope that ever causes him to aspire, and again to aspire; that never lifts a hand in aid because it cannot; that turns its back upon man because that is its tradition; a culture lost in ghostly *mésalliance* with abstractions, when what the world needs is courage, common sense and human sympathy, and a moral standard that is plain, valid and livable.

The damage wrought by the World's Fair will last for half a century from its date, if not longer. It has penetrated deep into the constitution of the American mind, effecting there lesions significant of dementia. [325]

2

THE NATIONAL GALLERY OF ART
Washington, D. C., 1938-1941

HENRY H. SAYLOR

The National Gallery of Art

Henry H. Saylor, *The National Gallery of Art* (Published by Henry H. Saylor, New York, 1941).*

In the late Andrew W. Mellon's letter to President Roosevelt, offering his collection as the nucleus of a national gallery of art, he expressed a wish to give to the people of the United States a building "suitable" to house these and other such works of art as may be given to the nation.

The building was constructed on a site on The Mall between Fourth and Seventh Streets, and between Madison Drive and Constitution Avenue, which was appropriated by the Congress to the National Gallery of Art, and the project was completed in accordance with plans and specifications approved by the National Commission of Fine Arts.

Among the many considerations that combine to make the National Gallery what the architects have created, are three major

* Reprinted with the permission of Henry H. Saylor and Eggers & Higgins.

factors: first, its specified location in Washington as an integral part of the L'Enfant plan; second, the fact that the building is to serve for a period limited only by the extent of our accumulated knowledge of what constitutes enduring construction; and third, the obvious necessity for unquestionable harmony between the building and the time-tested heritage of paintings and sculpture it is to shelter.

It was believed that the Gallery should be essentially a one-floor system of exhibition space lighted entirely from above, and by natural daylight as far as possible. This top lighting comes through several acres of wire-woven skylights and thence through the horizontal ceiling panels of a special diffusing glass which is shatterproof.

SIZE AND CONTENTS

All administration space, mechanical equipment, storage [1] and the like are kept off this Main Floor, to free it for the display of the major treasures. Galleries for auxiliary collections and for temporary exhibitions; an auditorium; a cafeteria and its kitchen; all the work rooms for restoring, copying, framing, crating; locker and rest rooms for guards and other employees—these numerous space requirements are met on the ground floor just below. In length the Gallery measures 782 ft.; in width over its extended wings, 303 ft., both exclusive of steps and approaches. This length is comparable to that of the Capitol and its wings.

A central Rotunda under the dome is reached through north and south lobbies, these being entered from the majestic porticoes on The Mall and on Constitution Avenue opposite Sixth Street. Poised over a fountain in the center is the bronze Mercury of Giovanni Bologna.

Surrounding the middle stem of the Main Floor, and the Garden Courts that terminate it, are 90 separate galleries, providing rooms for expansion needs of perhaps a [2] century. This Main Floor contains 179,000 sq. ft. There is nothing "frozen" about its subdivisions; the partitions that divide them are non-bearing walls, and can be moved and rearranged as may become desirable without affecting the structure of the building.

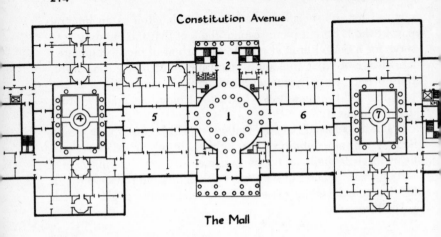

Constitution Avenue

The Mall

The National Gallery of Art, 1938-1941, Washington, D. C., designed by John Russell Pope and Eggers & Higgins Associates. The National Gallery offers an excellent example of the classical approach in its plan. Note how the central axis bisects the rotunda and how the wings are symmetrically balanced. 1: Rotunda; 2: North Lobby; 3: South Lobby; 4: West Garden Court; 5: West Hall; 6: East Hall; 7: East Garden Court.

LIGHTING

In Washington, actual measurements of daylight proved this to be adequate for 85% of the time the Gallery will be open. Artificial sources of the utmost flexibility in volume, color and direction, were devised to maintain ideal lighting at all times. So adaptable has the supply of light and its control been arranged, that it is possible to light each individual object as may be best for it, even where the needs vary widely in a single room. Certain objects are best seen in silhouette against a light background; sculpture needs directional rather than diffused lighting; painting, if glazed, must show no reflections; both side walls of a room must be evenly lighted, no matter what the sun's angle.

AIR CONDITIONING

Air throughout the interior is fitted not only to the [3] comfort of the visitors, both in winter and summer, but also to the requirements of the art treasures, in order that they may be preserved indefinitely. One such requirement is a constant relative humidity of about 50%. Another is the filtering of air and cleansing it of the sulphur dioxide fumes that injure paintings. A temperature ranging between 70° and 80° Fahrenheit is automatically regulated in its proper relation to the outside temperature. On a hot summer day the interior must be warmer than the ideal 72°, else the visitor would feel an uncomfortable chill upon entering. Warming the six changes of air per hour, and regulating its moisture content, are relatively easy operations, compared with the job of cooling it. Through the acres of glass roof the sun pours its own heat in tremendous volume. The space between the skylights and the diffusing glass of gallery ceiling has its air rapidly changed by blowers moving 700,000 cu. ft. per minute. Nevertheless, the engineers estimate that, under maximum heat conditions, there must be removed from the Gallery heat sufficient to melt 2,720,000 lbs. of ice in 24 hours. Obviating the necessity for making that much ice or its equivalent, the waters of the Tidal Basin are put to work. A great underground conduit brings over 5,000 gals. of water per minute through huge compressors in the basement to absorb heat and pass on underground to the Washington Ship Harbor.

Control of unwanted sound was particularly difficult in the galleries with reverberant stone walls. The dome of the Rotunda, of marble inside and out, rises to 103 ft. and is 101 ft. in diameter. Its inside surface and those of the entrance lobbies are broken by the architectural coffering, and the central unit of each coffer was provided with a sound-absorbing [5] element. On the balcony just below the dome, surfaces not visible from the floor below were covered with an absorbent material. Vaulted ceilings were likewise treated. All machinery was insulated from the structure and its base—lead, cork and rubber used for cushioning.

Foundations were a problem of major importance, the site being over an old swamp at the foot of Capitol Hill, with no rock bottom within reach. Friction is the support of the vast weight of masonry and steel—the friction of the earth with the surface of 6,800 deeply driven concrete piles.

MARBLE

For the exterior walls, no material other than the best could be considered worthy. Marble elected itself. But were quarries to be found equal to the unprecedented demands in quality and quantity?—for the Gallery is the largest marble building in the world. A deposit in the mountains of Tennessee proved adequate, but only after new quarries had been opened and older ones organized with these into a single operating source. Seven quarries supplied some 800 carloads of marble to Washington for this building.

The casual passerby would say that the marble is white. As a matter of fact, it is a comparatively narrow range of pinks, darkest at the base of the building, graded imperceptibly to a pale shell-pink at the top. Seven basic shades, and their 26 intermediate shades were charted—all so subtle as to be distinguishable only when the marble is wet. Each block as quarried from the 35-mile deposit in Tennessee, after being passed as flawless, was classified as to color by the architects' representatives, was cut to dimensions, and each of 35,000 individual pieces marked for its precise location in the wall before being shipped.

ROTUNDA

Twenty-four columns, over 36 ft. high, support an entablature [8] 16 ft. high, in the Rotunda under the central dome. Behind an encircling gallery the coffered marble dome terminates in a great circle of light—an *oculus* or eye, as in the Pantheon in Rome. The column shafts are of a dark variegated green marble—Verte Imperial. A search of the world's marble sources revealed the desired color and the necessary quantity high up above the west coast of Italy. After skidding down a mountain and being hauled by railroad to a dock, the great drums were brought across the Atlantic just before war would have prevented. Cut and turned in Vermont, they were painstakingly matched as to veining by revolving and transposing the great cylinders in a trial horizontal assembly, then marked for final position, polished and hauled to Washington, and the 10 tons of each lifted into place.

MASONRY PRECISION

For the walls of the Rotunda, and for the flanking East and West Central Galleries, Alabama supplied its Rockwood stone. Above the columns of the Rotunda the lintel stones [10] were cut to complete a ring 74 ft. in diameter. Machined to the finished profile near the quarry, they were shipped north, hoisted into position, end to end and when the last 22-ton stone was lifted to complete the great ring, it needed just ⅛ in. rubbed off the end to make a perfect fit.

A complete list of the various marbles used for interior walls, staircases and floors would read like something in a new language: Istrian Nuage, Phantasia Rose, Adorado, Red Levanto, Madre Alabama Cream, Nero Nube, Tavernelle Clair, Sterling Lunel, Italy's Botticino, France's Hauteville—mere names to most of us, but indicating the painstaking search for perfect harmony of color and texture throughout.

Marbles of various kinds, mosaic, broad oak planks and cork tile form the finished floor surfaces in different parts of the Gallery. For the exhibition galleries generally, wide laminated planking of oak is used, in a mellow brown color.

Many and various are the materials selected for the back-[11] ground surfaces in the exhibition galleries; travertine, buff limestone, plaster, painted pine, oak, walnut, damask—each chosen for its particular value as a foil to the treasures the room will shelter.

Large old boxwoods, evergreen trees, shrubs, hedges and ground cover effect the transition between the architecture and the broad lawns and elms of The Mall.

The Gallery has been erected with funds provided by the late Andrew W. Mellon of Pittsburgh, under the guidance and direction of Paul Mellon, Donald D. Shepard and David K. E. Bruce, trustees of A. W. Mellon Educational and Charitable Trust. The trustees, architects, builders, and all associated with the erection of the Gallery, appreciated and shared the great responsibility placed upon them.

DESIGN AND ADMINISTRATION

The trustees' building committee consisted of James L. Stuart, David E. Finley, Harry A. McBride and Alexander R. Reed. The architect was John Russell Pope and his associates, Otto R. Eggers and Daniel Paul Higgins, until August 1937, when Mr. Pope died. Messrs. Eggers and Higgins continued the architectural services without interruption until the Gallery was completed, just three years and three months after Mr. Mellon's death. Serving the architects in an executive capacity were Edwin Olsen in the New York office and James M. Allen at the building, assisted by Malcolm Rice, who also supervised work at the quarries. The builder was the Vermilya-Brown Company, Inc., of which Percy A. Vermilya is president; structural engineers, H. G. Balcom Associates; mechanical engineer, Clyde R. Place; lighting engineers, Stanley McCandless and Edward B. Kirk; landscape architect, Alfred M. Geiffert.[12]

HENRY H. SAYLOR

Mechanized Treasure House

Henry H. Saylor, "Mechanized Treasure House," Popular Science Monthly, CXXXIX (August, 1941).*

The casual passer-by will see the National Gallery of Art—Andrew Mellon's magnificent gift to the nation—merely as monumental architecture. It is really a complex and efficient machine. Behind that expanse of marble walls—longer, incidentally, than the Capitol itself—one will find not only one of the world's greatest collections of paintings and sculpture, but the last word in our scientific knowledge of building.

* Reprinted with the permission of Popular Science Monthly.

More than ten years ago, at the end of a day when Mr. Mellon left his desk as Secretary of the Treasury, he would often tell his chauffeur, "Just drive around." When he had found the site he wanted, he called in the architect, John Russell Pope, and his partners, Otto R. Eggers and Daniel P. Higgins; the engineer, H. G. Balcolm; the builder, Percy A. Vermilya. The problem he set before them must have seemed almost beyond accomplishment. The site was little better than a swamp, with no bedrock within reach for foundations. The land was no higher than the Potomac River's top flood level of 1932. The structure was to be built to endure for as long as American building genius could contrive. It was to present to the world a unified exterior, yet be capable of expansion sufficient to accommodate the art accessions of, say, two more centuries. In it were to be embodied the best fruits of our knowledge of lighting, air conditioning, and the protection of its priceless contents.

Lighting was a major problem. Experts said overhead daylight was the ideal. As a result the National Gallery's main floor is its top floor—a series of 90 exhibition rooms without side windows but with ceilings of a special diffusing glass, lighted by skylights and, when daylight fails, by floodlights. Thus acres of gallery roof are chiefly glass.

Below this main floor is one at street level, on which are located the administrative and work rooms, galleries for temporary exhibitions, a lecture hall, a cafeteria and its kitchen, receiving, repair, and photographic rooms. There is even a "delousing"[38] room for incoming works of art. Below this ground floor is most of the mechanical equipment.

Paintings are best viewed by diffused top light, but that is the worst light for sculpture. To see this three-dimensional art at its best, the light should be sharply directional, to give highlights and shadows. Moreover, the diffused top light for paintings must be equalized upon the four sides of a room, whatever the angle of the sun. That necessitated a considerable height between the ceiling glass—called "lay lights"—and the skylights, in places as much as forty feet.

Directional light for the sculpture was achieved by using a border of lenses around the lay lights in each gallery. So flexible is this system that paintings and sculpture can be ideally lighted even when they alternate around the room. And of course the lighting can readily be changed to suit rearrangement.

Another problem was reflections. Even unglazed paintings present annoying spots of glare when the angles of vision and of light are not properly related. The chief offenders are the tall canvases, where the line of vision turns strongly up. High ceilings, easily possible in this one-exhibition-floor [39] scheme, are the best answer.

Washington's weather, sun, haze, fog, smoke, and a few other factors were measured in a twelve-month survey, and it was found that the top lighting plan would give the gallery sufficient light 85 percent of the time it would be open. For the remaining hours, there are the flood lamps on steel tracks above the lay lights. Their light may be varied at will in volume and corrected for color by individual filters.

The lay lights offered some minor problems. Breakage and falling glass had to be guarded against. Wire glass sufficed for the skylights above, but such reënforcement in the ceiling would have made a distracting silhouette. One of the newer discoveries in glass making was the answer. It is a glass a quarter of an inch thick, both faces of which are in tension. A blow sufficient to break it causes complete disintegration, so that the broken pane would sift down as a fine powder.

One staggering factor results from the top daylight system. The sun pours its heat through the skylights unchallenged. That hot air between skylights and lay lights has to be taken out in a hurry, before it can unload its heat into the galleries below. Twenty-eight blowers are the guardians, going into action as they are needed, and they can remove 700,000 cubic feet of air a minute.

And that brings us to the Gallery's air conditioning. Visitors must be comfortable and the paintings must [40] be protected against too much or too little moisture, too much or too little heat. Fortunately, the two aims do not conflict. To prevent deterioration of the canvases, a constant relative humidity of about 50 percent is best, and that suits all of us. The temperature will vary between 70° and 80°, going up and down with outdoor conditions. . . .

Seventeen air-conditioning plants serve their respective

The National Gallery of Art, 1938-1941, Washington, D. C., looking southeast, with Constitution Avenue in the foreground and the National Capitol on the distant left. "The dedication of this Gallery to a living past and to a greater and more richly living future," said President Franklin Delano Roosevelt in 1941, "is the measure of the earnestness of our intention that the freedom of the human spirit shall go on too."

zones, and the ductwork for some of these, as seen in the basement, has all the complexity and grace of a cloverleaf highway crossing. Air in the gallery is changed six times an hour. On entering, the so-called "fresh air" (a poor thing compared to what finally goes into the galleries) is filtered through paper, preheated if cold, given moisture or robbed of it to achieve the proper degree of humidity, brought to the desired temperature, and delivered to the rooms. In addition practically all city air contains sulphur dioxide, an enemy of oil paintings, and this gas is neutralized by an alkaline spray, finely atomized, in each airconditioning plant, and never reaches the rooms.

Down in the basement, a large Diesel engine stands idle. Beneath the water-tight basement floor the site is practically a series of sumps, open to surface water and to the nearby Potomac when it is on a rampage. Electrically driven pumps in a series take out of these sumps what water may collect, but in a flood or if the city's electric power were disabled, the Diesel automatically would go to work behind them.

On viewing the gallery from the street, with its three-blocks length, it is a shock to be told that the building is held up by friction. Three hundred carloads of Tennessee marble went into its exterior walls alone, aside from the brick, concrete, tile, and steel that form its floor slabs, wall backing, and internal structure. Sixty-eight [41] hundred piles—pointed steel shells deeply driven and then filled with concrete—provide a frictional resistance with the soil that takes the place of foundation walls to bedrock. . . .

New methods of cutting stone were devised. In the two large garden courts, 32 columns of buff limestone support the glass superstructure. Each 24-foot shaft was cut from a single block weighing 40 tons, and turned to the precise taper desired, in a giant lathe. Sixty blocks were quarried and seasoned, to make sure of the 32 needed, and to one master mechanic was entrusted the lathe work.

Inside, the materials used cover a wide range. Quarries in Alabama, Vermont, Indiana, Tennessee, Missouri, contributed of their best; France was drawn upon; and from high up on Italy's west coast, 120 great ten-ton blocks of boldly figured dark green marble were put aboard ship just before war would have prevented. Oak, pine, mahogany, maple, teak, formed paneling and flooring; damask and other fabrics were specially woven to prevent sagging when stretched as wall backgrounds. Many of the individual galleries have unusually large wall areas of paneling; to avoid cracks, the wood is seven-ply veneer; to make possible the redivision of a wall, the background wood is one continuous sheet, and on this the stiles, rails and moldings may be rearranged at will.

Protection is provided through an extensive organization of watchmen and guards, connected through a control desk with fire, police, telegraph, and District of Columbia administration offices. Great bronze doors guarding the portals, each leaf of a pair weighing six tons, can be closed instantly by electricity....

Few of the thousands of daily visitors will see any of this mechanical ingenuity. That is as it should be, for all the ingenuity of the builders has been directed to creating a fitting background for great art, a background no more obtrusive than the clean air one breathes within these quiet rooms.[42]

ROYAL CORTISSOZ

Notes on Our New National Gallery

Royal Cortissoz, "Notes on Our New National Gallery," New York Herald Tribune (October 22, 1939), Section VI.*

During a recent visit to Washington I had the opportunity to make a survey, inside and out, of the new National Gallery presented to the country, with his collection, by the late Andrew W. Mellon. Construction is so far advanced that the exterior is virtually completed and the interior is a hive of industry which augurs well for the public opening in the early autumn of 1940. The huge building—measuring 785 feet in length—is a noble structure, proudly refuting the modernistic view that the classical tradition is played out. That tradition can never decline when it is handled by a man of genius, and that is what John Russell Pope was. He followed McKim as a major exponent of the grand style. He knew how to be majestic in architecture. His Scottish Rite Temple, also in Washington, long ago showed that. But he knew how to temper majesty with grace, with something that might almost be called elegance, and he designed the National Gallery in a singularly fine spirit. Dealing with mass, he saw to the perfect adjustment of proportions, so that the mass is not heavy, and then he relieved the imposing character of his great walls by a judicious play of line in the mouldings, in the beautiful cornice, and in the pillared portico on the Mall, which rises to a low pediment, in turn having for its background a dome that is again

* Reprinted with the permission of *The New York Herald Tribune*.

The National Gallery of Art, 1938-1941, Washington, D. C.; the main entrance on the Constitution Avenue side. An Ionic Order supports the entablature and pediment. "The expression of purpose is as little evident on the exterior as on the interior," wrote Joseph Hudnut in his criticism of the building. "Where no form exists in the interior it is scarcely possible to establish that conformity of outward aspect and inward purpose which is the first essential of a genuine architecture."

kept well in hand. The building has a vitalized unity, and its austere simplicity is somehow made doubly sympathetic by the pinkish glow of its Tennessee marble investiture. One is aware of beauty of color as well as of beauty of form. In every element of the design there is evident Pope's unerring taste. There is no teasing of the walls with decorative expedients. He preferred blind windows to niches for statues, and the few wreaths in the upper reaches of the walls are in the lowest possible relief. The cornice is as modest as it is beautiful, ideal to one who happens to be, like myself, a lover of good cornices.

Pope's art, indeed, was one of extreme delicacy, but what gave him peculiarly high rank in his profession was his essential strength, his power, his instinct for grandeur. It was not for nothing that he was an alumnus (the first) of the American Academy in Rome, early absorbed the lessons of the city's monumental buildings, and was, into the bargain, a disciple of McKim's. The sheer power they both possessed comes out in the portico aforementioned, in the prodigious scale of the rotunda, with its encircling march of heroic columns, and in the two garden courts, where columnar dignity is to be lightened by plants, shrubs and glittering fountains. The rotunda especially, in which the pillars made plain by the model are at present sheathed to avoid possible damage, has in abounding measure that majesty to which I have alluded. It is as impressive as the Pantheon, spacious and lofty, truly monumental. Yet as I use that last word I am impelled quickly to add again that Pope could magically blend the grand style with a very gracious touch. The rotunda is monumental, yes; so are the garden courts and so, in a lesser degree, is the central corridor. But when he came to the framing of his plan this resourceful architect recognized the necessity of providing galleries on a comparatively small scale. I stood in one of them, temporarily painted and supplied with its skylight for experimental purposes of illumination, coloring and so on. It could not have been more than thirty feet long, and it was not quite as wide. A single picture on one of the walls gave an idea of the ease and effectiveness with which the exhibits will be observed. In the upshot the building will be filled with really intimate rooms, fit places in which to study and enjoy the works of art they are to contain. The ceilings, I must also mention, are not too high, and I may note in passing that, having regard to the summer heat in Washington, the building will be air-conditioned throughout. Altogether, the impression I received was of a museum uniquely designed to house great treasures. . . .[8]

KENNETH G. CRAWFORD

Andy Mellon's National Gallery Is About to Open . . . And Critics Are Beginning to Look the Expensive Gift Horse in the Mouth

Kenneth G. Crawford, "The 55th Column," PM, March 4, 1941.

Washington, March 4. . . . The reason Mr. Mellon's memory deserves tolerant handling right now is that his friends and executors are about to open the $15,000,000 National Gallery, his gift to the nation. Already the experts are looking this gift horse in the mouth through microscopes. They are saying ungrateful things about it—that the late John Russell Pope's building isn't good classic in an age when classic is inexcusable even if it is good; that the late Lord Duveen, eminent art dealer, unloaded some phonies on Mr. Mellon, and that the whole conception of a National Gallery dedicated to the glory of art's dead past, rather than its living present and unknown future, is mistaken. . . .

Every one seems agreed that the Mellon and Kress collections, as well as the Widener collection, which will be installed later, contains some of the world's finest paintings. Everyone concedes, too, that Mr. Pope's plant is an improvement on the Louvre and probably the best picture arcade in the world. What the faultfinders are saying, in effect, is:

"It's art, but is it pretty?"

They insist that the building is incongruous in its time-place and that many of the old canvases are hidden behind so many coats of varnish that they've lost their value except as expensive curios.

Moreover, some persons, gross New Dealers at heart—are going so far as to say that the $50,000,000 Mr. Mellon is supposed to have spent on his pictures and the $15,000,000 he laid out for the building might have been used to better advantage providing airier garrets for living artists. (The National Gallery will buy only the works of the honored dead.)

All these questions will be subjected to querulous debate in the art journals, I have no doubt. . . .[12]

ARTHUR UPHAM POPE AND KENNETH G. CRAWFORD

Letters to and from the Editor of PM

"Letters to and from the Editor," PM (April 16, 1941).*

Dear Editor:

PM's reporters of the Washington National Gallery dedication treated a noble and significant occasion rather flippantly, apparently victimized by a propaganda campaign which is still struggling, with 20-year-old cliches, to deride established values in art.

Mr. Kenneth Crawford, able and brilliant as he is, was taken for an intellectual ride by anonymous "experts" whose credentials he evidently forgot to examine. He quotes them as saying:

"The late Lord Duveen, eminent art dealer, unloaded some phonies on Mr. Mellon." This charge is serious for it accuses Lord Duveen, the world's greatest art dealer, of being either a scoundrel or an ignoramus, and Mr. Mellon, as well as the many eminent specialists who have studied and approved his paintings, of being dupes. Will Mr. Crawford designate the assertedly fraudulent Mellon pictures, name the critics making these charges, and provide us with summaries of their evidence? Or are these the familiar hit-and-run attacks of smart-alecks seeking to fortify their own self-esteem, challenged by a great occasion. . . .

* Reprinted by permission of Dr. Arthur Upham Pope.

Mr. Crawford. . .—or the "experts" speaking through . . . [him, is] equally haphazard and contemptuous of the building itself.

"It's not good classic," complains Mr. Crawford.

It doesn't pretend to be strictly a classic building, but it is one of the most movingly beautiful buildings in the country and perfectly adapted to its purpose; and it is classic in purity of outline, lucid and harmonious proportions and perfection of detail. Mr. Crawford says in our age the "classic is inexcusable even if it is good." More dogma and more nonsense, a complete failure to understand the relation of the past to the present, an echo of the Cafe Montparnasse chatter of some 30 years ago when Clive Bell (now repentant) was urging the destruction of all extant works of art between the Ravenna mosaics and Cezanne. His imitators today frequently advocate the closing of all museums, these fountain sources of enlightenment and happiness for millions.

Mr. Crawford, or his anonymous advisers, protests the dedication of the building to "the glory of art's dead past, rather than its living present and unknown future." Both recommendations spring from a quite superficial notion that "our age" (dates please) must discard the past and find wholly new modes of expressing itself—something that no great age in art ever did or could do. But what is the living present? How long does it last? The flash of an electric spark and the geological present which covers several hundred thousands of years can both be called the present. Since when was the art of the past dead? Our language, literature, jurisprudence, science, all of the practical arts, institutions and traditions which sustain the present are from the living past which never dies. Neither Pericles' funeral oration nor the Gettysburg address is dead, nor is the Parthenon or Saint Paul's, both of which are today sources of inspiration for heroic achievements. The very means of expression are given from the past and are based on fundamental and formative factors in our experience, for some of which time is meaningless.

Some of the derision of the past comes from bored sophisticates, but more from incompetents who haven't had the modesty or wit to learn from it nor the industry to master a craft and hence find it easier to substitute exhibitionism and noisy verbalism for sound achievement. Some of these so-called "experts" imitate the Nazi tactics of shocking and extravagant opinions, apparently on the ground that sheer audacity will get them a hearing. The Nazis burn books. Many modernists condemn with similar violence basic and indispensable documents in the history of culture.

Perhaps they are uncomfortable in this reserved and stately building and the intense and noble art that it honors, feeling in its dignity, poise and fine breeding a rebuke to egotism and complacency. At least it is a most dangerous challenge to their theories.

To deny that the "experts" quoted by Mr. Crawford have any authority or said anything useful is not to deny the necessity of continuous advance in the world of art. Ruskin's dictum, "invent or die," was a profound truth but useful inventions do not emerge from vacuums. Many who have tried to invent without knowledge, experience, discipline, or any tested groundwork of values, are busy mumbling in our insane asylums while the less eccentric, the shockers and the charlatans, end up in neglect for which they and their friends shrilly blame the wicked and stupid public. The great inventors—Bach, Beethoven, Phidias, Michaelangelo and Giotto—yes, even Cezanne himself, and all the other heroes that have built the resplendant palace of art have labored mightily in the vineyard of the past from which they drew their nourishment and their inspiration. In the new National Gallery these splendors are gathered in a noble setting. They are a record of man's great adventure in civilization, a consolation and an inspiration to the present, guide and promise for the future.

New York   Arthur Upham Pope

I find it almost impossible to question the judgment of anyone whose appraisal of me is as accurate as Mr. Pope's. But I must insist that Lord Duveen's fallibility has long since been proved (see his testimony under cross-examination in the Mellon tax case). Also that steel and glass have left us small excuse for copying Greek architecture. As to the importance of the gallery and its collection, I do not disagree with Mr. Pope. Perhaps I should stick to politics.

Kenneth G. Crawford [2]

FRANKLIN DELANO ROOSEVELT

Address at the Dedication of the National Gallery of Art

Address by President Franklin Delano Roosevelt at the Dedication of the National Gallery of Art. *The New York Times* (March 18, 1941).

It is with a very real sense of satisfaction that I accept for the people of the United States and on their behalf this National Gallery and the collections it contains. The giver of the building has matched the richness of his gift with the modesty of his spirit, stipulating that the gallery shall be known not by his name but by the nation's.

And those other collectors of paintings and of sculpture who have already joined, or who propose to join, their works of art to Mr. Mellon's—Mr. Kress and Mr. Widener—have felt the same desire to establish not a memorial to themselves but a monument to the art that they love and the country to which they belong. . . .

There have been, in the past, many gifts of great paintings and of famous works of art to the American people. Most of the wealthy men of the last century who bought, for their own satisfaction, the masterpieces of European collections ended by presenting their purchases to their cities or to their towns. . . .

But though there have been many public gifts of art in the past, the gift of this National Gallery, dedicated to the entire nation and containing a considerable part of the most important work brought to this country from the continent of Europe, has necessarily a new significance. I think—I think it signifies a relation—a new relation here made visible in paint and in stone—between the whole people of this country and the old inherited tradition of the arts.

And we shall remember that these halls of beauty, the conception of a great American architect, John Russell Pope, combine the classicism of the past with the convenience of today.

In accepting this building and the paintings and other art it contains, the people of the United States accept a part in that inheritance for themselves. They accept it for themselves not because this gallery is given to them—though they are thankful for the gift. They accept it for themselves because, in the past few years, they have come to understand that the inheritance is theirs and that, like other inheritors of other things of value, they have a duty toward it.

Discovery by the People

. . . The people of this country know now, whatever they were taught or thought they knew before, that art is not something just to be owned, but something to be made: that it is the act of making and not the act of owning which is art. And knowing this they know also that art is not a treasure in the past or an importation from another country, but part of the present life of all the living and creating peoples—all who make and build; and, most of all, the young and vigorous people who have made and built our present wide country.

Symbols of Human Spirit

It is for this reason that the people of America accept the inheritance of these ancient arts. Whatever these paintings may have been to men who looked at them a generation back—today they are not only works of art. Today they are the symbols of the human spirit—symbols of the world the freedom of the human spirit has made, and, incidentally, a world against which armies now are raised and countries overrun and men imprisoned and their work destroyed.

To accept, today, the work of German painters such as Holbein and Durer, and of Italians like Botticelli and Raphael, and of painters of the low countries like Van Dyck and Rembrandt, and of famous Frenchmen, famous Spaniards—to accept this work today on behalf of the people of this democratic nation is to assert the belief of the people of this democratic nation in a human spirit which now is everywhere endangered and which, in many countries where it first found form and meaning, has been rooted out and broken and destroyed.

To accept this work today is to assert the purpose of the people of America that the freedom of the human spirit and human mind—which has produced the world's great art and all its science—shall not be utterly destroyed.

Words of Lincoln Cited

Seventy-eight years ago, in the third year of the war between the States, men and women gathered here in the capital of a divided nation, here in Washington, to see the dome above the Capitol completed, to see the bronze goddess of liberty set upon its top.

It had been an expensive, a laborious business, diverting money and labor from the prosecution of the war and certain critics—for there were critics in 1863—certain critics found much to criticize. There were new marble pillars in the Senate wing of the Capitol, there was a bronze door for the central portal and other such expenditures and embellishments. But the President of the United States, whose name was Lincoln, when he heard those criticisms, answered: "If people see the Capitol going on it is a sign that we intend this Union shall go on."

We may borrow the words for our own. We, too, intend the Union to go on. We intend it shall go on, carrying with it the great tradition of the human spirit which created it.

The dedication of this gallery to a living past and to a greater and more richly living future is the measure of the earnestness of our intention that the freedom of the human spirit shall go on too.[8]

ANNE O'HARE McCORMICK

Europe. Washington Turns from War to Europe of National Gallery

Anne O'Hare McCormick, "Europe. Washington Turns from War to Europe of National Gallery," *The New York Times* (March 22, 1941).*

Certainly no one timed the opening of our first National Gallery of Art for the moment when the American people face, for the first time consciously, the greatest crisis in their history. To dip even superficially into the cross-currents and contradictions of the American mind these days is to realize that the passage of the lease-lend bill and the President's speech last Saturday awakened the country to a sense of danger people in general did not feel before. The sense of emergency quickens throughout the land. With the full recognition of our involvement and our explicit commitment to a British victory the reality of war has been brought very near. . . .

There is confusion. Underneath the excitement of speed-up and action run dark backwaters of uncertainty. The course is set, but the oracles are silent; nobody can see the end of the road ahead. It is a strange moment for opening a national museum of art. Yet what event could be better timed to meet and counteract the despair with which civilized peoples contemplate the savagery of war?

Washington's new museum is perhaps the most beautiful gallery of art in the world. From the magnificent rotunda in the middle every vista is serene and noble. The paintings and sculptures collected in rooms as calm and luminous as a Vermeer interior are only in a few instances the masterpieces of the artists who produced them. In a dozen vast galleries, including the

* Reprinted by permission of *The New York Times*.

The National Gallery of Art, 1938-1941, Washington, D. C.; the Rotunda
and central fountain. The bronze statue of Mercury by the Italian
Renaissance sculptor, Giovanni da Bologna, adorns the marble basin.

Metropolitan, there are more and greater single works of genius. But nowhere else are they shown in this clear daylight, and the effect of color in the Alba Madonna, for instance, and in the Raphael portrait of Bindo Altoviti on the opposite wall, is so dazzling that you perceive that you have been looking all your life at the dim shadows of pictures. Though you are familiar with many of the canvases in the glorious parade of the Italian schools, you find that you have never really seen them before. The Rembrandts glow with an astonishing luster.

BEAUTY THAT ENDURES

But the gallery itself, incomparable as it is, the collection itself, splendid as it is, are less impressive than the effect they produce on the visitors. Every day this week the rooms have been crowded. . . . It is quiet, contemplative life, an oasis of lucidity and tranquillity in the fog of Washington. Almost an oasis of happiness; not for years has this observer seen so many happy faces as those who looked upon Desiderio da Settignano's "Bust of a Little Boy"—the eternal little boy, still touching and expectant after the wars of nearly half a dozen centuries.

Andrew Mellon's Medicean gesture in giving this museum to the nation may have been a signal that an epoch was ended. Or it may be the beginning of an epoch.

In a way it signalizes our maturity as strikingly as the heavy sense of world responsibility that begins to oppress the American people.

The folly and the glory of man meet at the door where one turns from the picture of war to the masterpieces of human genius, and one knows that they represent the Italy, the Germany, the England and the America that endures. One knows, too, that no people can enjoy the increment of civilization without bearing the common burden and paying the price of maintaining its values. "I feel cleansed and steadied," said a well-known sculptor leaving the gallery the other day. "Now I know it's worth fighting for."[14]

THE ARCHITECTS' JOURNAL

Flashback

"Flashback," *The Architects' Journal*, XCIII (June 5, 1941).*

On the following pages the *Journal* illustrates a building which it believes will very soon take a prominent place in the history of architecture: it believes that the United States National Gallery of Art, accepted on behalf of the nation by President Roosevelt on March 17 this year, will within a decade be regarded as the apotheosis, and the end, of an architectural outlook and endeavour which have had immense influence in this country, as in the U.S.A., for nearly 75 years. It believes that the architects of both countries will realize that along this road one can go no further.

The National Gallery of Art represents perfection in Neo-classical design in the Grand Manner, so far as an ideal site, unlimited money, the highest possible skill and unlimited care by some of the best craftsmen in the world, can achieve perfection. Its plan in balance, axis and vista is the perfect Beaux Arts plan; its external massing has the subordination and symmetry of Neo-classicism at its best; its detail—as might be expected—is superb. Other architects, handicapped by worse sites, limited means and worse craftsmanship, may claim in future that their Neo-classic designs have greater æsthetic merit. It is doubtful if the world will admit their claim: the National Gallery of Art observes all the definite rules of a rigid school of design. Once these rules begin to be broken in structure or plan Neo-Classicism breaks down and becomes increasingly an anachronistic veneer on the face of a building which cannot conform to Neo-Classic rules in all that really matters.

If, therefore, the National Gallery of Art seems insipid, even

* Reprinted with the permission of *The Architects' Journal*.

lifeless, it is because time has carried architects past Neo-Classic and nothing will ever bring it to life again. The architects who succeeded John Russell Pope seem to have feared this charge of insipidity for they published this apologia before the building was opened:

"The National Gallery has been designed with the aim of achieving harmony with neighbouring buildings, and making it a worthy element in the L'Enfant conception and plan of 1901 for the City of Washington. In the inception of the design and in the later execution of details, the architects have felt it proper to keep constantly in mind the belief of both Washington and Jefferson that the style of architecture for the Capitol City should not depart, under any temporary pressure of vacillating ideas, from the original broad base of the Classic. There will undoubtedly be voices raised in protest that the design is not in the spirit of a 1941 broadcasting station, or the latest steel-frame office building—something specifically representative of our day. If contemporary thought alone were permitted to determine the architectural style, the building might have been Richardson Romanesque, French Renaissance, Art Nouveau or Venetian Gothic, according to the year in which it was conceived. The National Gallery is built in the thought that it may serve its purpose for many centuries. America's finest architectural traditions—those of which the vast majority of Americans never tire—have seemed to the architects the one straight beam of light pointing the way through an epoch strongly marked by perplexity and irresolution. Time and the leisurely judgment of the American people will eventually decide whether that light has suddenly become a will o' the wisp."

To British architects, in the midst of war building problems, the National Gallery cannot but have an appearance of fantasy. Built almost wholly of marble at a cost of over 3½ million pounds, encased in solid marble of graded pink of which only about a sixth of that quarried was actually used, the Gallery must seem to British architects to belong to a world that is past. They will be glad that it has been built, glad that it is America that has built it. But they will feel that in achieving the *ne plus ultra* of Neo-Classicism, the National Gallery has also achieved contemporary architecture's greatest FLASHBACK.[370]

JOSEPH HUDNUT

Architecture and the Spirit of Man

Joseph Hudnut, *Architecture and the Spirit of Man* (Cambridge, Harvard University Press, 1949).*

THE LAST OF THE ROMANS

Ever since Thomas Jefferson, in 1785, sent from France his model of the *Maison Carrée*, we have been trying to create an American architecture by the imitation of European masterpieces. Today, after ten thousand experiments, the futility of this process is not yet amply demonstrated; one more effort was needed, it appears, if only to prove the hardiness of the neo-classic thesis. The National Gallery of Art combines again the portico of the Temple of Diana and the dome of the Pantheon.

Winckelmann, who invented the Greeks, invented also the idea of a beauty untouched by time and place. When he had abstracted from the lush Apollo Belvedere and the rounded Niobe that world of "noble simplicity and tempered wisdom" which he called antiquity, architects, imitating this imitator of imitations, abstracted from the gorgeous Parthenon their white and absolute temples—and made these the pure symbols of the most turbulent and scandalous of nations. The theory of a universal architecture, of an ideal beauty composed of column, arch, and dome, a beauty realized once for all by the Greeks and Romans, was thus offered to the triumphant rationalism of our young republic. Jefferson, the American exponent of France, a builder of constitutions, as ready to follow up his deductions in art as in politics, found no difficulty in accepting an architecture which could be proved to be beautiful by the syllogisms of authorities.

* Reprinted by permission of Harvard University Press, copyright, 1949, by the President and Fellows of Harvard College.

An international style, based upon the study of the antique—generalized, documented, unweighted by reality, the [49] work of aesthetes rather than of builders—became the *American style*.

Since Jefferson's day the idea has undergone periodic reconstructions. Like the Greeks of Winckelmann it preserves in spite of the assaults of common sense an eternal youth. Each generation returns to it in one form or another. Beauty in architecture is perennially reëstablished as a harmony of absolute forms accessible to the intelligence and embodied in the Roman masterpieces. No relation to time or place is necessary, no reference to humanity in forms thus emptied of purpose. The columns which clothe with dignity the home of the Supreme Court will do quite as well for the Archives Building or the Temple of the Scottish Rite; the dome of the Pantheon is as serviceable for a university library, a railroad station, or the pillared churches of the Christian Scientists. These suffer differences in arrangement, not in response to use or structure, but in accordance rather with the rules of a game intelligible only to the players—the peculiar solace of architects in a world too uncomfortably transformed by the cumulated successes of science.

I can understand the seduction which such a theology of architecture exercises over the minds of those prepared for it by that discipline in irrelevancies which, until recently, went by the name of architectural education; but I have never been able to explain its hold upon the imaginations of the rich and the great of our day. That men who have participated as leaders in the rise of American industry, who have shared its magnificent upward progress, its ceaseless and inexhaustible ferment, should turn for expression to the pale temples of an imaginary Greece is, I think, one of the strangest phenomena in the psychology of idealism. I should suppose—unless indeed, as some believe, our ideals are necessarily our complementary opposites—that such men more than any others would wish (to borrow a phrase from the *Poetics*) to attain and make evident in art that form towards [50] which their own age—the age they have created—is moving. Is it not reasonable to assume that when after a lifetime of effort and success they felt at length the need of a monument, they would wish to continue into whatever constructed forms they might essay at least some aspect of that world of which their own lives had formed so plenary a part? I can guess at the mind of Jefferson, "violently smitten with the Hotel de Salm," to whom the temple was both discovery and adventure, but I cannot explain the complacency of the Virginia legislators, willing to compress their explosive energies in that tight little box which the American ambassador sent them from Paris. I think that I can catch some hint at least of the mind of McKim and share the delight which must have been his when he arranged the peristyled terminal of the Pennsylvania Railroad; but the mind of the Pennsylvania Railroad is beyond my reach. The railroad, I think, could have had no secret joy in neoclassic abstractions, still less in pale translations of the garish vaults of Caracalla. Was it prompted, then, by modesty or shame thus to cover its iron bones with the debris of an ancient civilization? Or by a clandestine pleasure in the vision of those unhappy beings who for generations must carry their baggage across those vast unnecessary vistas? And that princely person who crushed the Harvard Yard with the prodigious peristyle and steps of her library: what was there in his life so apposite to the Corinthian mode that he should wish to leave unexpressed, not himself merely, but that America of which he was so characteristic and notable a part?

Of all types of buildings the museum of fine arts has offered the most favourable field for this pious collaboration of wealth and power with the priesthood of the Roman tradition. The museum, born in a palace, nevertheless built its first homes—in Munich, Berlin, London—out of the pages of antiquarians; and from that day to this its blank walls, its static functions,[51] its learned and leisured attributes have invited the attention of classicists, impatient even of windows. We know, for example, with what intransigeance these have exercised their art upon the Metropolitan Museum of New York: the preface of mighty steps, arches, and columns; the terror-inspiring vestibule; and then the interminable stairway which, I am sure, leads like those of the Mayan and Cambodian temples to some gruesome sacrificial platform. The architect of the Brooklyn Museum wept when the director, insensitive to the dignity of exterior steps, removed these and admitted the public directly to his exhibits; and Philadelphia, which always thinks in superlatives, has pedestaled its

The National Gallery of Art, 1938-1941, Washington, D. C.; the hall of
sculpture with its balance of spaciousness and repose. Over each of
the side doors, a cornice held by consoles; over end door, which is set
in a blind arch, a pediment resting on **consoles.**

museum upon a mountain at the base of which not one but three mighty flights challenge the knees of the hardy visitor, his soul being kindled by as many porticoes.

Forty granite steps of majestic width lead up from the Mall to the main entrance of the National Gallery of Art. They are placed there, not to be used, but to be admired. They are there in accordance with the rules of the game "for their own sake." A mighty portico crowns these steps: that too exists for its own sake, as does also the stupendous doorway, disdainful of human ants. For their own sake the great *vérde* columns of the central rotunda appear to sustain the weight of an angle-iron Pantheon and sumptuously cage the blithe little Mercury of Giovanni da Bologna. For their own sake were built the huge vaults, plaster on metal lathe, covering the nave-like corridors which lead right and left to the girder-supported gardens which nurture, not trees, but columns.

The columns, for their own sake, support nothing. Across the wide spaces which separate art and reality a sacred forest invites at every step the astonishment of the visitor, seducing him with expense and weight, crushing him under its firm assertion of authority. All of which adds nothing of delight or value to the objects exhibited: nothing, that is to say, which could not [52] have been added simply, directly, unpretentiously, at one fourth of the cost.

What is a museum? Surely not an opportunity merely for the virtuosity of architects. A box, then, for the display of curiosities and susceptible therefore of rich encrustations? A theater built for our entertainment and therefore congenial to the flattery of bronze and marble? Perhaps an apparatus of the schoolmasters, to be made less tedious by a coating of gilt? Those who think thus have never known a museum or felt the genuine magic that a museum may enfold. What is a museum? An invitation to a voyage; a window opening on the music of other times and of other spirits; a *means* always, never an *end*. The beauty conserved and guarded in the National Gallery of Art is made less, not more, accessible by this clamorous prelude; nor does the high language of neoclassicism assist in any way the quiet happiness to which that beauty entreats us.

Museums of art, although addressed as a rule to the use of other generations no less than to our own, are yet serviceable buildings. The source of whatever dignity they may attain is service, the inevitable source of all dignity in architecture. I mean, of course, not practical service merely—although that is included—but also whatever service architecture may render the spirit of man. I know of no one who would approve a stark utilitarian building on the Washington Mall; still less an undistinguished building for the collections of the National Gallery of Art. But where has beauty ever been discovered in an architecture which was not a social form, grown out of social needs? It is that which the temple itself teaches us and which Greece and Rome would teach if we could but see them clearly. This temple reaffirms that lesson even now when it is torn from its setting and made the frontispiece to a museum gallery. If we were not atrophied to the meanings of form we could not bear the dissonance so clearly proclaimed in these opposed shapes.[53]

The trouble is that we are thus atrophied. Because we have been taught that architecture is something embedded in history, that it is somthing precious, imported, and remote, this art which might illumine our lives does not even impinge upon them. In this mist of make-believe we have never experienced architecture. We have never learned to discover the genuine power inherent in useful space and the energies of constructed shapes, or to know nevertheless be developed from, not added on, to these.

Not the tradition of the temple codified in his books, but those facilities in which function is fulfilled—that is to say, the exhibition galleries—should have been the first concern of the architect of this building. That these should be clear, luminous, and peaceful enclosures, arranged in a rational order easily apprehended, is a principle which ought not to have needed a demonstration; nor should it have been necessary to remind the architect that these enclosures, welded into an organized crystal of space, unified by harmonious shapings and rhythmic intervals, by developing and unfolding sequences, should form the heart of his pattern. Yet we have in the exhibition rooms of the National Gallery neither order nor sequence other than the primitive order of the *enfilade*. The areas left over at the edges of the grandiose center are partitioned into *salles carrées* as if these were slices cut from a cake. Casual in the extreme is their relationship to the pomp and circumstance which they surround.

The expression of purpose is as little evident on the exterior as on the interior. Where no form exists in the interior it is scarcely possible to establish that conformity of outward aspect and inward purpose which is the first essential of a genuine architecture. Nevertheless, if the long wings had expressed even the rabbit warren that is inside them, they would have been more evocative than in their present role as the awkward accessories [54] of a temple. They would have then our respect if only by a blunt truthfulness: all the more so if the steel framework could have been set free from the oppression of the heavy masonry forms which deny the true nature of its lithe energies. I think that an architect must be somewhat naïve who supposes that the public will find in massive windowless walls of marble an expression of the conserving and guarding function of a museum. The public is not so innocent as to have failed to guess at the steel fabric which these mask or to know that the building will endure only so long as this endures. And those heavy interior partitions which appear to support arches of such a prodigious width and weight: that visitor is incurious indeed who is not aware of the hollow pipes and conduits with which these are stuffed. What is there so shameful about steel? Or about those felicitous mechanisms threaded through this structure which bring to every corner clean air, even temperature, security from moisture and accident? Are not these the true conservators and guardians? I understood the pride of the engineer who showed me in the attic the superb structure of his roofs and in the basement the miracles of his machines, and I marveled that an architect could ignore elements of expression so evocative. By this I do not mean, of course, that pipes and conduits should be everywhere visible, but only that their presence should be confessed—that the fabric of our building should be illumined by the wonder of our mechanical progress. But there is no precedent for that, I suppose, in the Parthenon.

It is said that we are bound to this dissimulation by the conditions of our site. There is a "prevailing style" in Washington to which architecture is chained; our fathers cast the expanding organism of the government in this iron mold and that mold must not be shattered. What then is the prevailing style? Two thousand years separate the Egyptian monument of Washington from the Doric temple of Lincoln; and seven hundred years more lie [55] between Lincoln and the imperial symbol which quaintly canopies Thomas Jefferson; and a span of another sixteen hundred years lies between Jefferson and the Georgian White House. There are nine different styles of architecture in the Triangle; nineteen face the Mall from the Folger Library to the heights of Arlington; and the National Gallery itself is compounded of at least three.

Nor is the character of this building imposed upon us, as is so often said, by any sanction discoverable in the magnanimous plan of L'Enfant. The garden forms of L'Enfant—a Mall surrounded by planted areas—were never intended to be crowded with structures so vast as to defeat a parklike quality in the ensemble; nor did his scheme admit any building so grandiose as to challenge the supremacy of the Capitol. Garden and city were to be parts of a single design; and no greater reproach can be made to the National Gallery of Art than the evident fact that not only does it shatter the balance and scale proposed by L'Enfant but also that it blocks forever one of the avenues which might have assisted the unity of the central garden form and the vaster dimensions of the growing city.

A cold invigorating wind is blowing these days over our national architecture. A new temper, impatient of make-believe, of professional hocus-pocus, of an art existing "for its own sake," is everywhere felt. I find, I hope not entirely as a consequence of wishful thinking, some hints of a coming change in the buildings built for the use of our government; and that change is foreshadowed by our judgments of buildings already built. People seem to admire less fervently such aberrations as the Archives Building; a strange silence even now surrounds the Jefferson Memorial. Architectures are born sometimes from that concord of spiritual experience which is engendered by crises faced and collectively overcome. Surely the time cannot be far distant when we shall find the means to open this city of Washington,[56] symbol and temple of the nation, to the rekindled soul of America.

Yesterday, when I passed the mighty steps of the National Gallery of Art, I thought that I could discern over its doorway the inscription, dim but growing slowly distinct: ULTIMUS ROMANORUM.[57]

LORIMER RICH

A Study in Contrasts

Lorimer Rich, "A Study in Contrasts," *Progressive Architecture*, XXII (August, 1941).*

We have more than a passing interest in Washington, its buildings, its monuments, and its great Mall scheme extending from the Capitol to the Washington Monument, the Lincoln Memorial and beyond. We have seen this mighty dream gradually unfold during the past forty years. It is thrilling and we are proud of it. The development of Washington is the one project that claims the common interest of all American architects. It is therefore natural that we should be concerned about all the elements that compose it, past, present and future.

To be commissioned to design buildings of this type is a great privilege and a great responsibility. These are the top honors in our profession. It is for opportunities such as these that architects strive. To design a successful building on the Mall in Washington carries with it the golden crown of achievement. Such buildings should have a real and beneficial effect upon American Architecture.[497]

. . . The National Gallery is impressive. Here is a marble building nearly eight hundred feet long; as long as the Capitol. It stands in a superb setting. The cornices and columns are all in accordance with the best classical precedent. The composition and mass are good. The workmanship and materials are of the best. The building conforms to accepted standards of design of the past 50 years and yet it does not seem alive, vital, and

* Reprinted with the permission of *Progressive Architecture*.

organic. Examine the Lincoln Memorial—each column, each bit or ornament, each block of stone is a vital and important part. Take one of them away and it falls apart. The National Gallery on the other hand seems loaded with surface decoration. It is a panorama of pilasters, double pilasters, breaks, panels, blank windows, and belt courses. Most of the vocabulary of neo-classic architecture has been assembled on this one building. One receives the impression that the budget was too liberal and the draftsmanship too perfect. Sophisticated delineation may have devoured intended simplicity and force. How else can one explain a main angle of the building and cornice making five separate breaks in turning its corner.

The interior is magnificent in its spaciousness and its materials. The detail is correct; the exhibits are well-lighted. Yet the same lifeless feeling that impresses you about the exterior has somehow invaded the interior. It is all too reminiscent of the old Metropolitan Museum and has the same air of yesterday. We have suddenly moved past such grand treatment of space and we desire that the architecture of our galleries be more subordinated to the exhibits. Here we are too conscious of gridironed ceiling lights, cornices, coves, and door trim. These elements all assail us and detract from the pictures. The Museum of Modern Art and recently remodeled picture galleries of the Metropolitan have shown us that a gallery can be simple, low, and visually quiet—and that the pictures themselves *gain* with such a background. There seems to be in the National Gallery continual strife between the architecture and the exhibits; so the visitor comes away impressed with the monumental character of the building but somewhat defeated in his effort to enjoy fine masterpieces to the utmost.[499]

. . . Public buildings stand for years and they must look well and wear well over a considerable period of time. A building that is too stylish is dated and may soon seem out of style. I like public architectural progress in less violent form. Perhaps that is impossible. . . .

. . . To my mind no single building can menace the Mall composition. This composition is really the splendid rows of trees—four deep—which will gradually attain a height of eighty or more feet. It is the great greensward spreading from the Capitol to

the Washington Monument and flanked by these trees that is
the backbone of the whole composition. Individual buildings, no
matter what their design, are powerless to menace this tremendous conception. As time goes on, the great trees will keep
all the buildings in a subordinate position. I see the buildings on
the Mall standing as milestones in our architectural development
and ever improving in character and style. I see them through the
trunks and foliage—all brought into harmony by the great elms,
the real guardians of the Mall.[500]

3

THE UNITED NATIONS BUILDINGS
New York City, 1947-1952

THE SECRETARY-GENERAL OF THE UNITED NATIONS

Report to the General Assembly of the United Nations on the Permanent Headquarters of the United Nations

Report to the General Assembly of the United Nations by the Secretary-General on the Permanent Headquarters of the United Nations (United Nations, Lake Success, New York, United Nations Publications, July, 1947).

Architecture that is worthy of the name can not be classified as either utilitarian or monumental. Every human gesture, all human action, is a symphonic rendering of a complicated association of ideas. The hiker who carves his walking stick from a hazel branch, the engineer who conceives a bridge or a machine, the architect who builds a shelter or a temple, are engaged in creating a symphony that is dominated by one intellectual goal: to do the work well. And work well done is the blending of the beautiful, the functional, the physical, and the economical; there is not only one need to be satisfied but a series of needs which make themselves felt successively and in a hierarchic order. The aesthetic need is as imperative as the most objective material needs. The lyrical is a human function of the same order as walking or breathing. We cannot, therefore, admit the possibility of a choice between a crassly utilitarian architecture and a hollowly monumental architecture.

In the final analysis architecture is a visual event, something to be seen within and without. But it is also to be lived in, and is made of real objects—organs—which are co-ordinated into an organism. . . .

On the headquarters site of the United Nations in the spaciousness afforded by the East River, will rise contrasting architectural masses—the General Assembly Hall, the low-lying meeting halls, the verticality of the Secretariat Building. Among these salient elements of the architectural composition, a harmony of proportion is to be created. Rarely has such an opportunity been presented to bring into a harmonious whole masses of such significance and on such an imposing scale; to establish, after a century of mounting urban disorder, a landmark of order in the heart of a great city.[74]

GERTRUDE SAMUELS

What Kind of Capitol for the U. N.?

Gertrude Samuels, "What Kind of Capitol for the U.N.?" *The New York Times Maga-zine* (April 20, 1947).*

THE ARCHITECTS SAY THEY WILL EMPHASIZE THE FUNCTIONS OF THE BUILDINGS, NOT SYMBOLISM

On the twenty-seventh floor of the RKO building of Rockefeller Center is the workroom of a group of men of many nationalities. Their surroundings are commonplace and incomplete, but the men are oblivious of them. They are working hard—and in haste.

It is an immense oblong room. Pushed together in the foreground are three tables with green blotters, white pads and neat

* Reprinted with the permission of Miss Gertrude Samuels.

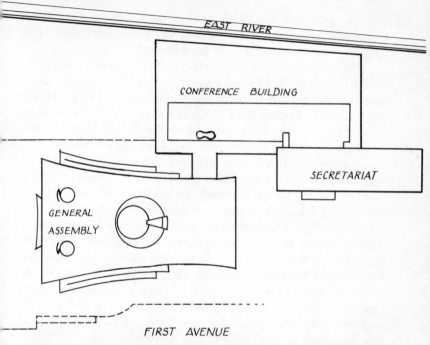

The United Nations, 1947-1953, New York, designed by an international board of architects with Wallace K. Harrison as its chairman. The plan, in contrast to the symmetry typical of the classical, shows the asymmetrical placing of building which is part of the Modern Style.

stacks of yellow pencils; at the windows are several drawing tables. In between are raised tables bearing clay buildings which can be pushed about at will, and a heliodon, a device for showing the sun's apparent motion.

Walls are covered with detailed studies of zoning, blueprints of housing, building conceptions, aerial photographs of a six-block site near the East River, Manhattan. Finally, there are studies of floor space, footage and staff requirements of the unique organization which has drawn on the planner's skills—the United Nations.

These men are the architects and consultants of the Big Five powers and five smaller countries, and this is their "planning and conference room" where they meet daily for two-hour conferences.

For the past few weeks they have been pitting their ideas, experience and philosophies against the greatest building challenge of their careers—the U. N. headquarters.

The emphasis is on early agreement. They will submit their finished plans to the General Assembly as soon as possible. Once the plans are approved, work can begin on the site—an $8,500,000 gift of John D. Rockefeller Jr.—which covers about eighteen acres of land bounded by East River (Franklin D. Roosevelt) Drive, Forty-second Street, First Avenue and Forty-eighth Street.

Tentatively, the design calls for three to four groups of buildings, probably eight buildings in all. The aim is to have a building for the Secretariat ready for occupancy by next March, the General Assembly's home by about August, 1948.

From what is known of the plans, it is possible to forecast what a visitor to U.N. headquarters in 1949 will see: three thirty-five to forty-five-story skyscrapers—one at the south or Forty-second Street end of the site for the staff of the Secretariat, two at the north or Forty-eighth Street end for specialized agencies. He will walk around a newly created park dotted with fountains. He may pause for a critical appraisal before the straight, clean, vertical lines of the Secretariat building, "which will have a conspicuous lack of modernistic scribbling"; wander through the three low chambers of the Councils which flank this structure, or continue to the General Assembly building in the central plaza.

Somewhere along the way he may want to examine the paintings, sculpture, murals and interior decoration or he may head directly for the conference chambers with their glassed-in booths for translators and their radio, press and movie sections. He may want to look over the offices of foreign delegations, the International Labor Organization and World Health Organization in the twin skyscrapers at the north end of the site. He may drop in at the U. N. library or visit the arcade of shops.

But all this is in the future. What keenly interests architects and laymen today is how—or whether—the monumental hopes of the United Nations, pledged to world unity, peace and the worth of the human person, can be reflected in the headquarters.

Of the League of Nations building in Geneva it was written that "to sustain the lasting homage to peace, three qualities were required—the strength of a fortress, the lyric grace of a temple and the stateliness of a palace." Should this new center of international affairs be a symbol of the world's post-war hopes? Can the idea best be reflected in classical architecture, or by combining classical, or "traditional," with modern architecture? Should it, on the contrary, be Cartesian—throwing imitations and tradition overboard and following the modern idiom to reflect confidence in the here-and-now? Or should it be detached from man's high aspirations, and simply be a functional mass drawn to requirements like any new factory or commercial building?

In the popular mind, because of the limitations of the site and because modernists were called in [9] to do the job, the feeling has been that Rockefeller Center with its gaunt, upward sweep, its murals, sculpture and metal-work was perhaps the preview of what to expect from the U.N. designers. The architects agree that the Center is structurally one of the best-planned masses in the world but, they add with grim insistence, "The U.N. will definitely not be like this." Their reasons are many and varied, and appear to go to the heart of the function of new architecture.

In the first place, they have a violent dislike of "building with symbolism." They deplore the idea of starting with a preconceived sketch—as with the one chosen from ten thousand plans entered in the League of Nations competition—and then raising a monument to fit a drawing. The work to be done inside a building, they say, must alone determine the height, arrangement and form of it; character, they argue, will automatically grow out of its perfect working order.

From the purely functional point of view, they agree, U.N. buildings must be prepared to serve the most complex, dynamic civilization in history. Rockefeller Center was started in 1931. As much time has elapsed between 1931 and 1947 as, say, between the Woolworth Building and Rockefeller Center. So why, they ask, should we have it look like anything else when we must plan not only for today but for tomorrow—for an epoch geared psychologically not only to the machine but to atomic energy?

Like the architects of each successive age, they are concerned with beauty—but to achieve beauty, they say, with stone, steel and glass, the design must grow out of the [55] basic, practical problems—in the U.N.'s case, building-to-building television; rapid facsimile transmission of vital documents; the relationship of the General Assembly, which usually functions for only two months of the year, to the Security Council, which is in constant session, and the relationship of both to the Secretariat and the press. There are matters of water and power supply, air conditioning, and finally, "of equal importance, because no one likes to work in a dump," how much sun, space, trees and green they can create space for.

Wallace Kirkman Harrison, American director of the group, who helped to build Rockefeller Center, takes this over-all view:

"Building is a matter of stone on stone and steel on steel, air conditioning and elevators that run. The layman thinks that all we have to do is come in with a beautiful sketch, and out of that everything is going to function. Just the opposite is true. These U.N. buildings can only grow out of requirements, now and for five or ten years hence. They must have stateliness and dignity. But the question is, are we building some phony Greek temple for a Greek god, or are we building to accommodate human beings in a complex civilization?

"The best building in Rockefeller Center," he went on, wheeling around in his chair to point out of the window, "is the big one. Why? Not because we decided to raise the best and biggest building in the world, symbolizing something, but because we decided how deep in from a window an office could be and still be a good place for a person working away from the light. That building grew out of our problems—not out of any philosophical concept. The test of these U.N. buildings will be whether the people in them like to be there."

Nor will the headquarters give one a feeling of government, as in Washington. Why should it? Mr. Harrison asks. Architecturally, Washington reflects the spirit of the past. Why cannot the U.N. group, by functioning well for tomorrow, have the same beauty and dynamics that Washington had for its time?

"We're not," as Mr. Harrison puts it, "building another Department of Commerce building. I had an office there behind four-foot stone columns and found the general pompousness and lack of light very disagreeable. Make a thing beautifully functional, and it will be beautiful."

Stanch support for his views comes from Charles-Edouard Jeanneret—better known as Le Corbusier—outstanding prophet of the modernists. His dictum is "A house is a machine for living. . . . The time is ripe for construction, not foolery."

"The group must be in such harmony that it will contrast with the violence of New York," said the French architect. "I take the words of the fifteenth-century poet, Charles d'Orleans— 'riant, clair et beau' ('smiling, clear and beautiful.') But I do not see all this as a symbol—as, for example, a world capital, or a temple of peace as it has been called. It is too soon to use such fine phrases, non? The U.N. simply does not exist yet. The nations are not united. The U.N. is not proved. It is simply a poste de combat—a battle post.

"I see it as a meeting center, as office buildings efficient to the last detail, for conference meetings, for the preservation of documents, with air, space and gardens around for perfect working conditions. There is no symbolism in all that. You will absolutely have a symbol?"

To this, Nikolai D. Bassov, noted engineer of the Soviet Union, who helped with the mass moving of Russian factories to the Ural Mountains during the war, adds:

"Symbolism in architecture is unnecessary. All symbols are growing old. If you incorporate symbols of today into architecture, and tomorrow those symbols will grow out of date, the architecture will look ridiculous."

Two other U.N. architects take a different view while upholding the emphasis on functionalism. They are Oscar Niemeyer of Brazil, widely admired for his work with glass facades, and Dr. Ssu-Ch'eng Liang, professor of architecture at Tsing Hua University, Peiping, and visiting professor of Far Eastern art at Yale. Both men find a direct psychological relationship between man's political aspirations and the house he builds.

"When we make a building for the U.N.," said Mr. Niemeyer, "we must have in mind what is the U.N.? It is an organism to set the nations of the world in a common direction and give to the world security. I think it is difficult to get this into steel and stone. But if we make something representing the true spirit of our age, of compression and solidarity, it will by its own strength give the idea that that is the big political effort, too."

Dr. Liang, who calls himself more of a historian than a creative architect, added:

"I think simplicity is always a virtue. My feeling is that this group of buildings should be not only international in character, but un-national—expressing no country's characteristic but expressive of the world as a whole. If a commercial building like [56] Rockefeller Center gave people in it the feeling that they were the United Nations, I would say that the building was not well designed. And vice versa, if the U.N. group gave the people in it the feeling of Rockefeller Center, I would say that it was not well designed."

Confronting this array of talent and range of views are leading architects who differ both with them and among themselves.

In his office near Park Avenue, furnished with rough-hewn benches, shining brass andirons and old prints of New York, William Adams Delano, who served on the National Park and Planning Commission in Washington for twenty-six years, deplored the ultra-modern intentions and the lack of emphasis on the spiritual approach.

"Of course, these buildings must symbolize peace and security," he declared. "They can show that they are buildings of character. They must indicate that they are performing a public service, and if possible an international service. To put it concretely, the buildings must show stability and wide purpose.

"For instance, if the designers build with glass, or with lots of glass parts, that wouldn't indicate stability. On the contrary, buildings of glass look neither stable nor dignified. And they certainly haven't a monumental appearance.

"Most important," he added, "is that these buildings have got to combine traditional architecture—things which have been designed in the past—with present-day ideas. I think the world and architecture have a lot to profit from in past experiences. Or else it's more of a damn-fool world than I think it is. It must reflect past achievements and mistakes, and so indicate that it's reaping the benefits of both."

Sharply attacking this point of view—but chary also of the U.N. designers—is Walter Adolf Gropius, professor of architecture at Harvard since 1938, the modernist who developed the "Bauhaus" school of allied building arts at Weimar and Dessau.

The United Nations, 1947-1953, New York, as seen from across the East River, looking west. To the left, the glass-walled Secretariat; in the foreground, the low horizontal Conference Building and on the right, with the dome and swept-up roofline, the General Assembly Building.

"We absolutely cannot combine traditional architecture with our modern conceptions," he said. "What is tradition? A dead language. It is not our language, any more than the clothes, science and architecture of a century or five centuries ago would suit us today. All great architecture of the past was created to express its [57] own period. Like the Egyptians, Greeks, Romans and the Gothic builders, we have to find an expression of our own. We cannot imitate.

"As for building with glass, that is one of our good, new materials, and in a sense, uniquely symbolic of our civilization since it is clear, practical and beautiful.

"What really matters," he said, "is the spirit of the designers, how they put such a building or group of buildings together be-

yond the purely utilitarian needs. This can't be accomplished or
thought through in a few weeks. It's not just an office problem,
or a structural problem. The psychological union of the whole is
as important as the utilitarian. I hope that the terrible rush with
which the building plan has been attacked will not affect the
ultimate result. I can't imagine that, if the U.N. is really growing,
this site will be sufficient."

Whatever final design emerges from the drafting boards and
blueprints of the "planning and conference room," the architects
agree on one point—that it will be the spirit of those who are to
work in the buildings which will be the paramount factor. No
doubt their work will be made easier by ultra-modern conveniences, but by their acts they will decide whether the headquarters is to become a living symbol of peace or another tomb
of Geneva.

As Mr. Harrison puts it for the architects: "For the people
who have lived through Dunkerque, Warsaw, Stalingrad and Iwo
Jima, may we build so simply, honestly and cleanly that it will
inspire the United Nations, who are today building a new world,
to build this world on the same pattern."[59]

'WE MUST SHAPE TRUE INSPIRATION'

*In connection with the discussion of what form the United
Nations headquarters should take, The Times asked Frank Lloyd
Wright, distinguished American architect, for any comment he cared
to make. His reply follows:*

By Frank Lloyd Wright

Scottsdale, Ariz.

Enlightened democracy is still in search of a form and has no
great official building it could honestly call home. Like the
cuckoo, it nests in homes devised by its adversaries. Language
may conceal thought, but when the thinker builds he cannot hide.
Limitations and false reactions are then on record to stay.
Anachronisms like Michelangelo's dome (a great arch high up in
the air on stilts) become symbols of authority.

So, in so far as the U. N. is democratic, the U. N. is in a

fix. But, with little hesitation and no embarrassment, the U. N. is willing to make shift. *The Times* wants to know what the makeshift should look like. I believe a number of architects are to answer. No doubt, being total masters of the makeshift, they can. But holding democracy an organic ideal, I believe no man entitled to build anything until individual entity is achieved. The same goes for democratic institutions established in his name.

Isn't his very building just what a man knows about "institution" in a very real sense? He knows the city skyscraper is exploitation, therefore abuse of privilege. So he must know skyscraperism to be a sinister emblem for world power. But if the policeman needs even more glory, the skyscraper would be it.

And empty monumentality like the building that was proposed for Flushing Meadow, showing architecture to be an utter sterility, would bear no comforting assurance of U.N. wisdom nor would it indicate the possession of any depth of humane feeling. So why not wait? Plant grass there on Flushing Meadow. Grass the ground where the proposed U. N. skyscraper would stand. Buy a befitting tract of land, say a thousand acres or more, not too easy to reach. On the land put a simple, adequate shelter where the U. N. mind, without artificial stimulation or immediate recourse to our popular flesh-pot—the big city—might be less likely to "mistake the driver for the passenger or mistake the passenger for the driver" in the peace of this world.

When a man has fever he doesn't take stimulants, though he may crave them. Humanity is now man-in-a-fever and is that fix likely to yield to the sanity of order by further concentrations and excitements of the standard sort?

In short, no overcrowded urban street is a better place for humane concentration upon the ethics of human progress than a graveyard.

Sequester the U. N. Why does it not itself ask for good ground where nature speaks and the beauty of organic order shows more clearly the true pattern of all peace whatsoever? Then build there in perfect accord adequate shelter for the body and, if possible, shape some true inspiration for the sham-less democratic soul of this world's greatest hope.[59]

THE ARCHITECTS' JOURNAL

Astragal

Astragal, The Architects' Journal, CVI (August 28, 1947).*

ASTRAGAL cabled FRANK LLOYD WRIGHT "please cable comments on design for UNO HQ." Frank Lloyd Wright replied:

ARCHITECTURE HAS NEVER COME OUT OF COLABORATION ALIVE. EACH LABORER COULD DO BETTER BY HIMSELF. OUT OF THIS COMMITTEE FOR DESIGNING UNHQ HAS COME A SINISTER EMBLEM FOR WORLD POWER. THIS MONSTROUS COMMERCIALIZED TOMBSTONE FOR THE GRAVEYARD OF PEACE.

UN THEREIN IS ON THE RECORD FOR DOLLAR FASCISM WHILE NAMING ITSELF ANTIFASCIST. MUST ITS ARCHITECTURE LIKE THE SITE ITSELF BE A MERE SUBSIDY IN THIS AFFAIR BETWEEN NATIONS?

FRANK LLOYD WRIGHT.

I asked Frank Lloyd Wright for his comments on the new UN headquarters illustrated in the AJ last week, and from Spring Green, Wisconsin, came the cable reproduced above. Though it appears there was a surprising measure of harmony at the discussions of the "committee for designing UNHQ," and the final plan was unanimously approved, the whole process has aroused great comment in architectural circles throughout the world. . . . Frank Lloyd Wright, his vision by no means impaired, expresses an uneasiness about the whole headquarters story that many others feel. . . .

ASTRAGAL [183]

* Reprinted with the permission of *The Architects' Journal*.

EDWARD PASSMORE

The New Headquarters of the United Nations

Edward Passmore, "The New Headquarters of the United Nations," *Journal of the Royal Institute of British Architects*, Series 3, LVII (July, 1950).*

It was Max Beerbohm who once said (and it was most certainly in his youth!) 'there is always something rather absurd about the past.' All familiar with 'Max's' viewpoint will know that for 'absurd' could be read nostalgic, quaint, charmingly whimsical or what have you; and that for once he was giving voice to a particularly trite form of 'amabilis insania'. The new United Nations building was not conceived in an atmosphere of 'pleasing delusion'; the beauty of its plan form or the sheer force of its contrasting elements may, or most certainly will not be appreciated by all, but the urgency of its purpose is expressed so thoroughly in terms of contemporary design (and incidentally infinitely more in the line of true traditional development than its predecessor at Geneva!) that one suspects that even the most reactionary critics will eventually see in it an inevitable beauty as expressed by its basic purpose.[348]

* Reprinted with the permission of the Royal Institute of British Architects.

The United Nations, 1947-1953, New York; the giant slab of the Secretariat as seen from the south, with the domed General Assembly in the background. The building in the foreground, which temporarily housed the U. N. Library, has since been razed. "Architecture that is worthy of the name can not be classified as either utilitarian or monumental—" *Report to the General Assembly of the United Nations.*

WALLACE K. HARRISON

The United Nations Building in New York

Wallace K. Harrison, "The United Nations Building in New York," *Journal of the Royal Institute of British Architects*, Series 3, LVIII (March, 1951). Paper read before the Royal Institute of British Architects, 20 February 1951.*

. . . André Gide has said: 'Having arrived at a certain point in history, there is nothing which does not present a problem. . . .' There is architecture today. Architecture not only *presents* but *is* the sum of the problems of the day. One of the greatest I've ever had to face, with fourteen other composer architects, was that of trying to build, quickly and well, a headquarters for the United Nations.

In April 1947 the Secretary-General of the United Nations, Trygve Lie, a truly great man, assembled in New York a group of architects and engineers (speaking at least 10 languages and from 14 different countries) to design, as a group, a home for the United Nations. We disagreed, we fought, but we worked hard and each day we returned ready to start anew. We knew we had to succeed. I should like to tell you something about these men, for the United Nations Headquarters is certainly no more, and perhaps is less, than their collected experiences. You probably know their names as well as I, but they are so much a part of the whole that I would like to pay tribute to them individually. The 14 architects appointed by the various member nations were:

John Antoniades, Greece; Nicolai Bassov, U.S.S.R.; Vladimir Bodiansky, France; Gaston Brunfaut, Belgium; Josef Havlicek, Czechoslovakia; Charles Le Corbusier, France; Ernst Cormier, Canada; Ssu-ch'eng Liang, China; Sven Markelius, Sweden; Oscar Niemeyer, Brazil; Matthew Nowicki, Poland; Howard Robertson,

* Reprinted with the permission of the Royal Institute of British Architects.

United Kingdom; G. A. Soilleux, Australia; Julio Vilamajo, Uruguay; Ernest Weismann, Yugoslavia.

Julio Vilamajo, Uruguay's distinguished architect, was a sick man when he came to help us. Unfortunately, he has not lived to see the completion of his effort as he died the following April.

The youngest of all, Matthew Nowicki, the brilliant Polish designer, was killed tragically in a plane crash in Egypt when returning from India.

Nicolai Bassov, Russian specialist in construction and foundations, was responsible for rebuilding plants destroyed by Germany during the siege of Stalingrad. He is an engineer of architectural breadth. He worked all one night to bring proof that a man would walk less, if the elevators were put in the centre of the building. I remember particularly how he illustrated his points by proverbs:

'The quality of the leather in my boot is unaffected by the feelings of the calf from which it came.'

'Drink and you die; don't drink and you still die; so let's drink.'

'If you have made your bed everyone wants to lie in it.'

Sven Markelius approached the U.N. from the point of view of its relationship to the city, and spent much of his time on approaches, the gardens, parking, etc. He also laid out a plan for the long range relationship of the U.N. site to the City of New York.

Oscar Niemeyer, one of the great designers of this world, held to the theory of open spaces and spaces around buildings. I believe his ideal is almost the Greek one, that each building should be complete and perfect in itself; and simple forms should all have space around them.

Liang would constantly vote against placing the Secretariat Building with its axis running north and south. He wouldn't say anything, just vote against it. Finally, hoping for unanimity, if we could get it, I asked why. He answered, very quietly: 'We have run our buildings from east to west in China for three thousand years and it's very satisfactory. I see no reason to change.'

Howard Robertson, a modernist, constantly tried to get us to introduce court-yards, and when I walk across the wide open spaces in front of the Secretariat in winter, I know he was right. I may say that without the tact, courage and diplomacy of Howard Robertson, there would be no U.N. Headquarters today.

There is no greater problem in this world than to face a sheet of blank white paper. What to do next?

Some architects are able, as though improvising, to search their souls and find the proper symbolic solution for the problem at hand. This may result in such great monuments as The Invalides or St. Paul's. Or an architect may have an idea, a conviction, a philosophy—call it what you will—that the structural system must dominate the composition. This may result in an Orly hangar or an Eiffel Tower. But in each case, man becomes a little dot in the empty spaces of the composition, left to his own devices to find his place, just as he did in the days when he explored caves for a home. It is architecture by man—but not *of* man or even *for* man.

We took as our first problem this man who, in the vast growing scale of world enterprises still stays 6 ft. high with a seat not over 2 ft. 6 in. In the Secretariat building, for instance, we had 4,000 people to take care of. They had to work together for the various bodies—the Assembly, the Security Council, the Economic and Social Council, the Trustee Council, and in 20 conference rooms.

Knowing that a man will seldom be over 6 ft. tall, we had to allow at least 2 ft. of space over his head for safety and comfort. As you know, the thickness of a floor in a modern office building, with air-conditioning, lighting, plumbing, and wind-bracing, is another 2 ft. 6 in. to 3ft. 6 in. in height. So we have a floor height of between 10 ft. 6 in. and 12 ft. 6 in. from floor to floor. This floor height of 12 ft. comes from the height of a man working in an office.[171]

We found we needed an area of 96 sq. ft. for desk, chair, files, etc. Studying the depth to which good light will penetrate a room from a window at one side of the room, we find that when the head of the window is 8 ft. from the floor daylight will efficiently enter about one and one-half times the height of the head of the window, or about 12 ft. into the office. That gives us an office 12 ft. deep. When we divide this into 96 sq. ft. of floor area, we have a minimum office 8 ft. by 12 ft.

The United Nations, 1947-1953, New York; part of the main lobby of the Secretariat. "Make a building functional, and it will be beautiful," said Wallace K. Harrison, chairman of the international board of designers of the United Nations.

Generally we find that the ideal office building plan is an outside office about 8 ft. by 12 ft. and inside that another 8 ft. by 12 ft. office for a secretary, reception space, or files. This gives a depth of 20 ft. to 24 ft. To this we must add a corridor of 6 ft. making in all about 30 ft. of outside space.

In a building with a population the size of the Secretariat, elevators have to be about 6 ft. by 10 ft., or 6 ft. by 8 ft. to let people in and out efficiently. And elevators have to work in groups of six or eight to keep the interval of waiting at any floor at a minimum. With elevators in banks of six or eight, and with a corridor between them, we find that the distance from centre of bank to centre of bank of elevators is from 24 ft. to 27 ft. This determines the location of our wind-bracing in office skyscrapers. Stairs, toilets, ducts, are also standards related in size to the man. Also, in plan we have found that if a man has to walk more than 125 ft. from his office door to an elevator, he is wasting time and energy. Finally, we have found by experience that with conditions similar to those found on Manhattan Island, a building 25 to 45 stories high is the most efficient and economical.

And, when you have solved all requirements and added a study of the problem of the economy of the perimeter, the architect has a rather complete plan—almost fixed—and largely determined by the size and energies of this little animal, the human being.

There is another major factor that enters into the designing of a skyscraper. Every skyscraper must be built in units not more than 15 stories high, built one on top of the other. Thus at approximately every fifteenth floor you have a 'basement', for water tanks, elevator and air-conditioning machinery, and fire protection. At this point we combine our facts of plan and section on paper and it is only then that adjustments are made for exterior delight.

In the Secretariat buildings of the United Nations Headquarters, we have provided well for the little man. We have: a population of 4,400; office space of 446,136 sq. ft.; meeting rooms and others of 365,176 sq. ft.; total area of 811,312 sq. ft.; area per person of 135 sq. ft.; building cube of 10,950,000 cu. ft.

Now, how do we plan the great council rooms where these men work together? We find that the same system used in planning office space can meet the needs of the conference rooms. Each room is worked out exactly as the office is worked out: one man after the other. As the engineer replied when asked, 'How can you build a railroad 3,000 miles long?' 'It's easy—I only build 1 ft. at a time.' We built one seat at a time.

I should now like to explore with you the prospects for future progress in the field of architecture. Since 1920 the technological side of architecture has been over-emphasized, probably in reaction to the Victorian and Beaux Arts period and in appreciation of the Greek standard of purity of line.

Some will say that man must also understand the supernatural, the fourth dimensional; and even the Dada. However, we don't often get jobs to build dream houses, except in Hollywood, and I will stick to the problems I have been faced with in the past.

I believe there are three essential parts of architecture: human, natural, and technological.

In the technological area we in the United States have developed many ·new materials, just as you have. One of our major problems has been that as buildings are built higher the wind, vacuum, rain, sleet, and snow bring up many new and more difficult problems. Every building is alive and moving. Sometimes the movement is considerable, as at the top of the Empire State Building. And there is no way with steel skeletons to stop this movement completely. If it is not caused by wind pressure, it is due to the differential between one side heated by the sun and the other exposed to a cold draught. This means that every joint, stone or brick is opening and closing all the time.

We have tried to find a solution to this problem by using metal, in one form or other, in place of heavy surface masonry. We must remember that when we take the masonry off a building it becomes more flexible and therefore we have to design more carefully for deflection.

There are important developments coming in air conditioning and insulating. The use of light has also changed considerably. We have found that we have to eliminate contrasts and raise the foot-candles to two or three times the quantities used in pre-war days. The use of silicones in some ways will open great new areas of development—and, of course, glass is just starting to be used for its various properties. In the U.N. we use a green glass which blocks the infra-red rays. When the sun is shining we have shown that the temperature is 10 degrees Fahrenheit less on the interior than with ordinary glass. . . .[172]

Let me get on to the second element in architecture—the natural. Human beings have been conditioned to nature and natural materials since the beginning of time. We can not forget this. Otherwise our architecture will produce technological schizophrenics.

Years ago Mr. Harrison and I were having lunch with Carl Jung in Zurich and talking about architecture. He told us that 'modern architects are all close to schizophrenia because they are getting too far from the animal and natural. You open the outside world into man's protective home, you even bring trees into his house—this can only end in insanity.'

He then told the story of an African chief who started to build his house, using certain trees that had protective gods associated with them. He rejected trees that were supposed to have hostile demons associated with them. For his home only the good and protective trees were used. It was the same with the stones and the fabrics—all were chosen for their beneficial qualities. . . .

The boring similarity of some of our mass housing projects, both public and private and perhaps of some of yours too, will drive a man to insanity or to the pubs here and in New York to the local bar.

In Liberia the Firestones tried to build nice brick houses for their employees, but the employees were so unhappy with brick houses that the company had to go back to the native form.

Your problem in England is completely different from ours or that of France or Switzerland. Why do we all try to put on the same corset of architecture? As the world becomes smaller it is essential that our cultures retain their personality. 'Digne de soi meme.' . . .

I believe in the inevitability of gradualness, but I like the shock of revolution. I'd like to see us really revolt against the idea that the machine will use man instead of man using the machine.

Where does all this lead us? Well, stated simply—the study of architecture is the study of man.

This brings me to the third element in architecture, the human. For example, I have found by personal experience that I don't like windows as large at 40 stories as at the second story. I have found that we have to develop new forms to give man greater assurance of security.

The Egyptians knew how to use architecture to give direct physical reactions to humans. For instance, a man walked through a brilliantly lit courtyard where the irises of his eyes were narrowed to a pin point. Then he entered a dim colonnade. From there he went into another dazzlingly bright courtyard. Finally he entered the Holy of Holies where the blackness blinded him for a minute. Out of the blackness the great god seemed to advance—lit by a 6-in. hole through 6 ft. of masonry. They used architecture as a means of enclosing light.

When we think of man we think of space around man, and the future of architecture depends on the way we manipulate that space.

We can not just draw plans.

We can not just draw elevations.

We can not just know techniques.

We can not just know mechanics.

We must know man.

We must know more about man than any of our predecessors—not less.

We must approach architecture simply, without fear, without pride—with faith in the human being.

When we reach this point, we have struggled through the thick woods and brambles up the hill to find ourselves on a precipice looking out over the vast expanse of the unknown. It is at this point that the great ones will be able to reach into that stratosphere of understanding too high for most men and bring down to this earth a little of that common inspiration which God grants his artists. This is the way that architecture is achieved.

Everything is ahead of us: The best play has not been written. The best song has not been sung. The best building has not been built.

Our job in building the U.N. was a difficult one—possibly

too difficult, but we have tried with all we had to build for man his Workshop for Peace.[173]

(The following is an excerpt from the discussion which accompanied the paper.)

PROFESSOR W. G. HOLFORD

. . . The serious comment that I wish to make is on the character of the building as opposed to what one might call a monumental building. It struck me as very interesting that it was almost a giant reflector of the moods and the atmosphere of the city, not only in a political sense but also in a material sense. The clouds and the reflections of all sorts which one sees in the glass façade show that the building must be a great many things to different people. A great public building of this sort may be seen as quiet and tranquil, dramatic or almost terrible, depending on the light and the time of day, the weather and various other things. It is interesting, I think, that this great building is exactly the opposite of a monumental building, that it is a mirror or reflector, as it were, of moods and atmospheres, and yet behind it there is an enormous hidden world of services and structure without which the more atmospheric character of the building could not be sustained. If I may add a tribute to those which have already been paid to Mr. Harrison, I would say that the real triumph of this building is that it is so simple that, in fact, it will mean a great deal to a large number of different people.[175]

S. ROWLAND PIERCE

The Architecture of Humanism

"The Architecture of Humanism," *The Architect and Building News*, CXCIX (March 9, 1951).*

The R.I.B.A. [Royal Institute of British Architects] was honoured and mightily interested in the paper on the United Nations Building by Mr. Wallace K. Harrison, the executant architect for the New York project—called the "Director of Planning". He not only gave the large audience something to think about in the way of large-scale organisation, with a view of the many problems in the realisation of the Headquarters, but he became almost philosophical and gave us some insight into his own personality and into that of his more humanistically-inclined countrymen.

The rather terrifying honeycomb of a building which has so far arisen from all the thought and planning is only the first unit of the whole scheme—the working office of U.N.—the Secretariat. It is a little strange perhaps to have to express doubts as to the extent to which humanism is expressed in such a structure.

The population of 4,400, equal to a small town, which is to be housed in its cells (rectangular—not hexagonal) have, we are told, been treated well; there are all the common office amenities and then some extra space and quality as well.

Mr. Harrison's emphasis, in summary, was on "Man". "We must know man . . . the study of architecture is the study of man". The engineer might similarly approach problems, yet get no further with his humanism. "The study of pumps is the study of liquids—we must know hydrostatics". This massing of the human spirit into a thing called "man" can become a dangerous sort of philosophical indulgence unless it is carefully watched.

* Reprinted by courtesy of *The Architect and Building News*, and the author, S. Rowland Pierce, F.R.I.B.A.

It can run away into the realms of the inhumanism of totalitarianism without much stretching of the imagination. The personal and humble soul-searching approach of Mr. Harrison certainly eliminated this possibility from his own thoughts, but it is not quite possible for us to forget that those 4,400 U.N. Secretariat people are each one a man or a woman. In fact Mr. Harrison admitted that the fact worried him at some broader level than that of his present problems—"we must approach architecture simply, without fear, without price and with faith in the human being . . . I believe there are three essential parts of architecture: human, national and technological". (*Pace!* Alberti—*pace!* Isaac Ware.)

The fact is that what really matters in architecture and in any sort of design are the relationships between the factors of the programme as much, if not more, than the factors themselves. It is man's relationship to man—each man and each woman to his or her contemporaries—the relationhips (and their resultants) of the "human, national and technological" parts of architecture that matter to architects.

The approach can be neither "idealistic" nor "materialistic"; these are, like science and art, interdependent and their interactions must, and inevitably will, determine the results. Mr. Harrison deplored the boring similarity of the repetitive utilitarianism of many housing and other schemes of to-day. Are they [273] not the result of the non-realisation of the relationships, the deliberate setting-aside of some of the factors? "Man" is not just one entity to be designed for or to be planned; humanism is not concerned with one bulk thing only—called, for better or worse, humanity. It is here that architecture, if it still exists and is to continue to develop for the service and for the pleasure of men and women, is fundamentally different from the all-too sectional activities that have dogged its steps and even led it astray during the last few decades. In this period it has revolted against and developed away from the sordid parts of the past— the pastiche of tradition—but at the same time it has hitched its wagon to some very doubtful stars and, what is more, has given names to them to prove its self-accredited rightness—functionalism, cubism, technics, existentialism. How soon, in the history of humanism, do these things get thrust aside, leaving their little contributions to a common development. One-sidedness will not keep "neo-chaos" at bay.

We must thank Mr. Harrison for coming over here and making us think. Looked at in one way, of course, he has been presenting an interim statement to one of his Clients—we congratulate him on his Progress Report. He, having done so, leaves us with the building he has called "Man's Workshop of Peace", to look at and to comment upon. How we could wish that it was more "human"; how we could wish that it was more isolated and not backed-up by a town-scape of so many other experiments in the worst type of experimental sky-scraping. What a symbol it could be—in its present form and shape—without the flanking rivalry of Woolworth and Empire State towers.

It is exactly here, perhaps, that something has gone slightly awry—in the interaction and relationships of two of the factors— the symbolism of humanism and the humanism of symbolism.[274]

JOURNAL OF THE ROYAL ARCHITECTURAL INSTITUTE OF CANADA

Editorial

Editorial, Journal of the Royal Architectural Institute of Canada, XXV (March, 1948).*

The astonishing thing about the new buildings for the United Nations is the apparent unanimity of opinion of its designers in favour of contemporary architecture. To most of us any other approach would be unthinkable, but that such a problem could be solved, without compromise, by a committee composed of architects of many races and many points of view shows how far we have come in just over one hundred years. As recently, architecturally, as 1844, the Houses of Parliament at Westminster were won in competition by Sir Charles Barry. In that heyday of

    * Reprinted with the permission of the Royal Architectural Institute of Canada.

eclecticism, the designs submitted covered the whole gamut of architectural styles, and Sir Charles, the winner, played the field with twelve, of which "Gothic" won by several lengths over "Italian Renaissance".

Perhaps even greater confusion reigned in the International Competition for a design for the Peace Palace at the Hague. By 1907 more picture books were available, travel was easier and the architect was unworthy of the name who was not on intimate archaeological terms with Amiens Cathedral, the Parthenon, the Alhambra at Granada and the Pyramid of Cheops. We have a portfolio in which the winning and commended designs for the Peace Palace are illustrated, and it is as instructive to the student of history as the pages of Banister Fletcher. However, if the exteriors were drawn from the masterpieces of the Christian and pagan world, there was a consistency in planning. Over all was the dead hand of the Ecole des Beaux Arts on the Rue of that name. The winning design was in a flamboyant French Gothic manner, which succeeded in being Gothic, but failed to be flamboyant. All the frustrations, all the humiliations, all the failures of a generation seem to be frozen and embodied in that dreary mass of stone and brick. It offered no hope—it seemed unconcerned with peace.

It has been observed on many occasions that the winning design in International Competitions is inferior to the second prize. It is as though international juries, fearful of the implications of their decision, recognized ability and imagination in design, and passed it by in favour of the safe and mediocre. It was so with the Tribune Tower where Saarinen came second to the pseudo Gothic Tower of Hood, and with the League of Nations Building in Geneva where Le Corbusier's design will long be remembered by architects after the winner's design is forgotten. The United Nations decided wisely against a competition with all its delays, its wasted effort, and with the foregone conclusion that the best design would remain for ever on paper in second place. Instead, the architects were appointed immediately. They proceeded with the job with their client, the world, looking on; their sketches have been illustrated in popular and technical magazines, and if we don't like them we can say so, either publicly or privately, through our national representative who is a member of the designing committee.

It has been said that the Chicago Exhibition of 1851 [*sic*] was remarkable for the fact that it was not designed by Louis Sullivan: that the New York Fair gained notoriety from the fact that it was not designed by Frank Lloyd Wright. Posterity cannot say that the U.N. building suffered from the absence of Le Corbusier. However good his colleagues may be, and some of them have proved their worth in many lands, a board of architects, speaking many tongues, from countries as vastly different as Canada and Russia might easily produce a Tower of Babel. Le Corbusier commands the respect of the team—he seems to be as articulate in speech as he is on paper, and, from what one hears, he is no shrinking violet when he has a point to make. . . .

Editor [68]

JOURNAL OF THE ROYAL INSTITUTE OF BRITISH ARCHITECTS

Correspondence on the U. N. Building

Correspondence, *Journal of the Royal Institute of British Architects*, Series 3, LV.

June, 1948

THE U.N. BUILDING

Sir,—In the ARCHITECTURAL RECORD of December 1946 the editors illustrated my Shell Building at The Hague, and some other work, together with an article entitled *Mr. Oud embroiders a theme.* In this they reproached me for being less functional than I ought to be in relation to my past and, at the end, they asked me for an explanation.

In the ARCHITECTURAL RECORD of March 1947 I answered in a short article *(Building or Architecture?)* and I quote from it:

'Architecture itself—old or new— can and must give emotion. It has to transport the æsthetic vision of one man (the architect) to another one (the onlooker). And why should it not? Are we in our modern times so condemned that we dare not set our own stages? Are we really so dried up that we don't allow ourselves to play a bit now and then? It is a very important fact which is too often forgotten in the case of new architecture.' And further: 'Why should it be forbidden to give functional doing a spiritual form? Functioning alone as a leading principle—my experience taught me this—results in æsthetical arbitrariness. Don't forget this.'

Mr. Howard Robertson spoke very interestingly before the R.I.B.A. recently about 'The American Scene', including the 'U.N. Building'. But he has not led me away from my conviction that the form in which the 'U.N. Building' was conceived is a shame in relation to the greatness of architecture! If the Union of Nations signifies to the world not only a practical means of administration but also an expression of peace and good brotherhood, then we have as architects to protest against the mill of world peace that is going to be erected in New York.[363]

This belief of mine has nothing to do with a wish either for 'a dome' or for 'a flop': modern architecture has its own means of showing its dignity. It has only to do with my respect for the noblest spirit of architecture which is going to be violated by the way this design came into the world!

'Collectivism' may be a wonderful thing now and then, but in our time architecture is not yet ripe for it. I agree with Mr. Russell Hitchcock: 'We have architecture of bureaucracy and architecture of genius'. Can a building for the Union of Nations do with less than 'architecture of genius'? We should not content ourselves with a peace factory designed by some of the best architecture-engineers of the world. We want a *symbol of peace* built by an *architect!* Architecture, like peace, is, in its essence, a matter of *faith*—not of *brains.*—Yours faithfully,

J. J. P. OUD° [*Hon. Corr. Member*] [364]

° By permission of J. J. P. Oud.

July, 1948

THE U.N. BUILDING

Sir,—I have a great deal of sympathy with the views put forward by Mr. J. J. P. Oud. In my view the finest architecture can not arise from designing in committee, though I would not care to argue that it can not arise from the joint efforts of a firm of architects accustomed to work in unison and harmony.

The U.N. Board of Design was, I feel, a solution to the difficult problem of collaboration between nations. It attempted to go a certain distance, *i.e.* to find a preliminary planning solution to complex requirements on a difficult site. At the stage when its Report was submitted the plan form and broad geometrical masses of the buildings were alone determined. The model, it may have been noted, showed no final expression of detail. It was, in essence, a developed esquisse for a solution.

I think I am right in saying that the collaborating architects felt that the architectural development of the scheme, and consequently complete freedom to modify the conception as set down in its first broad lines, would become the responsibility — and consequently express the personality—of the chief architect in charge, Mr. Wallace Harrison.

The difficulty about symbolism, and expression generally, is that architects, like painters and sculptors and all artists generally, are seldom agreed on contemporary achievement—a fact which history has so often demonstrated.

Time, and familiarity, are required in order to form a true sense of perspective; few architects today, struggling earnestly and competitively in the contemporary field—or critics, for that matter—are in a strong position to pass an authoritative or irrevocable judgement.—Yours faithfully,

HOWARD ROBERTSON* [422]

* By permission of Howard Robertson.

August, 1948

THE U.N. BUILDING

Sir,—Few people will not sympathize with Mr. J. J. P. Oud in his sensitive reaction to the criticism of his work recently published in the ARCHITECTURAL RECORD. It would, however, seem to be the fate of all architects who produce work of a distinctly personal kind that the waves of fashion in architectural thought are certain at one time or another to run counter to their own viewpoint. This, nevertheless, is a chance all designers must take as long as freedom of criticism is to be preserved.

While in no way wishing to make this letter a *cri-du-cœur* for misunderstood designers, I would like to stress the value of the catholic approach to contemporary problems; for only in this way will the seeds of a new architecture of humanism be sown. The need for eclecticism in all aspects of design was never so vital as it is today.

The U.N. project in Manhattan is a good case in point. Its mass architect-engineer approach, so unpopular with Mr. Oud, has at least succeeded in removing the traditional spectre of monumentality as an architectural expression of Peace, and with commendable dexterity the designers have managed to produce a scheme which steers the course, which has so far proved illusive to many modern architects, that of a compromise between utility and visual formalism. Faults the scheme undoubtedly has, if Mr. Hugh Ferris's perspective drawings among other things, are intended to be taken seriously. The human figure, still as efficient a standard of measure in design as any, has apparently been taken for a short ride and bundled unceremoniously in East River, and the comparative scales of the various components of the scheme appear to be somewhat adrift from each other.

But to all who know this particular stretch of riverside Manhattan, which shows the marks of mis-development at its worst, the clearing of the site and the general form and line of the buildings appear to be a particularly satisfactory solution to a problem so bristling with difficulties and pitfalls.

I am sure most architects in this country will righteously feel

that Mr. Oud's defence of his own particular creed was at once
a notable gesture of his faith and of an artist's sensitivity towards
what he feels to be best in architecture, but he can assuredly
find consolation in the fact that criticism of the kind which has
been levelled at his work invariably follows in the wake of fame.
—Yours faithfully,

EDWARD PASSMORE* [473]

October, 1948

THE U.N. BUILDING

Sir,—The reactions of Mr. Robertson and Mr. Passmore to my
letter on the U.N. Building compel me to clear up my argument
in some way. I am thankful to both correspondents for their sympathy, but they have somewhat misjudged the essence of my
words and my convictions.

The essence of my argument was that New Architecture is
capable of more than the jejune U.N. office building which is to
be erected in New York; also that it can produce a building of
greater dignity and nobler character within its own limits. It is
wrong to suppose that this argument of mine has anything to do
with the need for eclecticism that Mr. Passmore has discovered
to be necessary among the public. A need like this, if it really
exists, is due to the fact that functional building in its higher
aspects is of too little interest to hold the attention of the public.
This objection could be avoided by criticizing functional building
on these grounds, and by trying to stimulate modern architects
to some idealism above the mere matter-of-fact work which functional building tends to promote. This is what I am trying to do
—not by recommending eclecticism—but by asking that the possibilities of new architectural expression should be sought.

I did not write—as seems to be suggested—because my own
work has been misunderstood, but merely on behalf of the development of New Architecture. Pioneering thirty years ago in
functional building, I met misunderstanding; today fighting to
help functional building to rise to art-in-building, I shall meet
misunderstanding anew; this is clear but is of no importance.

* By permission of Edward Passmore.

The importance is only that functional building at the moment is in a phase of self-sufficiency which is the best state to lead it quickly and totally to an end, and, as a matter of fact, by eclecticism if we are not attentive!

We ought to be aware of the fact that functional building is the basis of New Architecture, but that it is not yet New Architecture itself. It is not yet art-in-building. New Architecture is more than the solution of present practical needs with contemporary building machinery. It is above all the result of idealism in the mind of the architect. It is the outcome of his force of æsthetic expression. We want a lot more idealism than functional building generally offers today. Æsthetic expression is the language of architecture. Without this expression a building is 'deaf-mute'. The U.N. Building planned for New York is nearly 'deaf-mute'. The effort Mr. Harrison makes to work out the scheme of the Committee is useless. A building is an organism as a whole, not an indifferent core slightly re-formed to give it an acceptable shape. Its growth should not be allowed to resemble the process of dressing a woman who is going to be made beautiful by changing and disguising her figure. This leads to fashion, not to style. For the U.N. Building, we must claim style!

The organism of a building like that for the U.N. has to be a creation from the very first beginning, based on and in continual interaction with the essential conditions. It will never become a creation by remodelling a preconceived neutral scheme. It is a mistake to think that the impersonal effect of teamwork like this can be at the same time the expression of a universal spiritual idea. By no means! A spiritual idea in architecture is never unintentional. Lacking such an idea, a work of building activity may be a clever piece of engineering science but it will fail to move us. As there is no emotion in it, it lacks perceptible well-being. It is not architecture!

And the site? Yes, the site chosen for the U.N. Building is a very bad one. It should have been rejected for a building of so high a standard! The aim of a building for the U.N. is not to cure the town planning of New York but to lift up the world!— Yours faithfully,

J. J. P. OUD* [*Hon. Corr. Member*] [560]

* By permission of J. J. P. Oud

IAN McCALLUM

Architecture by Co-operation

Ian McCallum, "Architecture by Co-operation," *The Listener*, XLVII (April 10, 1952).*

THE AESTHETIC PROBLEM

. . . An architect is always having to make some compromise or other between the facts of finance, the requirements of function, and his aesthetic preferences. If finance and function are sometimes victims of the struggle, so long as convenience and health are not ignored unduly, and the client can be squared, good may come of it. It is the job of the critic to try to decide whether it has, whether the sacrifice was worth while. Let us try to imagine, therefore, the aesthetic problem as it presented itself to the architects.

The design of a world parliament building is a very special case. Its only predecessor is the League of Nations building. No purpose is served by repeating the whole shameful story of that building now. Briefly, le Corbusier, who won the competition for it with a quite outstanding design, was not-so-gently dropped in favour of a number of other competitors who combined to produce a group of buildings remarkable only for a half-hearted monumentality, using debased classical motifs in a quite unsuccessful attempt at symbolism. There was fortunately no question that the particular architects chosen by the United Nations would follow this example. However, though the architecture of our time has rejected the symbolism of earlier styles, the desire still remains sometimes to give expression to ideas that go beyond the functional solution. Opinions differ as to how this can be done. Some people argue that the architect cannot conjure a new set of symbols out of thin air; the process that

* By permission of Ian McCallum.

might produce them is a long one, demanding the close participation not only of the other visual arts, but of the community as a whole. Others believe that a set of decorative symbolical devices will merely produce a superficially new version of the old symbolism—sermons in stone for moderns. We have advanced, or we must advance, this group suggests, beyond such fancies. They do not say what shape, if any, the new symbolism will take. What they do say is that we must go on building without worrying over imagined shortcomings of this kind. So long as we build truly and adventurously, in the long run we shall find the rest has been added to us.

The architects of the Secretariat seem to me to have decided on a position mid-way between these two groups. It is clear that they could not dissociate their solution of the requirements from their ideas of what the building stood for. But while there is no trace in the design of the Secretariat of an attempt to use any of the other arts to preach a sermon in stone, there is evidence of an attempt to do more than merely satisfy the functional requirements as imaginatively as possible. In fact the architects seem to have attempted by size, simple geometry and the scale imparted by a repetitive surface pattern, to achieve the kind of abstract magnificence associated with great monuments like the pyramids—a quality of timelessness, signifying much but symbolizing nothing in particular. . . .

A BUILDING DEDICATED TO UNITY

The final factor which conditioned the design of the Secretariat was, I believe, the character of the New York skyscraper landscape. If you accept the necessity for the Secretariat to be a high building (there are those, among them Lewis Mumford, who hotly dispute this necessity on any grounds); and if you accept the desire of the architects to express as forcefully as they could the significance of the United Nations idea it becomes clear at once that, in a landscape dedicated in glorious anarchy to commercialism, the one thing a building dedicated to unity and idealism has to be is different. Nearly all the skyscrapers in Manhattan, for zoning or other reasons, step back become thinner as they rise in height. Here, then, was a reason why the Secretariat should not step back. Then, nearly all the skyscrapers are tower shaped, that is square or cruciform in plan; here was a possible reason why the more compact multi-winged solution was rejected. The long axis of the New York street block runs east-west, which means that the slab effect occurs piecemeal and accidentally almost everywhere. The long axis of the Secretariat runs north-south and counteracts this strong directional emphasis of the New York block. Then there is the matter of the surface treatment. The surrounding buildings nearly all emphasise either the vertical or the horizontal in the arrangement of their windows and walls. None of them gives almost equal stress to both as the vast glass and aluminium network of the Secretariat does. Certainly none of them has two walls entirely of glass and two entirely solid.

Whether or not all these factors did consciously influence the architects, they would probably find hard to say. But they are, I believe, relevant to the matter of deciding the success of the undertaking. It is everyone's privilege to make his own judgment; it is, after all, everyone's building. For what it is worth, my opinion is that on balance the design is justified, the aesthetic gains just outweigh the functional losses. And I hope those who work in the building and suffer from its functional defects will not consider this too presumptuous.

It should be clear by now how unique a problem this was, and [586] consequently how dangerous it could be as an architectural precedent. The sincere desire to symbolise a great idea is the basis of a very real conflict between form and function in the Secretariat, and this is a situation that the present-day architect very rarely has to face. One of the many things in favour of the architecture of our time is the fact that it provides no ready-made symbols for architectural pretension. As its influence grows, banks, insurance offices, factories, cinemas, railway stations and homes drop their borrowed symbols and begin to be themselves, and what is more look extraordinarily good as themselves. It would be a disaster if the United Nations buildings gave any opportunity for a revival of pretension in architecture; if aspects of its design should be borrowed by, say, large shops or offices merely because the ideal it represents had given it some kind of international snob value.[587]

HENRY STERN CHURCHILL

United Nations Headquarters —
A Description and Appraisal

Henry Stern Churchill, "United Nations Headquarters. A Description and Appraisal,"
The Architectural Record, CXII (July, 1952).*

The buildings for the United Nations constitute what is probably the most important architectural work of the century. They constitute a World Capitol, and as such draw the eyes of the world as a symbol of hope for world peace and the visible expression of world government. Therefore these structures deserve careful critical comment as to both function and purpose.

The site for the United Nations buildings is seventeen and a half acres, bounded by the East River, Forty-second Street, First Avenue and Forty-eighth Street. The Franklin D. Roosevelt Drive, an expressway, runs along the river edge, and part of the buildings are cantilevered over it.[104]

The original scheme was to have cost about $85,000,000, as a loan without interest from the United States, repayable over 32 years. This was cut to $65,000,000 by the U.N. itself, to scale down its request for presentation to a Congress dubious of the whole idea.† The cut necessitated a general scaling down of areas and cubage. This was done without altering the original approved design. In fact the main elements of plan, section and general conception, as approved by the Design Consultants and the U.N., have not been changed in any essential respect whatever.

Let us consider each of the group components in some detail, starting with the Secretariat. This building is 544 ft. high, 287 ft.

---

* Reprinted with the permission of Henry Stern Churchill and *The Architectural Record*.

† Recently the U.N. has appropriated an additional $3,000,000 which was needed for completion of the work.

The United Nations, 1947-1953, New York; the northern façade of the General Assembly Building. This, the public entrance to the General Assembly, consists of vertical strips of translucent marbled glass and of marble. "The north front, meant to be imposing is," said Henry Stern Churchill, "quite unconvincing."

long, 72 ft. wide and has 39 floors and 3 basements. Visually it completely dominates the group; when one thinks of U.N. one thinks only of the vast green-glass, marble-end slab, although in plan it forms only a small part of the total building area. This visual dominance is probably as it should be, for in governmental organizations today the clerical worker with his paper-shuffling and the permanent heads of departments, divisions, bureaus, sections are the people who get the work done, subtly influence policy, and see that the wheels go 'round. Without the typists, the file-clerks, the men and women in the little cubicles, not only U.N. but all our businesses would collapse. The office building has consequently become the characteristic [111] form of American architecture, and it is in the technique of office buildings that our greatest advances have been made. It is somehow fitting that the Secretariat should become the symbol of the U.N.—an up-ended filing case for human beings, their hopes, their fears and their aspirations for a steady job. That is the new American Dream, a steady job, that is what we hope a United World will bring us, in the terms of peace and security; and of that the Secretariat is a just, if unconscious, expression.

Unconscious expression because actually the Secretariat is more than an American office building. It houses people from many nations with greatly differing cultural backgrounds. This raised a lot of technical problems, from how to provide tempera-tures and working conditions for a variety of physiological na-tures to psychological problems of adjustment to mechanical devices and personal habits, to questions of elevator controls and signs. Since there are practical limits to providing for national whims, the answer was to make the process of adjustment to our ways as painless as possible. The result is, of course, a forceful expression of Our Way, not theirs.

Seen from a distance the Secretariat is very handsome in-deed. It has, on the whole, remarkable clarity, and a quality of brightness. The utility floors are differentiated from the others by a kind of tracery, repeated at the top in the form of a high grille intended to hide the pent-house. The location of these bands could have been more carefully studied. They have no rhythmic relation to the whole surface and so they are disturbing, whereas careful placement might have enhanced the scale and dynamic effect of the façade. The top grille is also most unfor-tunate. It does not hide the pent-house, which is actually a very simple shape and could very well have been left visible. The grille, against the sky, seems frivolous, a little rococo, like the lace on men's eighteenth century sleeves.

As a mechanism the Secretariat works exceedingly well. The impression on entering is one of great openness and space; there is easy access to elevators and to the big lobby with the floor-to-ceiling windows which give it [113] its spaciousness and extension to the outer world. It is with details that most fault can be found: the entrance canopy which, though intended to be only part of a flamboyant two-story entrance motif, is in its present state only reminiscent of hotels and broadcasting stations; the restlessness of the ceiling; the poor handling, both inside and outside, of the narrow end-returns of the marble slab-ends where they come down through the first floor.

The office floors are efficient and simple. The big windows are pleasant, but raise a question of technology. The windows on the utility floors, although far smaller, seem to distribute just as much light with less glare: one questions the actual value of the big glass areas, so carefully contrived with venetian blinds to cut the glare and with heat resistant glass to keep out the hot western sun. Incidentally this glass was used on the east side as well, where it was not needed for technical reasons, in order to preserve the visual color balance within the office space. Psychologically this was a wise decision, for the difference in color would have required continual adjustment of the eyes.

There was trouble with the glass wall too, at first, from leakage resulting from the up-draft of air. Leaky walls are common enough on sky-scrapers. As with the leaky roofs attributed to Wright's houses, the prominence of the work has made it a target for snide criticism.

The floors are all laid out for maximum flexibility. The air conditioning is individually controlled for each bay, and all windows are openable. This was a concession to the great variety of desires as to "climate" expected from the differing national backgrounds of the personnel, paying off in better morale, and probably in fewer respiratory troubles. The use of double-hung sash also permits the windows to be cleaned in the ordinary way. (A wall-washing machine, once considered, was abandoned when cost estimates were found prohibitively high.) The electric lighting (fluorescent in sunken troffers) and the ventilation outlets are spaced on a modular system; and in practice it has been found that very little shifting of equipment has been needed in installing the many office partitions. . . .[114]

Below the street level of the Secretariat and Conference Building, both structures where the flow of words is unimpeded, are the printing plant and recording rooms where the flow is dammed and immortalized on paper and tape. The huge plant prints everything—delegates' speeches, reports of international portent, daily menus for the restaurant, forms. Here too are carpenter and upholstery shops, metal working and electric shops for the maintenance of the vast project. Here is the equipment for the heating, ventilating and refrigeration of the air-conditioning plant and the other mechanical needs. Here is a complete fire-fighting section, with a control room into which trouble in any part of any of the structures is automatically flashed on light panels. Here is the communications control room; from every device leads come back here to a control panel. Here are the well separated truck entrance, the auto-repair station, and general services such as locker rooms and storage. Below all this for two levels, and extending under the General Assembly and entrance courts as well, for three levels, is parking for 1500 cars.

Coming back up, there is the General Assembly, the real center of the Parliament of Nations. This, not the Secretariat towering in its green and gray brilliance, nor the half-hidden Conference Building, this and not those working areas is the symbolic core of the world's hopes. This the unborn World's Hypostyle Hall, its Parthenon, its Temple of Supreme Harmony, the emblem of Government rising, like that of London, Paris or Washington, over a noble river.

The architects felt this, of course. The General Assembly is, in plan, the focal point of the composition, and the flowing form of the structure was to characterize and emphasize its difference and its importance.

To me it lacks dignity and strength; it has a certain grace, but no beauty. The concave sweep of the wall, the concave droop of the roof make it weak and uncertain. A catenary held between two verticals has power and precision, but this curve is amorphous and is chopped off at points that have no visible relation to the curve or to each other. The dome of the Assembly Hall and the little pill-boxes that enclose the elevator machinery are inept and unrelated to the composition. The dome neither dominates, as one feels a dome should do, nor is it a decorative element, as it, together with the elevator enclosures, might have been. There are other curious discordances: the north front, the public entrance, is of so completely different a character from the south front—which opens out to the delegates' garden and the Secretariat entrance court—that although they are never seen at the same time the memory of the one comes as a shock when one looks at the other. The south front is of a piece with the other [120] buildings, a great window in a simple frame, and completes the composition of the court on which it faces. The north front, meant to be imposing, is quite unconvincing. On it, the use of photo-sensitive glass between the marble piers was intended to give a "solid" effect, which it momentarily does, and then one understands it is not solid at all, but a veneer seeming very thin and fragile and still somehow forbidding (though, of course, the building is still under construction). And on the west side, the First Avenue façade, the simplicity of the curved wall is marred by the rigidity of the ramps and the unbearably heavy canopy of the delegates' entrance.

The inside cannot be fully judged as yet. However, the plan is again thoroughly coordinated and excellent. The public enters into a huge hall, open to the roof and lighted by the strips between the piers with a very cold and gray light. Great ramps lead up to the public galleries, and it will no doubt be most impressive in scale. To the left of the foyer the public goes into a large space with big windows opening to the garden; the windows are cut across by a ramp similar to the one on the First Avenue side. The ramps provide fire exits from the main delegates' floor. This hall will be used for exhibitions and displays, and goes on to the connecting element between the General Assembly and the Conference Building with its Council and Conference rooms. Delegates enter from the First Avenue side, and go down to coat rooms and another large conference room, or up a double stairway with escalator in between to their lounge overlooking a garden and the Secretariat court. The garden is reached by a flight of free-form steps which, together with the proposed two-story marquee over the Secretariat entrance, was intended as a foil and diversion to the prevailing severity. From their foyer the delegates can go to the Assembly Hall or Conference Building without conflicting with the public.

The Assembly Hall itself will undoubtedly be a most impressive room. It will have a great scale, and every effort has been made to achieve a dramatic setting for the august body it will house. Like the other meeting rooms it will be acoustically perfect, and equipped with every device for hearing, recording and publicity.

The planning of the U.N. group is a triumph of clarity and ingenuity, a putting together and sorting out of an almost incredible variety of elements and functions. It is also a triumph of technical skill, of structural ability, of mechanical engineering. Almost every possible device of a mechanical nature has been used to further the comfort of the users of the buildings, to speed up communication, to disseminate information quickly and accurately. It is, in other words, a very fine example of American architectural skill.

It is not, however, much more than that; and perhaps it could not be. Our architectural genius today, and in the United States particularly, lies in the design of buildings for the use of business. Our most successful structures, esthetically as well as technically, are office buildings and factories. We are accomplished in the design of residences, too; but none of these classes of architecture speaks to the deep symbolic needs of our being, they have little emotional impact. The Secretariat is the U.N. to the world. By its simplicity of form and dominating mass it has become the symbol for U.N. The General Assembly building does not dominate either by its physical presence or its spiritual content. It is not that the effort to have the General Assembly provide the symbol was not made: it was. The failure is not the fault of the architects, but of a time in which no emotional symbols are possible because there is no deep belief, no emotional content in our lives. Symbols are not "created": they exist or they do not exist. The non-existent symbolism that was consciously striven for in the General Assembly got transferred subconsciously and necessarily to the real and existing symbol, the building which houses what we most believe in—paper-work, files, reports, pay-rolls, publicity. Symbols, great art, are not created *ad hoc*; they are inherent in the cultural and emotional heritage, and appear as such, whether we like them or not.[121]

JOHN DOS PASSOS

Architect of the U. N.

John Dos Passos, "Architect of the UN," New York Herald Tribune, This Week (October 19, 1952).*

We are standing in the tall strangely shaped north lobby of the Assembly building, looking out through huge glass doors across a stretch of rubble that's going to be a landscaped park towards the East River Drive where the sunlight flashes on the moving traffic and the river and the island full of hospitals and the ugly barrier of the 59th Street bridge.

Nothing could be further from the elegant dogmatism of the European Modern, with its obsessing memories of the permanence of the ancient styles, you think as you look up through the grim cold light at the ramps and girderwork contrived to lead crowds of walking people by the easiest possible slope into the hall beyond. There's a raw look of improvisation. This is American Modern.

You remember looking up at the gleaming blue glass flank of the Secretariat before you walked in and seeing the western sky and the incongruous buildings of midtown Manhattan mirrored in it. Could anything be more suitable? Here's an architecture that mirrors America's greatest strength, America's ability to change. Steel frameworks sheathed with glass are as removable as the tents of the Bedouin. If the United Nations doesn't work we take it apart and put it together again. Each experiment adds to the know-how. Next time we'll know better.[39]

* Reprinted with the permission of John Dos Passos and *The New York Herald Tribune.*

HENRY-RUSSELL HITCHCOCK AND PHILIP C. JOHNSON

The Buildings We See

Henry-Russell Hitchcock and Philip C. Johnson, "The Buildings We See," New World Writing, I (1952).*

Parallel in some ways with the belated success of the Barcelona chair is the situation that arose several years ago regarding the United Nations Building in New York. There was no competition for this international capitol, such as had been held for the League of Nations Building in the mid-twenties—the curious machinations by which Le Corbusier's winning project of that earlier Geneva edifice failed of execution perhaps played some part in the decision not to hold a competition this time. Instead, top professional representatives of the various nations met in New York to prepare a joint [114] design. That design was eventually executed under the direction of Wallace Harrison. The "slab" skyscraper was certainly an idea contributed by Le Corbusier, who was the official French representative among the architects. As his own late projects for North African cities illustrate, however, he had long ceased proposing slabs as slick and scaleless as what eventually came to execution.

For the 1920's, the executed design which we have seen rising beside the East River would certainly have been revolutionary. Only Le Corbusier, moreover, would then have had the imagination and the courage to conceive it. But by the late 1940's the slab concept for tall office buildings had become widely accepted, indeed almost platitudinous. This particular version, having been developed by a committee of architects, lacks the strongly individual expression which might have given it a more positive character.[115]

LEWIS MUMFORD

From the Ground Up

Lewis Mumford, *From the Ground Up* (New York, Harcourt, Brace and Company, Inc., 1956).*

U N MODEL AND MODEL U N

. . . The Board of Design Consultants did not begin to function until February of this year. "Speed," we read, early in the document, "was the essence of the problem." "Some fifty basic designs were created, criticized, analyzed, and resynthesized," we are told a little later. Those two statements, taken together, account for the fact that when it became necessary to reach a decision, the Board fell back upon the architectural stereotypes of the early nineteen-thirties. So far, their headquarters is a combination of Le Corbusier's breezy City of the Future and the business-like congestion of Rockefeller Center, a blending of the grandiose and the obvious. . . .

As I have just pointed out, the worst problem facing the architects who are laboring on the United Nations project is the site. Architects should not, of course, be blamed for the errors of their clients. Is this site the right one for such an institution, and is the area adequate? There is no question in my mind but that the [21] headquarters for the United Nations should be in the heart of a metropolis. There is also no question but that an organism that is bound to grow and to attract to its neighborhood other institutions fostering international activities should be a real city within a city, dominating its site even more conspicuously than Vatican City does. The site for such a headquarters should eventually embrace around a thousand acres, or at least be not less than the size of Central Park, which is around eight hundred and fifty acres. (The United Nations site, in its present form, is only seventeen and a half acres.)...[22]

Before Mr. Rockefeller bought the United Nations site, the land had been assembled by a group of private operators, who had engaged Mr. Harrison to prepare plans to develop it as an apartment-house and business center. The rise in the cost of building may well have made this project, conceived during the war, seem a dubious prospect, and the fact that Mr. Harrison was one of the major architects for Rockefeller Center may have made it a little easier for the principals in the present undertaking to get together. Once Mr. Rockefeller's gift was accepted, the appointment of Mr. Harrison—about whose outstanding abilities as architect and organizer there is no question—as the chief architect of this enterprise seemed an almost inevitable step. This essay in genealogy is not designed to look a gift horse in the mouth. It is merely intended [24] to show that this particular site, though it might have served business well, is too cramped adequately to serve the United Nations even as working quarters. And what can be built on it will hardly be a fitting symbol of a just and orderly world. What might be a good short-term realty speculation is not necessarily a good long-term investment in the interests of the welfare and the comity of the peoples of the earth....[25]

BUILDINGS AS SYMBOLS

... The problem that faced the distinguished Board of Design Consultants, of which Mr. Wallace K. Harrison is the head, was determined by two main considerations: the size and nature of the site, and the work that the United Nations is doing now and may be expected to do in the future.... The architects, to judge by the report, are better satisfied with the area than I am, for they say, "The East River site, extending fifteen hundred feet from Forty-second Street to Forty-eighth Street, and from First Avenue to the edge of the water, has sufficient scale for applying the fundamental elements of modern urbanism—sunlight, space, and

The United Nations, 1947-1953, New York; the interior of the public
entrance to the General Assembly Building. Of this Lewis Mumford
observed: "The main public entrance hall has a noble scale."

verdure. Protected by the wide expanse of the East River, the
site has [27] breadth enough to be made into a living unity of
strength, dignity, and harmony."

. . . The Board of Design Consultants are, I am afraid, a
little like Browning's Last Duchess, "too soon made glad, too
easily impressed." One could readily forgive them such amiable
faults if they had succeeded in making the best possible use of
the seventeen and a half acres that have been put at their disposal. Severe limitations of the sort encountered on this inadequate site are sometimes spurs to the imagination, so I examined
the model and the plans carefully to see whether in this case they
had had any effect. With great reluctance—indeed, with pain
and embarrassment—I must cast a negative vote. Symbolically,
these buildings are far from being an admirable expression of

the idea of the United Nations, and functionally, they do not make the necessary provisions for extension, change of purpose, and future development.

. . . Toward the south end of the site will be a group of four buildings. The dominant one will be that of the Secretariat, a rectangular slab of skyscraper forty stories high, halfway between the river and First Avenue, and running from a point a bit north of Forty-second Street to a point halfway between Forty-third and Forty-fourth [28] Streets. Directly north of this, at about the center of the site, will be the slightly fan-shaped General Assembly Hall—a great auditorium, whose axis will be parallel to First Avenue, with an entrance for the general public on the north, reached by a roadway through the park from First Avenue. This building will be broad and, because of its function, nowhere near as tall as the [other] . . . I have just mentioned. The buildings of the Secretariat and the Assembly Hall will be connected by a wide unit, even lower than the auditorium, lying to the east and to be devoted to the councils and committees of the United Nations. South of all this, on Forty-second Street, near First Avenue, another structure is already in existence — a small office building erected by the New York Housing Authority and turned over to the United Nations before it was finished. Plainly, this last is a mixed blessing, very useful at the moment, when the United Nations needs administrative quarters in the city, but an obstacle to any free development of this part of the site. [It is now being replaced by the U.N. Library. Eds.]

In trying to view this design as a whole, one quickly becomes conscious that, aesthetically speaking, a whole does not exist. . . . Despite the variety of their national backgrounds, the architects have apparently not been able to shake off the stereotypes of New York architecture. . . . But to rely upon creating a similar effect in a city of skyscrapers is either to miscalculate the visual relationships [29] completely or to scorn them altogether. The neighboring R.C.A. Building is seventy stories high, the Chrysler Tower is even higher, and the nearer-at-hand pinnacles of Tudor City, set just southeast of the United Nations site, on a bluff that rises above it, must diminish the effect even of the forty stories of the Secretariat Building.

. . . In the United Nations headquarters, there is not only no

human scale, there is no transition from the intimate to the monumental. And it was a mistake to make the Secretariat Building
the monumental, dominant structure instead of the General Assembly Hall and the Conference Building, which should be the
focus of visual interest as well as the symbol of political authority.
If the Secretariat Building will have anything to say as a symbol,
it will be, I fear, that the managerial revolution has taken place
and that bureaucracy rules the world. I am sorry that the architects have apparently taken Mr. James Burnham's discouraging
thesis as an axiom, for the United Nations is an attempt to make
other ideas prevail.

Doubtless the Beaux-Arts architects of the last generation
would have tried to make the United Nations headquarters look
richly palatial and ancient—a classic forum or a baroque plaza
—and the result would have been as grisly as the new government [30] office buildings between Pennsylvania Avenue and the
Mall in Washington. Perhaps we should simply be thankful that
Mr. Harrison and his colleagues have saved us from that fate.
But the Beaux-Arts architects would at least have tried to do one
thing right; they would have taken care that the important buildings of the group would be visible at a distance, would have a
handsome setting, and would make a powerful aesthetic impression. The United Nations headquarters should not look like a
group of temples and basilicas, but it likewise should not look
like a few forlorn and temporary "taxpayers"* nestling under a
group of office buildings till the rest of the site is ready to be
covered by skyscrapers. That is just another kind of imitative
formalism. In view of the difficult conditions under which they
have worked, one could forgive Mr. Harrison and his associates
for their mistakes of detail. Their real failure is of a different
order; they have failed to create a fresh symbol, and that failure
is more serious. Their new World City is just a chip off the old
block. Even the architectural huggermugger of the World's Fair
of 1939 produced a Trylon and a Perisphere, those slightly embarrassing efforts toward symbolism, and if Mr. Harrison, their

* One-story commercial buildings of the simplest construction, designed
to derive sufficient income to pay the taxes on the building site; found
chiefly in New York.

designer, is trying to live them down, all I can say is that he has swung too far in the opposite direction.

. . . When Mr. Harrison handed in the preliminary plans to the Advisory Comittee, of which Mr. Warren R. Austin is chairman, he presented them with these words: "The world hopes for a symbol of peace; we have given them a workshop of peace"— almost as if to say that the symbolic part of architecture, the impression [31] it makes on the mind and the senses, is of minor importance. If he did not mean to say this, the architecture has said it for him. . . . Considering the genteel classicism of the winning design in the competition for the Palace of the League of Nations, the modernity of the United Nations plans must have seemed to many of the architects involved—especially to Le Corbusier, whose austere design for the Palace was rejected by the Geneva jury—a great triumph. Time, however, changes everything, including the meaning of "modern." To say that a group of buildings is not fake Greek, bastard Roman, cast-iron Gothic, trite Renaissance, or simply warmed-over hash is no longer sufficient commendation. By now, these negative virtues, along with sunlight, air, and verdure, must be taken for granted. This should be our point of departure, not our goal. . . . [32]

There are, I should emphasize, some thoroughly commendable points in the present design of the Assembly Hall and the Conference Building. The latter, for example, with its wide windows looking out on the river, with its top-level restaurants and sunny terraces, will offer the delegates the recreative resources of light and space and wide horizons — resources that will serve them, in their more harried moments, better than aspirin, whiskey, or sleeping capsules. I do not, however, understand why the designers have not provided the delegates with a private waterfront promenade, where they might stretch their legs, along with little bosky recesses, where they could, in solitude, conduct private negotiations or just recover their sense of humor. [33]

. . . The report says that room must be provided for expansion, but I can find no evidence in the plans that such provisions have been made. Here, as elsewhere, there is evidence of the failure to respect fundamental principles. The report [34] uses all the right words to describe the architecture; it emphasizes integration, organism, flexibility, expansion, and so on. But in the plans themselves one too often sees just the opposite—rigidity, confinement, lack of sound provision for growth.

. . . Whatever the United Nations headquarters should do or say, however many people or functions it must serve, the buildings should proclaim with a single voice that a new world order, dedicated to peace and justice, is rising on this site. These buildings should be as beloved a symbol as the Statue of Liberty, as powerful a spectacle as St. Peter's in Rome. Such symbols cannot be created by falling back on clichés, like statues, domes, and skyscraper towers, and they cannot be conceived overnight. Short of flatly rejecting the site, the architects should have worked out the right scale for their present project, suggested an effective way of taking care of future requirements, and then set their most imaginative members to work on the problem of symbolism, which is, at bottom, the problem of public relations for the new world order. . . .[35]

MAGIC WITH MIRRORS

. . . Whereas modern architecture began with the true precept that form follows function, and that an organic form must respect every human function, this new office building is based on the theory that even if no symbolic purpose is served, function should be sacrificed to form. This is a new kind of academicism, successful largely because its clichés readily lend themselves to imitation and reproduction. In the present instance, it has brought into existence not a work of three-dimensional architecture but a Christmas package wrapped in cellophane. Functionally, this building is an old-fashioned engine covered by a streamlined hood much embellished with chromium. . . .

From a distance, the Secretariat Building, two hundred and eighty-seven feet long, seventy-two feet wide, and thirty-nine stories high, is a great oblong prism of glass, marble, and aluminum. It connects, on its lower levels, with the General Assembly Building, to the north of it, and with the Conference Building, to the east and almost invisible except from the river. But by reason of its bulk and height, this huge slab is visually detached from them and reduces them to insignificance. The smallest buildings in Rockefeller Center are far enough away from the enormous R.C.A. Building and are sufficiently supported by buildings of intermediate height not to seem runty, but there are no such spacial gradations between the midgets and the giant in the United Nations composition; the success of the whole group depends almost solely upon this [37] central building. The exterior of the Secretariat is much less complicated than that of the R.C.A. Building, for there are no recessions or setbacks. At the north and south ends, this prism is a smooth, windowless sheath of mottled white marble; on the east and west faces, it is a smooth wall of green glass framed in aluminum. Even the spandrels and frames of the windows do not break the surface; in fact, the only interruptions in it are four horizontal grilles, each one a story high and running the full width of the facade. These grilles, set at intervals, conceal the several installations of elevator and ventilating machinery. The lattice effect they create is repeated above the roof, to a height of over twenty feet, to conceal the penthouse, which also contains machinery. This manner of visually dividing the building was the object of adverse criticism in a recent architectural symposium. But on the whole the change of form seems to me a happy way of externally acknowledging a change of interior function, and even the latticework at the top, though costly, is a justifiable liberty in a rigidly restricted design. . . .[38]

Unfortunately, glass and steel are not wholly satisfactory building materials. If steel is not insulated from heat, it expands and contracts in a fashion that presents serious problems, particularly in a tall building placed where other buildings or trees do not modify the climate. Glass transmits not only light but heat, and unless windows are completely sealed, they admit air in a high wind. And, as last November's hurricane once more demonstrated, particularly in the case of the Secretariat Building, large sheets of glass are perilously breakable. Therefore, the development of the skyscraper became possible only when architects learned to give as much attention to heat-and-fire-resistant materials as to the revealing qualities of glass and the structural possibilities of steel. Glass and metal do not burn, but they crack and buckle in the heat of a fire. . . . But the massive masonry of the ancient stone-and-glass cathedrals of Europe stood up under both fire and bomb blast during World War II while the buildings around them were reduced to cinders and rubble. Glass not only admits a great deal of heat on sunny days, even when the windows are closed; it likewise radiates heat to the outer air on cold days. In his own design for the Secretariat, Le Corbusier proposed to overcome these defects with two special devices. One was the permanent sun screen, or *brise-soleil*, which was used on the sunny sides of the Ministry of Education and Health Building in Rio de Janeiro in 1937—a building on which Le Corbusier served as consultant. The other was a double glass wall, inside which he intended to circulate cool air in the summer and hot air in the winter. When these elements in his design were thrown out, he wrote an indignant [39] letter to Ambassador Warren Austin, the head of the United Nations building committee, declaring that the steel-and-glass building that has now been erected would be uninhabitable. There was good reason to avoid the *brise-soleil* in New York's climate, since menacing icicles might form on it, and there is also reason to avoid a double glass wall anywhere, since the cost of cleaning what would amount to a continuous double window would be enormous. But there was an even better reason for turning down this wall. Glass should give one a clear view of the outside world, and in the form of the window—that admirable invention—it provides direct contact with fresh air and sunlight. A solid glass wall sacrifices one of these advantages, and a double glass wall sacrifices both.

. . . Aesthetically speaking, the main function of these great glass walls is to serve as a mirror in which the buildings of the city are reflected, in which the western sky sometimes plays in delicate counterpoint to the eastern sky. No building in the city is more responsive to the constant play of light and shadow in the world beyond it; none varies more subtly with the time of day and the way the light strikes, now emphasizing the vertical metal window bars, now emphasizing the dark green of the spandrels and underlining the horizontality of the composition. No one had ever conceived of building a mirror on this scale before, and perhaps no one guessed what an [40] endless series of pictures that mirror would reveal. The aesthetic effect is incomparable, but, unfortunately, when the building is most effective as a looking glass it is least notable as a work of architecture. . . .

Here, then, is the Secretariat Building from the outside: two thin white vertical marble slabs, connected by two vast glass mirrors that are broken only by horizontal white aluminum grilles; a building chaste, startling, fairylike in its cold austerity, a Snow Queen's palace, exhaling by night a green moonlight splendor. Paraded as pure engineering and applied geometry, this new skyscraper proves really to be a triumph of irrelevant romanticism. If anything deserves to be called picture-book architecture, this is it, for all the fundamental qualities of architecture seem to have been sacrificed to the external picture, or, rather, to the more ephemeral passing image reflected on its surface. . . .[41]

In planning the Secretariat, the architects were not, like most designers, confined to the constricted space of the conventional Manhattan lot, or even block, and they could thus have designed a freestanding building, or a series of freestanding buildings. . . . A freestanding building can have light on all four sides, but the architects of the Secretariat have blanked out two sides of it with solid walls of marble. . . .[42]

Apparently, though, the Board of Design Consultants were hypnotized by Le Corbusier, and Le Corbusier has long been hypnotized by the notion that the skyscraper is a symbol of the modern age. But the fact is that both the skyscraper and Le Corbusier are outmoded. Skyscrapers conceived without respect for human scale or insight into human requirements and values are indeed symbolic, but they are symbols of the way specious considerations of fashion, profit, prestige, abstract aesthetic form —in a word, "the package" of commerce—have taken precedence over the need of human beings for good working and living quarters.

What we have, then, is not a building expressive of the purposes of the United Nations but an extremely fragile aesthetic achievement, whose main lines conform to the ideals of a boom period of shaky finance [43] and large-scale speculation. This sort of modernism goes only skin deep. As a conscious symbol, the Secretariat adds up to zero; as an unconscious one, it is a negative quantity, since it symbolizes the worst practices of New York, not the best hopes of the United Nations. So much for the outside of the building—impeccable but irrelevant. The inside of this package does not even live up to the elegant wrappings. On that matter, I shall presently have more to say.[44]

A DISORIENTED SYMBOL

Viewed from without, the thirty-nine-story United Nations Secretariat Building, whose east and west fronts form oblong green
mirrors, is the glass of present-day fashion. But, once inside it,
one discovers that it can make no claim whatever to being the
future mold of form. . . .[45]

   . . . The main entrance is marked on the outside by a curving
marble bay and an irregularly curved aluminum marquee that,
alas, recalled the *"modernique"* of the Paris Exposition of 1925.
The absence of a fine sense of scale here is conspicuous, for the
entrance, only one story high, is crushed to insignificance.

   On the inside, the ceiling, low enough as it is, seems much
lower because of the length of the lobby. The interior walls and
columns parallel to the east and west green glass façades are
faced with green marble. Those parallel to the north and south
façades, which are unbroken surfaces of mottled white marble,
are faced with the white marble. The floor, which is made up of
large squares of black and white terrazzo, calls attention to itself
too emphatically. The happiest feature of the lobby, humanly
speaking, is the long bench at the south end. This should be a
convenient place—like the information desk at Grand Central—
for meeting people. The lack of such a feature is a weakness in
most office-building design. (Some day, perhaps, this bench will
be turned to face the splendid East River view.) Otherwise, the
interior is in the frigid, impeccable taste that is the modern
equivalent of what the architectural bureaucrats in Washington
seek when they invoke the classic. If you like the Mellon Gallery
interior, you should like the Secretariat interior, even if its proportions are not so noble.[46]

   . . . If the decoration of the interior is without notable dash
or elegance, it is also inoffensive. In general, the color scheme of
the working floors is gray—light gray walls, dark gray floors—
relieved only by the blue of the doors, the sky blue of the United
Nations flag. This, incidentally, is just about the only symbolic
indication in the whole building that it has anything to do with
the United Nations.

   The plan of the working quarters is simple. The elevators,

at the center of the building, open on corridors, one on each floor, that run north and south. Since the windows are continuous along the two glass façades, the office space can be arranged and rearranged, when that is necessary, without the interference of external columns; at the moment, the smallest cubicle is two windows wide. Yet even the lucky executives with an ample office at one corner of the structure cannot have the luxury of cross-ventilation, because of the blank north and south outer walls.

The problem of making such a building livable as well as comely was a tremendous one. Let us consider first the matter of orientation. The Secretariat's long axis runs north and south. If the building had been turned so that it was parallel to Forty-second Street, it would not merely have blocked out, for those [47] approaching the General Assembly Building, the unkempt industrial district I have referred to but would have shielded the Secretariat's occupants from our intolerable summer sun, which can turn the completely exposed rooms on the east and west fronts into big bake ovens unless the Venetian blinds are drawn and the air-conditioning system is working full blast. Furthermore, the building could, like the Conference Building, have jutted out over Franklin D. Roosevelt Drive. It would then have been conspicuously visible for great distances north and south, especially when it was lighted up at night.

The engineers concerned estimate that the present orientation of this narrow building, because of exposure to the sun during the summer, puts a load on the cooling system that raises the operating cost two and a half per cent. The human cost is greater; many of the occupants are compelled to work a good part of the day under artificial light behind their drawn Venetian blinds. Thus it is sadly necessary to remove the view the walls of glass were designed to reveal and to cut off the sunlight they were designed to admit. Even when the summer heat presents no problem, there is no possibility of natural ventilation or a pleasant natural light to work in, despite the vast amount of window space. . . . [48]

The result of misorienting the Secretariat and using glass so exuberantly is to create a building that functionally is often windowless on all four sides. On this matter, the architectural his-

torian Professor Henry-Russell Hitchcock seems to me to have
said the last word. "The most significant influence of the Secretariat," he recently observed, "will, I imagine, be to end the use
of glass walls in skyscrapers—certainly in those with western ex-
posures, unless exterior elements are provided to keep the sun
off the glass.". . .

The standard floor of the Secretariat contains offices of various sizes. Because of the shallowness of the building (no point
in the interior is very far from the windows, except on the blind
ends of the building), this seems an admirable arrangement. Unfortunately, it produces far from ideal working conditions for the
secretaries, who occupy the interior offices, where the only daylight is what seeps through the semi-opaque glass partitions that
separate the outer rooms from the inner ones. . . . [49]

. . . By opening up the blind walls, and by moving some of
the lavatories that are unaccountably on the perimeter to the
interior, the designers could have given a certain number of the
secretaries decent exterior working quarters instead of the stuffy
interior chambers they occupy. . . . [50]

I am aware that I am putting in a minority report on the
Secretariat Building. But those who praise it without severe res-
ervations do modern architecture a disservice by judging it mainly on its superficial elegance. A building to house an international
personnel devoted to bringing about world cooperation and world
peace should be more than a slick mechanical job—and, as I
have said, even the mechanical details of this structure are sometimes far from slick. Such a building should, by its zealous attention to human functions and human needs, itself symbolize the
great purposes it serves. It should give at least a preliminary [51]
glimpse of the new world, the world in which human considerations will be uppermost and will set the mold for all our organizations and institutions. It should be both a visual and an
operational symbol, and its beauty should arise out of the due
fulfillment of all its functions, graded in the order of their human
importance. That is almost the last merit one could impute to
the new United Nations Secretariat Building. [52]

UNITED NATIONS ASSEMBLY

The group of buildings that forms the United Nations head-quarters reaches its architectural anticlimax in the recently completed General Assembly Building, a fairly low, sort of oblong structure with incurving side walls and a roof that droops in a long, graceful curve between the two ends. This building is the home of what must in time be the most important deliberative body in the world. But there is nothing in its shape, its position, its external treatment, or its relation to the two other United Nations buildings—the Conference Building and the Secretariat—to indicate its importance or that of the organization it serves. The architects who created it would have a hard time defending its exterior even if they had been designing a modern motion-picture palace, which is the only thing it resembles. It is the moving-picture palace of 1950, as the Music Hall was the moving-picture palace of 1930. Instead of a big mural by the conventional Ezra Winter, there are big murals by Fernand Léger, decorative yet equally empty and—is this a heresy?—equally conventional. But as a home for a great institution that seeks to establish peace and cooperation between the nations of the world, it is a painful simulacrum, the kind of thing Hollywood might have faked.

The main axis of the Assembly Building, like the main axes of the two other buildings, runs north and south. Its southern façade gives on the great entrance [53] court that faces on First Avenue, to the west. To the southeast of the building, and joined to it by a three-story passageway, is the low and oblong Conference Building, and farther to the south is the narrow but towering Secretariat. Unlike either of these structures, the Assembly Building has the look of a blank wall from almost every aspect. The only real break in its monotonous expanse of flat stone is the vast window that takes up the whole of the southern end. . . .

. . . Making no attempt to modify these expanses of stone by the application of any detail—sculpture or even inscription—the architects were content to quite literally draw a blank; even the letters "U.N.," which could have been as proudly displayed as the old Roman "S.P.Q.R." or the French "R.F.," are absent. . . .

Moreover, there is no approach to the building, for either the delegates or the public, except a sidelong, glancing one. The advantage of a frontal approach, enabling one to see the architectural features, was forfeited by the designers, perhaps for the good reason that they had provided nothing to see. The delegates' entrance, near the southwest corner, is marked only by a panel of marble above the marble-sheathed marquee. The public entrance, at the north end, and as far away as possible from the major subway [54] stops, is equally banal; were it not for an improvised street sign and a modest marquee, one would have no clue to its whereabouts . . .

Only one façade of this building, indeed, has any positive architectural quality — the great window, with gigantic square panes, running across the southern end and boxed in by a projecting marble frame. This window dominates, with a certain aesthetic assurance, what one excusably mistakes for the main entrance to both the Conference and the Assembly Buildings. But it wastes its monumentality upon the desert air, for it is not an entrance at all. A small stairway and platform, issuing dramatically from one side of the window, reveal its true purpose; it is a fire exit, and only that. The one part of this monumental structure that visually says "Come In!" is therefore actually saying "Stay Out!" Since this false entrance is of no use for getting [55] in, what purpose does it serve those within the building? This question is not easily answered, for though the view through the great transparent panel is almost unobstructed, the delegates on the ground floor, and the public and the press on the floor above, look out on the sordid industrial wasteland to the south of the United Nations site. Thus a bad site plan, which reveals what it should have taken pains to conceal, is capped by a bad building plan, which compounds this error with interest, in the manner of dwellers on cramped suburban lots whose picture windows face their neighbors' garages and clotheslines.

The three other sides of this building are innocent of any aesthetic decision, and there is little to say of its general form and silhouette except that they tell nothing about the interior. At one stage of the planning, there was a reason for this kind of structural envelope; it was to take care of two separate auditoriums. That accounts for the bulge at each end and for the rise in the

The United Nations, 1947-1953, New York; the Auditorium of the General Assembly which stands beneath the dome. In the background, the semi-circular wall, slanting inward is ribbed with wood fluting that is covered with gold leaf. In the middle, over the rostrum, a huge bronze shield bears the blue-and-white emblem of the United Nations.

roof line. When the decision to build but one auditorium—and ovoid, at that—was reached, the architects had become so committed to this structural envelope that they retained it unaltered, which is all the odder because the auditorium is at the center, the narrowest point of the building. The only outside indication that this auditorium exists is a blisterlike dome of lead-covered copper, too small to be of any positive visual consequence, though it manages to spoil, from certain angles, the one merit the roof could have had, as a sweeping, unbroken curve. Neither functional use nor aesthetic purity can account for this design. Happily, viewed at one point—from the north, along First Avenue—the two visible buildings (the Conference Building is con-

spicuously absent) suddenly become a vision of delight, when the
steep down curve of the Assembly roof, looking somewhat fore-
shortened from below, intersects the steep marble slab [56] of the
Secretariat, to the south. If one could stand permanently at that
point, one could forgive all the architectural lapses. Genuine
four-dimensional architecture would present a succession of such
miracles as one moved around from this point and into the buildings, but the United Nations design, unfortunately, offers only
one clean architectural hit. . . .

. . . The main public entrance hall has a noble scale, but the
details are, so to speak, consistently jumbled, from the marbled
glass, whose only intrinsic value is to hide the dirt that accumu-
lates on unwashed window-panes, to the parabolic arches that
support the ramp leading to the first of a series of projecting
balconies, a device that reminds one of nothing so much as a
Meyerhold stage setting of the 'twenties. As for the balconies,
whose billowing forms, finished in white plaster, define the upper
levels, they recall the imaginative black-and-white drawings of
"plastic" concrete structures that Eric Mendelsohn published
some thirty years ago. . . .[57]

At the core of the building is the General Assembly Hall,
which is topped by an open-ribbed dome painted powder blue,
with encircling lights pointing down on the delegates. The south
half of this hall, which gives on the delegates' lounge, is a semi-
circular wall, slanting inward toward the dome, ribbed by wood
fluting covered with gold leaf, and unbroken except for the
speakers' rostrum and the two continuous side panels of windows
for the radio and television booths. The other half is open to
the press and the spectators, who [58] are accommodated in a tier
of seats rising from the floor and in a balcony above it. Thus this
hall is a combination of parliamentary chamber and theater auditorium. A speaker on the rostrum faces both delegates and spectators. Above him is the desk of the presiding officers, and above
them is a large bronze shield bearing the United Nations emblem
in white, surrounded by large plastic medallions, covered with
gold leaf, that will eventually bear the insignia of the component
nations. But when one considers that the United Nations has
only sixty member countries, the proportions of the hall seem
overwhelming. That is not the fault of the architects; rather, as

the late Matthew Nowicki, one of the special consultants of the board of design, once observed, it reveals the weakness of the Charter of the United Nations, which, under the formula of "sovereign equality," provides the smallest state with as many seats as the biggest powers. As a result, the Assembly, even while in session, often seems empty, thus defying the conditions Mr. Winston Churchill holds essential to good parliamentary debate. It seems not to have occurred to anyone that this constitution is amendable, and that the composition of the organization could change, in which case even less seating space might be required. Here, as throughout the entire scheme for the United Nations buildings, what is saliently lacking in both the thinking and the architecture is the quality that differentiates modern design from the immobile and ponderous monumentality of the past—the ability to anticipate change and to provide for it. In the Assembly Building, as in the Conference Building, the future is frozen solidly in the form of the present. This lack of flexibility is a serious failure in planning for an institution that may undergo many constitutional changes before it solidifies into a durable mold.[59]

. . . The monumental weakness of this building—or the weakness of its monumentality—probably stems from the architects' ambivalent attitude toward the purpose of architecture. In the name of functionalism, they have perpetuated formalism, and under the illusion that they were designing a useful workshop, they have failed to meet the United Nations' greatest practical need—the kind of plan that could be adapted to new uses. Despite this sacrifice, all three United Nations buildings fail to meet the condition that would justify the subordination of practical need to aesthetic form—the creation of an endearing symbol of the purposes and meaning of the United Nations: order out of chaos, unity out of diversity, peace and harmony out of anarchic belligerence.

These three buildings do not in any way suggest in architectural idiom the dawning concept of world government or make visible the love and cooperation that are needed for its success. The arid neutralism of this architecture reflects neither paternal power nor maternal love; without any warmth of feeling, without any impressive image of human vitality, these buildings have only one climax; the thirty-nine-story skyscraper Secretariat, a type of building that to distant peoples is a stock emblem of the things they fear and hate—our slick mechanization, our awful power, our patronizing attitude toward lesser breeds who[60] have not acquired the American way of life. . . .[61]

WORKSHOP INVISIBLE

Architecture can be produced in a hurry only when the type of building is a well-established one. The lack of good types was a sufficient handicap, but an even tougher problem dogged all who were concerned—the difficulty of formulating a program for these buildings, of deciding, after it had been in operation only a few years, what the needs of this new organization were and how they should be met, considering the limitations of time, space, and money. Today the purely architectural consideration—i.e., the visible structure—is only a small part of the architects' problem. The matter of putting together its mechanical equipment, including such specialties as air-conditioning and radio and television equipment, is extremely complicated, and the prevailing obsession with invention may have inclined everyone involved to sacrifice the permanent function of the United Nations—the pooling of collective wisdom for the sake of world peace—to the novel possibility of dramatically reproducing its procedures by photography and sound and television, though there were voices in the United Nations that warned at the very beginning of the danger of this. . . .[63]

The Conference Building performs three wholly unrelated functions: it provides quarters for the councils and committees that run the United Nations, it houses most of the social activities of the delegates, and it serves as a concourse between the Secretariat and the General Assembly Building. . . .

Perhaps the most important factor about the Conference Building is that it is almost invisible. One of Le Corbusier's published sketches for the U.N. shows that it was consigned to oblivion at an early stage in the designing. Thus the architects threw away one of the greatest advantages of this site. These seventeen acres afforded an opportunity to design a group of modern freestanding buildings in harmonious aesthetic relationship. Were the architects afraid to take attention away from their skyscraper, their precious symbol of "modernity"? As if to support this possibility, the part of the three-level passageway visible from the entrance court has, because of its great glass windows heavily framed in stone, no relation, in scale or treatment, to either the Conference or the General Assembly Building, the two structures it connects. It looks as if it had been there long before these two [65] were erected and, like the Housing Authority Building, could not be absorbed into the composition.

In plan, the Conference Building is simple. This four-story oblong, sheathed in limestone, is two and a half times as long as it is broad, widening slightly toward its north end, and cantilevered out over Franklin D. Roosevelt Drive. It is surrounded on the second (or Council Chamber) floor by a balcony that juts still farther toward the water and leads, by a flight of stairs, to the still unfinished delegates' garden, which faces a mountain range of confused industrial architecture to the south. On the water side, the building is a seemingly solid wall of glass windows. Behind these windows are the big Council Chambers (Economic and Social, Trusteeship, and Security). Mr. Harrison has said that the architects' only aim was to make these buildings not a monument but "the best damn workshop we could," yet even that limited effort was handicapped by a lack of forthright thinking on matters of comfort, convenience, and function. The immense windows of these chambers do not open, there is no attempt at natural ventilation, there is insufficient provision for easy exit, during a recess, to the balcony for a refreshing turn in the open air. Since the enormous volume of light the windows admit must be screened, even the view of the sky that more functional windows would have given is lost. Le Corbusier once said that it is now possible to have a window three hundred feet wide, and the United Nations architects seem to have taken him at his word, without asking themselves why, at this particular point in this particular building, an all-glass façade was required. The Conference Rooms, the smaller counterparts of these auditoriums, on the floor below, come nearer to being workmanlike [66] because of their simpler furnishings and their less dramatic atmosphere.

The United Nations, 1947-1953, New York; looking south along First Avenue on the west side of the General Assembly building. Lewis Mumford: "Happily viewed at one point,—from the north, along First Avenue—the two visible buildings (the Conference Building is conspicuously absent) suddenly become a vision of delight. When the steep down curve of the Assembly roof . . . intersects the steep marble slab of the Secretariat. . . ."

There is an even huger window in the limestone wall of the north side of the building, which houses the delegates' lounge, as well as a bar and a writing room. Here the architects, by using vertical hangings, have broken the glass wall into a more conventional alternation of solids and voids, with a contrast of light and dark sufficient to create a pleasant interior. But they have abandoned the upright wall that surrounds the rest of the structure for a window frame that slants inward from top to bottom, as if this façade were a shop window from which it was necessary to remove any reflection. If one cannot call this art for art's sake, one certainly can call it the cliché for the clichés sake. The architects have overlooked the aesthetic function of the north façade as a pedestal for the Secretariat, to the south, and as a counterfoil to the almost completely blank curving flank of the Assembly Building, to the west. Black granite might have given the composition the aesthetic vitality the shadowy limestone completely lacks. . . .[67]

The interiors of the great Council Chambers are an attempt to do justice to three quite different sets of requirements—those of the members, engaged in discussion; those of the public and press, admitted to the gallery of these chambers; and those of the mechanical organs of publicity, whose radio and television booths take up a whole side of the walls, picking up sounds and images and sending them to other parts of the building and the outside world. The elaborateness of this equipment is fantastic. Because of it and the air-conditioning units, the floors and ceilings of the Conference and the Assembly Buildings harbor a maze of ducts and pipes, complicated to plan and expensive to execute, absorbing the time, money, effort, and imagination that in a simpler culture went into the production of architectural forms. The architect of the Economic and Social Council Chamber— Sven Markelius, of Sweden, one of the original consultants—has even tried to dramatize this unavoidable fact by leaving the rear part of the ceiling exposed. As a consequence, when the delegates' section is lighted up and the public section is in semidarkness, the room looks like nothing so much as a movie set. . . . The lack of conviction, the element of exaggeration, the recurring touch of uncertainty that pervades the whole design makes even these elegant rooms less workmanlike than they should be. Yet the interior is the only aspect of the Conference Building that deserves to be called architecture. All in all, this structure must be rated a magnificent perversity — a potentially monumental building effectively disguised [69] as a corridor. By missing every opportunity for good site planning and architectural counterpoint, the architects managed to wall out of sight one of the three buildings they were given to design. That would be a hollow triumph even if this building were—as, alas, it is not—the "best damn workshop" in the world.[70]

As a contrast to the comments on the United Nations, the editors offer the following quotations from letters of Thomas Jefferson, George Washington and others on the kind of architecture they desired for the United States, particularly in connection with the National Capitol. While the first three, written by Thomas Jefferson, are associated with the Capitol of Virginia at Richmond, they reveal his concept of public architecture and, for that reason, apply with equal validity to his part in the building of the National Capitol.

THOMAS JEFFERSON

Letters

Thomas Jefferson, *Papers*, Julian P. Boyd, ed., Mina R. Bryan and Elizabeth L. Hutter, assoc. eds. (Princeton, Princeton University Press, 1953), VIII.*

TO JAMES MADISON, WITH ACCOUNT ENCLOSED

Paris Sep. 20. 1785.

DEAR SIR

. . . We took for our model what is called the Maisonquarrèe† of Nismes, one of the most beautiful, if not the [534] most beautiful and precious morsel of architecture left us by antiquity. It was built by Caius and Lucius Caesar and repaired by Louis XIV. and has the suffrage of all the judges of architecture who have seen it, as yeilding to no one of the beautiful monuments of Greece, Rome, Palmyra and Balbec which late travellers have communicated to us. It is very simple, but it is noble beyond expression, and would have done honour to our country as pre-

---

* Reprinted with the permission of the Princeton University Press.
† Maison Carrée

senting to travellers a morsel of taste in our infancy promising much for our maturer age. I have been much mortified with information which I received two days ago from Virginia that the first brick of the Capitol would be laid within a few days. But surely the delay of this peice of a summer would have been repaid by the savings in the plan preparing here, were we to value it's other superiorities as nothing. But how is a taste in this beautiful art to be formed in our countrymen, unless we avail ourselves of every occasion when public buildings are to be erected, of presenting to them models for their study and imitation? . . .

   . . . Adieu. Your's affectionately,   TH: JEFFERSON [535]

Thomas Jefferson, *Papers*, Julian P. Boyd., ed., Mina R. Bryan, assoc. ed. (Princeton, Princeton University Press, 1954), IX.

TO WILLIAM BUCHANAN AND JAMES HAY

GENTLEMEN   Paris Jan. 26. 1786.

    I had the honour of writing to you on the receipt of your orders to procure draughts for the public buildings, and again on the 13th. of August. In the execution of those orders two methods of proceeding presented themselves to my mind. The one was to leave to some architect to draw an external according to his fancy, in which way experience shews that about once in a thousand times a pleasing form is hit upon; the other was to take some model already devised and approved by the general suffrage of the world. I had no hesitation in deciding that the latter was best, nor after the decision was there any doubt what model to take. There is at Nismes in the South of France a building, called the Maison quarèe,* erected in the time of the Caesars, and which is allowed without contradiction to be the most perfect and precious remain of antiquity in existence. It's superiority over any thing at Rome, in Greece, at Balbec or Palmyra is allowed on all hands; and this single object has placed Nismes in the general tour of travellers. . . .[220]

. . . We know that the Maison quarèe has pleased universally for near 2000 years. By leaving out a column, the proportions will be changed and perhaps the effect may be injured more than is expected. What is good is often spoiled by trying to make it better. . . .[221]

TH: JEFFERSON [222]

Thomas Jefferson, *Papers*, Julian P. Boyd, ed., Mina R. Bryan and Frederick Aandahl, assoc. ed. (Princeton, Princeton University Press, 1955), XI.

Nismes, Mar. 20, 1787

To Madame de Tessé

Here I am, Madam, gazing whole hours at the Maison quarrée, like a lover at his mistress. The stocking-weavers and silk spinners around it consider me as an hypochondriac Englishman, about to write with a pistol the last chapter of his history. . . . From Lyons to Nismes I have been nourished with the remains of Roman grandeur. They have always brought you to my mind, because I know your affection for whatever is Roman and noble . . . At Orange too I thought of you. I was sure you had seen with rapture the sublime triumphal arch at the entrance into the city . . . I thought of you again, and I was then in great good humour, at the Pont du Gard, a sublime antiquity, and [well][226] preserved. But most of all here, where Roman taste, genius, and magnificence excite ideas analogous to yours at every step, I could no longer oppose the inclination to avail myself of your permission to write to you. . . .

[From a correspondent at N]ismes you will not expect news. Were I [to attempt to give you news, I shoul]d tell you stories a thousand years old. [I should detail to you the intrigue]s of the courts of the Caesars, how they [affect us here, the oppressions of their] Praetors, Praefects &c. I am immersed [in antiquities from morning to night]. For me the city of Rome is

Photo Marcel Louchet, Courtesy French Government Tourist Office

Maison Carree, 16 B. C., Nimes, France, the best preserved Roman temple in existence. The Virginia Capitol at Richmond was modeled upon it. "Here I am, Madam, gazing whole hours at the Maison quarrée, like a lover at his mistress," wrote Jefferson to a friend in 1787.

actually [existing [227] in all the splendor of it's] empire. I am filled with alarms for the [event of the irruptions dayly m]aking on us by the Goths, Ostrogoths, [Visigoths and Vandals, lest they shoul]d reconquer us to our original bar[barism. If I am sometimes ind]uced to look forward to the eighteenth [century, it is only when recalled] to it by the recollection of your goodness [and friendship, and by those sentiments of] sincere esteem and respect with which [I have the honor to be, Madam, your] most obedient & most humble servant,

Th: Jefferson [228]

GEORGE WASHINGTON

Letters

The Writings of George Washington, John C. Fitzpatrick, ed. (Washington, United States Government Printing Office, 1939), XXXI.

TO DAVID STUART,* FROM PRESIDENT WASHINGTON

PHILADELPHIA, 8 March 1792.

DEAR SIR:

The doubts and opinions of others with respect to the permanent seat have occasioned no change in my sentiments on the subject. They have always been, that the plan ought to be prosecuted with all the dispatch the nature of the case will admit, and that the public buildings in size, form and elegance, shou'd look beyond the present day. I would not have it understood from hence that I lean to extravagance. A chaste plan sufficiently capacious and convenient for a period not *too* remote, but one to which we may *reasonably* look forward, would meet my idea in the Capitol. . . .[505]

* One of the three Commissioners of the District of Columbia.

George Washington, *The Writings of,* John C. Fitzpatrick, ed. (Washington, United States Government Post Office, 1939), XXXII.

TO THE COMMISSIONERS OF THE DISTRICT OF COLUMBIA, FROM PRESIDENT WASHINGTON

MOUNT VERNON, July 23, 1792

GENTLEMEN, Your favour of the 19th accompanying Judge Turner's plan for a Capitol, I have duly received, and have no hesitation in declaring that I am more agreeably struck with the appearance of it, than with any that has been presented to you....

There is the same defect, however, in this plan, as there is in all the plans which have been presented to you: namely, the want of an Executive apartment: w[hi]ch ought, if possible, to be obtained. The Dome, which is suggested as an Addition to the center of the edifice, would, in my opinion, give a beauty and granduer to the pile....[93]

Could such a plan as Judge Turner's be surrounded with Columns, and a colonade like that which was presented to you by Monsr. Hallet (the roof of Hallet's, I must confess does not hit my taste) without departing from the principles of Architecture, and would not be too expensive for our means, it would, in my judgment, be a noble and desireable Structure. But, I would have it understood in *this* instance, and *always*, when I am hazarding a sentiment on these buildings, that I Profess to have no knouledge in Architecture, and think we should (to avoid criticisms) be governed by the established rules which are laid down by the professors of this Art.[94]

Courtesy Virginia State Chamber of Commer

The Virginia Capitol, 1785-1792, Richmond, designed by Thomas Jefferson, third President of the United States. ". . . I cannot explain the complacency of the Virginia legislators," Joseph Hudnut has written, "willing to compress their explosive energies in that tight little box which the American ambassador [Thomas Jefferson was our Minister to France at the time] sent from Paris."

THE COMMISSIONERS OF PUBLIC BUILDINGS AND GROUNDS OF THE CITY OF WASHINGTON AND DISTRICT OF COLUMBIA LETTER TO THE MUNICIPALITY OF BORDEAUX

Documentary History of the Construction and Development of the United States Capitol Buildings and Grounds, United States, 58th Congress, 2nd Session, House of Representatives. Report No. 646 (Washington, United States Government Printing Office, 1904).

The Commissioners to the Municipality of Bourdeaux [Sic]

CITY OF WASHINGTON, 4th Jany. 1793

SIRS, We have the Honor to be intrusted, by General Washington, President of the United States, with the Commission of raising the public buildings, for the accommodation of Government, in the Capitol of the American States, and conducting the affairs of this new City—An honor that swells our ambition, to express in some Degree in the Stile of our Architecture, the sublime sentiments of Liberty which are common to Frenchmen and Americans. We wish to exhibit a grandure of conception, a Republican simplicity, and that true Elegance of proportion which corresponds to, a tempered freedom excluding Frivolity, the food of little minds. Our Country is young in Arts—from whence may we better expect Assistance than from the only nation who think and act as America on the End of Government and the rights of man? where the Arts have been sedulously cultivated for ages and whose peopled Cities cannot feel the emigration of a number most useful here in cementing the Fraternal Affections of the two nations. . . . We are with sentiments of high Respect and Esteem, your &c.,

TH. JOHNSON,
DD. STUART,
DANL. CARROLL.[21]

George Washington, *The Writings of*, John C. Fitzpatrick, ed. (Washington, United States Government Printing Office, 1939), XXXII.

TO THE COMMISSIONERS OF THE DISTRICT OF COLUMBIA (Private), FROM PRESIDENT WASHINGTON

PHILADELPHIA, January 31, 1793

GENTLEMEN: I have had under consideration Mr. Hallet's plans for the Capitol, which undoubtedly have a great deal of merit. Doctor Thornton has also given me a view of his.[324] These last came forward under some very advantageous circumstances. The Grandeur, Simplicity, and Beauty of the exterior; the propriety with which the apartments are distributed; and œconomy in the mass of the whole structure, will, I doubt not, give it a preference, in your eyes, as it has done in mine, and those of several others whom I have consulted, and who are deemed men of skill in Architecture. . . .[325]

George Washington, *The Writings of*, John C. Fitzpatrick, ed. (Washington, United States Government Printing Office, 1939), XXXII.

TO THE COMMISSIONERS OF THE DISTRICT OF COLUMBIA, FROM PRESIDENT WASHINGTON

PHILADELPHIA, March 3d, 1793

GENTLEMEN, This will be handed to you by Doctor Thornton of this City, who goes forward to lay before you a plan which he has prepared for the Capitol to be built in the federal City. Grandeur, Simplicity and Convenience, appear to be so well combined in this Plan of Doctor Thornton's, that I have no doubt of its meeting with that approbation from you, which I have given it under an attentive inspection, and which it has received from all those who have seen it and are considered as judges of such things. . . .[363]

THE COMMISSIONERS OF PUBLIC BUILDINGS AND GROUNDS OF THE CITY OF WASHINGTON AND DISTRICT OF COLUMBIA LETTER TO PRESIDENT WASHINGTON

Documentary History of the Construction and Development of the United States Capitol Building and Grounds, United States, 58th Congress, 2nd Session, House of Representatives. Report No. 646 (Washington, United States Government Printing Office, 1904).

To President Washington

GEORGE TOWN, 11th March, 1793.

SIR: Doctor Thorntons Plan for a Capitol has been laid before us. . . . We have no estimate accompanying the Plan, nor can one be found soon which could give much satisfaction: In our Idea the Capitol ought in point of propriety to be on a grand Scale, and that a Republic especially ought not to be sparing of expences on an Edifice for such purposes. . . .

We are Sir, with great regard and true esteem, your most Obt. Servts.,

TH. JOHNSON,
DD. STUART,
DANL. CARROLL.[24]
[Commissioners of the District of Columbia]

The Capitol of the United States, 1791-1863, Washington, devised by many architects. Dr. William Thornton was responsible for the basic design, but Benjamin Latrobe, Charles Bulfinch and others worked on it over the years. Thomas U. Walter was responsible for the dome which George Washington very much desired. "The dome," he wrote, "which is suggested as an addition to the center of the edifice, would, in my opinion, give beauty and grandeur to the pile."

WELLS BENNETT

Stephen Hallet and His Designs for the National Capitol, 1791-94

Wells Bennet, "Stephen Hallet and His Designs for the National Capitol, 1791-94,"
Journal of the American Institute of Architects, IV (October, 1916).*

In the general composition of his designs Hallet initiated a still more important type—the Capitol with balancing wings and a high central dome, which is now almost universal in American legislative buildings and has been widely followed elsewhere. Although justly criticized as giving undue emphasis to the central feature, which is primarily but an element of circulation, the scheme has the surpassing merit of a powerful expression of the majesty of government. This scheme, which dominates governmental architecture even today, is found for the first time, yet already fully developed, in the first study of Stephen Hallet.[417]

* Reprinted with the permission of the American Institute of Architects.

TURPIN C. BANNISTER

The Genealogy of the Dome of the United States Capitol

Turpin C. Bannister, "The Genealogy of the Dome of the United States Capitol," Paper presented before the Society of Architectural Historians, Boston, Mass., January 29, 1948; Journal of the Society of Architectural Historians, VII (January-June, 1948).*

Let us admit that in art, as in life, too much purism and too much logic can lead us down a very dark blind alley. No narrow argument can vitiate the transcendent power of Amiens, the shining glory of Justinian's miracle, or the crystaline lucidity of Athena's sanctuary. We need not deny to those who wish to assume the dogma of rationalism the right to do so if they please; but they should be reminded that such an assumption does not thereby attain universal validity. There are those who acknowledge the existence of beauty itself and regard it as a sufficient goal.

If, therefore, Walter's† dome performs its simple function as an effective focus for building and city, if its soaring mass lifts the observer's spirit and arouses within him a feeling of graciousness, dignity, serenity, and confident repose, if through its eloquence it requickens his awareness of our common aspirations, we should be generous enough to bestow the accolade such quality deserves. Walter poured out his genius in unimpeachable service to his fellow citizens. In turn they should accord his memory and his reputation such an acclaim as will in some degree requite the shabby neglect he received in his later lifetime. His masterpiece remains for us one of the most memorable treasures of our common heritage.[9]

* Reprinted by courtesy of the Society of Architectural Historians, from "The Genealogy of the Dome of the United States Capitol," *Journal of the Society of Architectural Historians* VII (January-June, 1948), p. 9.
† Thomas U. Walter.

4

LEVER HOUSE
New York City, 1952

ENGINEERING NEWS-RECORD

Glass-Walled Skyscraper

"Glass-Walled Skyscraper," *Engineering News-Record*, CXLVIII (May 1, 1952).*

Delicate and transparent, a narrow shaft of glass 24 stories high pierces the New York City skyline, its mirror-like exterior incongruously reflecting its massive, opaque skyscraper neighbors.

Its broad, two-story high base keeps surrounding buildings at a respectable distance. This glass tower was designed to be seen by the man in the street, as well as to capture daylight for interior illumination.

It is the new headquarters office building of Lever Brothers Co., manufacturer of soap, detergents, cosmetics, toothpaste and oleomargarine. Built at a cost of $6 million, it will be solely occupied by the 1,200 employees of the company's four divisions.

Lever House occupies an entire block front on plush Park Ave., between 53rd and 54th St., less than a half mile north of Grand Central Terminal. This location, the company figures, will save both it and its employees time and money. It is convenient to the offices of the many people with whom the company does business. And it is excellent for subway riders and commuters.

NO SETBACKS ABOVE THIRD FLOOR

In planning Lever House, the company had one primary objective—a building with 130,000 sq ft of office area that would be adequate for present needs and future expansion.

An 8-story building would have been adequate if it covered the entire site (200 ft on Park Ave., 155 ft on 53rd St., and 192 ft on 54th St.) and had no setbacks. While the city's zoning law would have permitted this, such a structure would have extensive interior areas far from windows—a condition that might affect employee efficiency adversely.

The zoning law would also have permitted a tall building with setbacks, like a tiered wedding cake. But this design, too, has disadvantages—relatively high construction costs, unsatisfactory appearance, possibility of close neighbors obstructing light, to mention a few.

Lever Brothers decided instead to take advantage of a provision in the zoning law permitting a building of any height that does not occupy more than 25% of its lot. Their tower starts as low down as the third floor, to conserve the maximum amount of daylight for its occupants and neighbors.

This design permits wings to be erected at the rear of the site when additional space is needed in the future. More than 25% more desk space can be added in this way without interfering with the present office arrangement.

For more immediate expansion needs, the entire sixth floor has been set aside. It is now used for storage.

DOES IT STAND ON STILTS?

The building, which is completely air conditioned, contains 21 office floors, plus three floors for mechanical equipment on top. A garage in the basement accommodates 50 automobiles. Gross building area is 289,600 sq ft, net office area 131,000 sq ft.

Street level is occupied by an auditorium seating 200, a demonstration kitchen, service areas in the rear, including provision for off-street loading, and a glass-enclosed lobby, with stainless steel trim. Though there are entrances from the three bordering streets, the lobby is set back on all three sides, leaving space for an arcade and garden. Building columns outside the lobby thus are exposed to view from the street. Hence, the structure appears to be standing on stilts.

The second floor covers the entire lot, except for an open well directly over the garden. Purpose of the well is to admit daylight into the interior of the building base.

An employee recreation lounge on the second floor overlooks the ground-floor courtyard. The second floor also [79] contains the mail room, stenographic pool, business-machines operations.

Lever Brothers considered the possibility of locating retail stores in the base. A shopping-traffic survey showed, however, that the net return would be small compared with the required capital investment. Furthermore, stores would have needed basements, whereas the company wanted the basement for its garage and storage space. Finally, stores would have destroyed the dramatic effect of a building that seems to float in the air above a landscaped patio.

On the third floor, where the tower begins, is an employee cafeteria and a landscaped terrace atop the second-floor roof. The cafeteria can seat 300, accommodate the company's entire personnel within a two-hour period.

The rest of the tower, except for the mechanical floors, is occupied by offices and a vertical transportation core at the rear of the building. In plan, this 24-story tower is 180 ft long by only 50 ft wide. No desk is more than 25 ft from a window.

OFFICES SEALED IN GLASS

In a city saturated with skyscrapers, like New York, such a tower normally would hardly attract attention. What makes Lever House particularly imposing is the unique treatment of its exterior.

Non-opening windows occupying slightly more than half of the 12-ft 4-in. story height form a continuous strip around the building at each level. Above and below them are spandrels faced with wire glass. Backup is 4-in. solid cinder block and 2 in. of cellular-glass insulation.

Sills, mullions and heads are sheathed in 18-8 chrome-nickel stainless steel, the light color contrasting sharply with the blue glass.

The result, the architects say, is an easily maintained durable exterior that seals air-borne dirt out, keeps expensive conditioned air in. They estimate that if conventional construction had been used, two to three times as much cleaning work would be needed in the offices. Air conditioning and heating costs would be higher. Cost of installing movable windows would have been greater, and the washing schedule for window interiors would be longer.

WINDOW-WASHERS' SCAFFOLD

To simplify and speed up washing of the building exterior, Otis Elevator Co., in conjunction with the Lever House architects and the consulting structural and mechanical engineers, developed a power-operated scaffold for cleaners. They will work from a 28 x 2½-ft platform capable of moving up or down at 35 fpm. Suspended and powered from a crane on the roof, the platform will [83] run on vertical stainless-steel rails, which are spaced 28 ft apart. It has a gripper at the center to ride a rail and is braced at both ends through rollers against the stainless-steel mullions.

The crane runs on standard railroad tracks just inside the cornice. It weighs 10½ tons, including a 3½-ton counterweight, and travels at 25 fpm. A switching system permits crane and scaffold to be stored at the center of the roof, out of sight from the street, when not in use.

The crew controls vertical movement with pushbuttons. Horizontal movement is accomplished by raising the platform above the cornice to detach it from the rail, then shifting it until grippers automatically find the next rail.

The owner estimates that two men can wash Lever House and its 1,400 windows in only six days.

COLUMNS SET BACK

It is noteworthy that the exterior design does not permit structural members to interrupt the glass surfaces. The building has a structural steel frame with columns and spandrels set back 18 in. along the sides of the tower. Columns along the Park Ave. end are set back 10 ft.

The end arrangement resulted in a saving in foundation costs. It enabled the piers, which are founded on rock, to be built clear of the structure under Park Ave. that carries the tracks of the New York Central R.R.

In the tower office areas, there is only one row of interior columns. . . .

Skidmore, Owings & Merrill were the architects; Weiskopf and Pickworth, the structural engineers; Jaros, Baum & Bolles, the mechanical engineers. George A. Fuller Co. was the general contractor.[84]

THE ARCHITECTURAL FORUM

Lever House Complete

"Lever House Complete," *The Architectural Forum*, XCVI (June, 1952).*

From across Park Avenue Lever House is a horizontal streak of stainless steel and green glass suspended on rows of tall columns whose metal skins have a cool wavering sheen. Within the rows of columns, deep inside the large emptiness of the sidewalk plaza, is an open court around a proud little garden; this is set in a marble box, paralleling the island of green down the middle of New York's most majestic avenue. Up from the third floor of the new building rises another glass and metal streak, a vertical one, the tower.

* Reprinted by permission from the June, 1952, issue of *Architectural Forum* © 1952, Time, Inc.

The architectural significance of Lever is something beyond this flashing first impression, however; it is the *shape* of this building which is impressive, more even than the gleaming materials. For there are other buildings in the US which have the same sleek metal and glass excitement. You can find them in Portland, in Davenport, in New York City itself (and in the walls of 10,000 diners along the continent's highways . . . the short order cooks discovered stainless steel before the architects did). Behind their tense polished surfaces, these other office buildings have part—but only part—of the character of Lever House. They have walls which seem to say, "Here I stand in complete clarity, without mystery. Look, here are my structural columns, my office space, my circulation system—all visible, evident and obvious. It's easy to see I am completely expressive of this industrial age. Look at me and I'll reflect back your image, darkly—but no more dramatically than you would like really to be. My personality is the image of yourself you see in my shining walls, as you stand before me in a luxurious suit made in Rochester and wonderful shoes made in St. Louis, with an airline ticket to California in your pocket. I'm you. I'll be standing here [102] when you're gone, to say what you were like. I'm you, but I'm bigger than you."

The Lever Co. and Skidmore, Owings & Merrill obviously were not satisfied with this statement of physical appearance. So out of the machined surfaces of the slick hard walls with their blank, watchful industrial expression, the architects created a strong intellectual form, and this is their achievement. Declining to be hypnotized by the brilliant geometric patterns of their materials, refusing to submit blindly to the obvious zoning ordinance on their site, they shaped a building which is infinitely more spirited and dignified than any other commercial office building in New York.

Because of this, Lever is only a *small* skyscraper. It uses open space as significantly as enclosed space, filling only a fraction of its zoning envelope. . . . The sidewalk level is almost entirely open, save for services, an auditorium, and sheets of glass enclosing a reception lobby. Above, the second story does cover the whole site, except the court, but then the lean tower rises with extravagant restraint into Park Ave.'s valuable air, housing a set of small office floors. Compared with the usual rich (but tasteless) wedding cake office building of New York, Lever is a wafer. There is no office space to spare for rent; nobody lives here but Lever.

Within the general shape which the architects preserved for the building, one detail more than anything else characterizes Lever House. This is the notch which is cut into the Park Ave. facade where the tower begins. As much as the entire open first floor and the thin taut materials, this idea makes the building stand clear and light and multiplies the significance of its industrial components; at the same time this detail of design also asserts the architects' function in our civilization beyond that of being merely a good mechanic. When several thousand other architects from all over the country attend the AIA [American Institute of Architects] convention this month at the Waldorf-Astoria, just down the avenue from Lever House, this should mean something to them.[104]

A thin stack of offices on a broad base is the section . . . cut parallel with Park Ave. The outline . . . indicates a contrasting conventional approach to the construction of office space on this kind of plot in New York City; this tone marks the limits of the zoning "envelope" which local regulations would permit an office building on this plot to occupy. Following the letter of this law, Lever's 290,000 sq. ft. could have been housed in an eight-story building, and a higher scheme filling setback patterns to the limit might have added a great deal of rentable revenue-producing space. But Lever was interested only in housing its own staff, and in doing an outstanding job of it. So the architects took advantage of a provision in the zoning law which permits a tower of any height (without setbacks) if it does not occupy more than 25% of its lot. Lever's lot measures 200′ on Park Ave., by 155′ on 53rd St., by 192′ on 54th St. Tower floors measure 53′ x 180′. . . .[106]

The office space inside has the blessing of all the daylight in New York, and no desk is more than 25′ from the exterior wall. But Venetian blinds come in for plenty of use even on sunless north side to control glare. . . .[107]

Within the court flowers bloom and the spacious tradition of Park Ave. is more than maintained in this interpretation by

Lever House, 1952, New York, the first important all-glass office building in the United States, designed by Gordon Bunshaft of Skidmore, Owings & Merrill. The strong influence of Le Corbusier, who was the first to suggest the idea of a tall building on stilts, is evident.

Skidmore, Owings & Merrill. . . . Dark green color is the result of spraying green "cocoon" plastic on the back of tempered glass panels. Columns swathed with stainless steel take fingerprints, but are designed to be polished regularly to reflect the Lever Co.'s creed of cleanliness. . . .[108]

Within the building Raymond Loewy Associates did the decorating on a very firm basis of efficiency, sales atmosphere, and comfort (three executives asked for fireplaces in their top-floor air conditioned offices, and got them).

INTERIOR COMFORT IS PRODUCED MECHANICALLY

Air conditioning is by means of a split system—individual window units for the glazed periphery of the structure fed with high pressure water and air, and in the center of the office space a duct system (also high velocity) which distributes its air through special new ceiling diffusers. Heat absorbing glass blocks 45% of direct sun heat penetration compared with 10% by normal glass, cutting the cooling load considerably. This glass is also effective in fighting glare, although blinds still are necessary. The greenish color of the glass made interior decorating somewhat more complicated than it might have been. Emphatically *warm colors* were used to compensate for its cool tone.

Acoustical control in the glass-walled building is attained by use of absorbent ceilings of acoustical tile, perforated metal and acoustical plaster. Office partitions are 3" gypsum block plastered on both sides, connected to the 3½" mullions by metal fillers. Freestanding partitions are prefabricated, and can be moved.

Lighting is aimed at a level of 40 foot-candles at desk level and is provided by flush fluorescent fixtures in the ceiling, covered by glass diffusing lenses.

A total of five passenger elevators and one freight elevator serve the structure, but there is an elevator shaft now empty, for an additional elevator when needed.

In construction, cellular steel floors saved an estimated 30% of floor weight over conventional slabs, and went in faster.

Cost: original contract price for the building was slightly above $6 million on a lump sum bid. . . .

Neighbors on Park Ave. like this building, although some are worried about reflected glare. This fortunately is not a major problem in this neighborhood because the only tall building nearby is to the north and gets little reflected sunlight except in early morning. Slick walls reflect considerable heat too, particularly into the court.[109]

THE ARCHITECTURAL RECORD

Lever House, New York: Glass and Steel Walls

"Lever House, New York: Glass and Steel Walls," The Architectural Record, CXI (June, 1952).*

The exterior of Lever House—24 stories of blue-green heat-resistant glass and stainless steel—was a technical design problem which required the joint efforts of architects, engineers, general contractors and sub-contractors. Its glass-paned skin is designed to be kept sparkling clean (Lever Brothers, manufacturers of soaps and detergents, are naturally pleased at this) with minimum difficulty or expense. The building has no openable sash. This not only prevents the entrance of the big city's dirt and grime, but is a means of reducing the total air conditioning load. It also lessens interior maintenance.

The heat-resistant glass likewise reduces both the air conditioning load and sun or sky glare. Wire glass faces the spandrels, which the building code required to be of masonry. The structure itself is of conventional steel frame, with tower bays so laid out that only narrow vertical mullions, formed of paired channel shapes, interrupt the glass. Horizontal mullions and muntins are similarly light in section; all are sheathed with 16-ga Type 302 stainless steel which is secured to the exterior glazing channels with hand-driven screws. Glazing channels were in turn screwed to structural mullions; the operation . . . took

* Reprinted with the permission of The Architectural Record.

time and was obviously expensive. However, this office building was designed for sole occupancy by Lever Brothers—even its ground floor has no tenants; a reasonably high construction cost, commensurate with the aim of providing an imposing, almost institutional, edifice, was not inappropriate.

The openness of the ground floor (where much of the area is garden and pedestrian walks with only the essentials enclosed in glass) is also somewhat monumental if not in expression certainly in its fundamental regard [131] for the citizens of New York. In this aspect, the entire structure is thoughtful, pleasant and a decided advance over the average speculative building. Above the few lower stories the tower is so designed that its slim bulk permits what it can of a city vista—an impression heightened by the contrasting surroundings. This is something to be grateful for. Like the U.N. Secretariat . . . it is a narrow slab, which means that the typical office floor will contain few dark cubicles. The design is an enlightened venture in public relations, and is to be applauded; the glass and metal skin, also a source of public interest, becomes rather a stunt by comparison.

In plan, the enclosed ground-floor area contains display and reception space, waiting areas for visitors, a demonstration kitchen and an auditorium. On the second floor are employees' lounge, medical suite, general office facilities. On the third floor, lowest of the tower, is the employees' cafeteria overlooking roof terraces. The remaining floors, up through the 21st, house offices of the parent and subsidiary companies. Above are the equivalent of three floors of mechanical equipment. In addition to complete air conditioning, the building is fitted with what has been called "the most modern fire alarm equipment"; and with a conveyor system, newly developed, which not only picks up internal and outside communications and distributes them vertically, but also transports them horizontally to the mail room. In such technical aspects, Lever House is marvelously ingenious. [132]

HENRY-RUSSELL HITCHCOCK AND PHILIP C. JOHNSON

The Buildings We See

Henry-Russell Hitchcock and Philip C. Johnson, "The Buildings We See," *New World Writing*, I (1952).*

At Lever House Bunschaft [Misspelling for Bunshaft. Eds.] allowed the simple rectangular tower to rise from only a portion of his site. Thus he has saved, out of the excessively rentable upper air that flanks Park Avenue, a volume of empty space in which his tower can live and breathe—metaphorically as well as literally. Since the handling of the circumambient space is more controlled by neighboring structures than is the space around Mies's apartment towers in Chicago, there is somewhat less assurance of its survival in precisely its present form. But at the ground level an open court has been created that extends also under most of the tower, somewhat as does Wright's at the Johnson Wax Building on the infinitely less expensive soil of Racine, but with a less Italianate sense of order and calm. There is also less clarity and continuity in the expression of the structural elements than in Mies's handling of the recessed lower stories at the base of his Chicago towers. But Bunschaft's court has positive qualities of its own. Open at the ground level on all the three street-fronts, the enclosed space is defined above by a mezzanine which is carried all around the site.

By contrast with its too, too massive neighbors along the Avenue, the structural expression of Lever House may appear somewhat underscaled throughout; compared to the United Nations Building, however, Lever House has a clearer and more intelligible articulation of surface. This exceedingly prominent commercial monument has already attracted a great deal of public attention, most of it highly favorable, even [122] before it is finished. The public reception of the United Nations Building has been far less enthusiastic.[123]

LEWIS MUMFORD

House of Glass

Lewis Mumford, *From the Ground Up* (New York, Harcourt, Brace & World, Inc., 1957).*

For a long time after Lever House opened its doors, throngs of people, waiting patiently in great queues in the lobby, demanded admission so insistently that the elevator system, designed to handle only Lever Brothers' office staff of twelve hundred employees and a normal complement of visitors, was severely overtaxed. People acted as if this was the eighth wonder of the world, this house of glass approached through an open forecourt that is paneled with glistening marble, punctuated by columns encased in stainless steel, and embellished by a vast bed of flowers and—last touch of elegance against the greenish-blue windows and the bluish-green spandrels of the glassy building that rises above it—a weeping-willow tree.

In many ways, this popular curiosity, which in a sense is also popular judgment, is justified. Lever House is a building of outstanding qualities, mechanical, aesthetic, human, and it breaks with traditional office buildings in two remarkable respects —it has been designed not for maximum rentability but for maximum efficiency in the dispatch of business, and it has used to the full all the means now available for making a building comfortable, gracious, and handsome. This whole structure is chastely free of advertisement; the minuscule glass cases showing

* Reprinted by permission of Harcourt, Brace & World, Inc., Copyright © 1947, 1948, 1949, 1950, 1951, 1952, 1953, 1954, 1955, 1956, by Lewis Mumford. (All of the essays in *From the Ground Up* originally appeared in *The New Yorker*.)

life-size packages of Lever products in the glass-enclosed reception chamber on the ground floor would hardly be [156] noticed in the lobby of a good hotel. But the building itself is a showcase and an advertisement; in its very avoidance of vulgar forms of publicity, it has become one of the most valuable pieces of advertising a big commercial enterprise could conceive. For years, businessmen vied with each other in the attempt to put up the tallest building in the city; thus the Metropolitan Life capped the Singer and the Empire State capped the Chrysler in the effort to make the sky the limit. In keeping with this now deplorably old-fashioned spirit, there have lately been rumors of a hundred-story skyscraper. Possibly Lever House has pointed the way for a new kind of competition—a competition to provide open spaces and a return to the human scale. At all events, it is definitely not an example of the "swaggering in specious dimensions" that Oswald Spengler called a sign of a decadent civilization.

To understand what the architects of Lever House—Skidmore, Owings & Merrill, whose Gordon Bunshaft was chief designer—have achieved, one must go back to some of the buildings put up on midtown Madison Avenue in the early 'twenties. They are only twelve stories high, without setbacks, and they cover the entire site, providing not so much as an air shaft in the center. But though they have resulted in a heavier density of population than a wise zoning law would permit, they are immensely superior to the extravagant thirty- and forty-story buildings that followed them. So valuable have these older ones proved that one of them, 383 and 385 Madison Avenue, has now been completely renovated and given new elevators, an air-conditioning system, and numerous other embellishments at a cost as great as that of the building itself. Lever House returns to the more modest density achieved in this twelve-story structure. By not quite doubling that number of floors in the main part of their building, however, the architects of Lever House [157] have been able to house those twelve hundred employees comfortably while providing an unusual amount of open space that is secure against encroachment. For the main structure, though it runs the crosstown length of the site and abuts the structure next door on the west, is set back a hundred feet from the south building line and forty from the north and has the generous width of Park Avenue to the east. The result of this self-discipline is that this shaft, or "slab," which is less than sixty feet wide, is open to the light on three sides, and few desks are more than twenty-five feet from the continuous windows. Even the least-favored worker on the premises may enjoy the psychological lift of raising her eyes to the clouds or the skyscape of not too near-at-hand adjoining buildings. I know no other private or public edifice in the city that provides space of such quality for every worker.

The layout of this building is itself transparent. The tall, narrow, oblong slab, which houses the firm's offices, is set off-center on a roughly square pedestal, only two stories high, that covers the whole plot, the western block front along Park Avenue between Fifty-third and Fifty-fourth. This irregularly shaped site runs a hundred and fifty-five feet west on Fifty-third and a hundred and ninety feet west on Fifty-fourth. The pedestal is a hollow one, for there is a court open to the sky in the middle of it, just to the south of the slab. To the north of the court, on the ground floor, is the glass-walled main lobby, and to the west of the court are an auditorium and a kitchen laboratory. The court, and the lobby, can be reached from almost any direction, for the ground floor is completely open on three sides—north, south, and east—to the streets; there is no vestige of wall, or even of shop-front window, to shut out the passer-by. The second floor contains, among other things, an employees' lounge, handsomely done in dark green and mustard yellow, and a [158] spacious room that houses the stenographers' pool. The third story, the beginning of the slab, contains a kitchen and cafeteria, which can feed all hands in two and a half hours; this dining room, with its reddish-brown drapes and modern furniture, is able to hold its own in elegance with any restaurant on Park Avenue, and it has something that no restaurant in the city has offered since the old beer gardens disappeared—a thickly planted open-air roof garden that flanks it (and, of course, the slab) on both north and south. If it weren't for its almost hepatic sound the word "Leverish" might well take the place of "ritzy" as a syno-nym for the last word in luxury. This floor of the slab is indented a whole bay along the Park Avenue side, so the rest of the slab seems to hover over the base of the structure. The indentation

Lever House, 1952, New York; its open ground story broke with the traditional way of constructing a commercial building. Rental space at street level is sacrificed to achieve open space for pedestrians.

permits the bed of plants that borders the roof garden to be carried without interruption along this entire frontage of the building. Unfortunately, the bay is not deep enough to permit people as well as plants to make this journey from south to north. Thus no one can take a full turn on the roof-garden deck, and the architects' sacrifice of free promenade space to the unbroken bed of greenery must be set down as a piece of empty formalism —all the worse aesthetically because the movement of people across the front of the building would have given an extra touch of life to a somewhat glacial, if not oversimplified, composition. This seems to me a blemish, but it is not beyond remedy.

The office building proper ends with the executives' offices, on the twenty-first floor. Above them are three floors, outwardly punctuated by the horizontal louvers of the air intakes, behind which are the elevator machinery and a cooling tank. All this is surrounded by a shell strong enough to support the elaborate machine that moves around the perimeter of the roof to raise and lower the window cleaners' platform.[159] This piece of apparatus was necessitated by the fact that the entire slab, windows and spandrels alike, is—except, as has already been pointed out, on the west side—sheathed in glass, and the windows are all sealed. The windows are four and a half feet wide, and even the smallest private office has two of them. For a company whose main products are soap and detergents, that little handicap of the sealed windows is a heaven-sent opportunity, for what could better dramatize its business than a squad of cleaners operating in their chariot, like the *deus ex machina* of Greek tragedy, and capturing the eye of the passer-by as they perform their daily duties? This perfect bit of symbolism alone almost justifies the all-glass façade.

The slab is the traditional steel-framed skyscraper, with one or two special features. The outer columns are set back a little from the outer walls, so the windows are a continuous glassy envelope, and the mechanical core of the building—the passenger elevators, the conveyor that delivers outgoing mail to the postal department and incoming mail to the proper floors, the coat racks for the office force, the fire stairs—is concentrated in the west end of the slab. If necessary, therefore, a wing could be built south from this end, parallel to Park Avenue, without taking away any daylight from the existing working quarters. The only opaque feature in this house of glass is that demanded by prudence and the fire ordinances of New York—the fire stairs, which are enclosed in a shaft of light-gray brick at the west side of the site and connected with the slab by open passages at each floor level. At the base of the fire tower is the entrance to the fifty-five-car underground garage for the staff.

Aesthetically, the exterior of this building has a sober elegance; the stainless-steel window frames and spandrel frames are repeated without variation over the whole façade. The darker bands of the spandrels [160] give horizontal emphasis, while the gleam of the vertical metal framing, sometimes reinforced by the

columns behind, provides a delicate counterpoise. The effect is
of alternating bands of dark-green and light-green glass, and,
as is true of all glass buildings, this surface looks far darker than
it would if an opaque covering, such as white brick, had been
used. Paradoxically, a whole city of such buildings, so open to
light, would be somber, since a transparent glass wall is mostly
light-absorbing, not light-reflecting. When the framing of Lever
House was put up, it was protected by a coating of brilliant
chrome-yellow paint, and though the cost of maintaining this
brilliance might have been prohibitive, that chrome yellow,
playing against the green, would have given the building a gaiety
it lacks. Standing by itself, reflecting the nearby buildings in its
mirror surface, Lever House presents a startling contrast to the
old-fashioned buildings of Park Avenue. But if its planning innovations prove sound, it may become just one unit in a repeating
pattern of buildings and open spaces. . . .[161]

Because Lever House has many points in common with the
United Nations Secretariat, it is inevitable that the buildings
should be compared. On almost [162] every point, it seems to me,
Lever House is superior. To begin with, it is correctly oriented,
with its wide façades facing north and south, and though this
means that no direct sunlight ever enters the northern windows,
it also means that there is no need to cut light and view on that
side by drawing Venetian blinds. Since there are three air-conditioning systems—for the north side, the south side, and the
middle—in the winter, warm air can be introduced on the cool
side of the building while cooler air is circulated on the sunny
side. The United Nations cafeteria for employees is good, but the
one in Lever House ranks with the quarters provided not for the
U.N. staff but for the executives and delegates. And there is no
open space around the Secretariat that compares in charm and
comfort with Lever House's courtyard and roof garden, enclosed
as these are on two sides.

Few of the features that make Lever House superior are
the result of its having a more generous budget to draw on.
Though they are superficially similar, one may say of these buildings that the United Nations is the last of the old-fashioned
skyscrapers, in which importance was symbolized by height, while

Lever House is the first of the new office buildings, in which the human needs and purposes modify cold calculations of profit and nullify any urge to tower above rival buildings. In Lever House, quality of space takes precedence over mere quantity.

The building that Lever House really invites comparison with is quite a different structure, though equally bold and even more striking architecturally in its own day—Frank Lloyd Wright's now demolished Larkin Building, in Buffalo, the paragon of office buildings at the time, though set in the midst of an industrial slum it never succeeded in dominating or even modifying. It, too, was a by-product of the [163] soap industry. In that building, as in this one, every possible innovation was made—new desks, new chairs, new office equipment of every kind, all of it specially designed. The Larkin Building was a shallow structure, built about a great skylighted interior court, with natural light coming down through the roof. Wright's creation was a masterpiece of beautiful masonry—more monumental, in fact, than most public buildings, whether churches or city halls, that have sought to be. Lever House lacks the massive sculptural qualities of Wright's inspired masonry; it is, rather, in its proud transparency, "a construction in space." It says all that can be said, delicately, accurately, elegantly, with surfaces of glass, with ribs of steel, with an occasional contrast in slabs of marble or in beds of growing plants, but its special virtues are most visible not in the envelope but in the interior that this envelope brings into existence, in which light and space and color constitute both form and decoration. In terms of what it set out to do, this building— excluding the deplorable executives' floor and the wall encrusted with golden mosaic that faces one in approaching the elevators on the ground floor—is an impeccable achievement. Lever Brothers and Skidmore, Owings & Merrill, and above all Gordon Bunshaft, are entitled to a civic vote of thanks for taking this important step toward sane planning and building. Lever House is not, of course, the first all-glass building; the famous Crystal Palace, and the more recent Daily Express Building, on Fleet Street, in London, antedate it. But it is the first office building in which modern materials, modern construction, modern functions have been combined with a modern plan. In a sense, it

picks up the thread where the architects of the Monadnock
Building in Chicago, the last of the all-masonry skyscrapers,
dropped it two generations ago.[164]

On the surface, this seems about the best that current architecture can provide when limitations of cost do not, in any substantial way, enter into the picture. It will be a little while before
one can make a final appraisal of this building; that will depend
partly upon how comfortable the quarters have been in the
summer and how expensive it has been to keep them comfortable,
likewise on how satisfactory this building will be in very cold
weather. It is a show place and an advertisement, and costs that
can here be written off to publicity might prove too high for
more workaday business quarters. Though the uniform façade
of Lever House is aesthetically consistent, a different system of
fenestration on the south side, with or without sun screens, might
not merely produce better summer temperatures within but might
also reduce the need for shutting off the view with Venetian
blinds, a necessity that makes nonsense of the windows. It may
be, too, that a more flexible system of ventilation, which depended more frequently on untreated air and would use air-
conditioning only to counteract extreme temperatures, would
prove more satisfactory as well as cheaper. And in that event
Lever House's closed-in glass face, along with its amusing
window-cleaning apparatus, could be discarded in newer designs.
Surely no building so open to the direct rays of the sun—particularly the valuable ultraviolet rays of morning—should nullify
that advantage by "windows" that do not let these rays in. But
Lever House, by reason of the internal consistency in its design,
is at the very least a highly useful experiment. Fragile, exquisite,
undaunted by the threat of being melted into a puddle by an
atomic bomb, this building is a laughing refutation of "imperialist
warmongering," and so it becomes an implicit symbol of hope for
a peaceful world. In the [165] kind of quarters it provides for its
staff, Lever House even anticipates the "Century of the Common
Man." I don't know whether that is what the corporation had in
mind when it built this structure, but that, it seems to me, is
what Lever House itself says.[166]

ALINE B. LOUCHHEIM

U. S. Architecture Praised by Briton

Aline B. Louchheim, "U. S. Architecture Praised by Briton," The New York Times (July 7, 1953).*

There is much more going on qualitatively as well as quantitatively in architecture here than in England, according to Nikolaus Pevsner, English art historian, writer on architecture and design and Slade Professor at Cambridge University who has just been made a Commander of the Order of the British Empire.

. . . He was especially enthusiastic about New York's Lever House.

"The fact that such an extraordinary building was commissioned from a firm rather than an individual genius," he said, "is different from the Continent. Moreover, it really develops the Rockefeller Center idea of giving a skyscraper sufficient space around it. I see this as the beginning of something."[25]

* Reprinted with the permission of The New York Times.

FRANK LLOYD WRIGHT

Address at the Meeting of the Student Chapter Members, the American Institute of Architects

Address of Frank Lloyd Wright at the Meeting of the Student Chapter Members, The American Institute of Architects, on June 25, 1952. The Waldorf-Astoria, New York City.* (Transcribed at the meeting and later edited by Mr. Wright.)

So it might be a good beginning to cross-examine some of you, trying to find out if some of you *do* know *why* knowledge of this thing we call Organic-architecture is not as I would like it to be. As the Architecture of today is called "modern" it already grows more and more superficial. Yes, it is now called "modern architecture." Well . . . the real meaning, (the inner content) that would be so greatly beneficial in this thing (we call it Organic Architecture) is still missing. We *do* have something here and there of its appearances. Yes, and we do have some of the better effects. But we have seen and now again have to see the sporadic decline toward the historic box. This—"the left wing"—, let's say of Organic-architecture comes up for a time like an ill wind and again goes down. I, myself, started this war on left-wing architecture (architecture as a box) because as you know, no box is fit form for human freedom. Nor is the box fit symbol for Democracy. Is it? If you will think about it you will see that any box is a container. A symbol of division. The box as we see it now, naked. Well, you remember the story about little Johnnie who asked his papa why boxes had to have such skinny legs? That is my "why" too. Why so-called "modern architecture" had to go boxes, boxes put up on such skinny legs. As most of you must know, *I have tried to abolish the box as architecture!* Isn't

* Reprinted with the permission of the American Institute of Architects.

it true that Architecture during the Renaissance and during almost all this 500-year period that you boys have been looking back at it, has been the Box? The Box got various holes cut in it, or out of it, and "they" put columns, pilasters, cornices on the front of it as a kind of decoration?[2]

But in Organic-architecture must come a new ideal of integrity. Call it Democracy. We may call that ideal democratic because the dignity and worth of the *individual*, per se, as such, protected and used by government, is Democratic Freedom. The emotion of this democratic sentiment is now a motive for our own Architecture. How to express that new feeling in our society as an architecture of our own? How to get this sense of interior space to come free—come *through* in the buildings that belong to us in this—our own period; that modern era in which our architectural Declaration of Independence was made? Not too simple a thing. No, but anyway, it is not too difficult to see that any containment like the box, old or new, even if open like a crate, would be essentially the very negation of any idea of democratic-freedom for the individual. Wouldn't it? So if you all greatly love Architecture you would have to get into it something better than the four-sided old box.[3]

FRANK LLOYD WRIGHT

Frank Lloyd Wright Speaks Up

Frank Lloyd Wright, "Frank Lloyd Wright Speaks Up," *House Beautiful*, XCV (July, 1953).*

The "International Style" is neither international nor a style. Essentially it is totalitarianism, an old totalitarian cult made new by organized publicity.

The "International Style" is nothing but the old architecture of the box with its face lifted.

Any box is more a coffin for the human spirit than an inspiration. The box dominates, constricts, and constrains the individual into something made fit only for collectivism. Its champions now declare dictatorially that the old box is *it*. This is their great gift to the world—their "style."

So many university professors, museum authorities, magazine editors, feature writers, and critics seem to be trying hard to give notoriety to a group of architects imported, by a curious twist of fate, from the German Bauhaus to the New York Museum of Modern Art.

These Bauhaus architects ran from political totalitarianism in Germany to what is now made by specious promotion to seem their own totalitarianism in art here in America.

It is being more accidental than creative to mistake a disciplined sterility for austerity, mistake the plainness of bones or a barn door for simplicity (knowing nothing of *real* simplicity—the innate grace and significance of a wild flower). This is the mistake their promoters seem to make.

In their dubious champions, there is no sense of the depth called the third dimension. They operate on only two. Among these puppets of promotion, façades again become of uppermost importance. These façades all add up to the same thing—a cliché for tyros, teachers, and sycophants who crook the little finger and talk esthetics. Or by duped educators grasping something easy to teach, and approved as a foreign cult.

Sterilization is again mistaken for refinement. Provincial apostles of refinement name it "Classic," stupidly comparing it to frozen Greek classicism as though the ancient sterilization were a high virtue. But the cause of great architecture, the great truth of building beautiful buildings beautifully according to the nature of architecture, is travestied by this superficial mimicry, that always seems to follow in the wake of great ideas.

The classic or camouflaged old post-and-lintel box is still practiced in the glassed-in cage or the glass-walled dwelling, both approved by these publicists and this latest procession of callow-professionals, now baptized (by whom?) "International." But this latest form of glassification is no true revolt, no actual dissidence. This affection is for free Americans no more than the petty pretenses of small men.

Old Man Box merely *looks* different when glassified, that's all. The more the box is glassed, the more it becomes evident as the box. No new ideas whatever are involved as might easily be demonstrated by intelligent reference to the origin of their drawing-board façades. The old sham front has had its face lifted; the only change is merely one of outward appearance. It is a change of face, not of heart.

There are fresh ideas to be brought to life, if you learn to labor for them and are willing to work for them and wait. You must tire, as I do, of seeing these original forms merely renamed. All we have received from "internationalism," aside from the dropped coping, is merely: "Make the walls *all* glass, boys."

And what do we get now? The same old box, only you now really look inside and through the box and see that it is more of a box than ever. Thereby the tenant, as well as the poverty-stricken imagination of the architect, is mercilessly exposed.[87]

5

THE PRICE TOWER
Bartlesville, Oklahoma, 1953-1955

FRANK LLOYD WRIGHT

The Story of the Tower

Frank Lloyd Wright, *The Story of the Tower* (New York, Horizon Press, 1956).*

Principle is the only safe tradition. Organic architecture—natural architecture—is capable of infinite variety in concept and form but faithful always to principle. It is—in fact and in deed—itself principle. A natural architecture true to the nature of the problem, to the nature of the site, of the materials and of those for whom it is built—in short, of the Time and Place and Man. Building *of* these, not applied or imposed *on* them. Neither a mere facade nor a glass poster, set up or "put over," regardless of man or the elements in which he must live—and built regardless of the basic principles which are the blood and the sinews of architecture organic.

By way of illuminating this perennial—eternal—matter of principle inherent in the solution of any problem, principle which lives and refuses to compromise wherever compromise is death to the integrity of the concept, here is The Tower as "idea." Not since I first began to think around it and work on aspects of the structure in 1891 with Lieber Meister, Louis Sullivan; but since

* Reprinted with the permission of Horizon Press, Inc.

this form first took shape for me in the design of St. Mark's-on-the-Bouwerie:

1929

Here is a fresh development of "St. Mark's", the now realized design of individual modern building for centralization or decentralization that, as a type, fulfills modern requirements either way and utilizes machine age resources at work upon machine age materials in a characteristic machine age way! The straight line and flat plane architecture suited to the technique of the machine age is seen here in significant outline instead of monumental mass.[11] The *constitution* of the whole building emphasizing interior space in light, with a novel combination of offices and apartments.

The structure is the cantilever—steel in tension—light and strong as it looks: one third lighter yet three times stronger than the heavy masonry-encrusted box frame of steel. In the nineteen stories of this structure the equivalent of at least two floors are available to live in, instead of being thrown away to give place to useless destructive wall-weights. There is but ten percent more glass area as "exposure" than you may see in the average commercial building such as Gordon Strong's Republic Building down on State Street, corner of Adams, in Chicago.

The steel textile, embedded in concrete, a machine age product of great value and beauty, here clothes interior space inside the glass and allows more light or less light, more or less privacy as desired under changing conditions. All exposed surfaces of the building except the central mass and floors, the supporting structure itself, are of copper. Partitions and furniture are designed as one and fabricated in the shop. Conservation of much space is effected by this resilient construction and this also means that the equivalent of a five room apartment, cave style, may be had in two thirds of the usual space. Sunlight methods in arrangement are everywhere evident.

Economy is extraordinary here in every sense. In any operation on large scale such construction affords enormous economy. Astonishing release from the usual field waste is the result of this use of the skyscraper form.

Naturally somewhat strange at first sight, but the kind of beauty we see in the liner, the plane and the motor is here. Added to that in [12] the interior you will find a graceful sense of harmony in the whole, an imaginative touch in all detail that makes the parts sing in unison with the form of the whole. (Now The Tower is an apartment-building within an office-building, both more useful than ever.)

Beautiful? Let time say.

What is beauty?—yours—and yours—yes, and yours, my sophisticated savant! I hear you, I imagine your answer. Yours would simmer down to a mere matter of "taste", if you spoke the truth. "Taste" is usually a matter of ignorance, or some personal idiosyncrasy, trusted to overmuch in our culture.

Eclecticism must come to terms—to knowledge. None of the great architectures of the world ever grew up on such a flimsy basis as "taste." Even rare taste such as yours, my dear connoisseur! Nor is it yet calculated by aesthete philosopher or functionist. Great architecture grows as this building grew—true to nature, therefore to materials, method and men—aimed at greatest human benefits by way of least expenditure of money—spontaneous individual insight inspiring more individuals to ever increasing insight until a new technique of a new life is here and individuality is still free. So, this village "skyscraper" is not only the embodiment of human use and comfort; it is a true satisfaction to the *mind*. Not a satisfaction merely to the intellect for that would be as unsure as the satisfaction offered to the taste of this transitory-period. I mean a satisfaction to the mind that *is* a mind and includes a heart.

The fact is this tower-building gets fresh hold on the sense of beauty as a new sense of order, recognizing beauty as something that can never come by putting anything *on* anything at will. It [13] comes as a *quality* that must be found in the thing itself as reward for integrity of means to ends. Here is individual love of nature—in no "exterior" sense.

You see here an expression of the new city as it might be when decentralization proceeds—no further betrayal of machine increment to hold rents.

PREMISE: This type of tall building may enable you to imagine similar ones, though infinite in variety rising as gleaming shafts of light, tall as you please from every village in the country. Space in town, courting the sunbeams and the view—no masonry cavern standing on the streets—the areas thus thrown back into the village planted as green parks. Out of this varied mass of shade trees and flowering shrubs, see the spider—steel—spinning its web to enmesh glass—glass clear—glass translucent—glass in relief—glass in color. Irridescent surfaces of this light-fabric rising high against the blue out of the whole city, the city now seen as a park, the metal fabrication of the shafts themselves turquoise or gold, silver, bronze; the glass surfaces between the threads of the fabric shimmering with light reflected, light refracted—sparkling light broken into imaginative patterns. Eventually all buildings will stand free of each other in natural greenery. The cost of all this devotion to the value of sunlit space would be, all told, one half the cost of the stuffy caverns it replaces. Imagine the savings thus made, put into ground to free the city of demoralizing congestion, to enable men to live and let live by spreading out into the country and up into the air!

Imagine all these human benefits of our new freedom to be coming [14] alive again *by means of the Machine*. You will then have a glimpse of our forthcoming new machine age, where the man himself is more a man and happier because of his advantages, not allowing them to become disadvantages.

See art now as much nature as Nature is herself. We are developed enough as a people to desire such ultimate features as of "human nature."

We must ourselves *make* it. Artificers . . . all. But artificial only as humble means to a greater integrity of life with Nature. This is the great atonement . . . still possible to the human race in spite of expedient abuses. Without this atonement the race dies—should die. Usonia will never have been born.

1938

This skyscraper, planned to stand free in an open park and thus be more fit for human occupancy, is as nearly organic as steel in tension and concrete in compression can make it; here doing for the tall building what Lidgerwood made steel do for the long ship. The ship had its steel keel: this concrete building has its

Courtesy H. C. Price Co., Bartlesville, Okl

The H. C. Price Tower, 1953- 1955, Bartlesville, Oklahoma, the only skyscraper built by America's best known architect, the late Frank Lloyd Wright. A reinforced concrete core supports floors cantilevered like branches. White concrete, blue-green copper sheathing and golden glass are the materials used on the exterior.

steel core. A composite shaft of concrete rises through the floors, each slab engaging the floors at nineteen levels. Each floor proceeds outward from the shaft as a cantilever slab extended from the shaft, similar to the branch of a tree from its trunk. The slab, thick at the shaft, grows thinner as it goes outward in an overlapping scale pattern in concrete until at the final outer leap to the screen wall it is no more [15] than 3 inches thick. The outer enclosing screens of glass and copper are pendent from the edge of these cantilever slabs. The inner partitions rest upon the slabs.

There are three offices to each floor and one double-decked apartment to every alternate floor; each apartment is unaware of the other or the offices, as all look outward. The structure throughout eliminates the weight and waste space of masonry walls. The supporting members stand inside, away from daylighted space and carry elevators and the entrance hallways well within themselves. Two of the exterior walls of every apartment and office are entirely of glass set into metal framing. But the building is so placed that the sun shines on only one wall at a time and narrow upright blades, or mullions, project 9 inches so that as the sun moves, shadows fall on the glass surfaces and afford the protection necessary for comfort.

The building increases substantially in area from floor to floor as the structure rises, in order that the glass frontage of each story may drip clear of the one below, the building thus cleaning itself. Also, areas become more valuable the higher (within limits) the structure goes. The central steel reinforced masonry shaft extending well into the ground may carry with safety a greatly extended top mass. This building is earthquake-, fire- and soundproof from within by economics inherent in its structure. The structure weighs less than half the usual tall masonry encased building and increases the area available for living by more than 20 percent.

This is a logical development of the idea of a tall building in this age of glass and steel; as logical engineering as the Brooklyn Bridge or an ocean liner. But the benefits of modernity such as this [16] are not merely economic. There is greater privacy, safety, and beauty for human lives within it than is possible in any other type of building.

In plan a 1-2 triangle is here employed, because it allows

flexibility of arrangement for human movement not afforded by the rectangle. The apparent irregular shapes of the various rooms would not appear irregular in reality; all would have great repose because all are not only properly in proportion to the human figure but to the figure made by the whole building.

Also the building has complete standardization for prefabrication; only the concrete core and slabs need be made in the field. Our shop-fabricating industrial system could function at its best here with substantial benefits. Owing to the unusual conformations the furniture would properly be a part of the building as the metal (copper) furniture is designed to be. Here again is the poise, balance, lightness and strength that may well characterize the creations of this machine age.

1953-55

The first expression of a tree-like, mast structure was designed in a project for St. Mark's-in-the-Bouwerie, New York, in 1929. The skyscraper is indeed the product of modern technology, but not suitable if it increases congestion. It inevitably would unless it could stand free in the country. This was the one planned as a feature of the model Broadacre City—so those from the city wouldn't feel lost in that vision of the country, and the Johnson Laboratory [17] Tower is another such. But it was an idea that had to wait twenty-five years for full realization. It is actually built now by H. C. Price in Bartlesville, Okla. The total weight of the building is about 6/10 of the conventional structure of the Rockefeller Center type, due to cantilever and continuity. Now the skyscraper comes into its own on the rolling plains of Oklahoma.

The urban skyscraper, unintentionally, has hastened the process of decentralization. But, to the rolling plains of Oklahoma it goes as a fresh realization of the advantages of modern architecture yet unknown to the great city. As a tree crowded in the forest has no chance to become a complete entity—standing free it may establish identity and preserve it. The "upended street" by nature gains more natural advantages from natural use of the technical triumphs of steel and glass in pre-fabrication.

Individuality should be no less appropriate to American business, be even more appropriate than to other facets of American life. The Hal Price Company intends to enjoy all there is to be had through complete use of preferred, convenient, compact space open to air and sky; the Price people will be thus surrounded and have access to roof gardens and fountains. Here in appropriate splendid proportion they will defy climatic discomfort, enjoy supremacy, winning dominance at no man's expense but their own.

This type of sheltered-glass tower-building was first designed by myself in 1924 for Chicago and in 1929 for St. Mark's-in-the-Bouwerie in New York. The idea has since been used, more or less, all over the world.[18]

Has our country in the interval grown up to skyscraper status? No—the skyscraper takes a field trip of its own to the place where it belongs—in the country. I believe this type of structure, weighing but a fraction of Rockefeller Center structures, will become a "natural" everywhere in these United States for successful men, for aspiring commerce, for remarkable achievements in engineering such as the one this building tells us about and was built to serve.

Steel, the spider spinning, here serves the democratic principle well—the individual's healthy aspiration—with even more privacy and greater convenience than the lower structures or the ranch house type lower down in the dust in this region.

Freedom of use by interior and exterior occupation, also protection from excess light and air, are here. In this structure, shaded by copper blades and glazed with mellow tinted glass the air conditioning is less expensive and the occupant more comfortable while his "pump" is more likely to hold out where rash extremes of warm and cool now too frequently alternate to tear his human structure down. At his peril man divorces himself from his native climate.

The self-service elevator—now perfected—is part of that especial gadgetry to the advantages of which the American people are sufficiently awake. Someday they will waken to the "payoff" of good design in all their building projects—learning little by little to know good architecture when they see it.

Witness this release of the skyscraper from the slavery of commercial bondage to the human freedom prophesied by our Declaration of Independence.

Democracy builds . . .[19]

THE ARCHITECTURAL FORUM

Frank Lloyd Wright's
Concrete and Copper Skyscraper

"Frank Lloyd Wright's Concrete and Copper Skyscraper," *The Architectural Forum,*
XCVIII (May, 1953).*

The skyscraper Frank Lloyd Wright had been planning and replanning for nearly a generation goes into actual construction this summer—not in New York, not in Chicago, not in San Francisco, but in Bartlesville, Okla. (1950 population 19,228). It is 18 stories, 186' tall—and its tower floors will gross only 1,900 sq. ft.

This will be a jewel-like building, somewhat small in size but vast in reach; modest in area but rich in ordinance [Ordonnance is the correct word. Eds.]. It rates careful study for its engineering, for the 83-year-old master has ventured boldly into the integration of tomorrow's structure and tomorrow's mechanization. . . . It is worth study for its economics, for this will probably be the costliest office building ever erected and yet it may prove one of the most profitable. . . . It is charming in its human scale and intriguing for the way it combines business offices and residential apartments on the same floor. It is exciting for the way it seems from some angles almost all copper, from other angles almost all glass—glass not white, not green, but gold.

But none of these aspects is as important as the attitude toward style and the attitude toward location.

* Reprinted by permission from the May, 1953, issue of *Architectural Forum,* © 1953, Time, Inc.

THIS IS FRANK LLOYD WRIGHT'S CHALLENGE TO THE DOGMA OF "SIMPLICITY"

Here in concrete and steel and copper and glass is organic architecture's answer to the stripped vernacular of almost all today's commercial construction. Here is an office building that is all flowering ornament—ornament, in Wright's own words, "of the building, not on it." Here is a tower whose surfaces have depth, whose form is manifestly intended to "transcend function and be touched with poetic imagination."

At first glance such a tower might seem anachronistic in an age that delights to honor such flat surface masterpieces as Lever House, an age when even the bosses stamped into the Alcoa Tower and the spider-web on the UN Secretariat are called three-dimensional. And it is true that no thoroughbred business building has been so richly adorned since Wright's own "Lieber Meister" Louis Sullivan laced the entire envelope of his 1908 Guaranty Building in Buffalo with terra cotta cast in delicate patterns.

But this "anachronism" of ornament is studied, deliberate, and defiant. Is this then the last skyscraper of another age? Or does it mark a new swing of the pendulum which through all ages has alternated between the wealth of ornamentation and the elegance of simplicity?[98]

HERE IS A SKYSCRAPER STANDING IN ITS OWN SHADOW—AND ONLY IN ITS OWN SHADOW

Not since Goodhue gave his wheat sower a pedestal 338' above the plains atop the Nebraska capitol has a US elevator building been so deliberately stood up free—"in its own right, in its own park, casting its long shadow, on its own ground." And never before, to FORUM's knowledge, has it happened with a tall business structure. Never has so tall an office tower been built in so small a city.

In the business district of New York or Chicago an 18-story building would be cramped and dwarfed and might not be visible for more than 500'. In Bartlesville, this tower will be visible from 16 miles away. Its upper floors will command an unbroken view in all directions over 800 square miles of prairie and foothills.

This act is Wright's manifesto for the elevator building: for, "as trees crowded in the forest have no chance to become themselves (as they could if they stood alone) so the skyscraper needs to be freestanding in the countryside to become a human asset."

CERTAINLY THERE IS NOTHING ANACHRONISTIC ABOUT THE CONSTRUCTION OR ENGINEERING OF THIS TOWER

The structure will be as new as tomorrow, but the integration of engineering with design is peculiarly Wrightian and the basic concept has existed in his mind and in his drawings for at least 25 years. . . .

The structural system reverses completely the current—and modern—method of enclosing buildings from the outside in, of conjoining the structure with the box enclosure. This tower is carried literally from the inside out. The bearing elements are four separate hollow concrete fins, each 18' long, set like a cross or a pin-wheel near the center, producing a quartered building or, as Wright calls it, a "segmented quadruped." . . . Each floor is carried like a tray on four diagonal arm-walls set at an angle of 30°-60°.

This structure, revolutionary 20 years ago, is bold even today, for it means that the entire floor system can be considered as cantilevered—some of it perhaps even 20'. Only in the past five years has conventional construction moved the enclosure 2' to 3' beyond the skeleton to get continuous windows.

The structure is light. It takes advantage of cantilevers, light-weight aggregates and the happily lenient building code in Bartlesville which imposes no foolish fire safety requirements on the masonry under the windows of such a free standing tower.

And that is still not all, for there is another advanced idea: the structure not only carries the mechanical equipment; it is also an integral part of the mechanical equipment. The hollow fins and hollow floors are so [101] formed as to serve three separate functions in addition to structure—to serve the plumbing system for chases, the elevator system for shafts, and the air conditioning system for ducts and plenums. This last integration means the whole structure will provide supplementary radiant heating in winter, radiant cooling in summer. Supply air will be zoned with each fin serving a separate quadrant.

The cooling tower will be made to do double duty as three fountains atop the highest office floor (the fifteenth) and one fountain on the roof of the adjoining two-story wing.

As for its elevators, this Price Tower is perhaps the first office building erected since the war where service will be truly adequate—four elevators for perhaps 200 tower tenants on 17 floors. The cost of extra equipment will be largely offset by dispensing with operators. Moreover the elevator machinery is in the basement, not on the roof. Were this made general practice, what an improvement in maintenance and in the skyline of a thousand buildings whose penthouses would be rid of machinery and available for human use!

SUCH INTEGRATION WAS NOT THOUGHT OUT OVERNIGHT

The evolving idea of the Price Tower traces back to Wright's famous Chicago skyscraper project, the ill-fated National Life Insurance Co. building plan of 1924, close to 30 years ago; and when Wright drew that he had been in practice for himself for more than a generation.

The National Building had four wings and the cantilevers were carried on parallel rows of interior columns (exactly the scheme to be repeated in the proposed UNESCO building, by Italy's famed engineer Nervi)....

It was for the 1929 St. Mark's apartment tower scheme for New York that Wright changed the parallel row of supports into the "quadripartite" scheme of right-angled fin supports; and in 1940 that he arranged these towers in a long arched row for the Crystal Heights project for Washington.

THIS TOWER IS ALL WINDOWS—
BUT ALL ARE IN SHADE

And this brings the story full-cycle to the theme of structure as ornament. For although other architects around the world have worked indeed with fins and trellisses as sunshades, not yet has one of them so cunningly used metal vanes to suggest "not only the trellis but the vine." Laid horizontally against the three business quadrants of the tower, vertically against the domestic quadrant, these 20″ fins are of that exceptionally noble metal, copper.

The copper may be counted on to change color with the years—first red, then black, then verdigris; through the spring, winter and summer of the tower the harmony will persist, since the metal will lie against not only the concrete spandrels or parapets, but against glass that will be tinted gold.

Nor will that enrichment be all: for the matching copper facings of the alternate mezzanine spandrels are to be of a delicate stamped pattern as fine as the ones Wright has made familiar on his great houses.

AND WHAT ABOUT THE COST?

Wright himself believes the tower can be erected for no more than a conventional structure. Some builders, on the contrary, think it will cost more than $3 million; i.e., more than $60 a sq. ft. Some subcontractors have been scared by the unusual design, have bid as high as $450,000 for the exterior copper alone, more than $300,000 for the concrete.

The owner is satisfied that the building can be bought for much less than $3 million, is prepared to negotiate compromises on the specifications like substituting aluminum for copper on the fins and tile for stainless steel on the bathtubs, (on which bids have run as high as $1,400 each). At this stage, the two safest cost forecasts seem to be these:

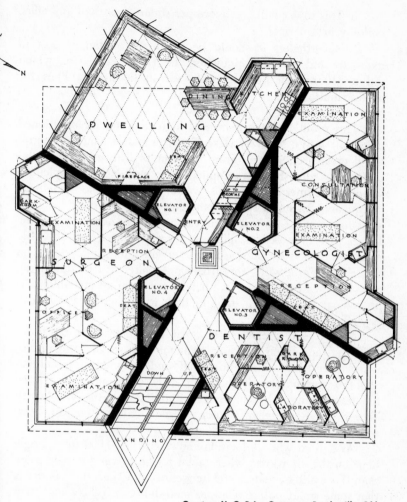

The H. C. Price Tower, 1953-1955, Bartlesville, Oklahoma, a typical floor plan. Here a complex asymmetry, which invariably delighted Frank Lloyd Wright, is clearly discernible. It also clearly entailed obvious complexities in construction.

1. This tower will cost more per square foot than any office building in America;

2. Nevertheless it should be worth more than its cost to its smart and well-heeled owner, the H. C. Price Co., which did a $10 million business last year in tie-in pipe lines for oil distribution.[102]

This profit is not a matter of high rents for airconditioned offices all with a two-way view. This is a matter which is central to all great architecture. From the time of Cheops, great architecture has almost always implied some element of conspicuous waste—sometimes conspicuous waste of decoration, sometimes conspicuous waste of space, sometimes both. But what has construction cost to do with the values of the Acropolis, or the Piazza in Venice, or Versailles—or, for that matter, with the little glass box which of late has conferred unwilling immortality on Dr. Edith Farnsworth for $76,000? Architecture is admittedly the costliest of the arts. Fortunately, it is also an art which has proved again and again that in time its intangible values can pay off.

In the end architecture, great architecture, is the most enduring—and often the most economical—form of "promotion," when advertising transcends itself and becomes the building and the presentation of character. How often must we relearn the lesson taught by the Singer Building and the Woolworth Tower, by Rockefeller Center, Corning Glass, Johnson Wax, Alcoa and Lever House?

At a time when television shows cost $100,000 for a single hour on the air waves, when talent for an evening is paid more than the world's greatest architect earns in a year, the wonder is that some smart public relations man didn't have his client snap up this little masterpiece long ago for its advertising value.

Today the Price Company is completely unknown outside its own industry. Tomorrow this little 40,000 sq. ft. gem of a building will make Price famous.[104]

FRANK LLOYD WRIGHT AND OTHERS

On the Price Tower in Bartlesville, Oklahoma

Frank Lloyd Wright and others on the Price Tower in Bartlesville, Oklahoma, *The Architectural Record*, CXIX (February, 1956).*

FRANK LLOYD WRIGHT,
Architect of the Tower:

This gentle skyscraper has escaped the big city to live in an American town in the country . . . To stand there in its own park, casting its own shadow upon its own ground. Reflected in a long slender pool it affords everyone everywhere in it a beautiful view of the rolling countryside that is Oklahoma.

The "skyscraper" in itself, where there is space, is a proper American circumstance; a triumph, not of landlordism, but of our own best technology. It should be a triumph of our architectural artistry as well. But such is not the case. The skyscraper of the big city where skyscrapers crowd upon skyscrapers is a rank weed in what otherwise might be a wholesome garden. The American skyscraper belongs, rather, to our smaller American towns like Bartlesville, where there is still a chance for the spirit of man to live and express itself in a free community that offers a better future to American democracy. The big city of today is servile and doomed by the eternal law of change.

This instance of the tall building in the country now seems to me to be one proper step on the way toward the inevitable, planned-decentralization of the giant-city: the city—a greedy monster—now being undermined by its own extravagance. The unplanned nature of this overgrown old pattern of the city—now so overcrammed with mechanized merchandise—is being accel-

---

* Reprinted with the permission of *The Architectural Record*.

erated to extinction by its own contrivances. This old pattern is
not for the modern free-world of democracy.

Look at this American skyscraper now upright in the American countryside. A natural! Its glass is protected by wide projecting copper blades (or blinds) and tinted gold. The occupant
is not only protected against actinic exposure; the whole building
is itself shielded against weather. This copper shielding is for the
liberation, comfort, and pleasure of those who live and work in
the building. Glass is here a blessing to the occupants.[154]

HAROLD C. PRICE,
Owner of the Tower and head of the H. C. Price Company:

The decision to engage Frank Lloyd Wright as the architect for
an office building for the H. C. Price Company was prompted by
our belief in his ability to create for us and our community a
structure of great and lasting beauty.

We were of the opinion that an office building could be
made beautiful without affecting its proper functioning. It seemed
to us that nearly all office buildings have followed a stereotyped
design—with variations—though many have proven very impressive upon completion.

It was not our intent to build a monument. We simply
wanted a functional office building that would possess a natural
beauty brought about through outstanding design. We wanted a
building of which our city would be proud. We believe that we
have obtained the desired result.

Working with Mr. Wright and his Fellowship over a period
of three years has been a liberal education in the appreciation of
the arts of decorative and functional design.

During the construction of a building, the client and Mr.
Wright do not always agree. When Frank Lloyd Wright is certain
he is correct, he objects to change. But, if the client has logic
in his argument, Frank Lloyd Wright will readily consider any
sensible changes suggested.

We particularly noted that Mr. Wright is never bound by his
original ideas. He will make changes as the work progresses,
whenever it is practicable and advantageous to do so. And, with-

out a single exception, during the construction of the Price Tower, every such change that was made resulted in marked improvement.

JOE D. PRICE,
Son of the owner; who took the photographs:

When only the bare structural form of the building had been erected, it possessed a basic poetry different from the rhythm of the ordinary post and beam and slab system—a beauty that was actually built in before the exterior was ever applied. The outer surfacing—when it was finally fixed in place—merely intensified the ingrained charm and grace of the basic form; a quality best described by Mr. Wright's own term "organic." [156]

When the windows were added to the skeleton, their big mullions tended to make the building appear heavy. This discouraging stage of construction lasted several months. But one day, when the louvers had been applied to the upper third of the tower, I was walking along Bartlesville's main street and looked up over the little box-type buildings all about me to find the Price building towering majestically over them. Then, for the first time, the true building itself became visible to me. There are no words to describe the intense feeling it gave me. Since then the building has grown in magnitude. As you drive through Bartlesville, down streets, past houses, through alleys, you keep seeing glimpses of the tower rising and thrusting nobly above the rooftops. Everywhere one goes he is aware of it—as a medieval cathedral, it dominates the town.[157]

EDGAR KAUFMANN, JR.,
Historian, author, critic:

The Price Tower culminates an extraordinary tradition that began in 1873 when Frank Lloyd Wright was four years old. Then Frederick Baumann published a pamphlet, *The Art of Preparing Foundations for all Kinds of Buildings with particular Illustrations of the "Method of Isolated Piers" as followed in Chicago*. At eighteen Wright went to work for Adler and Sullivan in the

Borden Block, one of the earliest tall buildings erected on isolated piers, and designed by the partners themselves in 1880. Similar piers supported Sullivan's later masterwork, the Wainwright Building. Wright wrote, "As he threw the 'stretch' on my desk with the first three bays outlined in pencil I sensed what had happened. . . . Until Louis Sullivan showed the way, high buildings lacked unity. They were built up in layers. . . . All except one . . . Root's Monadnock . . . a noble building."

In 1890, tall buildings achieved their first symbolic and purely exterior expressions of unity: the second Leiter building (structurally advanced); the Monadnock (structurally retrogressive); the brilliant Wainwright (structurally symbolic rather than directly expressive). Ever since, unity of surface has remained the admired expression of tall building design.

Beaumann's seed idea of the isolated pier was to yield a second harvest, however. In 1929 Wright, after his great skyscraper projects of 1912 and the early 1920's, grasped the isolated pier as the very core of tall building in his scheme for St. Mark's tower. Developing from a 60 feet wooden windmill he erected for his schoolteacher aunts thirty-five years earlier, this concrete and glass shaft achieved a technical and spatial expression of startling originality. Four separate, symmetrical segments were linked by ribbons of patterned copper; fire-stairs differentiated alternate sides of the building; pointed ribs of concrete, evidence of the mast-like structure, impinged on the sky to top it all.

Twenty years later, in the laboratory tower for S. C. Johnson and Son. Wright gave the isolated pier a yet more forcible expression. One great concrete shaft, sunk deep into the earth, rises to carry work-space cantilevered about it, smoothly sealed in bands of brick and glass; the surface the complete expression of the core.

When Harold Price requested a building combining offices and dwellings, Wright reworked and [158] refined his original scheme of a tower in quadrants. The proportion of three to one in favor of office space produces an exterior asymmetry of continual, graceful surprises. Fire stairs and core-walls rise to a coronet of offices for the owner. Blue-green copper—inside and out—counters the different blue of the sky; golden glass softens the strong prairie daylight or warms the dusk. Copper fins further modify the light—vertical over the apartment windows, horizontal elsewhere—ensuring in silhouette the vibrant dotted line Wright always prefers. The structural core of the Price Tower effloresces in movement, color, texture, ornament, and (in the penthouse mural) art, all held together and in scale by integration with the structure itself—inner unity and identity here embodied in an architecture that establishes as seldom before a new horizon.[159]

BUSINESS WEEK

Skyscraper Casts Its Shadow on the Plains

"Skyscraper Casts Its Shadow on the Plains," *Business Week* (February 18, 1956).*

Congested urban areas gave birth to the skyscraper, but now the full-grown child is leaving home and heading for the wide open spaces. Last week a 19-story office-apartment building was dedicated in Oklahoma that doesn't have to fight for a place in the skyline. For most of the squat buildings that make up Bartlesville, Okla. (population 22,000) barely reach above the new skyscraper's shoe tops.

Two men are responsible for bringing the symbol of the Big City to the Oklahoma plains. One is the country's best known architect—Frank Lloyd Wright. The other is Harold C. Price, president of H. C. Price Co. and a leading citizen of Bartlesville. He gave his own money and his name to what probably is the world's most modern office structure—and the most expensive per square foot....[114]

WRIGHT'S DREAM

Wright had just been waiting for someone like Price to come along. Twenty-five years ago Wright conceived the idea of con-

* Reprinted with the permission of *Business Week*.

structing a skyscraper tower, with concrete interior vertical shafts dividing the building into quadrants. He planned it as an apartment building because of the privacy afforded by the complete isolation of the four parts. But he couldn't find financial backers for the project.

Price's visit revived the architect's old dream. It meant a chance to put up his "quad" skyscraper. He felt this type of building ideally suited to Price's needs. By building up into the sky instead of spreading out on the ground, Wright argued, Price would get convenient compact space, an unusual amount of privacy—and plenty of fresh air and unobstructed views of the countryside.

And Wright has a strong conviction that the skyscraper belongs as much—if not more—in the open country as it [115] does in the city. In the country it isn't surrounded by other tall buildings. This means it's possible to bring the "outside" right into the building. And it makes it possible to give a skyscraper an individuality because it won't be swallowed up in a forest of giant structures. Wright looks at his "quad" skyscraper as a kind of "up-ended" street providing concentrated—yet uncongested, even isolated—living and office space on a scale suited for towns and small cities.

WRIGHT, THE SALESMAN

Speaking of Wright, Price said: "He quickly convinced me of the efficiency of a 19-story building over a three-story struc[ture] that we had in mind." The speed with which he did it led Joe Price to comment: "Wright's a better salesman than he is an architect." And he has a high regard for Wright's ability as an architect.

Of course, Wright and Price, both strong-minded individuals, had their differences. It makes Price bristle to hear Wright speak of bringing the skyscraper to the country. To him, Bartlesville is not a country town.

WORKING RELATIONS

And disagreements developed as the planning and construction of the building progressed. "We had our differences," said Price, "but Wright is no tyrant. I had been warned to get everything down on paper before starting construction because Wright has a habit or phobia for changing things as he goes along." That was one of the reasons given for the delay from the first talks to the actual construction a year later. . . .[116]

THE COST

As you might expect, a building of this type costs a pretty penny. Price says he laid out "around $2-million," although outside guesses have been much higher. Cost per square foot has been estimated at about $45 and this would come to about $2.5-million for the building itself. The structure contains 60,000 sq. ft. of floor space, but this includes some of the carport and parking area.

It would have cost even more to build the skyscraper Wright originally designed. But Price put his foot down and the architect modified the plans to scale down the cost.

BUILDING THE "QUAD."

At the time he put in a bid for Price Tower, contractor Haskell Culwell said: "We couldn't believe it would ever be built. It was just too extreme and too advanced in design when we first were asked to bid on it. One of our first problems was that of materials. Prices were hard to get from suppliers. It was hard to know ourselves what we would need."

And constructing the building was no easy job either. The structure was so slim that there wasn't room enough to move men and equipment around in it. Culwell described the basement interior as "like the interior of a submarine—every inch of wall space utilized."

An even bigger difficulty was having to erect the building more or less from sketches by Wright.

The tower, like other Wright structures, has had a tendency to leak like a sieve around the windows when the wind-driven, gusty rains come. So the windows have had to be fixed.

ADJUSTMENTS

And other adjustments [117] have been made, too. Wright designed the interiors and furniture in all nine floors of office space occupied by the Price Co., even down to the drapes in Price's office. He also arranged placement of desks, cabinets, and shelving. But not all of it has been to Price's liking or that of his officers.

Price sent back the world globe Wright designed for him and ordered another one. The one Wright designed didn't have Bartlesville on it.

And Wright is redesigning the executive chairs. Until the new ones arrive, the Price executives are suffering with the original chairs. One of them said, "They make you feel like you are about to fall on your face."

Many of the last minute changes, says Elmer Gallery, secretary-treasurer of H. C. Price, had to be made because "Wright didn't take into account the people for whom the building was to be built and their needs."

Apparently Wright paid little attention to acoustics. All of the offices are of masonry, glass, steel, and mahogany. But there is no sound-proofing in them. When one secretary uses an electric typewriter, you can hardly carry on a conversation, much less talk on the phone.

SOCIAL PROBLEM

On top of that, there is an embarrassing social problem. In the Price offices, the door to the washroom is located behind the secretary's desk. So some of the male office workers find themselves traveling to another floor rather than walking into the washroom while their secretary is in the office.

Courtesy Lever Bros.

Two Skyscrapers Compared: Lever House and the Price Tower. Frank Lloyd Wright called Lever House a "four-sided old box" and his own building "organic."

Courtesy H. C. Price Company, Bartlesville, Okla.

Generally, though, the Price employees are quite pleased with their new surroundings.

RENTALS

At the time of the dedication, about half the office space was rented. A small quadrant costs $135 a month, and the larger ones rent for $185. Among the tenants are a beautician, a lawyer, and doctors. Wright will design interiors and furniture for any of the tenants, but some, pointedly, have said they prefer their own.

One of the tenants, Public Service Co. of Oklahoma, which uses the two-story wing for its Bartlesville branch offices, is having troubles, too. Several of the lights burned out last week and the manager complained a scaffold would have to be built to replace them.

The furnished duplex apartments rent for $325 a month. As of last week, only one had been rented—to Bruce Goff, Tulsa architect, who is a follower of Wright. Price, of course, has one.

The townspeople have mixed feelings about their new landmark. But most prevalent comment of the tornado-conscious residents is this: "I sure would hate to be in that thing when it starts to blow." So far the building hasn't faced up to any really stiff winds.[118]

LEWIS MUMFORD

From the Ground Up

Lewis Mumford, *From the Ground Up* (New York, Harcourt, Brace & World, Inc., 1956).*

THE FUJIYAMA OF ARCHITECTURE

. . . As for the marriage of function with form, Wright never took seriously the doctrine Sullivan preached, that form must *follow* function, nor did he accept the earlier version given out by the sculptor Horatio Greenough,[76] who equated functional form with the absence of dress or ornament, with economy. In the evolution of Wright's architecture, his tendency has been toward demonstrativeness, toward dramatic exaggeration even when he is at work with the purely mechanical elements. Thus he turns the skyscraper from a cubical cage to an organic form like a plant, with a central core or stem, from which floors, in dramatic contrast to the older system of post-and-beam construction, are cantilevered out—though this more organic design imposes rigidities of its own in fenestration and in the disposition of interior space. Of the two fundamental Freudian types of personality, the hoarding and the spending kind, one tight and compulsive and the other released and generous, Wright belongs firmly to the second. His expansiveness, his exuberance, his inclination to put both form and function highhandedly at the service of his own singular genius are an essential part of his inexhaustible creativeness.

This very quality of personality, so richly interfused in all of Wright's buildings, imposes a great burden upon criticism; one cannot possibly criticize his buildings without making an estimate of his personality, and reckoning with his idiosyncrasies as

* Reprinted by permission of Harcourt, Brace & World, Inc., from *From the Ground Up*, by Lewis Mumford, © 1947, 1948, 1949, 1950, 1951, 1952, 1953, 1954, 1955, 1956, by Lewis Mumford. (All of the essays in *From the Ground Up* originally appeared in *The New Yorker*.)

well as his gifts. As Sir Herbert Read recently said of Wright's latest book, *The Future of Architecture*, "Carried to its logical conclusion, a sense of unity . . . implies that every house Mr. Wright builds is his own house and the people who live in them are not his clients but his guests." Speaking with all reverence for a great master, I must confess that Wright's dwelling houses sometimes put me off by persuading me that he is thinking not of the client's needs but of the architect's own desires and delights. . . . That willfulness,[77] for all the charm and aesthetic novelty with which it is cloaked, is not an uncommon quality of Wright's work. All great genius shows that tendency in some degree. . . . But in Wright this quality goes with one that was perhaps re-inforced by the bad example set by Sullivan. This tendency was one of the unhappy bequests of the Romantic movement, for it turned the artist into a Wagnerian superman, if not a god, whose intuitions became divine judgments, whose instinctive preferences become dogmas, whose word finally became law. Wright, fully aware of his own arrogance, has gaily defended it on the ground that arrogance is more decent than simulated humility. True, but arrogance is not necessarily better than real humility, the kind that learns, through self-examination, from its errors, that wrestles with its opponent instead of scornfully dismissing him and so be-comes stronger in the process, that surmounts the limitations of its education and its temperament by seeking to understand other ways of life, other temperaments, other purposes. Because his own world is so rich, he has little understanding of how much of other people's worlds he leaves out. . . .[78]

A PHOENIX TOO INFREQUENT

In his larger structures, even more than in his dwelling houses, Wright's university training as an engineer [80] has stood him in good stead. All these big buildings show, in one degree or another, the combination of qualities that makes up his specific genius—his fertility in technical invention and the endless play of his fantasy, largely in relation to new forms provided by the machine. Like sculptors who find heads and torsos and abstract forms in driftwood, Wright quickens in the presence of any building material; he can think of more ways of using glass and concrete, sheet metal and precast blocks, than any of his contemporaries. To respect "the nature of materials"—a phrase often on his lips—and to create original forms in harmony with the mechanical processes that shape them are perhaps his main concerns. These preoccupations override any regard for the varied natures of men whenever they are not in harmony with this effort. Add to this his respect for regular, geometric figures, which, he notes, "have acquired to some extent human significance, as, say, the cube or the square, integrity; the circle or sphere, infinity; the straight line, rectitude." From his willing submission to materials, mechanical processes, and geometric forms, he gets the deepest subjective satisfaction; indeed, to him all this has a moral quality that justifies his indifference to less architectonic human needs and desires. This aspect of his strength partly accounts for a human failing that goes with it: the client he seeks above all to satisfy is himself.[81]

. . . When thwarted, Wright seems to lie in wait for a client capable of matching his own audacity and sanctioning the new form. This gives some of his best designs a factitious air when they finally are built. Thus his idea for a skyscraper with floors cantilevered out from a utility core (elevators and the like), the whole to be sheathed in a curtain wall of glass and copper, was originally applied to a projected apartment house for St. Mark's-in-the-Bouwerie back in 1929, but only now has it finally found actual embodiment, in an office building in Oklahoma. . . .[82]

. . . In some buildings his logic overpowers his aesthetic sense: in his passion for geometric form, he turns the polygon into a paragon. Having seized upon a certain geometric form—a hexagon or a triangle—he will, for the sake of consistency, apply it to every nook and corner of his design, thus creating a far too insistent series of harsh, angular forms in the furniture he designs as well as in the meetings of beams, the shape of his windows, and the layout of his rooms. One's eye vainly seeks relief from this almost obsessive reiterativeness. . . .[84]

. . . To be free, for Wright, means to be free [87] from one's neighbors. That individuality may reside in the collective whole, as in a symphony, and that for the sake of this whole one might

willingly surrender some of one's individuality to have it given
back, enriched, at a higher level, is contrary to his philosophy of
life and his mode of design. In this inability to understand either
the urban or the urbane, Wright's attitude discloses the limitations of Romanticism, with its rebellion against everything that
demands conformity to a general social pattern. To the problem
of bringing individuality, personality, spontaneity, freedom back
into the huge mechanical urban collectives that now operate so
compulsively, he has no answer except "Clear out!" Thus he has
never faced the paramount problem of modern architecture—to
translate its great individual accomplishments into an appropriate
common form in which, by pooling economic and social resources
and cooperatively integrating designs, advantages that are now
open only to a wealthy few will accrue to a great many. If the
contemporary architect has not as yet found an adequate answer
to this problem, Wright characteristically has not even asked the
question.

As for the machine, Wright's approach to it has been ambivalent, not to say paradoxical. Though he was possibly the first
modern architect to freely accept the machine, in ornament as
well as construction, he has little use for its indigenous forms—
the impersonal, the typical, the anonymous. Le Corbusier gave
a fresh impetus to the modern movement by showing how much
good form had already been produced by the machine, in ordinary drinking glasses, pipes, bentwood chairs, and office equipment; Wright, on the other hand, saw machine production as a
way of producing new forms that would bear his unmistakable
mark. So his furniture, specially designed for his houses, has
fitted only his own unique architectural plans, both at [88] the
expense of the human carcass—he admits he always barks his
shins on his chairs—and at the expense of the influence that a
more neutral design might have exercised on furniture in general.
Wright's dislike for the typical and the generic is probably also
the explanation of his hostility toward those who have won favor
by using less personal forms. But surely one of the reasons for
the appearance of the cardboard-box style of architecture, which
he so violently detests, was the desire, in a world full of assertive
advertising and *art-nouveau* idiosyncrasy, for the almost monastic

simplicity and anonymity of Cubism and purism. Wright, it is true, had no need to participate in that revolt, for he had kept away from *art-nouveau* curlicues as rigorously as he had from moth-eaten historic furbelows. Indeed, in many of his earlier houses, which were disciplined by his love for Japanese forms, he had achieved a similar cleansing, a similar clarity, in his own right, long before Ozenfant, Le Corbusier, Mondrian, and Gropius had discovered abstract art's antiseptic charm.

How, then, is one to account for Wright's hostility to the "box," a hostility that seems to deny that it is one of the eternal, basic geometric forms? Is he not chiefly offended by the fact that its neutral background might allow for intimate choices and delicately personal needs—for a picture or a statue, for a set of fine chairs from the eighteenth century—that would be put out of countenance in a room with a more positive aesthetic character? Probably the answer for Wright is that the room itself, as molded by the architect, is the personality to be considered, not the user (he is as insistent as Le Corbusier that the client should replan his life to fit the new structure), and if this means discarding cherished possessions, giving up pictures on the wall, accepting the natural colors and textures of the materials used, it is for him a better solution than the toleration [89] of architectural anonymity or neutrality. Wright has identified his personal philosophy with "democracy" or "the Usonian [Wright for "American"] way of life," offering the implication that America must guard itself against all manner of foreign importations, especially architects. More than once, in expressing his opposition to the "box," he has spoken as if the work of his foreign-born architectural rivals were not merely "inorganic" but un-American. While Wright is sound in asserting the American architect's freedom from colonial servility, it is another thing for him to denounce architects of European origin, such men of integrity and humane understanding as Gropius, in language (and thought) that should be reserved for morbidly isolationist journals. The America First streak in Wright is a coarse, dark vein in the fine granite of his mind, and it has kept him from learning as much as he might have from those who by taste and temperament and training most differed from him. [90]

HARRIET MONROE

A Poet's Life

Harriet Monroe, A Poet's Life (New York, The Macmillan Company, 1938).*

In those days and earlier I saw more or less of Louis Sullivan, whose genius as the leader of the Secessionists and the designer of beautiful and original buildings I greatly admired. Sullivan and Frank Lloyd Wright, one of his students and followers, with others of this small group, had made Chicago "the center of the American rebellion against the historic styles in architecture," and though Wright was by no means Sullivan's equal, his genius for publicity prevented his being obscured by neglect and self-torture, as Sullivan had been in his later years. Three times the Architectural Club [of Chicago] gave Wright a separate gallery in their exhibition. There he showed houses rather than skyscrapers; indeed, his mind deals in smaller units than the commercial colossus requires, and his vision, I have always felt, is restless rather than serene. There are no great spaces in his architecture, no sense of bigness or peace.[210]

* Reprinted with the permission of Miss Monroe's heirs.

part III

For Discussion
and Themes

QUESTIONS FOR DISCUSSION

PART I. AIMS OF ARCHITECTURE

1. Compare the first four definitions of architecture. What factors have entered architectural controversy between antiquity and the nineteenth century? Examine carefully the assumptions that underlie each man's writing. Explore the polarities inherent in the definitions of Ruskin and Sir Gilbert Scott.

2. What is Abbot Suger's conception of the uses of beauty? Why does he feel that man needs beauty? Contrast this attitude with those of Alberti, Ruskin, Wright, and Le Corbusier. Discuss the concept of the "whole and its parts" in relation to architecture as presented by Palladio and other theorists included in Part I.

3. What is Wren's conception of the function of architecture? What role, if any, does an ideal beauty play in his thought? What is his attitude toward the introduction of the fanciful and novel into architecture? Compare his over-all attitude with that of Ruskin.

4. Contrast the views of Johnson and Burke on the relationship between beauty and utility (function) with those of Sullivan and Le Corbusier.

5. What is Ruskin's conception of the function and character of art? What is the relationship of art to originality? How does Ruskin conceive of the relationship between genius and invention? How would he define style? What new criteria does he introduce for the judging of architectural works? Examine the logical validity of his attitudes and use of language.

6. What is James's conception of "style"? How is it related to the idea of glory?

7. What benefits, if any, does Van Brunt perceive in the maintenance of tradition in architecture? How does he conceive of the relation of America to tradition? What is his attitude toward primitivism in a sophisticated society? Compare this attitude with those of Sullivan, Wright, and Le Corbusier.

8. Present an argument to show how Schopenhauer's views on architecture rest ultimately on a concept of "empathy." Contrast Schopenhauer's concept of beauty in architecture with those of Wright and Alberti. Pay particular attention to the use of such terms as *natural, rational, organic,* and *ornamental.*

9. What assumptions does Veblen make about the nature of beauty? How do his assumptions contrast with those of Ruskin, Alberti, and Burke?

10. What does Sullivan mean by *function* in his essay on the tall building? Examine the nature of his argument and its basic assumptions. How does he relate art and nature? Examine the terms of the analogy. How sound is the analogy? Compare Sullivan's and Van Brunt's attitudes toward tradition and rules in architecture. What is the justification for the architect's demand for freedom from precedent? How valid is it? Compare Sullivan's, Van Brunt's, and Tallmadge's conceptions of the relationship of architecture in America to foreign styles.

11. When Sullivan discusses historical styles, he says that architecture is "a serious attempt . . . to make a building grow naturally, out of all its conditions." Examine the logical assumptions underlying Sullivan's analogy between the design of a building and natural growth. How would Sullivan define a building's "conditions"? How comprehensive do you think his attitude is? Compare it with Alberti's and Ruskin's. Examine the logic of the substitution of the word *civilization* for *style.* Compare Sullivan and Alberti on the permanence of beauty.

12. In what sense does Wright make use of the word *machine?* Is a steel-frame building a machine? What reasons does Wright give for the effect of the machine on art of the past? Examine Wright's use of words such as *organic, simplicity, natural.* What do they suggest about his conception of the valid and invalid functions of art? Examine the political, social, economic, and cultural assumptions of his writing. How valid do these assumptions seem to be in discussing architectural beauty? To what extent do you think Wright's ideas would ultimately limit or restrict the artist's freedom to handle his materials?

13. What does Wright's reaction to his discovery of Lao-Tze suggest about his assumptions concerning originality? What is the relationship of truth or beauty to originality? Can you define Wright's conception of "Organic Architecture"? How precise is Wright's use of language? Upon what grounds does Wright

base the opposition he sees between tradition and common sense? Consider the question in the light of the role of tradition in legal or political institutions. Compare Wright's conception of beauty with those of Alberti and Ruskin.

14. Compare Le Corbusier's attitude toward custom with those of Alberti or Wren. To what extent are Alberti or Wren specifically concerned with styles of architecture? Contrast James's and Le Corbusier's conceptions of style. What does Le Corbusier mean by "intentions which do not speak the language of architecture"? Would Ruskin or Alberti agree with his strictures? Compare Wright's and Le Corbusier's attitudes on the machine-product and the capacity of the machine to create new forms of beauty or to make forms of beauty more available. Examine the concern for historical development and progress on the part of Le Corbusier and Wright. To what extent do their views differ from those of Ruskin and Alberti? What evidence does Le Corbusier offer for the pressing need of architectural reform? Compare his definition of the elements and aims of architecture, especially in the matter of decoration, with those of Ruskin and Vitruvius. Compare Alberti's and Le Corbusier's attitudes toward decoration. What basic premises seem to underlie Le Corbusier's concern for "primary masses"? Do these premises imply any restriction of the architect's vocabulary? Does Le Corbusier's final statement on the aims of architecture contradict his earlier views? Can you resolve any apparent contradictions?

15. Compare Walter Gropius's concept of beauty with similar concepts in the selections of writers from the nineteenth century and earlier. Does Gropius make clear why our epoch ought to seek "concrete" expression in "clear and crisply simplified forms"? Compare Gropius's interest in the effect of repetition of parts with James's interest in "visual glory."

16 Compare the aims of design on the part of architects who champion the "International Style" with those of Vitruvius, Alberti, and Wren. What visual symbols, if any, does the International Style condone? How much freedom in design does an architect of the International Style have? Compare the conception of decoration among advocates of the International Style with the attitudes of Suger, Alberti, Wren, and Ruskin. Why do architects of the International Style dislike ornament? How would Alberti or Ruskin treat the question of the *necessity* of ornament? What role does "function" and "organic design" play in the architectural outlook of the formulators of the International Style, and

how does this attitude compare with those of Sullivan and Wright?

17. Trace the occurrence of the fallacies analyzed by Geoffrey Scott in the selections from Ruskin, Sullivan, Wright, Le Corbusier, Gropius, and Hitchcock-Johnson. Compare Scott's analysis of the "conditions" of architecture with the classical and Modern statements on the nature and aims of architecture. Compare Scott and Modern architects on the problem of the architect's freedom to handle the elements of his craft.

18. After reading the selection by Katherine Gilbert, trace and assort the various uses of the word *clean* in the selections you have read by Modern architects. Note also the varieties of meaning and of emotional tone attached to the other key words that she cites. What words are most often used by those writers who favor the classical tradition in architecture? On the basis of different clusters of words used by pro- and anti-classicists, what distinctions can you make between the conceptions of each group as to the aims and values of architecture? Which words, if any, seem to have "real" or "visible" significance when applied to architecture? Which seem largely emotive?

19. Contrast the architectural perspective of Sedlmayr and Valéry with that of Wright, Gropius, and Le Corbusier. Consider Sedlmayr's assertion that the architect has lost the sense of his art in the light of statements by Wright and Le Corbusier on the role of the machine. Which perspective on the machine seems to you most persuasive, Sedlmayr's or Wright and Le Corbusier's? Why?

20. Can you find in the selections by Sullivan, Wright, Le Corbusier, and Gropius, as well as in those by apologists for the International Style, evidence of the conflict which Moholy-Nagy describes between self-expression (originality) and conformity? Analyze the various reactions to, and criticisms of, the Modern architectural idiom. What do recent critics find wrong with the path of functionalism? What alternatives do they suggest? How many of these difficulties encountered by architecture in a restless age have been predicted or foreshadowed in past statements on the problems or hazards of architecture? Can you find in warnings by Ruskin and Alberti, for example, any comments that have relevance to the contemporary situation?

21. Analyze the place and function of originality and innovation in architecture. What possible dangers can arise from the abuse

of original and novel elements (visual and material) in architecture? To what extent and in what ways do you think these dangers can be controlled?

22. On the basis of evidence presented throughout the selections of Part I, defend or attack Zevi's claim that a general architectural theory and practice, one that will unify the "two standards of judgment, one for modern and another for traditional architecture," is either *needed* or *possible*.

PART II. FIVE CONTROVERSIES

The World's Columbian Exposition of 1893

1. What were the chief aims of the architects of the Fair?

2. By what means were they attained? Consider these aims and means in the light of classical concepts of the nature and function of architecture as presented in the introduction.

3. Compare Van Brunt, Sullivan, and Schuyler on the question of originality in the Fair's architecture. What indication does Van Brunt's analysis of Post's building (this piece has been selected as an example from a series in which Van Brunt analyzes the design of each building of the Court of Honor) give of the reasoned evolution of form? How effectively does Van Brunt's analysis contradict Wright's and Sullivan's charges of the thoughtlessness and lack of care in the classical solution?

4. Distinguish between the concepts of beauty which underlie the classical solution and those which Hitchcock and Johnson point to as the aims of the International Style.

5. What was the effect of the Fair on distinguished visitors such as Henry Adams, William Dean Howells, Hamlin Garland, Paul Bourget, and others? What did they see in it, in terms of American culture? How adequate is Larkin's estimation of Adams' reaction? Consider the role of the Fair in bringing together all the arts under the patronage of architecture.

6. How do the attitudes of Van Brunt and Valéry on this question contrast with those of Wright and of designers in the International Style?

7. To what extent did the architects of the Fair satisfy needs for which functionalists, according to Eero Saarinen and other contemporary critics, have failed to provide?

8. What, in Schuyler's view, were the main lessons of the Fair?

9. Compare Van Brunt's and Schuyler's treatment of the subject of the Fair as an enduring contribution to living American architecture. On what assumption does Schuyler base his claim that the success of the Fair was largely one of "illusion," that it was not a "permanent and serious piece of building"? How would the classical concept of the aims of architecture counter these assumptions? To what extent do you think the qualities singled out as marks of the success of the Fair's architecture can be applied to architectural works in another style? To what extent will the values and aims of Modern architecture accommodate them?

10. Compare Louis Sullivan's account of the organization and development of the Fair with those of Moore, of Van Brunt, and of Hunt? How valid are Sullivan's portraits of Burnham (the man who "did his best and his worst, according to his lights") and of Hunt? Examine carefully the impact of Sullivan's rhetoric. To what attitudes in his audience does it cater? How, if at all, does Sullivan differ in this respect from Van Brunt? Would Sullivan's arguments fit into any of Scott's categories of fallacy? Explain.

11 Criticize the Columbian Exposition in terms of Schopenhauer's principle of rigidity-gravity (support-burden). Show how Schopenhauer would agree or disagree with contemporary critics of the Exposition.

The National Gallery of Art

12. What considerations influenced the architect in his stylistic solution of the problem of designing the National Gallery? How did they operate?

13. How "functional" is the Gallery? Consider particularly such elements as the Rotunda, on which critics disagree.

14. Compare the views of Royal Cortissoz, Anne O'Hare McCormick, Arthur Upham Pope, Joseph Hudnut, and Lorimer Rich on the aims and functions of a museum. Consider the problem raised by Hudnut whether noble surroundings detract from the proper effect of works of art on display.

15. Need there be antagonism between the view of a museum as a "means" and that of a museum as an "end"?

16. Contrast the attitudes of Arthur Upham Pope with those of Hudnut on the uses and endurance of the past.

17. Interpret this controversy in the light of conceptions of the relationship between beauty and originality which you have encountered in Part I and in the section on the Fair.

18. What does Hudnut mean when he calls classical architecture "unweighted by reality" and "emptied of purpose"?

19. Can you see any limitations in the use of the words *reality* and *purpose?* How would Ruskin or Van Brunt answer Hudnut's stricture that classical architecture lacks necessary "relation to time and place"?

20. What argument can be made that "relation to time and place" is a valid aim of any architecture? Upon what grounds does such an argument rest, and how valid in turn are they? How effectively can this criterion be judged contemporaneously?

21. How satisfactory is Hudnut's statement of the architectural aims of Jefferson (see the latter's statements in the section on the United Nations buildings)? Hudnut claims the various classical elements of the Gallery (steps, portico, etc.) exist "for their own sake." How would the classical theorists in Part I counter this contention?

22. Consider Hudnut's statement that beauty is a "social form, grown out of social needs." Would classical theorists be at all concerned with this idea?

23. Consider Hudnut's admiration for the machinery of the Gallery alone in the light of the selections from Sedlmayr and Moholy-Nagy in Part I.

The United Nations

24. Examine the architectural aims of the United Nations and of the architects at work on the design as they are presented in the Secretary-General's report, the interviews recorded in Gertrude Samuel's article, and in Harrison's speech. What common ground, if any, can be found to underlie any apparent differences? What elements are most stressed?

25. Do you find any indication—Harrison's assurance to the contrary—that function was not the primary factor in determining the choice of the "slab" as the basic form for the Secretariat?

26. Many of the critics who write on the United Nations complex discuss the problem of architectural symbolism in this World Capitol. Examine the ways in which they suggest a building can function as a symbol. Do you find any differences in their conceptions of how a building is able to symbolize certain concepts?

27. How do you think a building can achieve symbolic meaning? How extensive or simple a range of symbolism can buildings legitimately suggest?

28. Consider Geoffrey Scott's treatment of the romantic and ethical fallacies in relation to the problem of symbolism. What dangers relevant to the discussion of symbolism in the United Nations buildings does he help to clarify?

29. Examine the validity of the various analyses of symbolism in the United Nations complex. What seem to you the most important reasons given for the failure of the United Nations complex on the level of architectural symbolism? Do you agree?

30. How comprehensive is Churchill's account of the lack of adequate symbolism in modern architecture?

31. Does Churchill's view leave the architect powerless to use any existing form as a symbol? What would William Adams Delano's position be on this subject?

32. Compare the methods used to achieve adequate symbolism in our National Capitol and their results with those used to the same purpose in the United Nations and the results.

33. Harrison says that an architect searches in his soul and finds there a symbolic solution that is correct; he offers Wren and his Saint Paul's Cathedral in London as an example. On the basis of Wren's comments on architecture, do you think Harrison's description is an accurate summary of the method followed by Wren? Would it be accurate for any classical architect? Explain.

34. How compatible is the search for adequate symbolism in great public buildings with the aims of Modern architecture? How adequate from the point of view of the public aspects of the United Nations and its total needs of expression is Harrison's account of the considerations which determined the design of the complex? What are the implications of Harrison's reference to man as a "little animal"? On the basis of his illustrations what does Harrison mean when he says that architecture is the "study of man"? How comprehensive is his definition?

Compare it with classical statements of the meaning and aims of architecture. What tendency does S. Rowland Pierce fear in Harrison's speech? Why does he suggest that Alberti would disagree with Harrison's definition of the three essential parts of architecture?

35. Compare Mumford's analysis of the function and plan of the United Nations complex with Harrison's and other accounts of the architects' concern for function in the design of the buildings. How successful were the architects in their primary concern for function as a basis for design? What does Mumford mean when he calls the theory that shaped the design of the Secretariat "a new kind of academicism"? Examine the validity of his charge.

36. What would be the reaction of classical theorists of architecture to those qualities of the United Nations buildings which John Dos Passos finds exciting?

37. How successful is the United Nations complex if judged by the qualities that Hitchcock and Johnson list as essential components of the International Style?

Lever House

38. What qualities do critics single out for praise in the design or function of Lever House?

39. In what way does the building attempt to provide for human needs beyond the strictly utilitarian?

40. To what extent are the functional aspects of the building dependent upon its form? To what extent has consideration for such aspects revealed itself in the building's form?

41. What does *The Architectural Forum* mean when it says that the architects of Lever House have created "a strong intellectual form"? Would classical concepts of beauty support this assertion?

42. Why does *The Architectural Record* call the building "somewhat monumental"? Compare their criteria for judging monumentality with those of Van Brunt.

43. Why do some critics consider Lever House superior to the United Nations Secretariat? To what extent are the deficiencies pointed out in the Secretariat remedied in Lever House?

44. Mumford praises Lever House for its return to the human scale in design. What does he mean?

45. How successfully do you think the designers have catered to "visual delight" as a human concern?

46. What words are most frequently adopted to describe Lever House? Can Katherine Gilbert's observations in "A Study in Architectural Semantics" be applied to them?

47. Consider the merits of the form of Lever House in the light of such contemporary criticisms of architecture as those by Saarinen, Burchard, and Boyd.

48. How well does Lever House meet the standards of the International Style as outlined by Hitchcock and Johnson?

49. Classical architecture has been criticized by functionalists for its supposedly facile repetition of a repertory of forms. Compare the problems of composition involved in such a building as Lever House with those outlined by Van Brunt in his articles on the Chicago Fair.

50. Upon what grounds does Wright base his attack upon the "glass box" and the forms of the International Style?

51. How valid is his treatment of the symbolism of the box? Consider it in the light of Geoffrey Scott's analysis of fallacies in architectural thought.

52. To what non-architectural attitudes in his audience does Wright's argument address itself?

53. How valid is Wright's charge that the International Style has accepted sterility for simplicity? Would Ruskin or Alberti agree with Wright's charge and, if so, for what reasons?

Price Tower

54. Try to define Wright's use of the word *organic* as he applies it to the architecture of the Price Tower.

55. What concepts or clusters of ideas are attached to the word?

56. How does "organic" architecture differ in Wright's mind from the architecture of Lever House or that of the United Nations?

57. Contrast the architectural qualities of the Price Tower and Lever House. How do they contrast in the matter of ornament?

58. How does Wright's conception of ornament differ from the classical conception?

59. Analyze the part played in Wright's attitudes and feelings by his concern with Nature and the Machine. In constructing your analysis consider treatments of the subject by Geoffrey Scott, Sedlmayr, and Moholy-Nagy.

60. Analyze Wright's use of language. Does it emphasize more the communication of thought or of feeling?

61. What part do "poetic" devices such as repetition, rhythm, rhyme, alliteration, and assonance play in Wright's prose style?

62. What does Mumford mean when he calls Wright "romantic"? Can you illustrate this quality from Wright's architectural work? From his writings? If you can perceive any "romantic" qualities in his architecture, do you find they serve any function? Explain.

63. Criticize Price Tower in terms of Schopenhauer's principles of rigidity-gravity (support-burden).

64. Which contemporary critics included in Part I would be likely to approve, and which to disapprove, the Price Tower and on what grounds?

65. Consider Wright's concern for originality in the light of Ruskin's and Van Brunt's strictures.

66. How large a role does "fancy" play in Wright's work?

67. How valid is Wright's stress on the economy of his design?

68. How much is he concerned with function? How successful functionally is the Price Tower?

69. To what extent was the Price Tower designed for the easy reproductive capacities of the machine?

70. How much is Wright concerned with human comfort as opposed to the dictates of style?

71. Consider Wright's achievement in terms of the advantages and disadvantages of individualism as well as the classical and Modern concepts of the aims and values of architecture.

72. How would you define Wright's concept of beauty?

THEME TOPICS

Many of the questions appended to the texts, particularly those involving comparisons, will provide subjects for shorter papers.

Long Papers

Classical Aims and Values in Architecture
The Concept of Originality in Architecture
The Rationale of Functionalism
The Restlessness of Modern Architecture: Reasons and Causes
The Controversy over Ornament in Architecture
Tradition and American Architecture
Monumentalism in Architecture: Theory and Practice
Architectural Works as Visual Symbols
Architecture and Language: the Use of Words in
    Architectural Criticism

Write your own evaluation of the achievement of one of the five buildings or complexes studied in this book. Do not merely parrot authorities or sources, but use the entire critical apparatus provided by this book as a means to awaken, extend, and inform your own responsible perception of architectural aims and achievements.

Write a comparative evaluation of two (or more) of the buildings studied. You may find it necessary to limit the scope of your paper to one or two major points or concepts, as, for example, the following:

Unity and Monumentality in the Columbian Exposition and the
    United Nations Buildings
Lever House and Price Tower as Architectural Expressions of a
    Business Civilization
The National Gallery and the United Nations Buildings in Relation
    to the Concept of "Form Follows Function"
The Aesthetic and the Expressive Use of Materials in All or Several
    of the Buildings Studied
Lever House and Price Tower as Enrichments of the Vocabulary
    of the Modern Style

Contrast the classical buildings with the Modern on the basis of their achievements in satisfying man's capacity for pleasure of the senses in architecture.

Contrast the classical buildings with the Modern on the basis of their capacity to satisfy man's spirit and emotions.

Write a criticism and evaluation of a significant building in either classical or Modern style on your college campus or in a nearby city. Apply the total critical apparatus provided by this book to your task.

Compare a significant classical and Modern building on your college campus or in a nearby city. Be sure you choose buildings whose architectural qualities (e.g., social purpose, magnitude, etc.) provide a valid basis for comparison.

BRIEF SELECTED BIBLIOGRAPHY

A selected list of books on classical and Modern architecture

ANDREWS, Wayne, *Architecture, Ambition and Americans* (New York, Harper & Brothers, 1955). An entertaining, personal survey of American architecture from the Modern point of view. Well illustrated.

FLETCHER, Sir Banister, *A History of Architecture on the Comparative Method* (New York, Charles Scribner's Sons, 1950). A very useful encyclopaedia of world architecture in one volume. Lavishly illustrated with drawings and photographs.

GIEDION, Sigfried, *Space, Time, and Architecture* (Combridge, Harvard University Press, 1954). Architecture and city planning by one of the leaders of the Modern Movement. Beautifully illustrated.

HAMLIN, Talbot Faulkner, *The American Spirit in Architecture* (New Haven, Yale University Press, 1936). The best survey of American architecture in print. Well illustrated.

HAMLIN, Talbot Faulkner, *Greek Revival Architecture in America* (New York, Oxford University Press, 1944). A detailed survey of American architecture from 1783 to 1850 by an authority. Illustrated.

HEGEMAN, Werner, and PEETS, Elbert, *The American Vitruvius* (New York, Architectural Book Publishing Company, 1922). This carefully illustrated work is essential to any study of city planning and civic design.

HITCHCOCK, Henry-Russell, *Architecture: Nineteenth and Twentieth Centuries* (Baltimore, Penguin Books, 1958). A history of architecture in our time written by the leading American apologist of the Modern point of view. Illustrated.

MEYER, Franz Sales, *Handbook of Ornament* (New York, Dover Publications, Inc., 1957). The standard survey of ornament in a paperback edition.

MORRISON, Hugh, *Early American Architecture: From the First Colonial Settlements to the National Period* (New York, Oxford University Press, 1952). The definitive work on American architecture up to 1776.

MUMFORD, Lewis, *Technics and Civilization* (New York, Harcourt, Brace and Co., 1934). The widest read American critic of architecture, known for his column in *The New Yorker*, surveys our urban civilization, especially its architecture.

SANTAYANA, George, *The Life of Reason*, Vol. IV: *Reason in Art* (New York, Charles Scribner's Sons, 1955). A great American philosopher looks at beauty from music to architecture.

SUMMERSON, John, *Heavenly Mansions* (New York, Charles Scribner's Sons, 1949). A book of essays by a leading English critic explores the roles of Viollet-le-Duc, Le Corbusier, and others in shaping Modern architecture.

TUNNARD, Christopher, *The City of Man* (New York, Charles Scribner's Sons, 1953). A survey of city planning and civic design by a classical authority.

TUNNARD, Christopher, and REED, Henry Hope, Jr., *American Skyline* (Boston, Houghton, Mifflin Company, 1955; and New York, New American Library of World Literature, Mentor Series, 1956). The story of the forces that have shaped American cities and towns, with particular emphasis on the role of art.

VIOLLET-LE-DUC, EUGENE-EMMANUEL, *Discourses on Architecture*, trans. by Benjamin Bucknall (New York, Grove Press, 1959), 2 vols. The chief source for the theories of the man who is now generally considered to be the father of the Modern Style in architecture.

WHARTON, Edith, and CODMAN, Ogden, Jr., *The Decoration of Houses* (New York, Charles Scribner's Sons, 1897). The first book of the great American novelist, written jointly with the man who launched interior decoration as we now know it.

Glossary of
Architectural Terms

GLOSSARY OF ARCHITECTURAL TERMS

ABACUS. The upper part of the capital of a column, supporting the architrave. In certain orders it is square and flat, in others it is variously shaped and ornamented.

ABUTMENT. Solid masonry which receives the weight and thrust of an arch or vault.

AISLE. The side division of any building in which the interior is divided into parts by rows of columns. More particularly, aisles are side divisions which parallel the nave in a basilica or a church. See NAVE.

AMBULATORY. A passageway in a building for people on foot; often a covered walk in a monastery or a passageway around the sanctuary in a church.

ARCADE. A row of arches with their supports, or a passageway with a wall of the same. A covered gallery.

ARCH. A structural member or a set of wedge-shaped blocks which form a curve to cover an opening or a recess.

ARCHITRAVE. The lowest division of an entablature, which rests on the column. The term is also adopted for the molding or moldings found around a door, window, or other opening. See ENTABLATURE.

ART NOUVEAU. A style of decoration and architecture which flourished in Europe around 1900. It is distinguished by its use of sinuous natural forms based, for the most part, on the vine tendril. The chief force behind its adoption was an attempt to rebel against or secede from past traditions. In Germany it was known as *Jugendstil* (youthful style), in Austro-Hungary as *Sezession,* in Italy as *Floreale* (flowering) and in France and Belgium as *Modern Style* as well as *Art Nouveau.* In the United States Louis Comfort Tiffany initiated a similar style independently, as did Louis Sullivan, the leading Secessionist architect. The late Frank Lloyd Wright was a product of the American equivalent of the *Art Nouveau.*

ATTIC. A low story or garret above the main cornice of a building.

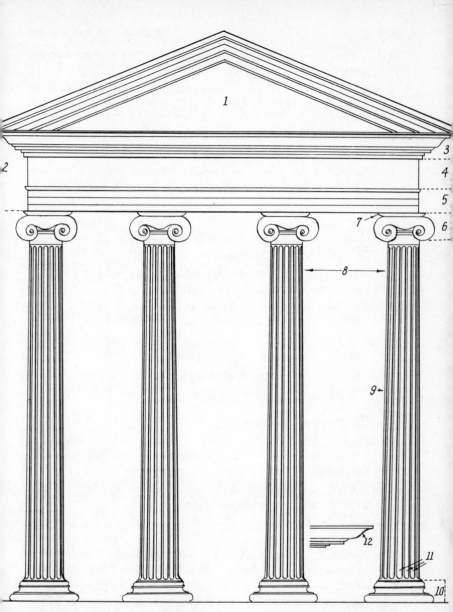

1: pediment; 2: entablature; 3: cornice; 4: frieze; 5: architrave; 6: capital; 7: abacus; 8: Ionic columns; 9: shaft; 10: base or plinth; 11: fluting; 12: cyma.

AXIAL, AXIS. A straight line which divides a plan into symmetrical parts.

BALUSTER. A short colonnette with base, shaft, and cap, serving as one of several to support a handrail or horizontal member. See BALUSTRADE.

BALUSTRADE. A railing composed of balusters carrying a handrail or horizontal member. See BALUSTER.

BARREL VAULT. A continuous arched roof or ceiling, usually semi-circular in shape and unbroken by ribs, over a hall or corridor.

BASE. The lowest part of a column, pier, or structure. See COLUMN.

BASILICA. A Roman hall of justice, rectangular in plan, with one main central part and side aisles. It was adopted for church buildings with the spread of Christianity.

BAY. The space between two repeating vertical members such as columns or pilasters.

BRACKET. A piece of stone, wood, or metal which projects from a wall to hold a beam, shelf, statue, etc. See CONSOLE.

BUCKY FULLER DOME. A prefabricated dome-shaped structure devised by the American inventor, Buckminster Fuller.

BUTTRESS. A particular form of abutment which is specially built to support a wall or vault. It projects from the wall. See ABUTMENT.

CAISSON. Same as coffer. See COFFER.

CAMPANILE. Italian for "bell tower." Here the word is adopted to denote a bell tower of Italian design, that is, one built apart from the church.

CANTILEVER. A horizontal beam which overhangs and which can hold a heavy load at some distance from its support.

CAPITAL. The topmost part of a column or pilaster. See COLUMN; PILASTER.

CLEARSTORY, CLERESTORY. A part of a building lighted with windows above a side- or aisle-roof. It is most often found in Gothic churches.

COFFER, COFFERING. A recessed panel in a flat or vaulted ceiling, almost always found together in numbers.

COLONNADE. A row of columns. See COLUMN.

COLUMN. An independent vertical member. In classical architecture it consists of a base, shaft, and capital.

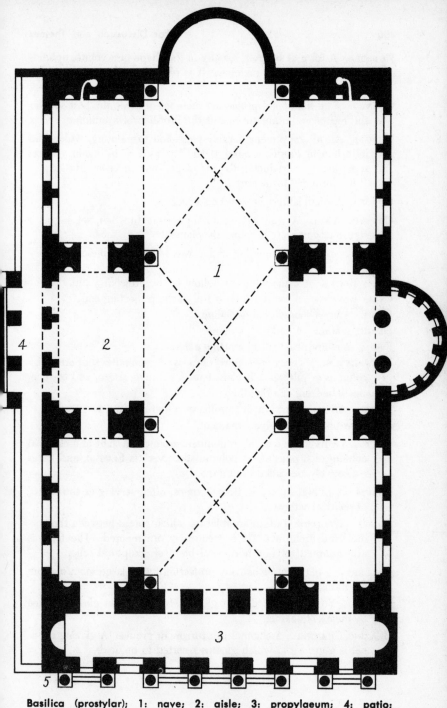

Basilica (prostylar); 1: nave; 2: aisle; 3: propylaeum; 4: patio;
5: colonnade.

CONSOLE. A form of bracket, usually in the shape of a volute, upholding a flat horizontal member. It is often found in numbers supporting a cornice.

CORNICE. The horizontal projecting member of a façade, best seen at the top of an entablature or at the roof-line of a building.

CUBISM. An art movement, largely restricted to painting, which had its origin in France around 1910. It was a revolt against representational art, reducing the art of painting to geometric shapes. It is a form of Abstract art.

CUPOLA. A small lantern or turret on a roof.

CURTAIN WALL. A wall having no supporting function, serving as a screen or curtain to keep out the elements.

CYMA, CYMATIUM. A molding with a wave-like or double-curved profile.

CYMA RECTA. A cyma which is hollow in the projecting end.

CYMA REVERSA. A cyma which is full in the projecting end.

DOME. A bowl-shaped roof or ceiling.

DOMICAL HALL. A hall with a dome.

DRUM. A cylindrical wall supporting a dome.

ENTABLATURE. The upper part of a wall generally supported by columns or pilasters. It consists of architrave, frieze, and cornice.

FACADE. The front of a building.

FINIAL. An ornament which terminates a spire, turret, or pinnacle.

FLAMBEAU, -X. A torch-like ornament.

FLUTE. A curved groove cut in numbers around the shaft of a classical column or a pilaster. A column so carved, is FLUTED, and flutes collectively are called FLUTING.

FORUM. A public square in Roman times, often serving as the center of political activity.

FRIEZE. The portion of an entablature which comes between the cornice and architrave. It is frequently ornamented. The term is also adopted for any horizontal band of sculptural relief.

GALLERY. A platform or balcony projecting into a large room or from a building.

GLAZING. To be furnished with glass. Also, to give a glossy surface by means of enamel.

GLAZING CHANNEL. A channel is a furrow or groove. A glazing channel is a groove in which glass is inserted to be held.

1: barrel vault; 2: arch; 3: spandrel; 4: entablature; 5: cornice; 6: frieze;
7: architrave; 8: capital; 9: abacus; 10: shaft; 11: base or plinth;
12: Tuscan column.

GONFALON. A flag or piece of cloth which hangs from a crosspiece or a pole.

HEAD. The upper part of a door or window frame.

HYPOSTYLE. A columned hall in which the columns support the roof.

LATTICE. An open grille of interlacing or criss-crossed wood or metal bars. LATTICED means with a lattice.

LINTEL. A horizontal beam of stone, wood, or metal which supports the weight of the wall above an opening.

LINTEL COURSE. A course is one horizontal row of brick or stone in a wall. A wall consists of a number of super-imposed courses. A lintel course is the particular horizontal row which is continuous with a row of lintels.

LOUVER, LOUVRE. A series of horizontal, usually movable, slats to allow ventilation while excluding rain or sunshine.

MODULE. An arbitrary unit of measure. In contemporary architecture, modular construction means that every dimension of the structure is a multiple of a given lowest common denominator (i.e., the module).

MONOLITH. A single large block of stone, which takes the shape of an obelisk and, more often, the shaft of a column.

MULLION. An upright or vertical member between the lights (panes of glass) of a window. The horizontal member is known as a TRANSOM. A LIGHT is a subdivision of a window.

MUNTIN. An upright or vertical member separating panels, as in a paneled door. Today it is mistakenly adopted for transom (see TRANSOM) by architectural journalists.

NAVE. The part of a church reserved for the congregation as opposed to the sanctuary which is reserved for the clergy. More often, it is the central aisle of a church or basilica whose interior is divided by parallel columns. See AISLE.

ORDERS. The architectural system of columns and entablature which is the basis of classical architecture. There are five principal orders: DORIC, IONIC, CORINTHIAN, COMPOSITE, and TUSCAN.

PANEL. A sheet of any material other than glass, held in a frame.

PARAPET. A low retaining wall on the edge of a roof.

PATIO. A courtyard enclosed on three or four sides.

PAVILION. A temporary building. The wing of a building. Also an ornamental building in a park or garden.

PEDESTAL. The base of a column or a statue.

PEDIMENT. The triangular space formed by the gable of a roof, espe-

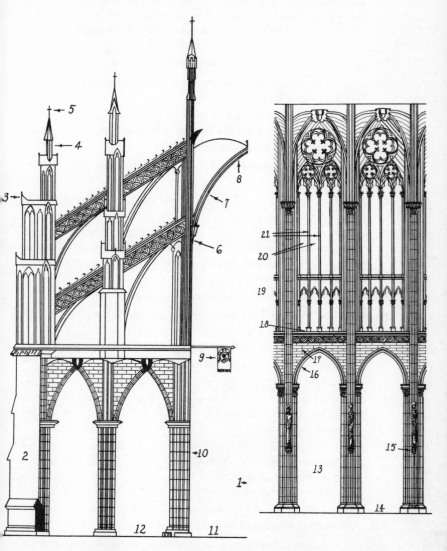

1: axis; 2: abutment; 3: parapet; 4: pinnacle; 5: finial; 6: buttress;
7: rib; 8: arch; 9: gonfalon; 10: pier; 11: nave; 12: aisle;
13: bay; 14: arcade; 15: bracket; 16: arch; 17: spandrel; 18: sill;
19: clerestory; 20: lights (glazing); 21: mullions.

cially in a classical building where it rests on the entablature (see ENTABLATURE). It is frequently used as a form of decoration in classical architecture where it is found over doorways and windows and its shape can be round as well as triangular and it can be broken.

PERISTYLE. A colonnade surrounding a temple or a court.

PIER. An upright support, free-standing or forming part of a wall, which carries a load.

PILASTER. The projecting part of a rectangular pier, extending from the wall, and architecturally treated with base, shaft, and capital. Pilasters are most often purely decorative.

PINNACLE. A vertical member of masonry used to top a buttress or a parapet.

PLINTH. The square base of a column or part of the bottom of the base of a statue.

PLUM, PLUMB. Vertically straight, exactly in line. To achieve a vertically straight line in a wall, the mason makes use of a PLUMB-LINE, a cord which has a metal weight at one end for determining the vertical direction.

PORTICO. An entrance porch, often very imposing.

PROPYLAEUM. An important entrance or vestibule to a temple or similar sacred building.

PROSTYLAR. A building with columns is so characterized when its columns are confined to the front.

PURISM. A form of Cubism (see CUBISM), devised by the Franco-Swiss architect, Le Corbusier, presumably derived from geometric shapes inspired by machinery. It is, like Cubism, a revolt against the representational.

PYLON. In Egyptian architecture, the portal of a temple built of two solid masses of masonry with slightly inclined walls that is, narrower at the top than at the bottom. It has come to mean any high, solid structure of masonry with such inclined walls.

QUADRIGA, -AE. A four-horse chariot used as a sculptural device.

RIB. A projecting member of an arched vault.

ROSTRAL COLUMN. A column decorated with prows of ancient ships.

ROTUNDA. A circular hall roofed by a dome.

SHAFT. That part of the column between the base and the capital. See COLUMN. Any high, relatively thin, upright object.

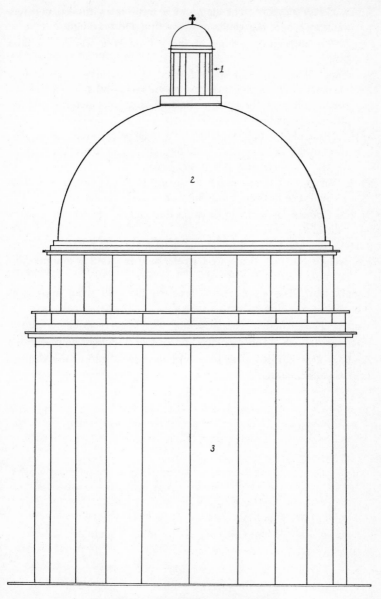

1: cupola or lantern; 2: dome; 3: drum.

SHELL CONSTRUCTION. The name of a form of reinforced concrete vaulting where the vaults are very thin and very light.

SILL. The horizontal member at the bottom of a window or door frame.

SPANDREL. The triangular space formed by the curve of an arch, a vertical line from the springing of the arch, and a horizontal line running through the apex of the arch. In contemporary buildings the wall panel beneath the windows.

STAFF. Stiff plaster held together by a fiber or horsehair. Found on the exterior of temporary buildings, notably in the instance of the World's Columbian Exposition of 1893.

STOA. An ancient Greek porch consisting of a wall at the back with a colonnade in front, affording a sheltered promenade.

STRING COURSE. A molding or projecting course which runs horizontally along a wall.

SUPPORTING MEMBER. Any part of a building which serves to carry weight. A steel beam in a steel frame building is a supporting member.

TEPIDARIUM. The warm room, between the cold room and steam room, of a Roman bath.

VAULT. The arched or curved ceiling of a large room or corridor.

VOMITORIUM, -IA. The entrance and exit of a Roman amphitheater.

ZONING. A legal instrument to restrict the use of land or the size and use of a building.